THE SIMPLE LIFE

THE SIMPLE LIFE

Plain Living and High Thinking
in American Culture

DAVID E. SHI

OXFORD UNIVERSITY PRESS
New York   Oxford

Oxford University Press

Oxford   New York   Toronto
Delhi   Bombay   Calcutta   Madras   Karachi
Petaling Jaya   Singapore   Hong Kong   Tokyo
Nairobi   Dar es Salaam   Cape Town
Melbourne   Auckland

and associated companies in
Beirut   Berlin   Ibadan   Nicosia

First published in 1985 by Oxford University Press, Inc.,
200 Madison Avenue, New York, NY 10016

First issued as an Oxford University Press paperback, 1986

Oxford is a registered trademark of Oxford University Press

Library of Congress Cataloging in Publication Data
Shi, David E.
The simple life.
Bibliography: p.
Includes index.
1. National characteristics, American.   2. Simplicity.
3. United States—Civilization.   4. United States—Social
life and customs.   I. Title.
E169.1.S556   1985   306′.0973   84-12212
ISBN 0-19-503475-9
ISBN 0-19-504013-9 (pbk.)

Printing (last digit):   9 8 7 6 5 4 3 2 1
Printed in the United States of America

For Bill Leverette

Acknowledgments

Tracing the history of the simple life in the United States has entailed synthesizing many strands of American thought and behavior. Fortunately, I was greatly aided in this effort by the spadework of previous researchers, and I gratefully acknowledge my debt to those works cited in the notes. In addition, a number of scholars, including Joyce Appleby, Sacvan Bercovitch, Rowland Berthoff, Timothy Breen, Edwin Bronner, Peter Clecak, James Gilbert, Daniel Horowitz, Michael Kammen, John Kasson, Jackson Lears, William Leuchtenburg, David Levin, Drew McCoy, Forrest McDonald, Edmund Morgan, Gary Nash, and Robert Shalhope were kind enough to read parts or all of the manuscript at various stages. Their comments were penetrating and comprehensive, and I only hope that I have done justice to their many incisive suggestions.

To Joe Kett I owe a special debt of thanks. He read the original drafts of each chapter as they were completed and provided prompt, detailed evaluations of their strengths and weaknesses—especially the latter. My colleagues at Davidson College—Malcolm Lester, Earl MacCormac, and Randy Nelson —also furnished discerning assessments of various chapters and offered much-needed encouragement.

I also want to express my appreciation to the National Endowment for the Humanities and the Davidson College Faculty Research Committee for providing generous financial assistance and a timely sabbatical. A fellowship from the National Humanities Center enabled me to spend most of 1983 at that scholars' paradise. Two Center staff members, librarian Rebecca Sutton and typist Karen Carroll, were especially instrumental in expediting my work there. During my stay at the Humanities Center I also gained valuable insights into the simple life from my discussions with the bright and varied Fellows, particularly Richard Bjornson, Hiram Caton, Dewey Grantham, Martin Melosi, Harold Perkin, Ken Severens, Lance Stell, and Larry Thomas.

The assistance provided me by the staff of the Davidson College library was typically gracious and invaluable. I also want to thank Ann Callahan, who was an accurate and speedy typist, and Rachel Henning, my indispensable and charming student assistant. In addition, I benefited greatly from the careful reading provided by Oxford's Leona Capeless. Sheldon Meyer was a patient and inspiriting editor, and his trenchant suggestions greatly improved (and shortened) the manuscript.

The working scholar is too often a distracted husband and father, and my study of the simple life unfortunately served to complicate the lives of my wife, Susan, and our children, Jason and Jessica. Yet they tolerated my inattention with affectionate understanding and cheerful encouragement —at least most of the time. Occasionally I did look up from my desk to discover two imploring kids, coloring books in hand, requesting, at the prodding of their mother, that I put my pen to more significant use. In doing so they reminded me that the most enriching simplicities are near at hand.

Finally, my greatest professional debt is owed to William Leverette, Jr., of Furman University. A luminous teacher driven by a sanely passionate love of ideas, Bill Leverette first exposed me to the enchantments of intellectual history and to the rudiments of narrative prose. Since then he has been an abiding friend and patient counselor. For the past several years, he and I have worked closely together in studying the theme of simple living in American culture, sharing materials and insights, and collaborating on several articles, parts of which have been integrated into the following chapters. Without his assistance and support, this book would have never been written, and for this, and for much else, it is dedicated to him.

Davidson, N. C.   *D. S.*
March 1984

Contents

THE SIMPLE LIFE

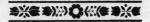

Introduction

"Less is more!" So say those for whom small has become beautiful in recent years. Since the 1960s, the energy and ecological crises have combined with persistent inflation to persuade many Americans to embrace "simpler" ways of living. In doing so they have helped sustain a rich tradition of enlightened material restraint in the American experience dating back to the colonial era. This book describes and evaluates that tradition in its various manifestations over the years.

The simple life is almost as difficult to define as to live. In contemporary parlance the phrase has developed into one of those imprecise rubrics that tantalize journalists and copywriters. Perhaps it is most often associated in the popular mind with unadorned country living. Yet having taken on somewhat of a faddish cast, it is also frequently employed in newspaper and magazine articles as an omnibus label to characterize such activities as the back-to-the-land movement, arts and crafts revivals, organic gardening, environmental conservation and recycling, anti-nuclear demonstrations, urban cooperatives, wilderness expeditions, consumer frugality, and the like.

Indeed, the precise meaning of the simple life has never been fixed. Rather, it has always represented a shifting cluster of ideas, sentiments, and activities. These have included a hostility toward luxury and a suspicion of riches, a reverence for nature and a preference for rural over urban ways of life and work, a desire for personal self-reliance through frugality and diligence, a nostalgia for the past and a scepticism toward the claims of modernity, conscientious rather than conspicuous consumption, and an aesthetic taste for the plain and functional. Over the years, individuals and groups have varied in the emphasis placed on these attitudes. As a result, there have been, and still are, many *forms* of simple living representing a wide spectrum of motives and methods. Their common denominator has been the core assumption that the making of money and the accumulation of things should not be allowed to smother the purity of the soul, the life of the mind, the cohesion of the family, or the good of the commonweal. As I have employed the concept, therefore, the simple life represents an approach to living that self-consciously subordinates the material to the ideal.

Of course, such a philosophy of living is by no means distinctively American. The primacy of the spiritual or intellectual life has been a central emphasis of most of the world's major religions and philosophies. The great spiritual teachers of the East—Zarathustra, Buddha, Lao-Tse, and Confucius—all stressed that material self-control was essential to the good life, and many Americans, particularly Thoreau and the "hippies" of the 1960s, drew much of their inspiration for simple living from its Oriental tradition. By far, however, the most important historical influence on American simplicity has been the combined heritage of Greco-Roman culture and Judeo-Christian ethics. Most Greek and Roman philosophers were emphatic in their praise of simple living, as were the Hebrew prophets and Jesus.

Socrates was among the first to argue that ideas should take priority over things in the calculus of life. "Men are to be esteemed for their virtue, not their wealth," he insisted. "Fine and rich clothes are suited for comedians. The wicked live to eat; the good eat to live." Socrates advocated a golden mean between poverty and wealth, and so, too, did his famous pupil Plato. But it was in Aristotle's writings that this classical concept of leading a carefully balanced life of material moderation and intellectual exertion was most fully articulated. "The man who indulges in every pleasure and abstains from none," Aristotle observed, "becomes self-indulgent, while the man who shuns every pleasure, as boors do, becomes in a way insensible; temperance and courage, then, are destroyed by excess and defect, and preserved by the mean."

A similar theme of simple living coupled with spiritual devotion runs through the Old Testament, from the living habits of tent dwellers of Abraham's time to the strictures of the major and minor prophets against the evils of luxury—in terms both of material excess and of excessive sophistication in thought. As the author of Proverbs prayed, "Give me neither poverty nor wealth, but only enough." Likewise, the career of Jesus represented, from start to finish, a protest against Greek sophistication and luxury. Jesus repeatedly warned of the "deceitfulness of riches," noting that superfluous wealth too easily led to hardness of heart toward one's fellows and deadness of heart toward God. Experience had shown, he argued, that it was "easier for a camel to go through the eye of a needle than for a rich man to enter into the kingdom of God." Jesus therefore urged his followers to seek their "treasures in heaven" rather than on earth.

So much for the ideal. In practice the simple life prescribed in classical philosophy and early Christian thought has proven far more complex, protean, and volatile than such summary descriptions imply. The necessarily ambiguous quality of a philosophy of living that does not specify exactly how austere one's mode of living should be has produced a welter of different practices, several of which have conflicted with one another. The same self-denying impulse that has motivated some to engage in temperate frugality has often led others to adopt ascetic or primitive ways. During the classical period, for instance, there were many types of simple living, including the affluent temperance of the Stoics, Cicero, Seneca, and Marcus Aurelius, the more modest "golden mean" of Socrates, Plato, and Aristotle, the ascetic primitivism of Diogenes, and the pastoral simplicity of Virgil and Horace. An equally wide spectrum of practices developed among early Christians. In asserting the superiority of spiritual over worldly concerns, some gave away all of their possessions and went to the desert to live as hermits. Others joined monasteries, and a few engaged in prolonged stints of abstinence and mortification. Yet, at the same time, many officials of the early Catholic church preached Christian simplicity while themselves living in considerable comfort and even luxury.

Since ancient times similarly diverse versions of the simple life have been practiced by poets and priests, businessmen and philosophers, monarchs and scientists. Simplicity has been an especially salient theme in Western literature. Chaucer repeatedly reminded readers of Christ's life of voluntary simplicity. Boccaccio took cheer in an open-air search for the spontaneous; Dante called upon his readers to "see the king of the simple life"; and Shakespeare offered the happiness of the greenwood tree. The Romantics of the eighteenth and nineteenth centuries likewise promoted a simplicity modeled after the serene workings of nature.

In addition to providing a compelling literary image, simplicity has often been embraced as a stylish fad. Benjamin Franklin's self-conscious decision to wear an old fur cap and portray himself as a plain Quaker while serving as a diplomat in Paris reflected his shrewd awareness that a Rousseau-inspired rustic simplicity had become quite fashionable among the French ruling elite. Marie Antoinette's famous Hameau, constructed on the grounds of Versailles at a cost of millions of francs, was a monument of extravagant simplicity. The toy village had its own thatched cottages, a dairy barn with perfumed Swiss cows, and a picturesque water mill. When the lavish life at court proved tiresome, the Queen and her retainers could adjourn to Hameau, don peasant garb, and enjoy the therapeutic effects of milking cows and churning butter.

For such bored aristocrats, simplicity was clearly an affectation. But there have been many through the centuries who have practiced simplicity rather than played at it. The names of St. Francis, Thomas More, John Milton, William Blake, Blaise Pascal, John Wesley, Prince Kropotkin, Leo Tolstoy, Albert Schweitzer, Toyohiko Kagawa, Mahatma Gandhi, E. F. Schumacher, and Mother Teresa come readily to mind. For them, simplicity frequently entailed what the English poet William Wordsworth called "plain living and high thinking." The degree of plainness differed considerably from individual to individual, as did the nature of the "high thinking." They simplified their lives in order to engage in a variety of enriching pursuits: philosophy, religious devotion, artistic creation, revolutionary politics, humanitarian service, or ecological activism.

American practitioners of simple living have displayed a similar diversity in putting the ideal into practice. Simplicity has been advocated for both religious and secular reasons. In addition, class biases, individual personality traits, and historical circumstances have combined to produce many differing versions of the simple life in American culture. Several enthusiasts have been quite affluent, a few have been almost primitive. Some have espoused the simple life as a conservative, even reactionary, instrument of social control, finding in it an ideological means of preserving the status quo by impressing upon the masses the virtues of hard work, social stability, and personal contentment. Others have viewed simple living as an explicit rejection of the prevailing social and economic order or as a refreshing therapeutic or recreational alternative to the hedonistic demands of the consumer culture. In addition, some proponents have felt the need to withdraw from the larger society, while others have tried their best to sustain their personal ethic in the midst of a tempting and complex world.

This study examines the diversity of both motive and method in the practice of simple living from the colonial period through the present. I have not discussed every major advocate or manifestation of simple living. To do so would have required several volumes. Thus, readers interested primarily in the Amish, Shakers, Hutterites, Moravians, Mennonites, or other pietistic sects that have tended to shut themselves off from the outside world will be disappointed to find that they receive little attention in the following pages. Their story has already been told well and often. Benjamin Franklin, James Fenimore Cooper, Robert Frost, and the Populists are also not included in my cast of characters. To do them justice would have required more space than I could afford. Besides, they still confuse me. I have tried to select individuals and groups that reflect both the variety and underlying unity of the outlook through the years. Taken together, they demonstrate a persistent desire to elevate American life above the material and the mundane.

Tracing the fate of such an ideal mode of living amid an American society preoccupied with material standards of value is a complex undertaking, for it concerns not just what people said and did but also what people hoped they would do and be. In this sense the simple life has been both a myth of social aspiration and a guide for individual living. In both respects it has experienced frustrating failures. Yet it has displayed considerable resiliency over the years. Like the family, simplicity is always said to be declining but never disappears. No sooner do advocates in one era declare it dead than members of the next proclaim its revival. A major concern of this study is to trace the fluctuating popularity and underlying continuity of simple living as the nation itself has undergone striking changes.

As an exercise in intellectual history this book necessarily deals with the ambiguous border region where religious, ethical, aesthetic, and economic concerns converge. It concentrates on the ideas and practices of an intellectual and moral elite, a group of America's spiritual, philosophical, artistic, and journalistic spokesmen who articulated the meaning of human experience in the light of deeply felt principles. By its very nature, then, voluntary simplicity has been and remains an ethic professed and practiced primarily by those free to choose their standard of living. The sordid poverty suffered by those at the bottom of the social ladder is *not* the subject of this book.

When considered as an intellectual and cultural phenomenon, the simple life shares close affinities with several other concepts in the American experience that scholars have fruitfully examined. The pastoral urge, the agrarian myth, the Adamic identity, the noble savage, the Jacksonian persuasion, and the image of the New World garden have been recurring themes in American thought, themes that have frequently intersected with the ideal of simplicity. Yet these subjects have been analyzed primarily as enchanting psychic abstractions, as cultural metaphors, myths, images, or symbols that have been dreamed by intellectuals, preached by ministers, manipulated by politicians, sentimentalized by writers, and evoked by poets. Though stimulating, such studies have been essentially static and one-dimensional. The ideas treated seldom descend from the rarefied region of the imagination.

But ideas in the abstract are inert; they tell us little about the mystery of daily living. To bring texture—indeed, to bring life to the study of cultural beliefs—requires going beyond symbolic analysis; it entails examining how people have struggled to translate myths into practice. For this reason, I have treated the simple life both as a sentimental ideal and as an actual way of living, revealing in the process the personal implications for many of those who have tried to live according to its dictates. At the same time, I have also studied the way in which the larger public has viewed the simple life over the years. Doing so will no doubt tell us more about ourselves—perhaps more than some may want to know.

CHAPTER ONE

The Puritan Way

In 1920 the Spanish-born Harvard philosopher George Santayana observed that the American had always been "an idealist working on matter." Indeed, the tension between accumulating goods and cultivating goodness appeared early in the American experience and has lingered long. Colonists were attracted to the New World for reasons both mundane and visionary. Some saw America as an Edenic garden of economic opportunity, a land of milk and honey, full of furs, venison, fish, timber, and—gold. In 1616 Captain John Smith bluntly admitted that most of his countrymen were considering colonization primarily for reasons of material gain. "I am not so simple to think," he wrote, "that ever any other motive than wealth will erect there a Commonweal." Yet there were many who came to the New World with quite different priorities. Pious settlers hoped that America would be a sanctuary for saints rather than an entrepôt for adventurers. Though many of those who signed the Mayflower Compact in 1619 hoped to better their economic condition through emigration, they nevertheless affirmed that the voyage to America was undertaken primarily "for the glory of God and advancement of the Christian faith." Americans have since inherited these divergent, yet frequently intermingled perspectives on the good life, and the tension between the two has served to define and complicate the pursuit of happiness in the United States.[1]

Resolving the tension between prosperity and piety was clearly on the minds of the first generation of Puritan magistrates and divines who arrived in Massachusetts in the early seventeenth century. To ensure the success of their Bible Commonwealth they brought with them from the Old World a delicately balanced social ethic combining hard work, temperate living, civic virtue, and spiritual devotion. This original "Puritan ethic" had its roots in the social theory of late medieval Catholicism. Scholastic theology joined Biblical teaching and Aristotelian ethics in establishing a hierarchy of values in which commerce, money-lending, and other material pursuits were clearly subordinate to ethical and religious ideals. Thomas Aquinas spoke for most medieval theologians when he declared that "it is impossible for happiness, which is the last end of man, to consist in wealth." True happiness could be attained only through the "vision of the divine essence." Economic activity was thus inextricably linked with otherworldly priorities and moral restraints. Whether in the church or the counting-house, the true business of life was spiritual salvation. Hence, Aquinas and others developed the concept of the just price, outlawed the practice of usury, and viewed trade with suspicion.[2]

Upon these basic assumptions of Thomistic thought, John Calvin and his later Puritan followers built their own social philosophy. At the same time, however, they recognized that the economic life of sixteenth-century Europe was far more complex and dynamic than that of the thirteenth century. Restrictions designed for a relatively static, agricultural medieval society frequently proved unworkable in an expansive urban and commercial setting. Consequently, Calvin saw the need to relax somewhat the limitations placed on economic behavior by Aquinas and the schoolmen, allowing, for example, the charging of interest on investment capital. But such concessions to changing conditions should not be construed as giving sanction to "free enterprise." For Calvin, as for Aquinas, the glory of God and the good of the community outweighed individual freedom in the marketplace.[3]

Calvin was much more specific than the medieval theologians in explaining how people could serve the Lord in the world as well as in their hearts. In emphasizing the concept of the "calling," he dignified hard work in one's vocation, giving to common toil a respectability that earlier thinkers had at times denied by distinguishing between "sacred" and "secular" vocations. Like Martin Luther before him, Calvin rejected the notion that clergymen, monks, and nuns somehow received more providential favor than farmers, housewives, and shopkeepers. In criticizing those who piously withdrew from involvement in the affairs of everyday life, he bridged the gap between faith and work that had for so long troubled the Christian Church. Every Christian, Calvin asserted, has a spiritual and a temporal calling, both of which were imposed by God for the common good. One was a divine call, a spiritual summons to attain the salvation God offered through Christ. The other was a practical call to serve God diligently in one's profession, skill, or vocation. In this sense the Christian at his labor would be a steward in the service of God and the commonweal. Although Calvin spent much more time discussing the divine rather than the temporal calling, he clearly believed that both were necessary to a full Christian life. Faith without work was sterile, and all forms of honest work were significant in the eyes of the Lord. In Calvin's view, the conscientious pursuit of one's vocational calling represented in essence a Christian duty. One must work hard in order to avoid idleness, for the idle man makes an easy target for the Devil.[4]

Some commentators, following the pathbreaking research of Max Weber, have fastened on the Calvinist concept of calling in linking the Protestant ethic with the spirit of capitalism. Weber emphasized that Calvin's sanctification of work freed Christians from a sense of guilt about material pursuits. At the same time, the single-minded Protestant emphasis on frugality meant that the scrupulous would accumulate more and more wealth, thus unintentionally furthering the rise of modern capitalism. Had Weber concluded his study with this insight that the results of human actions are frequently the opposite of those intended, he no doubt would have avoided much of the scholarly criticism he has since received. But he went on to suggest in passing that Calvinism not only encouraged hard work but actually *enjoined* the systematic accumulation of wealth as a visible sign of sanctification. The attainment of wealth, he observed, "was a sign of God's blessing."[5]

Weber himself was careful to qualify this point by noting that Reformed theology frequently acted as a restraining influence on economic behavior. Some of his overzealous popularizers, however, ignored such qualifications and drew an intimate and willing connection between Calvinism and laissez-faire capitalism. Aldous Huxley, for example, saw in the Protestant ethic "all that was and still is vilest, cruelest, most anti-human in the modern capitalist system." Such a statement is dangerously misleading, for it fails to distinguish between early Calvinist and Puritan theory and later practice in the post-Restoration period. John Calvin, as well as the early English Puritan social theorists, never equated salvation and wealth; they remained thoroughly suspicious of the "inebriation of prosperity" and never would have embraced what has since become the capitalist way of life.[6]

Calvin's social ethic as discussed in his *Institutes of the Christian Religion* was in this sense much closer to Thomistic thought than to modern capitalism. To Calvin the primary rewards of work were to be spiritual, moral, and societal. He explicitly denied any correlation between material success and spiritual salvation, noting that God *may* reward the righteous with prosperity, but prosperity in and of itself was no guarantee of righteousness. Calvin emphasized that God cares more about attitudes than acquisitions: "There is nothing which God more abominates than when men endeavor to cloak themselves by substituting signs and external appearances for integrity of heart." The possession of superfluous riches was in fact a dubious blessing that endangered rather than enhanced one's spirituality. They "who are much engaged in the care of the body," he wrote, "are generally negligent of the soul." Calvin's alternative to the extremes of asceticism and profligacy was not a life of pinched frugality but a life of material moderation and spiritual devotion. The things of the world are not evil, he pointed out, but worldliness is.[7]

Calvin recognized that moderation as a standard lends itself to ambiguity. What is moderate for some may be considered excessive by others. The guideline he offered in such cases was that people "should indulge themselves as little as possible; that . . . they should perpetually and resolutely exert themselves to retrench all superfluities and to restrain luxury, and that they should diligently beware lest they pervert into impediments things which were given for assistance." Every human decision and action should be directed toward God's service and blessing. Temperance must prevent excess and luxury; otherwise man's passions would promote a selfish materialism and social strife. "Men are of so perverse and crooked a nature," he believed, "that everyone would scratch out his neighbor's eyes if there were no bridle to hold them in." Moreover, if material instincts were allowed free play, God would soon be displaced in men's hearts by Mammon. "Where is our acknowledgement of God," he asked, "if our minds be fixed on the splendour of our garments?" Should hard work and simple living result in an accumulation of wealth beyond a comfortable subsistence, Christians must share such excess with the deserving poor. "Riches," he concluded, "are a means to help the needy. That is the way to proceed and keep a happy medium."[8]

This "broad and middle way" of saintly living was what the first generation of Puritan settlers brought with them to the New World. They arrived in America intent upon establishing a New Zion in the wilderness. Their settlement would be "as a city upon a hill," a carefully regulated community of saints that would provide a beacon of piety and virtue for all the world to emulate. Thus convinced that they had received a special commission from the Lord, the Puritans shouldered a tremendous sense of moral responsibility, and the early spiritual and political leaders of Massachusetts Bay forcefully reaffirmed the medieval and Calvinist standards of Christian piety and social conduct. The original settlers retained the rigid social hierarchy of the Old World, with its explicit inequality and privilege. People were expected to know their rank or station and accept it. And to promote such compliance, they established a formidable array of socializing agencies. Family, church, community, school, and state were all considered interlocking instruments of social control and social continuity. Together they would serve to instill conformity and "reduce every affection within its proper bounds."[9]

The Reverend John Cotton, who arrived in Massachusetts in 1633 and quickly became the colony's dominant spiritual spokesman, emphasized to the settlers the crucial importance of their social obligations, stressing that the Christian had a duty to work hard at his calling, but he must always do so for the glory of God and the "public good," making sure to exercise "diligence in worldly businesses, and yet deadness to the world." Ideally, heavenly and secular callings should not interfere with one another; Christians could serve "both God and man." But whatever good fortune might accrue to the saint should be taken only "in moderation." Christians who prospered in their temporal callings must act as stewards of God's material blessings and must resist the temptation to live a life of selfish luxury. When a man succeeds at business, Cotton advised, he "does it heavenly and spiritually; He uses the world as if he used it not."[10]

Cotton echoed Calvin in proposing a prudent sufficiency as the standard for the Puritan settlers to follow: "We may desire wealth from God, partly for our necessity and expediency, and partly to leave to our posterity. Thus far a man may desire wealth. But we are never to desire more than we can make good use of." Early New England Puritanism, therefore, was not opposed to prosperity itself but to the selfishness and avarice that seemed to accompany it. Superfluous wealth almost inevitably diluted one's piety. "We are never more apt to forget God," Cotton wrote, "than when he prospers us." He envisioned an ideal Christian society with simplicity as its guiding virtue—simplicity of worship, dress, manners, and speech. The greater simplicity, he said, the "more evident witness to the truth of God," for the "holy and good man desires but a mean."[11]

The founding Puritans knew that "loving the world with weaned affections" would be no simple task, and no one was more aware of the problem of developing the well-ordered balance and harmony required by the Christian simple life than John Winthrop, the colony's first governor. Born in 1588, he initially followed the traditional career of a young country gentleman, attending Trinity College, Cambridge, and Gray's Inn before succeeding his father as lord of Groton manor in Suffolk. Winthrop remembered that as a youth he had been "very wild, and dissolute, and as years came on my lusts grew stronger." But at some point as a young man he underwent an intense conversion experience and soon joined the Puritan movement, determined to learn how to be good and do good in a vicious world. So he gave up hunting and card-playing in order to devote more time to prayer and Scripture study. In addition he tried to "tame his heart" by moderating his diet. Such sacrifices did not come easily. It was perplexingly difficult for Winthrop to learn to "love the world with moderation and God without."[12]

Winthrop's "conflicts between the flesh and the spirit" caused him to suffer pangs of conscience after succumbing to worldly pleasures. Periodically he would adopt the ascetic approach and try to cleanse his soul by resisting all such temptations. But this course also proved unsatisfactory: "When I had for some time abstained from such worldly delights as my heart most desired," he remembered, "I grew very melancholic and uncomfortable, for I had been more careful to refrain from an outward conversation in the world, than to keep the love of the world out of my heart, or to uphold my conversation in heaven." Asceticism, he decided, could be as dangerous as worldliness.[13]

After such moral trial and error, Winthrop fastened on the principle of worldly moderation and the diligent pursuit of one's calling in order to end his moral doubts and restrain his material instincts. Like Milton, he had discovered that it was better to wrestle with the sins and temptations of society, to combat them in the open field, than to avoid facing them. Such a stance required unflagging discipline in order to maintain a steady course. "I see therefore," Winthrop pledged, "I must keep a better watch over my heart, & keep my thoughts close to good things, & not suffer a vain or worldly thought to enter, etc.: lest it draw the heart to delight in it."[14]

By 1629 Winthrop was forty years of age, had a large family, and found himself in control of a floundering English estate that could not support his seven sons. Even more unsettling was the government's growing religious intolerance and the general decline in spirituality and sobriety among the English populace. "We are grown to that height of intemperance in all excess of riot, as no man's estate almost will suffice to keep sale with his equals." His personal situation and that of the larger social scene had deteriorated so much that emigration became an increasingly attractive alternative. In May 1629 Winthrop wrote his wife Margaret: "I am verily persuaded God will bring some affliction upon this land, and that speedily." Yet he assured her that God would "provide a shelter and hiding place for us and ours." Within a year they would be in Massachusetts.[15]

Winthrop knew as he led the Puritan colonists to America that their new home would provide them with plenty of "trials and temptations." In 1629, before leaving for New England, he stressed to his followers that the purpose of their expedition was primarily spiritual rather than material and that a simple life would be sufficient for their needs: "If we have foods and raiment (which are there to be had) we ought to be contented." He knew that life in America would at first be harsh and primitive, but argued that "if we have sufficient to fill the belly and clothe the back, the difference in quality may a little displease us, but it cannot hurt us." In fact, he suggested, the spartan conditions of the New World might prove spiritually beneficial, since "God will by this means bring us to repent of our Intemperance here at home, and so cure us of that disease, which sends many of us to hell."[16]

Yet Winthrop was also aware that after the initial hardships of settlement were overcome, the situation might change. During the voyage aboard the *Arbella* he delivered his famous lay sermon in which he warned the colonists that the economic opportunities awaiting them in the New World might prove too alluring. Material success could cause them "to embrace the present world and prosecute our carnal intentions, seeking great things for our selves and our posterity." Consequently, they must vigilantly ensure that the "good of the public oversway all private interests."[17]

Winthrop's economic outlook in this sense was as medieval as it was modern, and he joined other leaders of Massachusetts Bay in arguing that "the life of business be placed within a structure whose proportions had been drawn by the hand of God." Prices, wages, and markets had to be regulated for the good of the commonweal. Winthrop also took the lead in urging the colonial government to pass sumptuary laws. He felt that luxurious living was wasteful, enervating, and distracting. It also distorted important class differences. Winthrop and the other magistrates and divines were anything but social levelers. They insisted early on that Old World distinctions of rank and privilege be maintained. Winthrop reflected the static, hierarchical quality of Puritan social theory when he remarked in 1630: "In all times, some must be rich, some poor, some high and eminent in power and dignity; others mean and in subjection." To try to live beyond one's means and station thus endangered the social gradations and sense of subordination deemed crucial to communal order. In 1634 the Massachusetts General Court, concerned about the appearance of "new and immodest fashions" among all ranks, ordered that "no person, neither man or woman" shall make or buy clothes of "great, superfluous, and unnecessary expenses." Five years later they specifically prohibited "immoderate great breeches, knots of ribbon, broad shoulder-bands and rails, silk rases, double ruffs and cuffs," warning that such "superfluities" tended to "little use or benefit, but to the nourishment of pride."[18]

Winthrop recognized that riches would naturally tend to accumulate in the hands of the more enterprising colonists, but such wealth should not be idealized in itself, nor should it be flaunted. For this reason he felt compelled in 1632 to criticize Thomas Dudley, the deputy governor, for his usurious practices as well as for the extravagant expenditures he was making on his dwelling. Winthrop told Dudley that "he did not well to bestow such cost about wainscotting and adorning his house, in the beginning of a plantation, both in regard to the necessity of public charges, and for example." Dudley was not the only colonist frustrated by the limitations imposed by the Puritan social ethic. The emerging Boston merchant class especially chafed under the restrictions placed on their business and personal habits. Successful merchants, artisans, and traders struggled with the conflict inherent in a communal ethic that stressed both hard work and simple living. Inevitably, it seemed, the former took precedence over the latter.[19]

Winthrop soon found himself waging, along with John Cotton and others, a difficult battle against the combined forces of secularism, individualism, and materialism. From the beginning of the settlement there had appeared colonists who were prompted by other than religious and civic motives, and their number increased with the years. Moreover, many church-going Puritans themselves began to pursue profits at the expense of the public good that Cotton and Winthrop deemed supreme. The abundance of the colony's frontier environment and the entrepreneurial opportunities it afforded came to represent the rock that divided the economic and spiritual streams of Puritan social thought. Only two months after arriving in New England, a dismayed Winthrop saw the Devil amassing "his forces against us . . . so that I think here are some persons who never showed so much wickedness in England as they have done here."[20]

Obviously, Winthrop's initial hope that the colonists could walk the tightrope of moderation had been misguided. Promoting austerity, diligence, and piety in a land of increasingly lucrative opportunities and among an increasingly diverse citizenry was difficult, if not impossible. As early as 1635 popular resentment forced the repeal of wage and price regulations. Moreover, colonists soon began disregarding the sumptuary laws. An English trader noted the penchant for luxury goods among the supposedly temperate settlers when he wrote Winthrop in 1637, observing that "many in your plantations discover much pride, as appeareth by the letters we receive from them, wherein some of them write over to us for lace . . . cutwork coifes; and others, for deep stammell dyes; and some of your own men tell us that many of you go finely clad."[21]

By the middle of the seventeenth century, when John Winthrop died, the inability of many in the colony to live up to the ethic of the "middle way" seemed shockingly evident to those directly responsible for the governance of the commonwealth. Throughout the Massachusetts Bay Colony, it was reported, "men were generally failing in their duty to the community, seeking their own aggrandizement in the rich opportunities afforded by the land, commerce, crafts, and speculators, to the detriment of the community." Perhaps most disturbing to the new generation of magistrates was the desire among the laboring ranks to raise their social status and engage in costly display that went beyond their means and threatened the established social hierarchy. In 1651 the members of the Massachusetts General Court reported that "intolerable excesses . . . have crept in . . . amongst the people of mean condition, to the dishonor of God, the scandal of our profession, the consumption of estates, and altogether unsuitable to our poverty." To deal with this growing problem of maintaining traditional social distinctions, the Court issued a new sumptuary decree remarkable for its specificity and intent: "No person . . . whose visible estates shall not exceed the true and indifferent value of 200 pounds shall wear any gold or silver lace, or gold and silver buttons, or any bone lace above 2 shillings per yard, or silk hoods or scarves, upon the penalty of 10 shillings for every such offense."[22]

This development reflects the many-sided nature of the simple life as a societal ideal. The double standard inherent in the sumptuary legislation passed at mid-century suggests that many members of the new ruling group were more committed to the maintenance of a stable, hierarchical social order than to the universality of plain living. As the seventeenth century progressed, the frequent declamations against high living were almost always directed at common people, who were enabled by an expanding commercial economy to afford luxuries once confined to the elite. Ostentation thus came to be seen by the wealthy as a danger to the virtue of others but not so much to themselves, and the simple life in this sense, both then and later, ran the risk of becoming an ethic that one group wishes (or enforces) upon another.[23]

The self-interested paternalism reflected in the discriminatory sumptuary legislation may account in part for the unwillingness of ordinary folk to abide by such restrictions. For despite the passage of more sumptuary regulations, many colonists refused to be content with their lot, and the criticism of excessive getting and spending in Massachusetts Bay became a familiar litany in Puritan sermons and speeches. Materialism was coming to smother spiritualism, claimed minister Thomas Shepard, as more and more people raced to elevate their social and economic standing. The colonists were busily engaged in their callings, as indeed they should be, but many had lost sight of their priorities. "There is a number among us, young and old, of all sorts among us, that swarm up and down towns and woods, and fields, whose care and work hitherto has been like bees, only to get honey to their own hive, only to live comfortably with their houses, and lots, and victuals, and fine clothes, but not to live hereafter eternally."[24]

During the second half of the seventeenth century, such criticism increased in intensity as the disparity between ideal and real seemed to widen. The ministers, however, were faced with the logical dilemma inherent in the Protestant ethic. How could they limit social ambition without stifling economic enterprise? How could they promote opportunity without encouraging a fragmenting mobility? They railed at the dangers of materialism but could not condemn material success directly, since it was the result of the diligence they also preached. The puzzle of prosperity and piety thus limited the ministers and magistrates to attacking the love of wealth rather than wealth itself. What they emphasized time and again was that the colonists should strive to acquire a modest competency, not riches.

To accentuate the impiety and intemperance that they saw infecting their congregations as well as to provide examples of plain, pious living to follow, many second- and third-generation Puritan ministers and civic spokesmen highlighted the spiritual purity and material austerity of the original colonists. In his election sermon in 1663, John Higginson warned that young Puritans were casually abandoning the ideals of their ancestors in favor of the crass love of money. New England was "originally a plantation of religion," he concluded, "not a plantation of trade. Let merchants and such as are increasing cent per cent remember this."[25]

But to recall the past is not to renew it. Throughout the second half of the seventeenth century, ministers and magistrates went beyond issuing such jeremiads and created new institutional measures designed to enforce simple living. They passed laws ordering parents to fulfill their traditional roles as guardians of the civil and social order by paying stricter attention to the discipline and education of their children. To buttress family authority and to ensure the transmission of cultural values, towns were required after mid-century to establish schools. The impetus behind such mandatory public education was the fear that the Puritan ethic would be "buried in the grave of our fathers" unless something was done to transmit the original values of the colony to the younger generations. The Court also created new governmental officials called "tithingmen," whose stated purpose was to serve as social censors and snoopers, monitoring the behavior of the citizenry and upbraiding those who did not follow the "middle way."[26]

Yet such measures apparently did little to stem the tide of social upheaval and personal ambition. The pristine social vision of the colony's founders continued to be dashed upon the rock of selfish individualism. If one accepts the jeremiads at face value, New England society was rapidly developing along lines that ran counter to the pious communal ethic outlined by Winthrop aboard the *Arbella*. Liberalizing influences were gaining ground in pulpits and politics. And, at the same time, the original goal of economic self-sufficiency for the colony as the best way to preserve social unity by insulating its members from greed and corruption was quickly being supplanted by a thriving commercial system linking Massachusetts Bay with an international trading network. As profits and personal incomes increased, so, too, it seemed, did high living and spiritual deadness. Boston by the end of the seventeenth century was said to have strayed from its original backwater moorings into the mainstream of worldliness, having become a center of commercial activity and theological liberalism, ruled not by a clerical elite but by a merchant oligarchy. "The merchants seem to be rich men," one visitor remarked in 1675, "and their houses as handsomely furnished as in London." Should material concerns clash with affairs of faith, there were many now ready to choose the former over the latter. In 1714 a concerned layman deplored the "great extravagance that people are fallen into, far beyond their circumstances, in their purchases, buildings, families, expenses, apparel, generally in the whole way of living."[27]

Worldliness was not unique to the Boston area. Salem, New Haven, and other New England port towns were also witnessing the emergence of a high-living merchant aristocracy and an infectious commercial spirit. Even the backwoods settlements were beginning to feel the effects of creeping ostentation and declining spirituality. Solomon Stoddard, the powerful minister from Northampton, in western Massachusetts, was steadfast in his preaching against social status-seeking and energetic in his criticism of luxurious living. He once encouraged the prosecution of wealthy Elder John Strong's two daughters for wearing silk in a "flaunting" manner. Likewise, a Connecticut minister found that in his colony, at least, men were more eager to get "Land and Money and Stock, than they be about getting Religion revived, and securing the salvation of souls."[28]

Year after year, New England's ministers continued to preach jeremiads reminding the faithful how far they and their unchurched neighbors had strayed from the vision of the founders. Eleazer Mather, the influential Boston pastor, wondered aloud from his pulpit in the early eighteenth century whether there had been "less of the world" in the first years of settlement but more of the spirit. "Less trading, buying, selling, but more praying, more watching over hearts, more close walking, less plenty and less inequity?" As he surveyed Boston social life, Mather concluded: "Outward prosperity is a worm at the root of godliness, so that religion dies when the world thrives." Throughout the early eighteenth century, New England ministers reiterated their belief in the original Calvinist ethic, all the while many of their parishioners joined non-churchmembers in undermining its survival. In 1719 the Reverend Peter Thacher of Middleborough, Massachusetts, lamented: "Enormities among us show our departure from the natural simplicity and justice of the first generation."[29]

The jeremiad mentality of the seventeenth and early eighteenth century introduced what would become an important recurring element into the history of the simple life as a societal ideal. By constantly attributing "true" piety and simplicity to earlier generations, the Puritan reformers developed a nostalgic and self-flagellating mode of discourse that dates back to Aristophanes and Moses and has since become commonplace. Americans have inherited the burden of presuming themselves to be a people of providential destiny and therefore are repeatedly being told that they have sinned against the fathers.[30]

Actually, of course, there is no way of knowing the true extent of saintly and selfish behavior in society at a given time. Generalized assessments of cultural behavior and values, whether issued by ministers, social critics, or historians, are notoriously intuitive and therefore inexact. This was true for the Puritan jeremiads, and it has remained true for the tradition of disillusioned social criticism they originated. Too often the past seems far more virtuous, simpler, and happier than it actually was. The first generation of settlers was never as saintly as the jeremiads claimed, nor were later generations as debauched. The ministers often mistook the vices of their society for its norms, and their sermons were therefore more prescriptive than precisely descriptive. Certainly there were multitudes of decent folk who still conscientiously adhered to the ideal of pious simplicity, especially in the backwoods settlements. And there were undoubtedly many successful merchants who steadfastly retained a sense of civic responsibilty and individual piety.[31]

Yet, while acknowledging the distortions prevalent in such assessments of cultural behavior, one should not make the mistake of dismissing their relevance altogether. The jeremiads may have exaggerated the sinfulness of society, but they did help sustain the ideal of simple, pious living in a society undergoing rapid change. What people select to contrast with the past or emphasize about the present reveals much about their guiding hopes and aspirations. Without memory there can be little meaning, and the patina of assuredness that nostalgia adds to the concept of simple living has been crucial to its survival over the years. Many advocates have found it immensely comforting to presume that such an ideal was widely practiced in the past. And, no doubt, the second- and third-generation Puritan saints were equally buoyed by such a scrupulous image of their forefathers. Hence, in developing the jeremiad style, the Puritan reformers provided a mythic idiom for nurturing moral concern and social revival that has proven both durable and influential, if not entirely reliable.

It is also important to remember that hidden among the edifying sentimentality of the jeremiads was more than a germ of truth. If the social ethic of the original settlers was never a universal actuality, it was certainly even less so by 1700. The first generation was indeed "simpler" in its habits and ways of living than its successors. Whether it was necessarily more pious or more virtuous remains a puzzle. But many ministers and concerned laymen were convinced that their ancestors had indeed been more saintly. And the rhetorical weight of their laments was enough to convince almost any doubter that such was indeed the case. Nevertheless, many of those who agreed with such a stylized depiction of the first generation did not always agree with its indictment of the present generation or its prescription for reform. The simple life may have seemed both necessary and reasonable to the original Puritan leaders faced with carving out a Christian utopia in a "howling wilderness." To many of their descendants a half-century later, however, the need for such spartan enthusiasm was less self-evident. Children growing up in relative comfort and stability rather than in the midst of royal persecution or the "starving time" of the first settlements were understandably less inclined to see the virtue of a stringent austerity and a static social order.

There were other factors at work that undermined pious simplicity. As New England grew in population during the first half of the eighteenth century, it also grew in complexity. Towns lost their original cohesiveness as the pressures of population growth and economic survival forced many sons to abandon the open-field system and either move to the port towns or establish new individual homesteads at some distance from the central village. Along the coast, urbanization, commercialism, and cosmopolitanism were also combining to introduce diversity into the heretofore homogeneous social order. Ships brought not only new goods but new people and new ideas. Such developments combined to weaken the unity of village life and undermine communal supervision of personal behavior. In the process, the original medieval impulse toward a consensual communalism was gradually displaced by a more modern Lockean individualism that separated economic activity from political and religious authority. Fewer and fewer people were willing to defer to the ruling elite. In the midst of such social turbulence, the original Puritan ethic did become an increasingly defensive and minority ideal in the seaboard towns. Arminian rationalism and Anglicanism grew rapidly as the eighteenth century progressed. The founders had never foreseen that Puritanism would come to represent the outlook of such a small fraction of its society. They could never have imagined that "emigration would bring to the shores of Massachusetts Bay such a horde of average lusty Elizabethan Englishmen."[32]

As time passed, the traditional appeal for the public to practice simple living and sacrifice their individual interests to the common good was seen by many among the laboring classes as a "rhetorical cloak employed by those enjoying elevated status and material wealth to hide their covert selfish interests." The belief that the magistrates and merchants harbored such a hidden agenda convinced many that they must play by the same rules in order to survive and prosper. Thus, by the early 1700s, a new system of values that legitimized profit-seeking for private gain as the best means of promoting the welfare of society began to surface in New England at the same time that such an economic liberalism was taking root in England. In the process the Puritan ethic began to be transformed into the secular entrepreneurial ideology found among eighteenth-century Americans and Englishmen by Max Weber and others. The self-limiting Puritans were becoming grasping Yankees. Admittedly, this creeping materialism and social fragmentation seems slight by twentieth-century standards, but to those New Englanders who still identified with the exacting standards inherent in the original social covenant, the gulf between profession and practice was dramatic.[33]

The process of changing social values is far more complicated than such a compressed summary implies. Transformations in cultural norms are rarely sudden or complete. Old ideals are rarely displaced altogether. Nor do new beliefs and practices emerge full-blown. Instead, the old ideology and ways of living persist alongside the new. Though less noticeable, historical continuity has been almost as influential as historical change in defining the American experience. In fact, it has been the constant friction between the two that has given shape to the national character. Americans have embraced progress and tradition at the same time. This was especially true regarding the Puritan ethic. Religious traditionalists held on stubbornly to their original social vision throughout the eighteenth century, long after it had been challenged by a more modern outlook. Others tried to accommodate themselves to new conditions without compromising essential values. In New England at the end of the seventeenth century, there were numerous examples of both resistance and accommodation. One of the most complex was Cotton Mather.

Mather was the pre-eminent religious spokesman in New England at the start of the eighteenth century, and he reflected the transition taking place in the spiritual and economic life of the colony.[34] For the most part, his attitude toward work and wealth was decidedly orthodox. In language reminiscent of Calvin and Cotton, Mather emphasized the communal significance of work and frugality: "God hath placed us, as in a common hive. Let there be no drone in the hive; every man is to make some fair way, that the whole hive may be the better for him." Mather likewise adopted the jeremiad style so popular among Puritan ministers. In 1706 he charged that a tragic spiritual and moral decline had occurred since the original settlements because the colonists had mistakenly exchanged pious simplicity for worldly excess. "The cursed hunger of riches," he maintained, "will make men break through all the laws of God." And the Lord would thereafter wreak his vengeance. "If you make an idol of this world, God will throw your idol into the Fire!"[35]

In his magisterial history of the Massachusetts Bay colony, *Magnalia Christi Americana*, Mather described with unfeigned adulation the simple habits and tastes of the Puritan fathers whose exemplary lives he held up as models for a fallen generation to emulate. He tried to shame his readers into restoring the "primitive principles and primitive practices" of the founders, chastising his peers for the "visible shrink in all orders of men among us, from that greatness, and that goodness, which was the first grain that our God brought from three sifted kingdoms into this land." He succinctly pinpointed the reason for the decline. Religion "brought forth prosperity, and the daughter destroyed the mother." Nature's bounty had caused the settlers to forget the primary reason for their "errand into the wilderness."[36]

Mather repeated this refrain in his sermons at the turn of the century, warning Boston's merchants that God would find "an eternity to damn the man who cannot find the time to pray." Too many of them, he observed, were "wasting grand capacities on trivial ends." Yet it was not too late for reform, and he put forth the traditional Christian ideal of self-conscious material limitation as a standard. "I will mention," he advised, "the example of some eminent merchants, who have set their estates at a moderate and competent elevation, and resolved that they would never get any richer than that. . . . Whatever gain carried their estates beyond a *set sum*, they devoted it all to pious uses." Mather was convinced that such "stinted estates" were the answer to the ambiguity embodied in a Puritan ethic that demanded both diligence and temperance.[37]

Yet at other times Mather appeared less orthodox in his practice of the traditional Puritan ethic. His own spacious three-story house on Hanover Street in Boston, some argued, befitted more a merchant prince than a minister. It was adorned with classic pilasters and lavish ornamentation. Nor was Mather a traditionalist in his view of certain other social practices. In 1691 he used his pulpit to defend the wearing of periwigs, saying that it was wrong "to be so zealous against this innocent fashion, taken up and used by the best of men." The crusty Puritan layman Samuel Sewall, always on the alert for such clerical backsliding, grumbled in reply: "I expected not to hear a vindication of Periwigs in Boston Pulpit by Mr. Mather." As illustrated by this incident, Mather in his personal life was a maze of contradictions, espousing values in public that he had difficulty practicing in private.[38]

Mather also frequently seemed less critical of business life and material affluence than many of his predecessors had been, and as time passed he focused more of his attention on the dangers of idleness and sloth than on the dangers of avarice and luxury. Though still concerned about covetousness, he seemed to accept more readily the possession of great wealth as a sign of God's blessing: "Tis neither skill nor chance," he said, "that brings our estates into our hand, but it is of God, of whom we are told, that he is the maker both of the rich and the poor." Mather recognized that the nature of

colonial society had changed dramatically since the first years of settlement
and that any reform program must reflect such new circumstances. Consequently, while never totally abandoning the original Puritan ethic, he tended
to spend much more time emphasizing the need for the affluent to use their
wealth to "do good" in the community than he spent chastising them for
their preoccupation with making and expanding their fortunes. Where Winthrop had envisioned an entire society "knit together" by common purposes,
Mather by the eighteenth century had to settle for what he called "bundles of
love," small bands of dedicated believers sustaining the Word and themselves.[39]

Mather's attempt to revive the spiritual life of the church through an appeal
to good works and philanthropy had little tangible effect. Eighteenth-century
Massachusetts was dotted with the reform societies he advocated, yet the
hoped-for regeneration of individual piety among the larger public did not
ensue. He grew increasingly frustrated at his inability to reverse such trends.
"In my continual addresses unto people of all sorts, to set upon the practice
of serious religion," he wrote in his diary, "I am still answered by them, that
they can't." People were "so taken up with secular and sensual matters that
they have no leisure to acquaint themselves with a precious Jesus." He was
finally forced to admit that it would take more than hortatory sermons and
doing good to restore the primacy of religion in the colony's hierarchy of
values.[40]

The widening distance between ideals and behavior that Mather and other
colonial spokesmen bemoaned created what Erik Erikson has called a "guilt
culture" which led them to explain social crises and catastrophes as the direct
result of their society's failure to live up to the values its founders had
preached. Thus it was with mixed feelings that Mather and other clerical
leaders greeted the disastrous earthquake that rocked New England on
October 29, 1727. While mourning the widespread loss of life, they saw in the
natural disaster a possible catalyst to produce a spiritual and moral transformation. The day after the earthquake, Mather interpreted it to his congregation as an explicit warning from God that spiritual renewal was
imperative. Among the causes of God's ire were the "excesses and vanities"
of the people. "The earthquake says to us," he thundered, "put off some of
your ornaments." A few days later he reiterated the point, cautioning his
parishioners not to "lay the main stress of our demands on things, which the
worst people in the world can as easily come to as the best . . . let all
exorbitances and extravagances be rebuked and retrenched." Across the city,
other ministers interpreted the earthquake in the same manner and made
similar pleas. Thomas Prince of Boston's Old South Church saw the event as
a violent token of God's displeasure with the colonists' lust for "extravagant
apparel, building, furniture, [and] expensive and pompous ways of living."[41]

For several weeks after the tremors subsided, religious ardor did seem to
return to many of the city's residents. By the time Mather died the following

year, however, the regenerative effect of the earthquake had worn off, and the diminution of religious intensity again came to monopolize Puritan sermons. One minister regretfully admitted that "tho' nothing but the most amazing thunders and lightnings, and the most terrible earthquakes could awaken us, we are at this time, fallen into as dead a sleep as ever." Like Mather, the Puritan ethic in its original guise seemed to be suffering from old age, unable to comprehend or adjust to the dramatic changes transforming New England society.[42]

Yet colonial spirituality and simplicity were not dead yet. Just as religious orthodoxy seemed to be falling into its final sleep, it was again awakened with a start. This time the catalytic agent was not an earthquake or epidemic, but a spontaneous series of revivals that began in the southern colonies in the early 1730s and quickly spread up the Atlantic coast. Whole towns and villages were swept up in the ecstasy of conversion or reconversion, and no group, denomination, or area seemed immune to the effects of this "Great Awakening." A Connecticut minister testified that the Awakening touched people of "all orders and degrees, of all ages and characters." Many of Boston's converts, observed Benjamin Colman, pastor of Brattle Street Church, were "among the rich and polite of our sons and daughters." Even sceptical Ben Franklin was inspired by a revivalist sermon to contribute to a charitable religious enterprise in Georgia.[43]

The causes of the Great Awakening were many and complex, but a central concern of many of the revivalists was to halt their society's headlong rush toward impious materialism and to restore felt religion and simple living among the colonists. The Awakening's "primary appeal seems to have been for a renunciation of contemporary worldliness and a return to the simple, uncorrupted, pious, and virtuous life of an earlier generation. . . ." In 1733 a minister trying to encourage a revival of piety and plainness emphasized that the "powerful love of the world, and exorbitant reach after riches, which is become the reigning temper of all ranks in our land, is enough to awaken our concerns for abandoned, slighted and forgotten religion."[44]

In an effort to counter such disturbing trends, Jonathan Edwards, the towering figure in the New England Awakening, forcefully restated the Calvinist position that the gift of grace had no relationship to personal wealth. In fact, as he maintained, superfluous wealth was more apt to weaken one's religious faith than strengthen it. For Edwards himself this meant adopting a stringent personal ethic in order to redeem every possible moment for the precious business of religious study and family relations. The intensity of his piety initially led Edwards to sanction an extreme asceticism that went well beyond the "middle way" espoused by Calvin and Cotton. In January 1723, at age nineteen, he expressed his desire to "live in self-mortification, without ceasing, and even to weary myself for as long as I am in the world, and never to expect or desire a life of ease or pleasure." Self-denial, he observed, meant "denying worldly inclinations," and "forsaking and renouncing all worldly . . . enjoyments." In his almost total rejection of the material world, young Edwards came closer to expressing the monastic ethic than the Puritan ethic. Unlike John Winthrop, who had believed it neither desirable nor possible to deny material appetites or human passions altogether and who therefore chose to emphasize moderation as a guiding principle, Edwards seemed almost hysterically bent on self-mortification rather than merely self-control.[45]

Yet by the time Edwards assumed the Northampton pastorate in 1726, he had moderated his social outlook considerably. The same pious soul who a few years before had gloried in his monkish asceticism now lived in a comfortable manse on King Street and sported silver-buckled shoes, a wig, and clothes custom-tailored in Boston. Edwards had not developed a "craving disposition," as some of his more disgruntled parishioners asserted upon learning that he had purchased a "gold locket and chane" for his wife; he merely had come to recognize that some material comforts were not necessarily hostile to faith and were in fact commensurate with his role as a leading spokesman for the community. In a sermon devoted to the subject of living standards, Edwards denied that he was opposed to all "adorning the body." He insisted, however, that it was "very provoking to God when persons go beyond their rank." But he did not stop there. To him, simplicity was a standard for all ranks to follow. "Some fashions in themselves," Edwards stressed, are "ill—extravagant—very costly—immodest," regardless of a person's station in life.[46]

Judged by the ministerial standards of the era, Edwards and his family still led a conscientiously temperate existence. One of his early biographers emphasized that "wastefulness of any sort was not countenanced in the King Street home." George Whitefield, the stirring English evangelist who did so much to spread the Great Awakening throughout the colonies, confirmed this picture of Edwards. After visiting the Edwards household in Northampton in 1740, he recorded in his journal that "their children were not dressed in silks and satins, but plain, as become the children of those who, in all things, ought to be examples of Christian simplicity." In his public statements on the subject of Christian living, Edwards emphatically attacked the grasping for wealth and prestige he saw enervating the spiritual life of Massachusetts. "If one worm be a little exalted over another, by having more dust, or a bigger dunghill," he exclaimed, "how much does he make of himself!" Edwards attributed much of the prevailing social malaise to the emergence of a "false scheme of religion" that incorrectly attributed Divine favor to entrepreneurial success.[47]

The concerns that Edwards expressed were not limited to the Awakening in New England nor to the Reformed churches. Throughout the colonies, revivalists and concerned laymen of all religious persuasions pointed to the growth of materialism and rationalism as the primary causes of degeneration.

In Virginia, for example, Commissary James Blair upbraided his Anglican peers for their addiction to "all manner of gratifications of their luxury, stately houses, furniture, and equipage, plentiful tales, mirth, music, and drinking." At the same time, in South Carolina, the colony's chief justice, Benjamin Whitaker, urged his fellows to "abstain from that luxury and excess which within a few years past, has poured in upon us like a torrent" and so "greatly contributed to enervate and soften our minds, and to sink us into indolence and inactivity."[48]

But even more significant than the self-criticism among the ruling orders generated by the Awakening was the outspoken *popular* assault on the prerogatives and hypocrisies of the gentry elite. In this sense the Awakening backfired on those who had intended it to bolster church discipline and social order. Religious enthusiasm is not so easily manipulated, and in many ways the revivals proved more disruptive than reinforcing. The theology of individual conversion espoused by such popular exhorters as Whitefield, Gilbert Tennent, and James Davenport contained a potent new liberating element that would have far-reaching political and social implications. Although the Awakening's appeal initially cut across class lines, it proved more and more attractive to the lower ranks as it continued and spread. Tennent and Davenport, in fact, eagerly courted those at the bottom of the social scale—laborers, seamen, servants, artisans and craftsmen. By beseeching their listeners to renounce the established clergy and become the agents of their own salvation, the radicals sought to breed contempt for a new group of liberal church leaders whom they considered traitors to the original Protestant ethic. Their doing so served to erode even further the already crumbling edifice of a traditional deferential society.[49]

For the radical evangelicals, therefore, the Awakening was far more than a religious revival; it also represented an explicit challenge to gentry materialism and social control. Tennent, Davenport, and others were tired of hearing the ruling elite call upon the laboring classes to practice plainer manners and adopt more limited ambitions while they themselves enjoyed considerable luxury and status. And the popular preachers ceaselessly emphasized this contradiction in their assault on the rich and powerful. They pointedly contrasted those who were preoccupied with gaining "temporary wealth and riches" with the truly virtuous colonists who were contented with the "riches of Christ." It was time, the evangelists demanded, that the upper classes began living up to the same standard of plain living and public concern that they had for years tried to impose on the masses. "The Grandees," Tennent exclaimed, "grow in wickedness in proportion to their increase in wealth," and they would be called to account by a wrathful God and an aroused citizenry. Similar rhetoric appeared in sermons throughout the colonies. The Baptist revivals occurred somewhat later than the Congregational and Presbyterian Awakening in the North, but they exhibited the same contempt for the dissolute social behavior of the gentry. Baptists in Virginia adopted the austere ethic of other evangelicals, vigorously renouncing such "superfluous forms and Modes of Dressing . . . as cock't hats."[50]

Such inflammatory rhetoric terrified the upper classes, who claimed that the radical revivalists were breeding "anarchy, levelling, and dissolution." Genteel critics characterized the Baptists as a "contemptible class of people" making up an "ignorant . . . and illiterate sect" which "none of the rich or learned ever join." Charles Chauncey, the staid spokesman for the new liberal theology and friend of the Boston merchants who dominated his First Church, was equally scornful of the Presbyterian and Congregational Awakeners. He warned that the itinerant rabble-rousers were attempting to "destroy all property, to make all things common, wives as well as goods." This was utter nonsense, but its hysteria reflects the nervousness felt by the urban elite when called upon to practice the stringent social ethic of self-restraint and stewardship that they themselves preached.[51]

For a time during the 1730s and 1740s the revivalists reported startling evidence of both renewed piety and simplicity among the well-to-do. Edwards pointed out in his *Thoughts on the Revival* that during the early stages of the Awakening, people began abandoning "those things of which they were extremely fond, and in which they had placed the happiness of their lives." Everywhere in New England the "wealthy and fashionable," the "great beaus and fine ladies relinquished their vanities" and "extravagance in apparel." He observed in 1734 that in Northampton people seemed to "dread their former extravagances." In Boston the Awakening produced a "week of Sabbaths" during which taverns and social clubs, which "have always proved unfriendly to serious Godliness," were abandoned in preference for prayer meetings, and religious discussions were said to be "almost fashionable." Affluent young men and women conspicuously discarded their imported finery and strolled down the Boston Mall wearing the plain dress of their forefathers.[52]

But as had happened so often in the past, such regeneration was both exaggerated and fleeting. The Great Awakening, with its accompanying renewal of plain living, died out almost as suddenly as it had arisen, and the simple life continued its retreat in the face of the burgeoning economic growth of the colonies. By the late 1740s Edwards was forced to acknowledge that the revival of piety and plainness he had promoted in Northampton had quickly subsided. Between 1744 and 1748 there was not a single new applicant for membership in his church. And the simplicities he observed during the early stages of the revivals were likewise discarded. "We in this town," he remarked, "are evidently got to great excess. Boston is extravagant beyond London. And we, considering all things, I think beyond them." Not long thereafter, his congregation, grown irritated by his constant strictures, relieved Pastor Edwards of his duties.[53]

Throughout New England at mid-century the gap between professed ideals and actual behavior seemed to grow ever wider, and the Puritan ethic took on a meaning that bore little resemblance to the credo preached by the colonial founders. Successful New Englanders continued to devote more and more of their time and energy to the pursuit of their particular calling at the expense of their general calling. Hard work and the enjoyment of the fruits of one's labor became an ethic almost complete in itself, devoid of much spiritual content. As an indentured farmhand reported in the 1740s, his master never mentioned religion: "His whole attention was taken up on the pursuits of the good things of this world; wealth was his supreme object. I am afraid gold was his God."[54]

That Americans in the colonies came to emphasize material gratification more than pious self-restraint is not surprising. The simple life as expressed by early Puritans was circumscribed by a stringent set of limits. People were encouraged to work and prosper but not so much that they became crassly materialistic or intent upon living above their appointed station; they were reminded to be temperate in their style of living, since needless luxury for some meant penury for others; they were warned that individual liberty in the workplace and marketplace must always defer to the public good; and, they were told that by reducing their material desires they could afford more time for worship, their families, and community service. But such restraints no longer seemed appropriate either to many upwardly mobile Americans dazzled by the prosperous and seemingly fluid new society opening up before their eyes or to those already blessed with abundance. By the nineteenth century the British literary traveler Anthony Trollope could note that Boston still "calls itself a Puritan city, but it has divested its Puritanism of austerity." He then wryly added: "The Puritans of Boston are simple in their tastes and expense. Champagne and canvas-back ducks I found to be the provisions most in vogue among those who desired to adhere to the manner of their forefathers."[55]

CHAPTER TWO

The Quaker Ethic

The Puritans were not the only settlers who sailed for America intent upon establishing a plain and pious society. A little more than fifty years after John Winthrop and the *Arbella* arrived off the coast of Massachusetts, English Quakers began filtering into the Delaware Valley, determined to carry out their own "holy experiment" under the direction of William Penn. Like their Puritan counterparts, the Quakers came to do good in America and ended up doing too well. The same entrepreneurial opportunities that had proven irresistible in Massachusetts and Connecticut quickly challenged the unadorned social ethic that the Friends brought with them to the New World. At first, economic success caused many of the Quakers to undergo what observers labeled a decline in simplicity and spirituality similar to the Puritans'. Eventually, however, concerned Friends were able to revitalize their original ideals to a much greater degree. How they did so tells much about the strengths and limitations of the simple life as a collective enterprise.

The Society of Friends was formed soon after George Fox climbed atop Pendle Hill in Lancashire during the spring of 1652 and received a vision of a "great people to be gathered." Superficially, at least, Quakerism and Puritanism were manifestations of the same nonconformist impulse. But they were quite different manifestations. Each of the two groups, in fact, went out of its way to attack and irritate the other. In New England, the Puritan magistrates and divines were so terrified of Quakerism that they immediately outlawed the sect and proceeded to arrest, torture, and hang those Quaker martyrs who slipped into the Massachusetts Bay colony and began professing their disruptive beliefs.[1]

Why such animosity? By rejecting the Calvinist doctrine of predestination and insisting that God's grace was a gift offered to all, Quakerism raised the specter of antinomian individualism and religious toleration. The Quakers' perfectionist enthusiasm, insistent pacifism, and egalitarian implications placed them at the extreme left-wing of the Protestant spectrum, and the movement therefore posed a significant threat to the Puritan religious and political order.

Yet if the Puritans and Quakers differed theologically, driving each other to fury, they at the same time both promoted a "Christianity writ plain." The Friends echoed Calvin and the Puritans in emphasizing the virtues of thrift, sobriety, and hard work at one's calling. And it was only natural, they agreed, to enjoy the fruits of one's labor. God did not intend man to be poor and uncomfortable. But they also stressed that the material world of daily toil and daily bread was, after all, only transitory, and one's heart should be set upon eternal treasures. By living simply, by resolutely surrendering that which was not essential, the Friends could keep themselves free—free to speak their minds, free from the wiles of greed, free to devote themselves primarily to spiritual pursuits and social service rather than limitless material gains.[2]

Fox emphasized the liberating aspects of the Quaker simple life when he advised the Friends: "Neither be cumbred nor surfeited with the Riches of this World, nor bound, nor strained with them, and be married to the Lord." He realized that energetic and frugal Quakers would naturally increase their wealth, but he cautioned that after "Riches do increase, take heed of setting your Hearts upon them, lest they become a Curse and a Plague to you." His warning illustrated the perplexing challenge embodied in both the Puritan and Quaker ethics—how to live and work in a complex, tempting material world without coming to love it. Yet the early Friends were even more confident than their Calvinist counterparts in their ability to manage such conflicting tensions. Openly perfectionist in outlook, they believed that those who responded to the "Inner Light" could begin to control their base passions and serve God's will.[3]

The original Quaker ethic, then, was designed to teach Friends how to live rather than to make a living. Simplicity would not only serve as a testament to the rest of the world against the evils of conceit, greed, and superfluity, but also promote social justice. If a few lived in needless luxury, the Friends assumed, then the masses would be relegated to poverty. Early Quaker thought rejected the notion that the extravagant habits of the wealthy were necessary in order to provide jobs for the poor. George Fox suggested that those who believed such a theory should exchange their jewels, raiments, and mansions for money and then distribute the proceeds to the needy, a considerably more direct approach to the problem of poverty. He reminded affluent Quakers that "there is so much destroyed in your superfluity and vanity that would maintain the weak, lame, and blind."[4]

Quaker social thought did not expect everyone to have the same income or standard of living, but it did go beyond Puritanism in insisting that the widening gap between the wealthy and the indigent should be narrowed. Robert Barclay, the most articulate interpreter of early Quakerism, explained: "We say not . . . that no man may use the creation more or less than another; for we know, that as it hath pleased God to disperse it diversely, giving to some more, and some less, so they may use it accordingly." The key point was that personal expenditures should be based on need rather than impulse. "If a man be clothed soberly and without superfluity, though finer than that which his servant is clothed with," Barclay continued, "we shall not blame him for it; the abstaining from superfluities, which his condition and education have accustomed to, may be in him a greater act of mortification than the abstaining from fine clothes in the servant, who never was accustomed to them." Leading a plain and benevolent life, at whatever level, would benefit the community as a whole and would help ensure that one's heart was wedded to the eternal rather than the temporal world.[5]

Pursuing a simple Quaker life in England, however, grew more difficult as the seventeenth century progressed. As the persecution of nonconformist sects intensified, many of the normally tenacious Friends migrated to Quaker settlements in West Jersey and Pennsylvania rather than suffer continued harassment. In America, they hoped, the persecuted Friend could work and worship unhampered by the constant threat of being arrested or fined, and thereby be better able to "improve his talent, and bring more plenteous fruits, to the glory of God, and public welfare of the whole creation." The danger was that the new economic opportunities in America might divert the primary attention of the Friends from piety to profits. In 1682 George Fox warned a group of settlers boarding ship for Pennsylvania that they must remain steadfast in their convictions: "My friends, that are gone, and are going, over to Plant, and make outward Plantations in America, keep your own Plantations in your Hearts, with the Spirit and Power of God, that your own Vines and Lilies be not hurt."[6]

William Penn shared Fox's concern and was determined that his "holy experiment" in America not follow the same pattern of declining piety and rising materialism that had characterized the Puritan settlements in New England. At first glance the founder of Pennsylvania would seem an unlikely proponent of the simple life. Born in 1644, in the midst of the Civil War, Penn was the son of Admiral Sir William Penn, the conqueror of Jamaica and friend of both Charles II and his brother James, duke of York. The younger Penn reached maturity at the time of the Stuart Restoration, and he reaped the benefits of his father's high station. Throughout his life he would enjoy access to the drawing-rooms of the great and powerful. Impressionable, sensitive, and much given to mystical pietism as a youth, Penn received an excellent humanist education at Chigwell School, Oxford, Saumur (the Protestant university in France), and Lincoln's Inn. He then traveled widely in Europe with several other "persons of rank," and for a time he lived the carefree life of a gentleman at the court of Louis XIV. When Penn returned to London from the Continent in 1664, Samuel Pepys described him as being possessed of "a great deal if not too much, of the vanity of the French garb, and affected manner of speech and gait." The only surviving contemporary painting of Penn bears out this description. It shows him shortly after his return from France, infected with French mannerisms, bedecked in a suit of armor and wearing a flowing wig (his own hair had been severely damaged by the smallpox).[7]

Yet William Penn did not long remain an indulgent courtier. In 1667, while managing his father's estate in Ireland, he heard Thomas Loe preach of "the faith that overcomes the world" and was suddenly converted to Quakerism. "When about Two and Twenty Years of Age," he later remembered, "God took me by the hand and led me out of the pleasures, vanities and hopes of the world." Much to the dismay of his conservative father, William decided to devote himself completely to serving the Society of Friends, and he quickly became one of the sect's most influential proponents, a close associate of Fox, Thomas Ellwood, Isaac Penington, and other noted Quaker leaders.[8]

Expounding the Quaker gospel occasionally brought Penn into conflict with the authorities, and he was jailed several times. During one such period of confinement in the Tower, he produced the first version of his stirring social tract "No Cross, No Crown." Penn's social philosophy as expressed in "No Cross, No Crown" and other writings represented an almost complete rejection of the courtly style of living he had practiced before his conversion. The true believer, he asserted, must lead a life of self-denial, for Christ's cross represents the path to Christ's crown. Self-denial, however, did not require separating oneself from the world. Penn shared with Calvin and the Puritans the belief that the monastic ideal was bankrupt, a "lazy, rusty, [and] unprofitable" model. It was instead imperative that Friends work out the implications of their faith in the midst of everyday life, carrying the serum of the spirit into the veins of the larger society. The Christian was to live in the world, emulating the "plain and exact life" of Christ and taking care not to allow the world's attractions to clog the channels of the spirit. "The Cross of Christ," he said, "truly overcomes the world and leads a life of purity in the face of its allurements."[9]

Liberally buttressing his arguments with examples from Greek and Roman philosophy as well as the New Testament, Penn emphasized that the mere possession of wealth was not evil, but the luxury and avarice that frequently accompanied it were. "Riches serve wise men," he maintained, "but command a fool." Too often the insatiable appetite for more wealth blinded people to the higher goals of life, leading them to believe that "cumber, not retirement, and gain, not content, were the duty and comfort of a Christian." Those who blindly pursued riches were prisoners to their work and traitors to their faith: "Do we not see how early they rise; how late they go to bed; how full of the Change, the shop, the warehouse, the customhouse; of bills, bonds, charter-parties, etc., they are?" Serving and worshipping God, he declared, must always remain the primary business of life. In a letter to his wife and children, Penn advised how to avoid the snares of Mammon: "Let your industry and parsimony go no farther than for a sufficiency for life, and to make a provision for your children (and that in moderation, if the Lord gives you any)."[10]

Penn intended such advice to help preserve individual piety and promote both the national interest and social justice. He assumed that if most people adopted a simple life suitable to their social rank, the cost of labor would fall, as would retail prices, and a greater market would result, thereby enabling the country to reduce its dependence on foreign imports. In this way, he argued, "the temperance I plead for is not only religiously, but politically good." In addition, the simple life of hard work coupled with benevolence would help ameliorate the social inequalities prevalent in British society. Such a combination of virtues would help cure society "of two extremes, want and excess: and the one would supply the other, and so bring both nearer to a mean; the just degree of earthly happiness." There was, Penn claimed, "enough for all; let some content themselves with less; a few things plain and decent serve a Christian life."[11]

This was the simple social ethic that the aristocratic Penn hoped would flourish in his new American colony. His study of history had convinced him that societies declined when luxury and secularism appeared. In 1684, two years after Philadelphia was founded, he encouraged the colonists to keep their priorities in order: "Have a care of cumber, and the love and cares of the world . . . truly blessed is that man and woman who, in the invisible power, rule their affections about the visible things, and who use the world as true travelers and pilgrims, whose home is not here below." The Quaker colonists, he advised, should strive to maintain an essentially agricultural society. "The country life is to be preferred, for there we see the works of God, but in cities little else but the works of men; and the one makes a better subject for our contemplation than the other." This commitment to an ideal society of plain farmers led by what Penn called "natural aristocrats" closely foreshadowed the social outlook of John Adams, Thomas Jefferson, and other republican spokesmen a century later.[12]

At first there was considerable support among the original Quaker colonists for such a philosophy of living. Though prospects of economic gain undoubtedly tantalized many of the settlers, a significant number had sincerely responded to Penn's request for colonists who "have an eye to the Good of prosperity, and that both understand and delight to promote good Discipline and just Government among a plain and well intending people." James Claypoole, one of the first to land in Philadelphia, spoke for many when he testified that he was not "striving or making haste to be rich, but my Intent and desire is to go on quietly and moderately, and to have a regard to the Lord in all my ways."[13]

To help the Quakers maintain a simple life of hard work and piety as they carved out new colonies in America, Penn and the governing political and religious authorities in Pennsylvania and West Jersey carefully monitored the conduct of the settlers, believing that compulsion was frequently necessary to convince people "to do what they know is right and fit." In addition to his frequently utopian optimism, Penn retained a degree of authoritarianism. He believed that the mere planting of a colony did not guarantee order and piety, especially in a settlement that encouraged religious toleration. At least some legal and institutional controls were necessary to restrain men's baser tendencies. As he stressed in the preface to the Frame of Government of 1682, the first objective of government was to "terrify Evil-doers."[14]

Like John Winthrop, Penn demanded that wage and price controls and sumptuary laws be enacted to harness pride and prodigality. The monthly, quarterly, and yearly Quaker meetings also exercised considerable control over the Friends. They required Quakers to assume charitable obligations and to engage in ethical business practices and plain habits of living. Friends were cautioned not to trade beyond their abilities or needs. Vain, needless objects were to be avoided, and sobriety, simplicity, and modesty cultivated. Quaker meetings were as conscientious as the Puritan authorities in issuing detailed instructions on right conduct. But their sumptuary guidelines were to be followed by all Friends, regardless of their wealth or status. One meeting, for instance, urged in 1695

> that all that profess the Truth, and their Children, whether Young or Grown Up, keep to Plainness in Apparel As become the Truth and that none Wear long lapp'd Sleeves or Coats gathered at the Sides, or Superfluous Buttons, or Broad Ribbons about their Hats, or long curled Periwigs . . . or other useless and superfluous Things.

Five years later the same meeting warned children to avoid the "world's corrupt language, manners & Vain needless Things & Fashions."[15]

Yet in spite of such frequent reminders, many of the Quakers of Pennsylvania and West Jersey either did not share such convictions from the start or they gradually underwent the same departure from piety and simplicity experienced by the Puritans in Massachusetts. The history of Pennsylvania during the three generations that it remained a Quaker-controlled commonwealth is one of growing political friction and social divisions, rising prosperity, and diminishing plainness and spirituality. Rapid migration of German and Scots-Irish settlers into and through the Delaware Valley eventually transformed the ruling Quaker majority into a defensive and fragmented minority, and the political, social, and religious consensus of the original settlement disintegrated. By 1750 Friends made up only a quarter of the colony's population. Undoubtedly, much of the decline in Quaker spirituality also resulted from the lust for wealth and luxurious living that motivated more and more of the Friends themselves. Unimpeded by religious persecution and political oppression and having first access to the most fertile lands and promising trades, many early Quaker colonists quickly found the door to wealth wide open, and they rushed across its threshold.[16]

Honest, efficient, and energetic, the Quaker merchants, artisans, and farmers thrived. And just as Fox and Penn had feared, many of them adopted the worldly attitudes and trappings that their faith explicitly rejected. Reports of laxity in self-discipline were widespread in a colony that soon was the most tolerant and prosperous in North America. As early as 1690 George Fox feared that the American Friends were in danger of submerging themselves in the world rather than transforming it. "Take heed," he cautioned, "of sitting down in the earth and having your minds in earthly things, coveting and striving for the earth. . . . Some have lost morality and humanity and the true Christian charity." For the most part, however, his pleas had little effect. The changing mores and composition of the colony continued to erode its simple social ethic. An old Quaker saying pinpointed the problem: "A carriage and pair does not long continue to drive to a meetinghouse."[17]

Indeed, in Philadelphia especially, the countinghouse did soon replace the meetinghouse as the locus of activity and devotion. By 1697 Penn was shocked at the condition of his "holy experiment" and began to see his cherished Philadelphia as a modern Babylon: "The Reports are . . . that there is no place more run over with wickedness, sins so very scandalous, openly committed, in defiance of law & virtue, facts so foul, I am forbid [by] my common modesty to relate them." Philadelphia's Quaker merchants adopted a flamboyant way of life that openly contradicted their social creed, and the change from simplicity to sumptuousness grew even more visible as the eighteenth century progressed. One visitor to Pennsylvania observed in 1724: "According to appearances plainness is vanishing pretty much."[18]

Like their Puritan counterparts, many of the original Quaker settlers failed to transmit to their children their own religious zeal and social ethic. Samuel Fothergill, a leading English Quaker spokesman who during the mid-1750s tried to revive the declining spiritual discipline in Pennsylvania, emphasized this point in analyzing the colony's malaise:

> Their fathers came into the country, and bought large tracts of land for a trifle; their sons found large estates come into their possession, and a profession of religion which was partly national, which descended like a patrimony from their fathers, and cost as little. They settled in ease and affluence, and whilst they made the barren wilderness as a fruitful field, suffered the plantation of God to be as a field uncultivated, and a desert.

Growing up in a tolerant and bounteous Pennsylvania gave many of the younger Quakers a much different outlook from their parents, who had suffered religious persecution and economic hardship in England. The younger generation's attachment to the Society of Friends was often the result of inherited convention rather than personal conviction, and their lack

of self-discipline betrayed their superficial commitment. A young Philadelphia Friend gave a gloomy account of several of his former schoolmates:
"Poor P.S. . . . drinks very hard . . . John Cameron, John Relf, John
Baily, John Marsh and Dan Wistar are broke. . . . The meeting is disowning
many for sottishness and immorality, and has condemned D.W. for keeping
game cocks." He then added that "D.W." had also paid a girl a handsome
sum "to strip Stark naked before him." The Quaker principle of unadorn-
ment had indeed taken an unusual twist.[19]

As more and more Friends grew enmeshed in worldly activities and
values, tensions within Quaker communities throughout the colonies erupted
into open conflict. Many prosperous Quakers in the seaboard towns rebelled
against the austere personal and economic guidelines set forth by the monthly
meetings, which tended to be dominated by rural traditionalists. In response
to such irking criticism and supervision, some of the richest and most
powerful city Friends went so far as to renounce Quakerism altogether and
join the more fashionable and less severe Anglican church, with its popular
deistic doctrines, elaborate ritual, and social prestige. Penn's son Thomas
illustrated this development. In 1751 he remarked that he would "no longer
continue the little distinctions of dress" that Quakerism demanded, and he
joined the Church of England.[20]

Still other prosperous Friends illustrated the ambiguity inherent in the
Quaker ethic when put into practice. Before his death in 1718 William Penn
himself had demonstrated that plain living could be interpreted rather
broadly. In 1682 he had claimed: "I need no wealth but sufficiency." And on
another occasion he declared that "All Excess is ill." That was all well and
good, but judging from his own example one might question the usefulness
of his standard. Even after he had turned Quaker, Penn had retained many
of his aristocratic instincts and tastes. He loved stately living, good food, and
costly wine. Despite George Fox's explanation that Penn needed a wig to
warm his bald head, some Friends questioned why he needed *four* of them.
Pennsbury, his magnificent country estate overlooking the Delaware River,
with its broad lawns, formal gardens, thoroughbred horses, and numerous
outbuildings, seemed more appropriate to a feudal lord than a Quaker
leader. Staffed by five gardeners, twenty slaves, and several houseservants,
the estate boasted its own vineyards managed by a Frenchman brought to
the colony solely for that purpose. Penn had his steward order butter from
Rhode Island, candles from Boston, and rum from Jamaica. And, to carry
him from his country home to Philadelphia, he had a team of shipwrights
build a twelve-oared barge.[21]

Despite Penn's sincere pleas for plain living among his colonists, he
himself clearly lacked a sense of economy. But like many other upper-class
spokesmen for the simple life, then and since, Penn saw no contradiction
between his espousal of material moderation and his own princely style of
living. He occasionally reminded critics that his position as proprietor

dictated a certain amount of display in order to sustain the power and prestige of his office, especially since he would be in England much of the time. The estate is a poor surrogate for the man, he recognized, but at least it might serve as a visible reminder of his office. Moreover, Penn believed that his own wealth and elevated standing provided him with the power and the time to engage in spiritual reflection, civic leadership, and good works. As he had said in "No Cross, No Crown,"

> I must grant, that the condition of our great men is much to be preferred to the ranks of the inferior people. . . . For, first they have more power to do good: and, if their hearts be equal to their ability, they are blessings to the people of any country. . . . [since] they have more help, leisure, and occasion, to polish their passions and tempers with books and conversation.

Thus, for the masses he advised austerity; for himself and a few others like him, he supported enlightened gentility.[22]

Isaac Norris, one of the wealthiest of Quaker merchants, made this same distinction in 1707 when he responded to a fellow Friend's criticism of his lavish habits. Norris admitted that he and his family were living in considerable comfort, even luxury, and, he confessed, self-restraint was indeed a virtue to be preferred over self-indulgence. But he explained that temperance was a virtue relative to one's social standing. "Every man ought soberly and discreetly to set bounds for himself and avoid extremes, still bearing due regard to the society he is of." Norris and the other rich Quakers, like their Puritan counterparts, saw no inevitable contradiction between affluence and simplicity. One could be poor and simple or rich and seemingly unadorned. Quaker grandees such as Norris used this rationale to purchase household goods of the finest quality and highest price, as long as they were in a plain style. A well-to-do Friend reflected this practice when he requested from a London merchant two "Japan'd Black Corner Cubbards, with 2 Doors to each, no Red in 'em, *of the best Sort but Plain.*"[23]

Some of the more traditional Friends observed these developments with consternation. To them the supposedly temperate, yet in fact indulgent life of aristocrats like Norris was a transparent distortion of the original Quaker ethic. The Philadelphia Monthly Meeting concluded in 1756 that it "is too obvious . . . that there's a great declension in many professing Friends among us from the primitive Simplicity of our Forefathers. . . ." Nor was this an isolated assessment. By the middle of the eighteenth century, numerous Friends were interpreting the decline of the "holy experiment" in the same way. In 1764 John Smith, an elderly Quaker from rural Chester County, recalled the development of the colony in an address to the Yearly Meeting of Ministers in Philadelphia. At the beginning of the century, he observed, the Friends were "a plain, lowly minded people." A generation later, as wealth increased along with a general accommodation to the fashions of the world, the Quaker meetings "were not as lively and edifying." Now, he stressed, many Friends had grown rich, and luxurious living among the affluent had become the norm rather than the exception. Once simplicity had been abandoned, he concluded, it did not take long for the Quaker merchant princes to abandon their spirituality as well.[24]

Such often-repeated commentaries demonstrate that the Quakers were as adept as the Puritans in developing the jeremiad as an expository and rhetorical form. And, no doubt, their laments provide similarly exaggerated pictures of both past and present practices. Yet to a much greater degree than their counterparts in New England, the Quakers did more than just listen shamefacedly to such admonitions and then return to business as usual. A significant number of Friends conscientiously set about reordering their lives. Beginning in the 1740s and continuing for well over a generation, a remarkably sustained reformation occurred among concerned Friends in the Delaware Valley and eventually spread throughout the Quaker communities in all the colonies. Not long after Jonathan Edwards, George Whitefield, Gilbert Tennent, and others led a Presbyterian and Congregationalist revival, the Quakers experienced their own "Great Awakening."[25]

The impetus behind this dramatic reformation in Quaker life at mid-century was provided by a number of dedicated Friends determined to restore the community's spiritual basis and social ethic. Samuel Fothergill, Anthony Benezet, John Churchman, John Smith, John Woolman, and others launched a spirited assault on the worship of wealth and luxurious living that seemed most responsible for the erosion of orthodox Quaker beliefs and practices. In 1752, Churchman, a Chester County Friend, chastised his rich Quaker brethren, emphasizing that "those who were delighted in the pursuit of worldly treasures, and lived in the pleasures and pollutions of the world . . . were of the church of antichrist." Benezet was even more severe in his criticism of the worldliness that had infected the Friends. He especially cringed when affluent Quakers tried to rationalize their relentless pursuit of wealth and prestige as being consonant with God's will. "The desire of amassing wealth and of gaining the esteem of the world," he warned, "will no more unite with ye pure genuine spirit of ye Gospel than iron will unite with clay." Violation of the Quaker principle of plain, pious living was to him a spiritual felony, not a misdemeanor: "I cannot look upon the love of the world & giving way to desire for riches, as many do, as a pardonable frailty; but rather esteem it a departure from the divine life, which must either gradually kill all religion in the Soul, or be itself killed, by it."[26]

In 1755 the growing religious revival sponsored by Benezet and other Quaker saints began to spill over into the political arena. With the outbreak of the French and Indian War in 1754, Indians had begun attacking settlers in western Pennsylvania, and the Quaker members controlling the Assembly were confronted with a practical and spiritual dilemma. How could they provide for the defense of the frontier settlements and at the same time remain true to their pacifist principles? In March 1755 John Woolman and other concerned Friends at the General Meeting of Ministers and Elders wrote an epistle on the issue to the Friends serving in the Assembly. Referring to the conflict between France and England, it recognized the "commotions and stirrings of the powers of the earth at this time near us" and concluded that the Quakers must strive to be "sufficiently disentangled from the surfeiting cares of this life, and redeemed from the love of the world, that no earthly possessions nor enjoyments may bias our judgments, or turn us from that resignation, and entire trust in God, to which his blessing is more surely annexed."[27]

Such a plea on behalf of traditional Quaker values encountered stiff resistance. Some politically prominent Friends such as Isaac Norris II argued that defensive military action was justified. Others believed it only reasonable to provide arms for non-Quakers to use, if so requested. There was a small group of Friends in the Assembly, however, who could not in good conscience vote for any military appropriations. Late in 1755 James Pemberton led six other pacifist Friends in resigning from the Assembly, and their seats were soon taken by supporters of Benjamin Franklin's policy of vigorous military defense. Their withdrawal effectively ended Quaker control of the Assembly. Hence, where the Puritans had tended to sacrifice their spiritual beliefs in order to maintain their political and social power, the zealous Quakers decided that they must sacrifice political authority in order to save their religious principles.

Yet the end of Quaker political control may have been a blessing in disguise, for it provided a further stimulus to reform among many Friends, forcing them to renew their original emphasis on person-to-person relationships rather than political structures. They came to realize that, instead of transforming the world, they had been transformed by a too close accommodation to it. Many concerned Friends thereafter began an energetic effort to revive the piety and plainness of their sect. Some went from house to house, urging their peers to give up their pursuit of the vanities of the world and restore the simplicity dictated by their faith. At the same time, the yearly meetings began enforcing strict disciplinary codes. Friends were expelled for marrying non-Quakers, for violating the principle of plainness in dress and deportment, and for supporting military action. Quaker toleration had discovered its limitations.

In the process of this revival, many more Friends began a searching re-examination of their religious life and its relationship to their temporal callings. Those undergoing such personal "awakenings" included some of the most prominent and prosperous Friends in the colony. It was reported, for instance, that Israel Pemberton, Jr., certainly one of the richest merchants in Philadelphia, was so zealous in his renewed piety that he gave "friends daily uneasiness by his froward conduct." In 1757 Anthony Benezet noted the growing transformation in the religious life of Pennsylvania: "I may with pleasure say, that there continues to be a great shaking amongst our dry bones, the Hearts of many amongst us, especially the youth, are touched with love and zeal for God."[28]

Among the leaders of the mid-eighteenth-century Quaker reform movement, none was more inspiring than John Woolman. In fact, he may be the noblest exemplar of simple living ever produced in America. Woolman did not have the towering intellect of Jonathan Edwards, but he was much more openly humane than his more famous counterpart. It was easy enough for a William Penn and other wealthy reformers to tell the lower classes to be contented with a simple way of living while they themselves enjoyed the comforts of their high station. But to command the sustained respect of commoners required a saintly willingness to share some of their austerities. Woolman displayed such a practiced empathy, and in doing so he became a figure both believed and beloved. Woolman was a true Quaker in the mold of George Fox, at home among the common folk of his time, intensely concerned about their welfare as well as understanding of their weaknesses. In his quiet and humble way he served as both an apostle of simple living and an early crusader against slavery, urging those around him to abandon their worship of worldly treasure and leisurely ease and redirect their devotion to the service of God and all of humanity. Then and since, his life of Christian simplicity and good works has served as an inspiration to countless others around the world. Samuel Taylor Coleridge observed in 1797 that he "should almost despair of that man who could peruse the life of John Woolman without an amelioration of heart."[29]

Born in 1720 into a large Quaker family in Northampton, West Jersey, about twenty miles east of Philadelphia, John Woolman lived his first twenty-one years at home on his father's farm. He was raised in a household of strict Quaker piety where the Bible "or some religious books" were read aloud every Sunday. Like most youths, Woolman occasionally succumbed to the world's temptations. He spoke of himself as a plant "which produced much wild grapes." Yet through all his youthful waywardness he "retained a love and esteem for pious people." In time he learned to avoid the "snares" of youth, and by regularly attending Quaker meetings and reading the Bible and such works as Fox's *Book of Doctrinals* and Penn's *No Cross, No Crown*, he learned, like St. Francis, to "love and reverence God the Creator and to exercise true justice and goodness, not only toward all men but also toward the brute creatures."[30]

Once his inward life was securely grounded, Woolman began planning his outward life. He decided as a youth that farming was not to be his calling. Farm work was more than his frail physique could manage, so at age twenty-one he left home and moved to the nearby village of Mount Holly, where he began work as a clerk and bookkeeper in a general store. After several years working with the same merchant, however, he began to worry that such a busy life of trade would prove distracting both to the mind and to the spirit. All around him he saw fellow Quakers on the make, eager to garner quick profits, frequently at the expense of their religious values or family obligations. This he determined not to do.

> My mind through the power of Truth was in good degree weaned from the desire of outward greatness, and I was learning to be content with real conveniences that were not costly, so that a life free from much entanglements appeared best for me, though the income was small. . . . I saw that a humble man with the blessing of the Lord might live on a little, and that where the heart was set on greatness, success in business did not satisfy the craving, but that in common with an increase of wealth the desire for wealth increased. There was a care on my mind to so pass my time as to things outward that nothing might hinder me from the most steady attention to the voice of the true Shepherd.

Woolman consequently decided to apprentice himself to a tailor, and in 1746 he established his own small clothing and dry goods store, hoping thereby to "get a living in a plain way without the load of great business and have opportunity for retirement and inward recollection."[31]

Woolman's careful choice of his vocation allowed him to spend more time pursuing his spiritual calling, actively promoting the Quaker gospel as an itinerant minister. The Quakers, of course, had no salaried ministry, but they did recognize certain of their number whose personal witness was particularly edifying. In 1743 Woolman had been designated such a "public minister" by the Burlington Quarterly Meeting of Ministers and Elders, and he soon began traveling to other meetings to share his personal message and to advise Friends in right ways of conduct. Before his death he would make some thirty excursions throughout the colonies, from New England to the Carolinas, exerting a profound personal influence on American Quakerism.[32]

Woolman spent much of his early ministry crusading against slavery. It was especially distressing for him to see so many Friends owning and abusing other humans. In 1746, at the age of twenty-six, he visited Quaker meetings in Virginia, Maryland, and North Carolina. There for the first time he saw "the dark gloominess" of slavery practiced on a large scale, and he determined to do all he could to end such a barbaric practice. During his trips to the southern colonies, he paid for his lodging in the houses of Quaker slaveholders rather than accept their hospitality, since it was unpaid slave labor that made such hospitality possible. He also gave up using both sugar in his food and dyes in his clothing because they were products of slavery.[33]

Yet Woolman was able to adopt such strict practices without appearing sanctimonious or alienating the slaveholders. He realized the complexity of the problem and the difficulty of changing overnight a deeply entrenched economic system and way of life. He was as much concerned for the harm that slavery did to the owner as to the slave, so he listened patiently to the slaveholders defend their forced labor system with arguments that would become hackneyed by the ante-bellum period: slavery rescued the Negro from heathen primitivism; Negroes were naturally lazy and needed paternalistic guidance; God had destined the black race for a life of servitude. Woolman saw more rationalization than justification in such statements and was disturbed at the "darkness of their imaginations." The actual reasons for slaveholding, he was convinced, were selfish and crass. "The love of ease and gain are the motives in general of keeping slaves, and men are wont to take hold of weak arguments to support a cause which is unreasonable." Slaves toiled so that their owners could live in unnecessary comfort, and such a labor system flagrantly violated the basic Christian principle of the universal brotherhood of man. In 1758 he and Benezet convinced the Philadelphia meeting to disown Quakers who continued to buy slaves.[34]

As demonstrated by the confidence expressed in him by the Philadelphia meeting, Woolman by mid-century was emerging as a recognized leader of the growing movement dedicated to a revival of Quaker piety and principles. When the Quaker majority in the Assembly disintegrated, and it was obvious that Penn's "holy experiment" based upon Quaker political control of the colony had failed, Woolman, along with many other Friends during the crisis of 1755-56, wondered what would happen to the Quaker faith and its social ethic. Would the Friends respond to the failure of their Quaker commonwealth by turning inward and adopting an isolated quietism? Or could they somehow find a workable middle way between ruling civil society and leaving civil society?

Woolman grew convinced that it was possible for the Friends, now shorn of their controlling political power and representing a minority among the colonists, to bridge the gap between the spiritual and the temporal world as private citizens. They could indeed live in modern society, with all its diversity and perversity, without necessarily compromising their original ideals. But to do so would require both a restoration of inward spirituality and a conscious reordering of personal priorities. "Great reformation in the world is wanting!" he exclaimed in his *Journal*, and, true to his prescription, Woolman began practicing what he preached. In 1756 he systematically set about reducing his own involvement in material affairs.[35]

From the outset of his career as tailor and merchant in 1743, Woolman had rigorously applied his religious scruples to his business practices. He tried to keep his poorer customers from going into debt by dissuading them from purchasing beyond their means. He also refused to appeal to their vanity by selling items that he considered mere luxuries. Yet despite such unorthodox business practices, or perhaps because of them, his trade prospered. And with prosperity, he, too, began to experience the tension between piety and profits embedded in the Protestant ethic. More than most of his peers, however, he was genuinely troubled at the implications of too much commercial success. As he disclosed, the "road to large business appeared open, but I felt a stop in my mind." His business was becoming more of a burden than a blessing. Did not his obligation to serve God and man demand the bulk of his time and attention?[36]

By 1756, the same year that he began writing his famous *Journal*, Woolman decided he must reorder his affairs. "Through the mercies of the Almighty," he wrote, "I had in good degree learned to be content with a plain way of living. I had but a small family, that on serious consideration I believed Truth did not require me to engage in such cumbrous affairs." After several unsuccessful attempts to curtail his growing business, Woolman gave his customers fair warning and then abandoned merchandising altogether. Thereafter he would make his living as a tailor. To supplement his income, he occasionally taught school, tended an apple orchard, and served as a scrivener. An Irish Friend who visited Woolman during this period testified to his simple way of living, describing him as a man "whose life and conversation shines in Christian piety. His concern is to lead a life of self-denial: pomp and splendour he avoids. . . . His house is very plain, his living also and yet he enjoys plenty of the good things that are necessary for Christian accommodation: we dined with him and were kindly entertained." Woolman was by no means a poor man, but he self-consciously set limits to his vocational pursuits and to his standard of living.[37]

Woolman believed that this fundamental sense of personal economy and spiritual devotion provided the key to revitalizing not only his own life but also that of society. In his *Journal* and other writings he developed a systematic social and economic philosophy based upon Quaker principles. Where Winthrop's journal was stiff and formal, concerned primarily with the problem of maintaining social order, Woolman's was quite intimate, devoted to moral and social justice, the plight of the slaves and Indians, the poor and the young. At the root of the problems facing the "great family" of man, he observed, was the corrosive effect of wealth, luxury, and covetousness. War, slavery, poverty, and most other social evils resulted directly from man's insatiable material appetite and his carnal pride. "We cannot go into superfluities, or grasp after wealth in a way contrary to his wisdom without having connection with some degree of oppression, and with that spirit which leads to self-exaltation and strife." The "least degree of luxury," he argued, "hath some connection with evil," since the more wealth acquired the more wanted, until gradually one's original faith and sense of social responsibility become submerged in the avaricious and ambitious.[38]

In observing the bustling economic activity in Philadelphia and the Delaware Valley in the middle of the eighteenth century, Woolman was convinced that men were devoting much more of their time and energy to their secular vocations than Jesus, Fox, or Penn had advised. Those in pursuit of an ever higher standard of living not only worked themselves too hard; they also demanded more from indentured servants or slaves than "pure wisdom" allowed. Landowners and moneylenders tended to charge excessive rent or interest, and those forced to pay such high charges in turn tended to be more callous in their own business dealings. If only people would learn to rest content with a "plain, simple way of living," he pleaded, then much of the grinding labor that they and their servants toiled under would be relieved, and all could devote more time to serving the Lord, their families, and their communities. "Moderate exercise, in the way of true wisdom, is pleasant to both mind and body. Food and raiment sufficient, though in the greatest simplicity, are accepted with content and gratitude." Woolman also recognized that some would inevitably acquire more possessions than others, and as long as such goods were used "faithfully for the good of all," he had no objection. But those who consciously caused "men and animals to do unnecessary labor in order that they themselves might have money to spend on luxuries were acting contrary to the design of the Creator."[39]

Woolman forcefully dismissed the argument that widespread unemployment would result from the rich simplifying their consumptive habits. The luxurious living of the rich, he felt, had resulted in a crass economic system that forced a few to labor overly hard at producing the essentials of life while most were employed to produce luxury objects to satisfy the vain desires of the wealthy. If the rich moderated their tastes, more laborers could return to the production of staples rather than baubles. Workdays could thereby be reduced so that a man's vocation could again become a source of pride rather than drudgery. In the process, he hoped, more workers would be free to return to a life of self-sustaining farming rather than wage labor. As he emphasized, "I know of no employ in life, more innocent in its nature, more healthy, and more acceptable in common to the minds of men, than husbandry, followed no further than while action is agreeable to the body only as an agreeable employ." Like so many proponents of simplicity, Woolman clearly preferred rural to urban living. And during his lifetime it was not such a romantic notion; most people were then living off the land.[40]

Supported by his own example of successful self-restraint, Woolman began earnestly preaching his gospel of the simple life as he visited wealthy Friends throughout the colonies in the 1750s and 1760s. He felt an inward call to promote a "humbler, plain, temperate Way of Living: a life where no unnecessary cares nor expenses may encumber our minds, nor lessen our ability to do good." Woolman recognized that leading a simple life of piety in the face of alluring entrepreneurial opportunities and social pressures was not easy; it required an inner discipline that was difficult to develop and even harder to maintain. In this regard he sympathized with those wealthy Friends who "have at times been affected with a sense of their difficulties, and appeared desirous . . . to be helped out of them," yet lacked the spiritual foundation necessary to do so. But he assured them that God would show the way. "There is balm, there is a physician!" he stressed. Christ's example "teaches us to be content with things really needful, and to avoid all superfluities, and give up our hearts to fear and serve the Lord."[41]

In 1770 Woolman was forced to curtail his ministerial travels when he almost died from pleurisy. The personal crisis led him to survey his life. As he did so, he took some comfort in the reformation then taking place among the Society of Friends. During a bedside conversation with his daughter Mary, he reflected:

> I feel a pure and Holy Spirit in a weak & broken Constitution: this Spirit within me hath suffered deeply and I have borne my part in the Suffering, that there may come forth a Church pure & Clean like the New Jerusalem, as Bride adorned for her husband. I believe my Sufferings in this broken Nature are now nearly accomplished, & my Father hath showed me that the Holy Spirit that now works within me, may work in young lively Constitutions & may strengthen them to travel up and down the world in the feeling of pure Wisdom, that many may believe them & the purity of their Lives & learn Instruction.

With this consoling thought on his mind, Woolman murmured to his daughter that he awaited death with a serene conscience. But he did not die. After several delirious weeks Woolman began to recover, and thereafter he spent most of his time in Mount Holly, tending his garden and orchard and readying his *Journal* for the printer.[42]

Then, in 1771, Woolman suddenly decided to undertake one more missionary journey. Late in that year he requested and received a certificate from the Burlington Monthly Meeting to visit England. He had learned of the considerable social misery in Great Britain caused by the enclosure movement and had decided to do what he could to help ameliorate the plight of the poor and oppressed. Woolman boarded ship in May 1772, fully convinced that his mission to England was providentially inspired. One of his close friends, James Pemberton, wrote a letter to a business associate in London, forewarning the English Friends about Woolman's intense piety and strict manner of living:

> Our friend Jno. Woolman embarked with Cpt. Sparks on a religious visit to some parts of your Island. He is a Friend in good Esteem among us, of blameless Life, a good understanding and deep in Spiritual Experience, tho' Singular in his dress and deportment. Is not a Censorious Mind, and I believe apprehends it his real Duty to appear as he does.

Woolman displayed his "singular" nature soon after boarding the *Mary and Elizabeth*. He quickly noticed that the cabins were decorated with "carved work and imagery" and "some superfluity of workmanship," and he could not in good conscience pay extra for such ornamentation. As Woolman explained to the ship's owner, the desire for such luxuries "entangled many in the spirit of oppression," and he could "not find peace in joining in anything which he saw was against the wisdom which is pure." So, he decided to travel in the steerage, where he shared for six weeks the hardships of the sailors, "their exposure, their soaking clothes, their miserable accommodations, their wet garments often trodden underfoot."[43]

Woolman's ship landed in June 1772, and he went directly to Devonshire House in Bishopgate, where the London Yearly Meeting of Ministers and Elders was in session. The English Friends were shocked at his unannounced entry and unusual appearance, the latter being heightened by his having just spent six weeks in steerage and his being dressed in simple undyed clothes and hat. They had seen enough such itinerant enthusiasts to make them especially wary of an American version. One of the English Friends recorded his fear that Woolman's garb "might in some Meetings draw the attention of the youth and even cause a change of countenance in some." After the American visitor presented his credentials, there was an awkward pause until an elder stood and suggested that "perhaps the stranger Friend might feel that his dedication to himself to this apprehended service was accepted, without further labour, and that he might now feel free to return to his home."[44]

Woolman was taken aback at such a cold and suspicious reception, and he began to weep. Composing himself after several strained minutes, he rose and addressed the company, humbly insisting that he could not return home without undertaking the personal mission that had called him to England. Yet in order to minister in England he needed the consent of the meeting. Since that consent was apparently not forthcoming, he requested that he be given employment until the meeting saw fit to authorize his visit. Another long silence followed. At length Woolman stood again, feeling "that rise which prepared the creature to stand like a trumpet through which the Lord speaks to his flock." He then delivered a stirring testimony that literally forced his listeners to take him seriously. The London Friend who had earlier suggested that Woolman return to America now rose, admitted his mistake, and urged his peers to do likewise, and the meeting quickly "welcomed and owned" Woolman. That evening one of the Englishmen recorded in his diary that he initially had strong doubts about Woolman, but the "simplicity, solidity and clearness of many of his remarks made all these vanish as Mists at the Sun's Rising."[45]

It was not London, however, that Woolman felt called to visit, but rather the northern part of England, where he had learned that social conditions were rapidly deteriorating. A week after arriving in London he began walking toward Yorkshire. He could not bear to ride in a stagecoach after hearing that in their haste they caused cruel hardships on men and horses alike. Traveling on foot also allowed Woolman to see more vivdly the daily life of the people and talk personally with some of them. As he walked along he was greatly moved by the sight of pervasive poverty. He agonized over the plight of the post-boys, riding the stages day and night, sometimes freezing to death during the winter months, all because the frantic quest for profits had infected man's soul: "So great is the hurry in the spirit of this world that in aiming to do business quick and to gain wealth the creation at this day doth loudly groan!"[46]

As Woolman saw many English Friends working in factories that produced superfluities bound for America and others openly engaging in the
slave trade, he "felt great distress" at the decline of the original Quaker ideal:
"the weight of this degeneracy hath lain so heavy upon me, the depth of this
revolt been so evident and desires in my heart been so ardent for a reformation, so ardent that we might come to that right use of things where, living on
a little, we might inhabit that holy mountain on which they neither *hurt nor
destroy*!" But he did not despair. Nature confirmed his faith in the possibility
and desirability of the simple life. "Under the weight of this exercise," he
observed, "the sight of innocent birds in the branches and sheep in the
pastures, who act according to the will of their Creator, hath at times tended
to mitigate my trouble."[47]

By mid-September, when Woolman arrived in York, he was exhausted.
While attending the Quarterly Meeting he contracted the much feared smallpox, then so common, that had earlier claimed his sister and cousin. As the
disease progressed, Woolman calmly accepted the inevitable. "This trial is
made easier than I could have thought," he reflected, "by my Will being
wholly taken away, for if I was anxious as to the Event, it would be harder
but I am not, and my mind enjoys a perfect calm." To the very end he
remained single to the truth, consistently leading the simple life he had long
before adopted. In dictating his funeral arrangements, he wrote that he
desired "an ash coffin made plain without any manner of superfluities, the
corpse to be wrapped in cheap flannel, the expense of which I leave my
wearing clothes to defray, as also the digging of the grave." A few days later,
he thanked those Friends who had faithfully attended him during his illness:

> How tenderly have I been waited on in this Time of Affliction, in which I may
> say in Job's Words, tedious days and wearisome Nights are appointed to me;
> and how many are spending their Time and Money in Vanity & Superfluities,
> while Thousands and Tens of Thousands want the Necessaries of Life, who
> might be relieved by them, and their distress at such a Time as this, in some
> degree softened by the administration of suitable things.

Three days later, on October 7, 1772, Woolman died, "without Sigh, Groan,
or Struggle."[48]

To many a modern observer John Woolman's life no doubt seems both
eccentric and extreme. At times he was overly simple in his social and
economic outlook. His sentimental agrarian vision and anti-urbanism occasionally did not penetrate the fact of contrary historical developments. Nor
did his absolute pacifism offer much consolation to those frontier families
facing slaughter by the Indians. The strength of his own moral and religious
principles also led him to be overly optimistic about the spiritual potentiali-
ties of society at large, and some of the restraints he imposed on himself could

be regarded as needlessly austere. Samuel Johnson, in reflecting on such Quaker scrupulosity, once remarked that a man who could not get to Heaven in a green coat could not get there any easier in a grey coat. William James made the same point years later when he used Woolman's life to illustrate the danger of excessive purity. After noting Woolman's decision not to use dyed clothes or hats, he concluded: "When the craving for moral consistency and purity is developed to this degree, the subject may well find the outer world too full of shocks to dwell in it, and can unify his life and keep his soul unspotted only by withdrawing from it." Woolman himself, of course, had never isolated himself from the world. But James correctly recognized that others following Woolman's advice might not be as success- ful in living a simple life of piety *in* the world.[49]

Yet such reservations should not detract from the remarkable example of pious simplicity that Woolman provided. He discovered and successfully maintained the material and spiritual equilibrium that Jesus had deemed necessary to keep the work ethic from devouring the spiritual ethic, finding in the combination of inner piety and outward activism the glue to hold the two competing strands of the Protestant ethic together. Woolman displayed an inward repose free of egotistical temperament and material ambition and in complete harmony with the divine will. His legacy in this sense was not a fixed pattern or rigid mold to be slavishly followed but rather an inspiration, a kindling life that provided a simple credo: "A supply to nature's wants, joined with a peaceful, humble mind, is the truest happiness of life."[50]

The consistency and the humility with which Woolman lived his simple life were a source of enormous inspiration to those around him. He did not have the vehemence of an agitator, but rather moved among men as an embodied conscience, demonstrating that religion was something to be lived as well as felt. Unlike Penn and other aristocratic exponents of plain living, there was nothing flabby nor hypocritical about Woolman's personal ethic, and he never hesitated to make the personal sacrifices that it demanded. He simplified his life in order to enjoy the luxury of doing good. "Conduct," he stressed, "is more convincing than language." And it was his conduct that helped him become the germinating center of the new group conscience that emerged among the American Friends at mid-century. During the Revolu- tionary era, thanks to the exemplary leadership provided by Woolman, Benezet, and other reformers, concerned Quakers continued to experience a "revival of ancient simplicity in plainness of apparel, household furniture, the education of youth, and a due and wakeful attendance of our religious meetings." The crisis of conscience produced by the imperial debate with Great Britain served to unify those Friends determined to remain true to their social and pacifist ethic. As one meeting expressed it: "Under the prevailing trials and difficulties we have a prospect that some are so loosened from outward things as to promote a more steady care to keep a true moderation and a true temperance."[51]

The Quaker ethic survived intact largely because the reformers were willing to sacrifice political authority and social leadership and to adopt the stringent disciplinary procedures required to purge those Friends who betrayed basic Quaker principles. In the process, however, the Friends paid a high price. Once a ruling majority, they became a disciplined minority, and they increasingly began to see themselves as a "quiet and peculiar" people set apart from society rather than integrated within it. Leading a simple life in a busy, abundant new republic proved either too difficult or too drab for the bulk of the Friends in the Delaware Valley. Plain and pious living required a sense of commitment and restraint that only a relatively few could maintain in the face of dramatically opposed social, economic, and intellectual developments.

That the Puritans and Quakers were unable to sustain the austere ethic of Reformed Protestantism on a societal basis seems, on reflection, to have been an obvious development. "The American mind," Perry Miller concluded, "discarded this notion of its personality because the ingenuity required to maintain it was more than men had time or energy to devise." In his view, the "fact of the frontier" and a "thriving commerce" won out over the simple life in shaping American attitudes toward things material. Seduced by the seemingly limitless economic and social opportunities available to them, more and more Americans chose the individual pursuit and enjoyment of plenty over the cultivation of piety, plainness, and the public good. The facts of history thus repudiated the colonial dream of a society of temperate saints.[52]

There is certainly much evidence to support such an interpretation. Yet it still leaves some questions unanswered. To say that these well-intentioned people brought with them to the New World a commitment to the simple life and then saw it increasingly eroded by the abundance of the American envionment answers one question but raises another. How committed were they to the simple life? That the founders of both colonies publicly professed the value of plain, pious living and quickly established sumptuary laws would seem to testify to their initial purposiveness. As noted earlier, however, such regulations went increasingly unenforced or were quickly revised to apply only to the lower classes. The social elite's abandonment of simplicity as a standard for itself, therefore, may not have been solely because they succumbed to material standards of value. Other forces may have been at work. Perhaps their commitment to traditional hierarchical social assumptions was stronger than their commitment to simplicity. Or perhaps they were genuinely convinced that they could combine high living and high thinking. Some, no doubt, simply found the idea of voluntary simplicity tiresome.

Similarly, many among the merchant and working classes may have decided that the diligent pursuit of their callings was a more salient value than pious simplicity. The notorious Boston merchant Robert Keayne, who was censured and fined for charging excessive prices, reflected this different sense of priorities when he lamented that he thought he was being a good Puritan, only to wake up one morning to find himself damned by his peers for being too good a Puritan. This is said not to deny that the simple life was an important strand in both the Puritan and Quaker mind. It clearly was. But there were many strands at work, and individuals showed varying degrees of loyalty to each of them. Eventually, some of these separate ideals making up the original Protestant ethic came into conflict, thus leading individuals to choose one over the other. In making such choices, colonists tended to reflect their own social condition or their degree of personal piety. Yet they were also influenced by the seeming abundance of material opportunities surrounding them as well as by the swirling forces of social change associated with colonial growth. Conflicting loyalties thus combined with tempting circumstances to dislodge the simple life from the list of operative assumptions guiding the behavior of many Americans.[53]

But I generalize too grandly. One must take care to differentiate between the collapse of the simple life as a dominant standard of behavior and its persistence both as an attainable ideal on an individual basis and as a sustaining myth of national purpose. In fact, the two different styles of simplicity that the Puritans and Quakers expressed, the former fatalistic, authoritarian, and elitist and the latter perfectionist, egalitarian, and humanitarian, would continue to appear in various forms thereafter. Both were reflections of the same impulse, but they were quite different reflections, and their differences are crucial to an understanding of the subsequent history of the simple life as both a societal ideal and as a personal ethic. John Winthrop and John Woolman would not be the last Americans to lead a simple life in an increasingly complex society, nor would temperate simplicity quickly give way to conspicuous consumption as an expressed social virtue. Even as they violated with abandon the command to love the world with weaned affections, Americans during the eighteenth century and after would tenaciously hold onto at least the rhetorical expression of the "broad and middle way" of pious simplicity. Their doing so illustrates the growing discrepancy in American life between promise and practice, values and actions, that has remained a central theme in the national experience.

CHAPTER THREE

Republican Simplicity

The Great Awakening had for the most part subsided by the middle of the eighteenth century, but the social tensions underlying the popular revivals had not. In fact, they increased as the century progressed. Beginning in the 1740s, an era of dramatic population growth and uneven economic expansion, interrupted and complicated by the French wars, produced social strains that further undermined the cohesiveness of colonial society. Although the bulk of the people remained small farmers and artisans of the "middling sort," the visible disparity between rich and poor widened. In South Carolina, for example, a visiting New Englander reported that the province was "divided into opulent and lordly planters, poor and spiritless peasants and vile slaves." Devereux Jarratt, a Methodist minister born in 1732 on a small farm in New Kent County, Virginia, likewise noticed that "the difference between gentle and simple" had become recognized "among all my rank and age."[1]

Colonial parvenus and descendants of old wealth alike seemed intent on setting themselves apart from the public "rabble." Country estates, sartorial finery, gilded carriages attended by liveried slaves, gala balls, fox hunts—all served to sharpen class distinctions and sow popular resentment. As always, such social tension was greatest during periods of economic decline, and this was the case during the turbulent decade of the 1760s, when commercial and political disruptions combined to exacerbate popular frustrations. That affluent conservatives often attributed the economic difficulties of the commoners to their supposed laziness and sottishness did not endear them to the masses. Equally grating to the lower ranks was the tendency among many of the urban elite to treat people of lesser status with what one observer called an "insulting rudeness." As a result of such actions, tempers flared, acts of violence increased, and discussions spilled forth from the lower ranks and their spokesmen concerning the fitness of the ostentatious wealthy for positions of public leadership.[2]

Jeremiads bemoaning the disintegration of communal unity and personal piety continued to resound regularly from American pulpits. Yet anxieties about the course of events were no longer the monopoly of the clergy. The pamphlets, correspondence, and diaries of concerned laymen were filled with disturbed accounts of an increasing preoccupation with luxury and a diminishing sense of civic virtue. After mid-century, imports of costly fashions and furnishings from London skyrocketed, as prosperous Americans aped the lavish style of living of their social counterparts in England. Doctor William Douglass of Boston observed in 1760 that "Idleness, intemperance, luxury in diet, extravagancies in apparel, and an abandoned way of Living" had enervated the "general character of many of the populace," not just in Massachusetts but in every colony. A New Jersey writer in 1768 placed much of the blame for such developments on the influx of paper money and the speculative mania occasioned by the French and Indian War. Such inflation had "relaxed industry, promoted idleness, encouraged running into debt, opened a door to profusion and high living, luxury, and excess of every kind." He was sure that the "most superficial observer must be surprised at the difference in living and dress between 1755 and the present time, besides the expensive diversions, and scenes of dissipation, unknown among us until of late. . . ."[3]

Similar descriptions were repeated in the southern colonies with striking frequency in the decade and a half before the Revolution. A resident of Annapolis contended that ostentatious living seemed to spread more rapidly among "polished and affluent" Americans than among many "opulent" Londoners. One participant in the high life of the Virginia aristocracy bore witness to such ostentation when he recorded in his journal an account of the social scene: "Most of the company went away this morning, soon after breakfast, in their phaetons, chariots, and coaches in four, with two or three footmen behind. They live in as high a style here, I believe, as any part of the world." That social "inferiors" were trying to live beyond their means in emulating the carefree life of the planter elite was equally worrisome to some gentry reformers. "Hence," as a prominent Virginian wrote, "extravagance, love of gaieties, the taste for modish pleasures, are in a chain of imitation carried down to the lowest people, who would seem to have a notion of what high life is, by spending more than they can afford with those they call their betters."[4]

Such pretentiousness on the part of the "lesser sort" still provoked considerable anxiety among the upper ranks, and the call for simple living remained for many as much an instrument of class discipline as it was a pristine ideal. But a surprising amount of the gentry's criticism of extravagant living was directed against themselves. In Virginia, for example, the wealthy planter Landon Carter lamented the wasteful and dissolute behavior of his boys who "play away and play it all away." His eldest son, William, was so notorious for his excesses that he acquired the nickname "Wild Bill." In

1766, one of Carter's fellow planters confessed that the only "Recipe that can be prescribed at this juncture" for their licentiousness "is Frugality and Industry, which is a potion scarcely to be swallowed by Virginians brought up from their cradles in Idleness, Luxury and Extravagance." William Nelson, whose family's superfluous expenditures eventually threatened him with bankruptcy, regretted in 1768 the "extravagance which hath been our ruin" and hoped that others would avoid the "luxury to which Virginians are too prone."[5]

These and other anxious observers, whatever their religious perspective, shared a disquieting feeling that, instead of serving as a beacon of spirituality and temperance to the rest of the world, the colonies now seemed but a sad reflection of the rampant materialism, social striving, and impiety infecting Europe. And this disturbing sense that America was losing its community identity and moral distinctiveness helps explain the surprisingly intense colonial response to increased British regulation and taxation after 1763. During the Revolutionary crisis, Whig spokesmen articulated a republican ideology that proved to be the most potent conceptual force shaping political and social thought among the intellectual elite between 1750 and 1800. Derived from the Latin term *res publica*, republicanism was never precisely defined. In its simplest sense it meant a rejection of monarchy and aristocracy in favor of a government representative of and responsible to the people. In eighteenth-century America, however, it came to embody much more than just a rationale for political independence and popular representation. For many colonial leaders, republicanism entailed a comprehensive moral vision that provided a secular analogue of the Protestant ethic espoused by John Winthrop, John Cotton, William Penn, John Woolman, and others.[6]

Even though most "classical" republicans felt more comfortable with the rational humanism of the Enlightenment than either the predestinarian theology of Puritanism or the mystical piety of the Society of Friends, they shared with those religious groups a basic assumption that forging a successful society depended upon maintaining a necessarily tenuous balance among power, liberty, and virtue. The first two factors—power and liberty—would ideally counterbalance each other. But such an equilibrium between force and freedom fundamentally depended on developing and sustaining a virtuous citizenry. The virtues to be sought—industry, frugality, simplicity, enlightened thinking, and public spiritedness—were almost identical to those valued by the early Puritans and Quakers. Virtuous republicans, like virtuous Puritans and Quakers, were to be industrious without becoming avaricious. And they were expected always to subordinate private interests to the larger public good.[7]

Such a republican social ethic was initially able to garner the support of both Protestant evangelicals and Enlightenment rationalists, gentry Whigs as well as patriot artisans and farmers. To those secular and spiritual idealists already worried about the cohesiveness of their society, the conflict with

England came to represent more than an opportunity to gain political independence. It offered a vital chance to cleanse America's soul of its impurities and halt the disquieting growth of a crass economic individualism that threatened to dissolve all traditional community and kinship ties. By doing so, republicanism added a "moral dimension, a utopian depth to the political separation from England—a depth that involved the very character of their society."[8]

Yet, while sharing many affinities with the Protestant ethic, republicanism differed in at least one crucial respect. Where the Puritans had directed their ethic of self-control and spiritual intensity in large measure at the masses in order to prevent material striving from upsetting the established social order, republican idealists, like the radical evangelicals and Quaker reformers such as Benezet and Woolman, increasingly aimed their protests at the upper ranks, the placemen, planters, patroons, and merchant princes who seemed more interested in selfish gain than social responsibility. "Is it equitable," a New Yorker asked in 1765, "that 99, rather 999, should suffer for the Extravagance or Grandeur of one, especially when it is considered that Men frequently owe their Wealth to the impoverishment of their Neighbors?" To ardent Whig moralists such as Sam Adams and Tom Paine, the ruling elites, not the toiling masses, were the primary source of political corruption, moral degeneration, and social decay. Instead of promoting deferential simplicity on the part of the common people, therefore, they stressed the need to replace officeholders of great wealth and luxurious habits with men of modest estates and demonstrated civic virtue. This transformation of the simple life from an instrument of social control to an agent for social change meant that the ideology was potentially far more sweeping in its effects than the Protestant ethic. Whether it would ultimately be more successful was another matter.[9]

In reorienting the Protestant ethic along more secular lines, American republican thought turned from theology to history for its wellspring, discovering a rich tradition of simple living in Western culture dating back to classical antiquity. Colonial readers especially identified with the pastoral poetry of Virgil and Horace and the histories of the late Roman republic written by Sallust, Cicero, Livy, Tacitus, and Plutarch. These and other Roman writers portrayed the Republic as a serene, pastoral nation of virtuous citizens. As long as the majority of Romans had remained simple, rustic husbandmen devoted to the public good rather than to selfish interests, Rome had thrived. But spectacular success on the battlefield during the second century B.C. proved too powerful an intoxicant for the sober republicans, and Rome began to experience a moral crisis from which she never recovered. Increased plunder from eastern wars produced increasing personal extravagance and massive inflation at home. The avarice of the ruling classes made itself felt in the misery and discontent of the masses, and class strife grew rampant in a republic gone sour.[10]

The colonists also learned about the virtues and fragility of classical republicanism from the English Opposition writers of the seventeenth century—James Harrington, John Milton, Algernon Sydney—and their eighteenth-century "real" Whig successors—James Burgh, Charles Davenant, Thomas Gordon, Richard Price, and John Trenchard. They likewise drew inspiration from the Tory Oppositionist Henry St. John, Viscount Bolingbroke. These outraged English Dissenters saw a striking historical analogy between the fall of the Roman republic and the contemporary condition of Great Britain. They repeatedly contrasted the pervasive luxury, immorality, and corruption of the Stuarts and Hanoverians with an idealized image of a simple, virtuous, pastoral British republic in the classical tradition, led by men of integrity, temperance, and public spirit. Bolingbroke insisted that the corrupt administration of Horace Walpole, so blatantly in collusion with financiers, speculators, and stock-jobbers, must be swept out of power. A republic could survive only as long as the majority of the people lived on and worked their own land. Otherwise, manly virtue would continue to give way to effeminate vices, and public spiritedness would continue to be discarded in favor of private interest. Bolingbroke and the Oppositionists agreed with Montesquieu that private restraint on behalf of the commonweal was the actuating principle of successful republics. It was "absolutely necessary," Montesquieu wrote, that "there should be some regulation in respect to . . . all . . . forms of contracting. For were we once allowed to dispose of our property to whom and how we pleased, the will of each individual would disturb the order of the fundamental laws." With this principle in mind, English radicals saw the experience of the Roman republic as providing a clear warning to their countrymen. The Romans, Thomas Gordon argued, initially led naturally simple lives, having "no Trade, no Money, no Room or Materials for Luxury." With battlefield victories producing seemingly limitless booty, however, the Romans first "grew less Virtuous, then Vicious."[11]

The Scottish-born dissenting schoolmaster James Burgh was one of the most effective Whig propagandists in England during the eighteenth century, and he was especially popular in the American colonies. John Adams once claimed that Burgh's books were "held in as high estimation by all my friends as they are by me. The more they are read, the more eagerly and generally they are sought for." Burgh's *Britain's Remembrancer*, occasioned by the Jacobite rebellion of 1745, enjoyed three printings in America between 1747 and 1759. It presented a scathing indictment of modern British life and drew directly on Roman precedents in explaining "this thoughtless and voluptuous age." Burgh noted that all great empires had collapsed "under Luxury and Vice" and warned that Great Britain was already mired in "luxury and irreligion . . . sufficient to rend any state or empire." From his study of the ancient republics, Burgh concluded that the "welfare of all countries in the world depends upon the morals of their people. For though a nation may get riches by trade, thrift, industry and from the benefit of its soil and situation . . . when their manners are depraved, they will decline insensibly, and at last come to utter destruction." As he looked about him at mid-century, Burgh lamented that his beloved England was following such a pattern. London was filled with scenes of "Wantonness, Pleasure and Extravagance."[12]

Americans visiting the mother country after mid-century confirmed this portrait of an increasingly corrupt, self-indulgent, and degenerate British society. The South Carolina planter Henry Laurens found the English "overwhelmed in Luxury and Corruption." From London, Virginia's Arthur Lee penned a similar account of British life in a letter to his brother in 1769: "Corruption has spread its baneful influence so universally that this country seems now to be nearly in a state in which Jugurtha found Rome." Four years later, while still in London, he predicted that the British empire "must fall as Greece and Rome have fallen, in the same manner, and by the same means. In this prospect there is but one consolation. That liberty, when she abandons this country, will not . . . relinquish us forever but will fix her favourite seat in the rising regions of America."[13]

The Pennsylvanian John Dickinson had said much the same while studying law in London during the 1750s. In 1754 he had written that "luxury and corruption" must be curbed by "a general reformation of manners, which everyone sees is absolutely necessary for the welfare of this kingdom." Such a "general reformation" was crucial not only for England but for the colonies as well. Dickinson maintained that the source of America's moral decline and domestic turmoil was not so much internal as external, the result of continued connection with a British empire that was clearly following the same lurid course toward self-destruction that had foredoomed the Romans. Britain was to America, he concluded, what "Caesar was to Rome."[14]

This was a captivating explanation of America's fall from simplicity and piety, for it not only justified resisting British imperial policies but also promoted a return to the standards of the fathers. Heretofore, American evangelicals and social critics had tended to pinpoint the source of their failure to provide a beacon of virtuous living to the rest of the world in their own moral depravity and weakness as human beings in the face of material temptations. But increasingly after 1763, numerous colonial spokesmen focused on the continuing attachment to England as the source of the cancer infecting the morals and debasing the piety of the colonists. "Alas! Great Britain," groaned one Virginian, "their vices have been extended to America! . . . The Torrent as yet is but small; only a few are involved in it; it must be stopped, or it will bear all before it with an impetuous sway."[15]

For those Americans concerned about the moral fabric of the provinces, it was easy to see in British mercantile policies a conspiracy to foster excessive consumption among the colonists in order to satisfy the insatiable greed of British merchants. A writer in the *Newport Mercury* asserted in December

1767 that the cause of New England's economic strains was the extensive "Luxury and extravagance in the use of British and foreign manufactures and superfluities." Americans, so the argument among more and more colonial observers went, must somehow prevent the further spread of the "poison of British corruption" to their own society. Only then could they resume the providential "errand into the wilderness" begun by their forefathers. In 1778 the colonial historian David Ramsay looked back to the pre-Revolutionary period and recalled that it was "the interest of Great Britain to encourage our dissipation and extravagance, for the two-fold purpose of increasing the sale of her manufactures, and of perpetuating our subordination." Had they not resisted British mercantile policies, "our frugality, industry, and simplicity of manners, would have been lost in an imitation of British extravagance, idleness, and false refinements."[16]

As Ramsay indicated, this fear of further contamination from a British empire in decline was reflected in the organized efforts during the 1760s and 1770s to reduce imports and thereby reduce dependence on a home country rife with corruption and ostentation. From the time of the passage of the Sugar Act in 1764, merchants, artisans, lawyers, editors, mechanics, farmers, and others demonstrated remarkable unity in boycotting British products. Historians have usually explained the nonimportation movement as an effort to pressure the British to repeal the noxious taxes and regulatory measures passed after 1763. Yet many colonial leaders also saw the boycotts as another way of "reaffirming and rehabilitating the virtues of the Puritan Ethic."[17]

British mercantile policies thus provided an incentive for Americans to revive the spartan virtues of their forebears and to re-emphasize the public good over private gain. Upon learning of the passage of the Sugar Act in 1764, Virginian Richard Henry Lee remarked to a friend in London that "this step of the mother country, though intended to oppress and keep us low, in order to secure our dependence, may be subversive of this end. Poverty and oppression, among whose minds are filled with ideas of British liberty, may introduce a virtuous industry, with a train of generous and manly sentiments." A writer in Pennsylvania shared this optimistic outlook a few years later when he argued that "the unconstitutional and oppressive Revenue Acts" might in fact "excite a Spirit of Frugality and good Economy, and thereby decline the use of luxurious Importations."[18]

Plain living thereupon became a symbolic measure of one's patriotism. A Bostonian claimed as much in 1768 when he argued that those who could not make the sacrifices necessary to preserve colonial liberties did not deserve the benefits of citizenship: "He, who cannot conquer the little vanity of his heart, and deny the delicacy of his debauched palate, let him lay his hand upon his mouth, and his mouth in the dust. Now is the time for the people to summon every aid human and divine, to exhibit every moral virtue, and call forth every christian grace." This was the same regenerative message preached by Samuel Stillman, pastor of Boston's First Baptist Church. The Reverend Mr. Stillman emphasized that "it is absolutely necessary to exclude *luxury* from the camp. The plainness and simplicity of our ancestors with respect to their manner of living, may reasonably be supposed to have contributed much, to that greatness of mind which they often discovered." Stillman was convinced that the colonists would find in the debate with the British government the stimulus to social reform that he and other ministers had so long desired.[19]

Much like the earthquakes, epidemics, Indian attacks, wars, and other calamities used in the past by colonial ministers to spur religious revivals, the imperial crisis with England thus came to be viewed by both spiritual and civic leaders as another providential signal for moral and religious reformation. Initially, at least, the Revolutionary crisis produced a more sweeping and prolonged revival of simple living than any previous event. With so much at stake, many colonial patriots appeared eager to reduce their material desires for the sake of a great public cause. During the 1760s newspapers throughout the colonies reported the success of the nonimportation societies and of new domestic manufacturing enterprises designed to reduce colonial dependence on British goods. "If we mean still to be free," one Pennsylvanian urged, "let us unanimously lay aside foreign superfluities, and encourage our own manufactures. SAVE YOUR MONEY AND YOU WILL SAVE YOUR COUNTRY." By the fall of 1765 most seaport towns had nonimportation associations. One such group, the Society for the Promotion of Arts, Agriculture and Economy of New York City, emphasized that its purpose was to "advance husbandry, promote Manufactures, and suppress Luxury."[20]

Soon the inland communities were establishing similar societies, as well as patriotic spinning, weaving, and knitting circles. The *Boston Gazette* reported in 1767: "It is judged that the spirit of frugality and Economy prevails in our country towns, as the demand for European superfluities is of late greatly diminished." The wearing of homespun was a distinctive sign of patriotism, as evidenced by the refusal of Harvard and Princeton graduates to don imported garb during their commencement ceremonies. Other colonists abandoned the traditional practice of wearing black at funerals, since fine black cloth was almost exclusively imported from Great Britain. John Dickinson's confidence that such measures alone would be enough to convince the British to rescind their hated ordinances was typical of many Whig leaders: "Homespun clothes are all the armour, spades and ploughshares all the weapons we shall use in this holy war. So gentle and so effectual are the means we shall employ."[21]

Evidence of renewed frugality and growing self-sufficiency gradually appeared in the southern colonies as well. One South Carolina planter, obviously exasperated by his own province's delay in organizing effective boycotts, urged his fellows: "Let us then, AT LAST, follow the example of our brother sufferers in the Northern Colonies, and encourage the making of our own manufactures. . . . Let us, Brother Planters, wear our old clothes as long as they will ever hang on us." His exhortation produced surprising support in a colony not known for its frugality. In July 1769, at an overflowing town meeting in Charleston, a nonimportation agreement was passed with considerable enthusiasm. "The Zeal of the People to enter into this necessary Measure," it was reported, "even far exceeded the Expectations of the Warmest first Promoters."[22]

These nonimportation associations, by encouraging austerity, self-sufficiency, and patriotism, were all of a piece with classical republicanism's emphasis on a virtuous, temperate, self-reliant citizenry being crucial to the preservation of liberty. John Dickinson, the wealthy, polished young Philadelphia lawyer who emerged as one of the most effective early spokesmen for organized colonial resistance, self-consciously assumed the mantle of republican simplicity in his famous *Letters from a Farmer in Pennsylvania* (1768) attacking the Townshend Acts. He began by confessing that he was "now convinced that a man may be as happy without bustle, as with it. My farm is small; my servants are few, and good; I have a little money at interest; I wish for no more; my employment in my own affairs is easy; and with a contented and grateful mind, (undisturbed by worldly hopes or fears, relating to myself,) I am completing the number of days allotted to me by divine goodness." He then stressed that temperate living should be accompanied by reflective thinking: "Being generally master of my time, I spend a good deal of it in a library, which I think the most valuable part of my small estate. . . ." Although Dickinson's self-portrait was highly idealized and embellished, it nevertheless attests to the renewed faith in the rhetorical appeal of the simple life engendered by the crisis with Great Britain. As he concluded, England's "unkindness will instruct and compel us, after some time, to discover in our *industry* or *frugality*, surprising remedies." Soon after *Letters from a Farmer* was published, a Boston town meeting sent Dickinson a commendation for his "Spartan, Roman, British Virtue, and Christian spirit joined."[23]

By the end of 1770 the intense American opposition to continued revenue acts forced the British to repeal many of the Townshend duties. At that point the colonial resistance movement began to show signs of fragmentation. Many of the leading merchants, having depleted their overstocked inventories, now withdrew from the nonimportation associations. As one Philadelphia importer admitted in 1769, he and other merchants had participated in the boycott of British goods primarily in order to "dispose of the great quantity of goods on hand, and contract their affairs." These "sunshine patriots" had little real sympathy for the republican emphasis on stinted estates, personal austerity, and an essentially agrarian economy. Colonial resentment toward the British was directed more against their restraining trade regulations than against a corrupt political economy and civil society. Once the regulations were removed, they eagerly resumed a thriving trade with Great Britain.[24]

During 1771 imports of British luxury goods soared to record levels. In June a friend reported to John Adams that in Boston "there is a greater flood of goods than ever was known." Imports into Philadelphia were described as "amazingly great." Such developments led some patriots to fear that selfish interests would again win out over public virtue. Arthur Lee sadly observed to John Dickinson in January 1771: "When I speak of my country it is in the despair and grief of my heart. She is undone. That virtue which alone could have saved her does not exist. . . . If our liberties are not worth the difference between a homespun and a broadcloth coat . . . on what are to be found our hopes of retrieving our rights?" Yet, despite widespread violations, the nonimportation movement did not totally collapse. Republican activists continued to call for boycotts, seeing in such self-sacrifice both political and social benefits.[25]

This same sentiment led some colonial leaders to support the formation of the Continental Association in 1774, a coordinated effort designed to end all economic relations between the colonies and an increasingly oppressive mother country. Adopted by most of the colonies, the Association charter declared: "We will, in our several stations, encourage frugality, economy, and industry, and promote agriculture, arts and manufactures of this country . . . and will discountenance every species of extravagance and dissipation. . . ." Local communities were responsible for enforcing such provisions, and public pressure was frequently used against recalcitrant individuals when voluntarism failed. A woman in Virginia, for instance, was forcefully advised not to give a ball she had planned, and she grudgingly acceded. Horse races in Virginia and South Carolina were called off, as were card games and lotteries. The Protestant social ethic seemed alive and well again—albeit in a new republican guise—not only in New England but throughout the colonies.[26]

The most persistent spokesman for republican simplicity in the years leading up to Lexington and Concord was Samuel Adams. "If ever a man was sincerely an idolater of republicanism," a visiting Frenchman commented during the Revolutionary era, "it was Samuel Adams. . . . He has the excess of republican virtues,—untainted probity, simplicity, modesty, and above all, firmness." Adams's personal life and public career were cut of one cloth; in both he consciously sought to resurrect and put into practice the virtues of his Puritan forefathers. John Adams remembered that his cousin's "inflexible integrity, his disinterestedness, his invariable resolution, his sagacity, his patience, perseverance, and pure public virtue, were never exceeded by any man in America."[27]

Sam Adams has frequently been referred to as "the last Puritan"—and for good reason. Born in 1722, he was the son of pious parents, and he inherited their intense spirituality. His father, Samuel Adams, Senior, a retired ship captain turned prosperous brewer and merchant, served devotedly as a deacon in Boston's Old South Church and was also active in local politics. Apparently, however, the pillar of piety in the family was Mary, Sam's mother. A person of "severe religious principles," she imbued her children with strict Christian ethics and insisted that they practice what she preached. Young Sam learned his religious lessons well, and when he entered Harvard in 1736, at age fourteen, his intention was to become a minister. But then he began reading Greek and Latin and his horizons widened considerably. Through the works of Plutarch, Cicero, Virgil, and Sallust, he discovered the heritage of classical republicanism, and thereafter his interests turned from theology to politics. He by no means abandoned his theological predilections or his personal piety, but he did decide that a career in the ministry was not for him.[28]

After leaving Harvard in 1740, Adams initially took his father's advice and began studying law. But when the elder Adams suffered tremendous losses in the Land Bank collapse, Sam gave up his legal studies as a favor to his mother, who was worried about the family's economic future. He then turned to business and began working as a clerk in Thomas Cushing's countinghouse. There he quickly revealed a lack of entrepreneurial interest and business talent that would be a lifelong characteristic. Adams stayed with Cushing only a few months before being dismissed. He then borrowed 1000 pounds that his father had salvaged from his catastrophic banking venture, with the idea of going into business for himself, but he foolishly lent half of the money to a shiftless friend supposedly in need, who promptly disappeared with it. His father, showing remarkable patience if questionable judgment, then took Sam into his brewery business, "where it may be supposed," one biographer has written, "he did little good for lack of capacity, and little harm from lack of responsibility."[29]

After the deaths of his father and mother in the late 1740s, Sam inherited one-third of the parental estate, including the brewery business and the commodious family home on Purchase Street. Within ten years, however, he managed to bring the once thriving brewery to the edge of collapse. His own financial condition reached its lowest ebb in 1758 when he barely succeeded in saving his house from foreclosure. Adams was not frivolous in his financial affairs; he was simply indifferent. The thought of monetary gain and the thrill of economic competition never intoxicated him, as they did so many of his peers. He once claimed that "a guinea had never glistened in my eyes." Politics, not profits, was his abiding passion, and he spent more time at mid-century and after debating political issues at local taverns than managing accounts at his brewery desk.[30]

One of the political clubs that Adams joined in 1747 began publishing a year later the *Independent Advertiser*, a newspaper devoted to political and philosophical discussion. The publication served as an organ for Adams's Puritanism and his growing patriotism. At mid-century he was distressed at how quickly a crass materialism had smothered the flames of revivalism in

Boston and other seaport towns. Rampant commercialism and luxurious living, he felt, were replacing "the good old New England spirit" of the founding generation. Unlike the clerical Jeremiahs of the age, however, Adams was concerned as much with the effect of the decline of plain living on his townsmen's political outlook as on their spirituality. He was convinced that as New Englanders grew more and more engrossed in material concerns, they inevitably became less and less protective of their political liberties. "Our Morals, our Constitution, and our Liberties," he argued, "must needs degenerate" under such conditions. In support of such a prediction he repeatedly referred his readers to the "dreadful example" of republican Rome's collapse into tyranny because of growing luxury and corruption.[31]

Sam Adams, like his Quaker counterpart John Woolman, practiced the republican virtues he espoused, and this helped endear him to the mechanics, laborers, and shipwrights who became his devoted followers during the 1750s and 1760s. Although the brewery was continually on the verge of failure and his house was in disrepair, Adams remained remarkably unconcerned about his financial affairs. He had learned that if he kept his material desires to a minimum he could live on his small income as a tax collector and still have time to devote to his political activities. Sam once told John Adams that he "never looked forward in his Life, never planned, laid a scheme, or formed a design of laying up Any thing for himself or others after him." This was no exaggeration. Sam Adams was devoid of economic ambition. John described him as a "universal good character," a "plain, simple, decent citizen, of middling stature, dress and manners," who prided himself on his frugality and his distaste for ceremony and display. He was known for wearing holes in his clothes before buying new ones and on more than one occasion limited himself to brown bread and milk when a guest at elegant dinners. Nor did he have any patience for the Boston merchant class and their extravagant "Decorations of the Parlor, the shining Boards of Plate, the costly Piles of China," that represented to him a shameful betrayal of the Puritan creed. Adams was, in fact, so singular in his indifference to possessions and in his criticism of the elite's lavish style of living that some of his townsmen censured him as "wanting wisdom to estimate riches at their just value." Joseph Galloway, one of Adams's ardent Tory opponents, acknowledged that the Whig firebrand "eats little, drinks little, sleeps little, thinks much, and is most decisive and indefatigable in the pursuit of his objects."[32]

After the mid-1760s the object that Adams pursued most single-mindedly was the colonial resistance movement. Convinced that the English were conspiring to sap American resistance by debasing the colonists' morals, he was determined to halt the incursion of British tyranny and corruption, and in the process he hoped that the colonies might witness a revival of simplicity. Adams was among the first to propose a boycott of British goods in response to the regulatory acts, not only to force repeal of the odious measures but also to encourage greater colonial self-sufficiency through local production and personal economy. This would promote, he hoped, both political liberty and Puritan morality. "As I am a hearty Well wisher to every Attempt towards a public Reformation," he explained in October 1764, "it gives me peculiar Pleasure to hear that Numbers of the inhabitants of Boston have entered into an Agreement to suppress Extravagance and encourage Frugality." To him such efforts represented New England's only hope for spiritual renewal and economic independence. "Nothing but FRUGALITY can now save the distress'd northern colonies from impending ruin."[33]

Throughout the 1760s Adams remained in the forefront of the organized resistance to British regulations. When the repeal of the Townshend duties in 1770 caused many of the colonists to abandon the boycotts and the spartan sacrifices of the previous decade, Adams was understandably distressed, but not really surprised. In explaining to a friend the collapse of the Nonimportation Association, he wrote that the merchants "held it much longer than I thought they ever would or could." Plain living, he admitted to Arthur Lee, was the most difficult path to follow: "Such is the Indolence of Men in general, or their Inattention to the real Importance of things, that a steady & animated perseverance in the rugged path of Virtue at the hazard of trifles is hardly to be expected."[34]

Yet, while admitting that human nature warred against prolonged self-restraint, Adams remained confident that once enough Americans recognized the severity of their situation, they would indeed be capable of both militant patriotism and moral transformation. To this end he continued to keep the issue of British corruption and American complicity before the public eye, hoping to shame his readers into renewed opposition. His effectiveness as an agitator may be judged in part by the rancor he aroused in the Tories he attacked. Governor Thomas Hutchinson, in referring to Adams in 1771, charged that "I doubt whether there is a greater incendiary in the King's dominion." Two years later the governor regretfully reported to the Earl of Dartmouth that Adams had refused to be bribed into silence. He "could not be made dependent and taken off by some appointment to a civil office."[35]

With the passage of the Port Bill and the other Coercive Acts in 1774, Adams was convinced that the moral and political revolution he so much desired was now imminent, and he called for the severance of all commercial relations with Great Britain. When some Boston merchants balked at such an extreme response, he put forward an uplifting picture of the early Puritans and referred his readers to his own example:

> The Virtue of our Ancestors inspires us—they were contented with Clams & Mussels. For my part, I have been wont to converse with poverty; and however disagreeable a Companion she may be thought to be by the affluent & luxurious who never were acquainted with her, I can live happily with her the remainder of my days, if I can thereby contribute to the Redemption of my Country.

As more and more colonists joined the resistance movement and support in the Congress mounted for more extensive boycotts, Adams grew confident that his faith in the people was justified. "I think our Countrymen," he wrote in October 1774, "discover the Spirit of Rome or Sparta." A few months later, he was even more effusive, declaring that the Puritan social ethic was reviving again among New Englanders. "Inheriting the spirit of their virtuous ancestors, they will, after their example, endure hardships, and confide in an all-gracious Providence."[36]

Sam Adams could look to his cousin John for a prime example of such an attitude. Despite sharp temperamental and political differences, the two kinsmen were remarkably similar in their social and moral outlook as well as their personal backgrounds. Born in 1735, the year that Jonathan Edwards was leading the revival in Northampton, John was the eldest son of Deacon John Adams, a farmer and cordwainer in the tiny rural village of Braintree, on the south shore, ten miles from Boston. Like Sam he entered Harvard intending to become a minister but while there changed his mind. "Necessity" forced him to, he said. Having become a freethinker, he worried that as a clergyman he would be preoccupied with theological debates that would distract him from tending to the needs of his congregation: "I perceived very clearly, as I thought, that the Study of Theology and the pursuit of it as a Profession would involve me in endless Altercations and make my life miserable, without any prospect of doing good to my fellow Men."[37]

Adams then turned to law as his chosen vocation, and, after spending two years under the tutelage of James Putnam in the backwater village of Worcester, he returned to Braintree in 1759 to begin his practice. There he adopted the outlook on the profession suggested to him by Jeremiah Gridley, another early mentor: "In the first place pursue the Law itself, rather than the gain of it. Attend enough to the profits, to keep yourself out of the Briars: but the Law itself should be our grand Object." To ensure that the law remained the primary object of his attention, Adams established a strict regimen that would have pleased the sternest of Puritans:

> Take my Advice, Rise and mount your Horse, by the Morning's dawn, and shake away, amidst the great and beautiful scenes of Nature, that appear at that Time of the day, all the Crudities that are left in your stomach, and all the obstructions that are left in your Brains. Then return to your Study, and bend your whole soul to the Institutes of the law and the Reports of Cases that have been adjudged by the Rules, in the Institutes. Let no trifling Diversion, or amusement, or Company, decoy you from your Books; that is, let no Girl, no Gun, no Cards, no flutes, no Violins, no Dress, no Tobacco, no Laziness, decoy you from your Books.

In this way Adams transformed the Puritan ethic into a professional ethic, keeping the daily code of conduct while discarding the Calvinist theology. As he mused in his diary in late April 1756, "Our proper Business in this Life is, not to accumulate large Fortunes, not to gain high Honours and important offices in the State, not to waste our Health and Spirits in pursuit of the Sciences, but constantly to improve ourselves in Habits of Piety and Virtue."[38]

Although he rejected the life of a Puritan clergyman, Adams, like cousin Sam, obviously did not discard his puritanism.[39] Throughout his long career he fought a running battle with his passions, determined to lead a classically balanced, temperate life devoted to study and public service. At age twenty he wrote in his diary: "He is not a wise man and is unfit to fill any important Station in Society, that has left one Passion in his soul unsubdued." Setting such high standards led Adams to feel guilty when he violated them. "I have smoked, chatted, trifled, loitered away the whole day almost," he sorrowfully admitted in language reminiscent of a John Winthrop or a John Woolman, and he reminded himself that he must always learn from such transgressions. "May I blush whenever I suffer one hour to pass unimproved."[40]

John Adams's most intractable passion, as he himself acknowledged, was pride. Early in his life he admitted that he was a creature of immense vanity; it was his "cardinal Vice and cardinal Folly." His egoism manifested itself not in a desire for ostentatious living or in "empty boastings of Wealth, Birth, Power, Beauty, Parts learning, Virtues or Conduct." Rather, he was vain in his overweening desire to be a "transcendent Success" as a public figure. As a law student he had confessed a "passion" for fame and had pleaded with himself to "wear out of my mind every mean and base affection, conquer my natural Pride and Self Conceit, expect no more deference from my fellows than I deserve, acquire that meekness, and humility, which are the sure marks and characters of a great and generous soul." Yet he never acquired such a self-effacing personality, and his vanity became notorious over the years. Humility was a virtue that always eluded Adams. His preoccupation with public acclaim was, he wrote, "admittedly a Weakness," but he explained it away as a universal trait among public servants. Certainly it was preferable to be vain about one's public accomplishments than to succumb to the baser vanity of "Avarice and Ambition."[41]

Adams was much more successful at conquering avarice than vanity. A life of moderate simplicity, he believed, was essential for himself, his family, and the nation. "Virtues, Ambition, Generosity, indulged to excess degenerate in Extravagance which plunges headlong into Villainy and folly." By the middle of the 1760s, he worried that Americans were engaging in such excessive living. In his *Dissertation on the Feudal and Canon Law* (1765) Adams emphasized how dangerous the growing consolidation of property into a few hands was to republican virtue. A modest sufficiency widely distributed was to him crucial to the stability of the social order. "We should preserve not an Absolute Equality—this is unnecessary, but preserve all from extreme Poverty, and all others from extravagant Riches." It was this middle ground between poverty and riches that Adams sought to occupy in his own life. "It has been my Fate," he observed in 1772, to be acquainted, in the way of my Business, with a Number of very Rich Men. . . . But there is not one . . . who derives more Pleasure from his Property than I do from mine. My little Farm, and Stock, and Cash, affords me as much Satisfaction, as all their Buildings, their vast Sums at Interest, and Stocks in Trade yield. . . . The rich are seldom remarkable for Modesty, Ingenuity, or Humanity. Their Wealth has rather a Tendency to make them penurious and selfish.

Although John Adams's standard of living was considerably higher than that of his cousin Sam, they both expressed the guiding principle of simple living in that they consciously sought to subordinate their material passions to their spiritual and public duties.[42]

Abigail Adams played no small role in facilitating her husband John's desire to lead a life of dignified simplicity and follow a career in public service. As Karl Marx once wrote, "Anyone who knows anything about history knows that great social changes are impossible without the feminine ferment." Certainly this was true of the American Revolution. And it has been true of the history of the simple life as well. Men may have been the most prominent spokesmen for the ethic, but women have most often been responsible for translating the ideal into domestic practice. Abigail Adams, for example, was an amazingly efficient manager of the Braintree household and fully shared her husband's commitment to republican morality. During John's extended absences from home she was able to keep the farm operating by carefully monitoring all expenses. As she explained, "Frugality, Industry and economy are the lessons of the day—at least they must be for me or my small Boat will suffer shipwreck." In 1774, as the newly imposed Port Bill began to strangle Boston's economy, Abigail wrote to John, then in Philadelphia: "If we expect to inherit the blessings of our Fathers, we should return a little more to the primitive Simplicity of Manners, and not sink into inglorious ease." He thoroughly agreed with her assessment and emphasized that such patriotic simplicity should begin at home. To this end, he later advised Abigail to have the family coat of arms removed from their carriage. She did so, assuring him that "I never placed my happiness in equipage."[43]

During the 1770s John Adams joined the chorus of republican spokesmen assaulting the corrupt influence of Great Britain on the colonies. He was convinced that "the Preservation of Liberty depends upon the intellectual and moral Character of the People," and that the character of the English ruling class was rotten. In his *Novanglus* essay, written in 1774, he described the English ship of state as so "loaded with debts and taxes" that she was frantically trying to bring the colonies down with her. It was not the debts incurred during the French and Indian War that had stimulated the British revenue acts but widespread corruption in England that, "like a cancer . . . eats faster and faster every hour. . . . until virtue, integrity, public spirit, simplicity, and frugality, become the objects of ridicule and scorn, and vanity, luxury, foppery, selfishness, meanness, and downright venality swallow up the whole society."[44]

That England was in such a declining state confirmed for Adams the need for the colonies to separate themselves as much as possible from the corrupting influence of the home country, and he wholeheartedly endorsed the nonimportation movement and other forms of resistance. He was, however, more sceptical than his cousin Sam that Americans could sustain the self-denial required of all successful republics. In 1775 he wondered about the colonists' commitment to a total boycott:

> How long will or can a People bear this? I say they can bear it forever. . . . We must change our Habits, our Prejudices our Palates, our Tastes in Dress, Furniture, Equipage, Architecture, etc., but We can live and be happy. But the question is whether our People have Virtue enough to be mere Husbandmen, Mechanicks, and Soldiers? They have not Virtue enough to bear it always I take for granted. How long then will their Virtue last? till next Spring?

A few months later he provided a more extensive analysis of the problem in a letter to Mercy Warren. Under a monarchy, he pointed out, the people could be as degenerate as they pleased; in a republic, however, they must be wise and virtuous. Therefore Americans should choose a republican form of government for their own, knowing full well, of course, that such a government could be maintained only by a citizenry committed to "pure Religion or Austere Morals," a citizenry with a "positive Passion for the public good."[45]

Since Americans no longer embraced a pure religion, did they have the necessary private virtue to sustain a republic? Again, Adams seemed pessimistic, noting that "there is so much Rascality, so much Venality and Corruption, so much Avarice and Ambition, such a Rage for Profit and Commerce among all Ranks and Degrees of Men even in America, that I sometimes doubt whether there is public Virtue enough to Support a Republic." The conflict with Great Britain, Adams suggested, could corrupt Americans as much as purify them. Yet as the Revolution opened, he buried such doubts, hoping that the conflict itself would work a miraculous transformation in the hearts of his countrymen. The day after Congress voted for independence, he shared with Abigail his hope that the Revolution would "inspire us with many Virtues, which we have not, and correct many Errors, Follies, and Vices, which threaten to disturb, dishonor, and destroy Us.— The Furnace of Affliction produces Refinement, in States as well as Individuals."[46]

The Adamses' commitment to republican simplicity was shared by many Whig spokesmen throughout the colonies. Benjamin Rush, who once observed that from "the time of my settlement in 1769 'till 1775 I led a life of constant labor and self-denial," was another distinguished exemplar of patriotic simplicity. His Philadelphia doctor's office was "crowded with the poor in the morning and at meal times," as he was selfless in his ministering to the illnesses and accidents of the needy. "While my days were thus employed in business," he recalled, "my evenings were devoted to study." Not content to preoccupy his thoughts with medical and scientific knowledge, he versed himself in the latest philosophical and political treatises and emerged as a well-informed spokesman for the colonial resistance. Rush agreed with his friend John Adams that American society was racked with the disease of materialism, but he was more optimistic that the patient could yet overcome it, since the ailment "has advanced but a few paces in luxury and effeminacy." The mass of Americans, he prescribed, must be "preserved from the effects of intemperance" by the "force of severe manners." As the Revolution began, Rush, too, hoped that it would introduce "among us the same temperance in pleasure, the same modesty in dress, the same justice in business, and the same veneration in the name of the Deity which distinguished our ancestors." Rush was confident that his countrymen would eventually develop the private and public virtues necessary for self-government. "Time will ameliorate us," he exclaimed in 1776. "A few more misfortunes will teach us wisdom and humility and inspire us with true benevolence."[47]

The prominent Virginia planter Richard Henry Lee was also influenced by the old republicanism of New England, and he self-consciously modeled himself after Sam Adams during the years before independence. As a young man Lee had been deeply influenced by the moral philosophy of the ancient Greeks. "The love of poverty, contempt of riches, disregard of self interest, attention to public good, desire of glory, love of their country," he recorded in his journal, were virtues that "cannot be repeated too often." When he sent his sons to London for schooling in 1772 he asked his brother William, who was in England, to get them settled: "You will readily see that my boys must be frugally clothed. The plainest, to be decent, will please me much the best. They will want a plain cheap furnishing upon their arrival." Lee's sense of frugality seemed out of place among the Tidewater aristocracy with whom he associated, and his peers frequently remarked on his "eccentricity." Perhaps it was such ridicule that led him once to admit that he hoped eventually to move to Massachusetts, where the civic leaders were "wise, attentive, sober, diligent and frugal."[48]

Like his republican counterparts in Massachusetts, Lee came to view the Revolutionary crisis as a means of producing a return to the hallowed values of an earlier generation. In a letter to Sam Adams on the eve of the Revolution he assumed a spartan perspective:

> Those who sail gently down the stream of prosperity are very apt to loose [sic] that energetic virtue so necessary to true happiness. It seems that discipline, and pretty severe discipline too, is necessary for the depraved heart of man, nor have we any right to expect security in the enjoyment of the greatest human blessings until we have learnt wisdom and moderation in the school of adversity.

This assumption that the conflict with Great Britain was as much a moral crusade as a struggle for political and economic freedom pervaded the rhetoric of Lee and other American republicans. In this way the Revolution came to be viewed by many Whigs as an "opportunity to close with one heroic effort the long-existing chasm between their societies and the social models they so much admired."[49]

But the chasm between the ideal and real had grown too wide to be closed quickly or easily. Within months after hostilities commenced, republican idealists were shocked to learn how badly they had misread the public temper. While promoting continued frugality and self-sacrifice among some patriots, the Revolutionary conflict also spawned an outpouring of greed, profiteering, and speculation. Financing the unexpectedly long war effort produced a dangerous increase in public and private credit, and the infusion of paper money into the economy resulted in a skyrocketing inflationary spiral. The removal of British economic regulations and the expropriation of hundreds of estates abandoned by fleeing loyalists helped create new chances for quick profits and entrepreneurial chicanery. And many Americans, then as since, eagerly took advantage of the profit-making opportunities produced by war. James Otis had predicted as much when he observed in 1776: "When the pot boils, the scum will rise." But hardly anyone expected the ensuing froth. Traders from Spain, France, and Holland raced to replace Great Britain as the supplier of luxury items to the Americans, and by 1777 colonial newspapers were again filled with advertisements announcing new shipments of European finery. A New England clergyman watching this development commented that "instead of a public spirit which should have been a moving spirit in us all, there has in many appeared the most insatiable avarice, and a greedy grasping at every thing within their reach, endeavoring, at the expense of the public, to draw every thing possible into the narrow circle of self."[50]

Many Revolutionary spokesmen feared that profiteering was endangering the war effort. South Carolina's Henry Laurens reported to General Washington from Philadelphia in 1778 that "almost every man has turned his thoughts and attention to gain and pleasure, practicing every artifice of Change Alley or Jonathan's." Throughout the war years Washington himself frequently complained that "speculation, peculation, and an insatiable thirst for riches seems to have got the better of every other of Men." He had never seen such a "dearth of public spirit and want of virtue, such stockjobbing, and fertility in all the low arts to obtain advantage of one kind or another." By 1782 Timothy Pickering could write home to his wife that while the soldiers remained poor, the "citizens in general in the United States indulge a luxury to which, before the war, they were strangers."[51]

The contrast between the thrilling austerity of the prewar nonimportation movement and the wartime activities of the citizenry was especially disheartening to those republican idealists who had predicted a moral as well as political revolution. While serving in Congress in Philadelphia, Sam Adams found it hard to believe the reports he heard describing the collapse of civic virtue in Boston. In 1777 he asked a hometown friend:

> Is it indeed true, my Friend that "Self Denial is a Virtue rarely to be seen among you"? How great a Change in a few years! The Self Denial of the Citizens of Boston, their Patience and Long Suffering under the Cruel Oppression of the Port Bill was astonishing both to their Friends and their Enemies. . . . God forbid that they should so soon forget their own generous Feelings for the Public and for each other, as to set private Interest in Competition with that of the Great Community.

Adams tried his best to minimize the implications of such disturbing trends, rationalizing at one point that the renewed "Spirit of Avarice . . . rages only among a few, because perhaps, the few only are concerned at present in trade." As the evidence of selfishness among the Revolutionaries mounted, however, he found it more and more difficult to remain optimistic. "I hope," he wrote his wife in 1778, "the Depravity of Manners is not so great as to exclude all Hopes of Children rising up and serving God and their Country in the Room of their Fathers. May Heaven grant us a Time of Reformation!"[52]

By 1780 it was clear that such a reformation was not in the offing, and Adams felt that his fellow New Englanders had again betrayed the heroism and self-sacrifice of their Puritan fathers. He especially resented the extravagance of John Hancock, who served as governor of Massachusetts during the early 1780s and who brought to that office a personal preference for pomp and display. To Adams it was scandalous for an elected official of the new republican commonwealth to engage in such high living, especially while the general public was being asked to make great sacrifices for the Revolutionary cause. "Does it become us," he asked, "to lead the people to such public diversions as promote superfluity of dress and ornament when it is as much they can bear to support the expense of clothing a naked army?" What a mockery Hancock and his consorts had made of their Puritan heritage, he charged. "Our Bradfords, Winslows & Winthrops would have revolted at the Idea of opening scenes of Dissipation & Folly. . . . I love the people of Boston. I once thought, that city would be a Christian Sparta. But Alas! Will men never be free!" As the war progressed, Adams put his faith in the spartan example provided by America's political and military leaders as the most effective way to influence the manners of the public at large. The "Men of Influence," he wrote in 1781, "must form the Manners of the People. They can operate more towards cultivating the Principles & Fixing the Habits of Virtue than all the Force of Laws." To that end Adams presided over several town meetings in 1780 and 1781 designed to encourage virtuous habits—but to little avail. The very people the meetings were intended to instruct were so indifferent as not even to attend.[53]

The successful Revolution thus brought political independence but had not resulted in the sweeping moral regeneration envisioned by so many republican spokesmen. Its failure to produce a classically organic society devoted to plain living and possessed of deferential civic virtue suggests that the ideal of republican simplicity had not penetrated very far into the social conscience. Many Revolutionary Americans apparently viewed the self-limiting political economy advocated by evangelical clergymen and classical republicans as at best only a temporary expedient. Despite the pervasive use of the term "republicanism" in patriotic pamphlets and newspapers, there was in fact little consensus among the various economic groups and geographic regions about the meaning of the term's social ethic. Abstract notions such as "power," "virtue," "liberty," "equality," and "simplicity" were pregnant with ambiguities that resulted in sharply differing perceptions of what the Revolution was intended to accomplish. As John Adams was led to admit, republicanism had come to mean "anything, everything, or nothing."

The Revolution was not simply an ideological crusade on behalf of liberty and virtue engineered by highly educated republican elites. There was a popular ideology of revolt as well, and it interacted with classical republicanism to give the rebellion its driving force. What did the Revolution mean to those workers, servants, farmers, and freedmen who participated in the Stamp Act demonstrations, supported the nonimportation movement, idolized Tom Paine, and fought with Washington and Greene? The hard evidence needed to answer such a question is scanty, and sorting out the differences in outlook among the various social ranks and occupations is extremely difficult. Nevertheless, recent scholarship suggests that public support for patriotic simplicity was greatest among the lower social orders—the common laborers, seamen, and servants, as well as the lesser artisans, struggling journeymen, and apprentices. These Americans were already living frugal lives by virtue of their vocational status and, significantly, many of them had been among those most affected by the moral appeal and emancipating rhetoric of the Great Awakening.[54]

Often literate but rarely learned, these "laboring poor" knew little of the classical underpinnings of republican simplicity. But they nevertheless responded enthusiastically to the Whig oratory in defense of classical liberty and virtue, just as they had earlier responded emotionally to the evangelical appeal for spiritual regeneration. To them, simplicity was a fact of life, not an abstract ideal. They lived according to what E. P. Thompson has called a "moral economy," harboring a traditional assumption that familial and community cohesion outweighed the private acquisition of wealth. They also still tended to view work morally, as a spiritual or civic calling, rather than selfishly, as the individual pursuit of gain, and they therefore despised speculators, hoarders, monopolizers, and gougers. During the war, these traditional attitudes found tangible expression in the demands of the urban and rural poor for a revival of the Calvinist concept of the "just price." Such government controls were necessary, they believed, to halt the dramatic inflation provoked by wartime profiteering and speculation.[55]

The shoemakers and tanners of Philadelphia expressed the outlook of many of the patriotic "laboring poor" when they declared in 1779 that their efforts had always brought them a "bare living profit," regardless of "however industrious and attentive to business, however frugal in manner of living" they had been. Nevertheless, they had been "contented to live decently without acquiring wealth" because "our professions rendered us as useful and necessary members of the community." An artisan made a similar observation in a Philadelphia newspaper: "Corruption, extravagance and luxury are seldom found in the habitations of tradesmen. Industry, economy, prudence, and fortitude generally inhabit there." Far from being self-seeking materialists, some lower-class colonists, particularly in New England, with its still potent residue of Puritanism, had in fact shown more fidelity to the traditional moral economy of republicanism than had its upper-class spokesmen.[56]

Among the more successful artisans and master craftsmen, however, this traditional "moral economy" apparently lost much of its appeal during the Revolutionary period. Many artisan entrepreneurs seized the opportunities created by war to expand their activities into the realm of the merchant class. In doing so, they began the transition from the medieval guild outlook to the more modern commercial mentality emphasizing laissez-faire, mass production, and the self-regulating marketplace. For these projectors on the make, the "way to wealth" aphorisms of Ben Franklin's "Poor Richard" and the compelling logic of the new economic liberalism espoused by Adam Smith and others had more attraction than the pleas for contented simplicity and a regulated economy coming from the clergy and republican spokesmen.

But the situation was more complicated than this. If the various elements making up the laboring classes differed in their economic perspective, they tended to be more of one mind in their political outlook. Journeymen and master craftsmen, day laborers and skilled artisans alike believed that productive labor, the making of tangible goods by hand and machine, entitled one to recognition as an equal member of the social and political community. The liberating rhetoric of the Great Awakening had in this sense remained etched in the minds of many of the workers, and they began in 1776 to "identify the millennium with the establishment of governments which derived their power from the people, and which were free from the great disparities of wealth which characterized the Old World." This producer republicanism thus conflicted in a fundamental way with the gentry republicanism of a John Adams or a Richard Henry Lee. The Whig patricians, despite their animus toward ostentatious Tories and their espousal of republican simplicity, nevertheless adhered to the traditional hierarchical social structure in which everyone knew their place and accepted it. Voting and office-holding privileges were still to be limited to those with a specified amount of real property.[57]

To many among the laboring ranks, however, the Revolution was intended to remove, not reinforce, such social barriers. Their motivating impulse, therefore, was egalitarian rather than deferential, more Quaker than Puritan, one might say, and they saw little practical *political* difference between being lorded over by corrupt placemen or by virtuous "natural aristocrats." Either way, they would continue to be denied full participation in the political process and be expected to accept their subordinate social status. Hence, though willing to support the learned Whig elite in the fight against British tyranny and corruption, many lower-class rebels approached the Revolution with expectations about their status in the new nation that quickly conflicted with the ordered social vision of classical republicanism.

The artisans, craftsmen, and laborers who for years had been under the political and social heel of the merchant class in the seaport cities seized the opportunity afforded by the Revolutionary crisis to assert an egalitarian ideology that threatened the very heart of the traditional deferential social system. By the early 1770s they were openly assailing the pretensions of affluent colonists who had the "impudence to assert that Mechanics are men of no consequence," who "make no scruples to say that the mechanics . . . have no right to be consulted; that is, in fact, have no right to speak or think for themselves." Such a leveling spirit was given added momentum when Tom Paine published his influential tract *Common Sense* in January 1776. Although it reflected the same basic argument for independence put forward by classical republicans, it differed significantly in style and intent from the pamphlets of the gentry Whigs. Paine explicitly appealed to the "producing classes" and supported broadened voting rights for non-landowners.[58]

To republican patricians such as John Adams, the "democratical" demands fostered by Paine and other radicals were as odious as the British regulatory measures. The specter of unlearned mechanics and laborers exercising political power horrified him, and he adopted an aggressively defensive posture reminiscent of Puritan magistrates and divines. The "one thing" absolutely required in the new republican governments being formed after 1776, he stressed to a correspondent, was "a decency, and respect, and veneration introduced for persons of authority." Benjamin Rush was likewise disheartened by the egalitarian tendencies unleashed by the struggle for independence. He opposed the democratic constitution drafted for Pennsylvania because it "presupposes perfect equality, and an equal distribution of property, wisdom, and virtues among the inhabitants of the state." Inequality, he pointed out, was the historical fact of life. Rush's arguments, however, failed to sway the public, and the Pennsylvania constitution became the most democratic in the newly united states. In the process, said one observer, it "split the Whig party to pieces." Rush remained bitter, calling his state government a "mobocracy." He appealed to men of "wisdom, virtue, and property" to reassert true republican principles. "A simple democracy, or an unbalanced republic," he emphasized, "is one of the greatest of evils." Rush's concerns about the upsurge of popular politics were shared by the Whig elite throughout the colonies, and such anxieties would play a major role in the decision to organize the Constitutional Convention in 1787.[59]

Revolutionary Americans, in sum, were of many minds about what the pursuit of happiness in the new nation meant. Some patriots had supported resistance in part as a means to increase individual freedom in the market-place; others viewed independence as an opportunity for greater participation in social and political life. And many, no doubt, combined both motives. Once the Revolution began, entrepreneurial and individualistic patriots used the same libertarian arguments that had been applied against British trade regulations to reject traditional restrictions on their own social mobility, political participation, or their style of living. Just as had occurred with Puritanism, therefore, the ideal of enlightened simplicity had become intertwined with other political and economic ideals making up republican social theory. During the Revolution, these divergent strands were kept from splaying completely by the exigencies of war. After 1783, however, individuals began to choose one over the other in assigning their priorities of value. And, in the process, traditional notions of simple living often became expendable. As John Adams had correctly observed, self-realization, not self-restraint, was the republican virtue prized most by the populace in the aftermath of the Revolution.

CHAPTER FOUR

Republicanism Transformed

If public behavior during the Revolution was disillusioning to classical republicans, postwar developments were even more threatening. The egalitarian forces unleashed by the conflict with Great Britain continued to erode the traditional authority of the gentry elite. Instead of enjoying a stable republican consensus, the new nation seemed plagued by a fragmenting factionalism. By the mid-1780s every state was witnessing the emergence of extra-legal popular associations designed to promote the interests of particular groups—debtors, farmers, artisans, seamen. Occasionally resorting to vigilante methods, they expressed their grievances and aspirations by intimidating government officials, demanding the printing of paper money, and resisting tax collections and foreclosure proceedings.

Equally disturbing to classical republican sensibilities was the raging materialism that seemed to energize all ranks. As if to offset immediately the privations of war, citizens rushed to enjoy the luxury goods they had earlier proudly renounced. Imported fineries, James Warren of Plymouth wrote in 1783, had destroyed all "Ideas of Frugality which Necessity had before given, and drained us of our Money." No sooner had the fighting stopped than British vessels began clogging American harbors, and British traders began offering easy credit to the former colonists. One newspaper reported that "British Frippery" was being shipped into Massachusetts in such large quantities that the General Court in 1785 felt compelled to try to reduce a flow of foreign luxuries "unknown to our ancestors." Mechanics were buying silk stockings and farmers' daughters purchased satin lace. A writer in the *Boston Gazette* blamed the newly arisen entrepreneurial elite for stimulating such a buying spree. "Are not our mushroom gentry, in conjunction with those from the other side of the Atlantic, introducing every species of foreign luxuries, not only in dress, but at their tables?"[1]

Confronted with such extravagance among the affluent and such rebelliousness among the aspiring, those Revolutionaries still committed to the ideal of republican simplicity were divided about how best to promote and preserve it. Traditionalists such as Sam Adams pleaded with the people to obey the laws and act in an orderly and temperate fashion. But he was most concerned about the unseemly behavior of the elite. He especially lashed out at those younger Bostonian nabobs responsible for the founding of the "Tea Assembly," an exclusive social club where dancing and card-playing were the primary diversions. Popularly called the "Sans Souci Club," it symbolized for Adams the aristocratic practices of the Old World that were inimical to the survival of republican virtue. "If there ever was a period wherein reason was bewildered, and stupefied by dissipation and extravagance," he wrote in a newspaper article attacking the club, "it is surely the present. . . . We are exchanging prudence, virtue and economy for those glaring spectres luxury, prodigality and profligacy." He then asked his readers to recall the history of the Roman republic, reminding them that as long as the Romans "continued their frugality and simplicity of manners, they shone with superlative glory but no sooner were effeminate refinements introduced amongst them, than they visibly fell from whatever was elevated and magnanimous, and became feeble and timid, dependent slavish and false." Adams's diatribe set off a storm of controversy, with letters of opposition and support dominating the pages of Boston's newspapers for almost two months thereafter.[2]

Yet by the time the dispute over the Tea Assembly faded from the public forum, it was apparent that Adams and other older proponents of classical austerity were losing their influence over the younger generation. After the lengthy newspaper debate concerning the social club, one writer sighed: "I am tired and disgusted with the 'Sans Souci' babble, noise and nonsense; and heartily wish our folks would employ their time, and pen, and paper, and tongues to better purpose." Instead of the respect they had enjoyed during the crisis years before 1775, Adams and his "puritan" supporters now found themselves ridiculed in fashionable circles "as *rigid republicans*, men of contracted minds. . . ." Adams was stunned by the disturbing course of events. "So great is the wickedness of some men and the stupid servility of others," he wrote in 1787, "that one would be almost inclined to conclude that communities cannot be free."[3]

James Warren shared Adams's disillusionment at the inability of their peers to live up to classical republicanism's restraining social ethic. In 1792 Warren complained that he had "lived long enough to feel pains too great for me to describe." He and other old patriots like Adams had "helped carry men through a time of change." But now that the crisis of war had passed, they "had no place in a time of stability. With the consolidation of the new order their acute Spartanism becomes uncomfortable, outmoded." By the 1790s Warren had despaired of reforming American society and spent his remaining years in rural isolation. "Public virtue, and an attention to the security of public liberty," he had earlier told Arthur Lee, "are seldom found in cities; they must be looked for in the sober and manly retreats of husbandmen and shepherds, where frivolous manners, commerce, and high stages of civilization, have not debauched the principles and reason of mankind." The simple life, he concluded, could be achieved only by a few in rural isolation, rather than by the many.[4]

Other Revolutionary idealists were not as hopeless. They argued that it was too much to expect a moral revolution to occur simultaneously with independence. It would take time and effort to teach the citizenry their new ethical and social responsibilities. As Benjamin Rush assured a despondent friend in 1789: "Remember, my dear sir, that we are at present in a *forming* state. We have as yet but few habits of any kind, and *good* ones may be acquired and fixed by a good example and proper instruction as easily as *bad* ones without the benefit of either." Rush believed that too many of his disillusioned countrymen were confusing the end of the Revolution with the end of the fighting. "On the contrary," he emphasized, "nothing but the first act of the great drama is closed. It remains yet to establish and perfect our new forms of government, and to prepare the principles, morals, and manners of our citizens for these forms of government after they are established and brought to perfection." The corrupt influence of British tyranny had been removed; now it was necessary to implant republican virtues in the American people.[5]

For Rush and other determined republican spokesmen, this cleansing process required gradually instilling in the public an appreciation for the fragility of republican government and its utter dependence on civic and private virtue. If such economic self-control and political restraint were not developed, then the new republic would eventually see its citizens "devouring each other like beasts of prey." The means proposed to produce such public enlightenment were many and varied. College students at Yale debated whether sumptuary laws should be revived. Ministers called for a new religious awakening. But with the massive migrations into the interior and with the disestablishment of state churches, the traditional moral authority of community and church was now even less effective than in the past. Ethnic, political, and religious pluralism was rapidly becoming the keynote of American social life.

In the face of such changes, a number of Revolutionary leaders in the early years of independence looked for new ways to help inculcate republican values. The most frequently discussed proposal was to establish public schools as agencies for moral and civic development. Benjamin Rush took the lead in maintaining that the younger generation be transformed into "republican machines" through education in state-supported schools with uniform goals and methods. In these public schools, as well as in the Sunday schools and in the national university Rush proposed, American children would not only be made literate but would also be taught to choose the public good over all private interests and concerns. He wrote, in a passage indicative of the way in which republican simplicity closely approximated the original Puritan ethic, that the new American "must be taught to amass wealth, but it must be only to increase his power of contributing to the wants and demands of the state. He must be indulged occasionally in amusements, but he must be taught that study and business should be his principal pursuits in life. Above all he must love life . . . but he must be taught that this life is not his own." Time and training, Rush was convinced, would demonstrate that Americans were indeed capable of developing republican virtue.[6]

Thomas Jefferson was equally hopeful that republican virtue could be nurtured in new generations of American citizens. The Virginia statesman-philosopher and gentleman farmer had constructed his own ideal of republican simplicity from a variety of sources. He borrowed freely from the French—Voltaire, Rousseau, Montesquieu, and the Physiocrats—as well as from Locke, Francis Hutcheson and the Scottish moralists, and the English Whigs. Yet his outlook was as much classical as contemporary, and he also identified closely with the philosophers of Greece and Rome. From an early age Jefferson was particularly attracted to the moral philosophy of the Stoics and Epicureans. He gleaned from Stoicism an emphasis on self-discipline. And his reading of Epicurus taught him to appreciate the power of reason and the joys of a contemplative life. "Their precepts," he once explained, "related chiefly to ourselves and the government of those passions which, unrestrained, would disturb our tranquility of mind. In this branch of philosophy they were really great."[7]

On several occasions Jefferson referred to himself as an Epicurean. For him, however, Epicurus was not the unbridled sensualist that many Europeans had mistakenly assumed. "I consider the genuine (not the imputed) doctrines of Epicurus as containing everything rational in moral philosophy which Greece and Rome have left us." Jefferson agreed with Epicurus that happiness is the aim of life, and he defined it as "to be not pained in body, nor troubled in mind, i.e., In-do-lence of body, tranquility of mind." To achieve such tranquility of mind required not hedonistic living, but temperate living in order to avoid "desire and fear, the two principal diseases of the mind." As Epicurus advised, to be "accustomed to simple and plain living is conducive to health and makes a man ready for the necessary task of life."[8]

In the aftermath of the Revolution, Jefferson shared the chagrin of other Revolutionary leaders at his countrymen's apparent eagerness to abandon republican frugality and in the process accumulate a dangerous indebtedness. "All my letters," he reported from Paris in July 1787, "are filled with details of our extravagance." Jefferson could not understand why patriots would want to discard the noble simplicity and rusticity they had displayed during the war years:

I know no condition happier than that of a Virginia farmer might be, conducting himself as he did during the war. His estate supplies a good table, clothes himself and his family with their ordinary apparel, furnishes a small surplus to buy salt, sugar, coffee, and a little finery for his wife and daughters, enables him to receive and visit his friends, and furnishes him pleasing and healthy occupation. To secure all this he needs but one act of self-denial, to put off buying anything till he has the money to pay for it.

Anyone who has ever visited Monticello knows that Jefferson's own life as a Virginia gentleman farmer was never so modest as this idealized description. His was a refined and learned form of simple living, much like that of his classical heroes Cicero, Horace, and Pliny. But, like William Penn, he never let his own cosmopolitan tastes nor his own careless financial management deter him from continually rhapsodizing about the virtues of republican simplicity and self-sufficient husbandry for the nation as a whole.[9]

To Jefferson the issue at stake for young America was momentous. Personal corruption was the greatest danger facing the new republic. If his countrymen could not quickly restrain their acquisitive instincts, they would eventually lose their liberty. Indebtedness could stifle individual and national freedom as much as British rule had done. Yet the mounting evidence coming from the United States indicated that much of the public seemed heedless of such dire consequences. The newly independent Americans were reported by a correspondent to be "a Luxurious, Voluptuous, indolent, expensive people without Economy or Industry."[10]

Jefferson, however, refused to accept such accounts at face value. From his vantage point in Europe, while serving as minister to France, American manners still seemed *relatively* restrained, and he was optimistic that such a distinction would become more evident in ensuing years. Jefferson suggested to a worried countryman that those who were disillusioned by American behavior should visit "London, Versailles, Madrid, Vienna, Berlin, etc." There they would see what "high living" was all about. Later, in speaking of America to a European friend, he offered that "though there is less wealth there, there is more freedom, more ease, and less misery."[11]

Like Rush, Jefferson based his hope for an increasingly virtuous American republic in large measure on the creation of state-supported schools. Public education, he stressed, was the very "keystone of our arch of government." In 1779 Jefferson had introduced his "Bill for the More General Diffusion of Knowledge" into the Virginia Assembly. It called for the creation of elementary schools throughout the state where all free children—male and female— would receive three years of education at public expense. Each elementary school would select its best student to attend a grammar or secondary school, and, in turn, each grammar school would choose one student to receive four more years of advanced education. "By this means," Jefferson suggested, "twenty of the best geniuses will be raked from the rubbish annually, and be instructed at the public expense, as far as grammar schools go." Through such a program the "laboring classes" would attain a basic literacy and an historical appreciation for the necessity of self-government. And, at the same time, the hierarchical filtering process would produce an enlightened, "learned" class of leaders, men who would form the "natural aristocracy" of talent and virtue necessary for the moral and political guidance of the republic. Jefferson was clearly for equal opportunity but not for equal status.[12]

Many of the founding fathers shared Rush's and Jefferson's faith that classical republican values could best be disseminated through public education. Sam Adams, despite his disappointment at the postwar behavior of his contemporaries, still cherished the thought that instructing the youth of the nation "in the study and practice of the exalted virtues of the Christian system . . . will happily tend to subdue the turbulent passions of men, and introduce that golden age." And, as governor of Massachusetts, he asked the state legislature to support a system of public education. Yet in almost every instance, the educational schemes put forward by these enlightened statesmen came to nought. Jefferson's plan for Virginia was repeatedly rejected. Wealthy Virginians opposed spending their tax money on schools that would mingle their sons "in a vulgar and suspicious communion" with the masses. The same fate awaited Rush's proposals in Pennsylvania and Adams's in Massachusetts. Consequently, the informed and sober citizenry envisioned by the educational reformers failed to appear.[13]

This development disappointed but did not surprise John Adams. Unlike Jefferson, Rush, and other enlightened optimists, Adams had grown convinced that Americans could not be so easily taught to control their material lusts once they had reached a level of comfortable sufficiency. How long, he asked, "will republicans be the dupes of their own simplicity?" Mere words and books and teachers were not enough to turn naturally passionate men into virtuous republican "machines," as Rush and Jefferson believed. "The modern improvers of society—ameliorators of the condition of mankind, instructors of the human species—have assumed too much. They have undertaken to build a new universe."[14]

After all, Adams pointed out in a letter to Virginia's John Taylor, education had been a dominant institution in the Old World for centuries, and there was little evidence that literate Europeans had come to control their baser instincts. "You may read the history of all the universities, academies, monasteries of the world, and see whether learning extinguishes passions or corrects human vices." Obviously, he admitted, education was a desirable asset. "Laws for the liberal education of youth, especially of the lower class of people, are so extremely wise and useful that to a humane and generous mind no expense for their purpose would be thought extravagant." Yet he had no great hopes that education alone would generate widespread appreciation for republican virtue. "The world grows more enlightened," but, Adams asked, "are riches, honors, and beauty going out of fashion? . . . The more knowledge is diffused, the more the passions are extended, and the more furious they grow." Moreover, since state legislatures were defeating most proposals for public education, he despaired of ever seeing education made "sufficiently general for the security of society."[15]

Adams reflected his Puritan heritage in placing primary responsibility for the shaping of character within the household. "The foundations of national Morality," he wrote, "must be laid in private families." John told Abigail that "above all Cares of this Life let our ardent Anxiety be, to mold the Minds and Manners of our Children." To this end they monitored the development of their children with meticulous care. John Adams could be remarkably concise in teaching his children the purpose of life. "To be good, and to do good," he stressed to his twelve-year-old daughter, "is all We have to do." Abigail was equally direct in her instructions to young John Quincy. After telling her son that the "due Government of the passions has been considered in all ages as a most valuable acquisition," she expressed the hope that he would learn "to govern and control" himself. "Having once obtained this self government you will find a foundation laid for happiness to yourself and usefulness to Mankind."[16]

But John Adams realized by the 1780s that such conscientious parental attention to the moral instruction of children was increasingly rare among the public at large. In response to a stream of letters from James and Mercy Warren describing the postwar scramble for wealth and status, Adams professed little shock. "It is most certain that our Countrymen," he told James Warren in 1786, "are not and never were, Spartans in their Contempt of Wealth, and I will go farther and say they ought not to be. Such a Trait in their Characters would render them lazy Drones, unfit for the Agriculture, Manufactures, Fisheries, and Commerce, and Population for their Country." He reminded Warren that after every other war during the eighteenth century, the American people had demonstrated the same eagerness to overindulge in foreign manners and fashions. "You will be very sensible that our Countrymen have never maintained the Character of every exalted Virtue. It is not to be expected that they should have grown much better." Adams had not abandoned his own preference for republican simplicity. He had simply come to feel in his conservative heart that, since most people were preoccupied with increasing their material possessions, political power, and social status, it would be better for them to be hard at work than indolent and indebted. At least that would tend to keep them busy and out of trouble. Since so many people were not inherently virtuous, at least they could be encouraged to behave virtuously. Active industry and enterprise, even though primarily excited by the prospect of material gain, thus became "virtuous" activities in their own way.[17]

In departing so from the classical republican presumption of widespread public virtue, Adams essentially revived the Puritan emphasis on the social benefits derived from individuals diligently pursuing their callings. He knew, however, that the Puritan ethic had been effective only as long as the agencies established to counterbalance *excessive* materialism—government, religion, family, schools, and community—remained viable and strong. By the 1780s, however, it was apparent to him that such agencies no longer checked acquisitiveness or contentiousness. Adams admitted that his outlook in this respect differed from that of Sam Adams and other traditional republican idealists, and therefore his proposals for the future must as well. Since he was convinced that the public as a whole would always lack a sense of classical restraint and be motivated primarily by private interest rather than the public good, only the state could contain popular ambitions and passions. The Confederation government, therefore, must be modified to reflect this consideration. Once republicans admitted that public virtue was not inherent in the American character and that neither parental attention nor public education could be relied upon to inculcate it, they would turn to government for the glue to hold the social order together. They would see with Adams that a stable republic demanded something "more efficacious . . . than moral song, ingenious fable, philosophic precept, or Christian ordinance." Only government itself, he concluded, was powerful enough to channel individual passions so as to serve the public good—and even its effects were limited.[18]

But what form of government was best suited to serve the interests of a young republic? To answer this question Adams wrote his famous *Defense of the Constitutions of the United States of America*, published a few months before the Constitutional Convention gathered in Philadelphia in 1787. History had demonstrated, Adams asserted, that man was driven by a vain desire for social distinction, which was most often expressed in the acquisition of increasing amounts of material wealth. "We may call this desire for distinction childish and silly, but we cannot alter the nature of man." And in a republic such as the United States, these natural tendencies were actually reinforced rather than reduced. Adams wrote that a "free people are most addicted to luxury of any. That equality which they enjoy, and in which they glory, inspires them with sentiments which hurry into luxury." During and after the Revolution, the United States had proven to be "more Avaricious than any other Nation that ever existed." Admittedly, some especially virtuous individuals still lived according to the dictates of the "golden mean," but they were, and would always be, few in number.[19]

Since history had shown that no government, no matter how well constituted, could eliminate man's natural propensity for self-love, Adams concluded that the objective should be to "find a form of government best calculated to prevent the bad effects and corruption of luxury, when, in the ordinary course of things, it must be expected to come in." Though agreeing with most other republican moralists that excessive luxury should be restrained as much as possible by public morality and law, Adams maintained that the root of the evil "lies in human nature," and that "must be restrained by a mixed form of government, which is the best in the world to manage luxury."[20]

Adams argued that by separating the legislative branch into two houses, one popular and one aristocratic, the upper classes would be balanced by the lower classes and vice versa, thereby checking each other's base tendencies while preserving each other's strengths. To him there would always be an aristocracy, even in a republic, made up of the "rich, the well-born, and the able." And there would always be those lower on the social scale eager to dislodge them. In Adams's mixed system of government, however, the ambition of commoners would be tempered by the haughty pride of birth. Such a mixed government, overseen by a separate executive branch, would have "all the advantage against general luxury which arises from subordination; and it has the further advantage of being able to execute prudent and reasonable sumptuary laws, whenever the circumstances of affairs require them." This interaction of the "one, the few, and the many" would ideally promote societal restraint while not totally suffocating the positive effects of individual ambition.[21]

Of course, the Constitution that was drafted in Philadelphia in 1787 closely resembled Adams's plan in its basic structure. And many of the delegates shared his opinion that the dream of establishing a decentralized republic of simple manners and civic virtue had proven illusory. Shays's Rebellion and other disruptive incidents indicated that many commoners were behaving in a dangerously unrepublican way. In state after state, a dramatic shift in political power had occurred since 1776. Men of humble origins and parochial interests began to displace the gentry in seats of power. The popularly elected state assemblies violated traditional property rights by printing excessive amounts of paper money and by staying judicial action against debtors. Such developments led many of the Revolutionaries who earlier had been optimistic about America's republican potential to reveal a defensive, conservative strain reminiscent of Puritan magistrates and divines. "*We have, probably,*" concluded George Washington in 1786, "*had too good an opinion of human nature in forming our confederation.*" John Dickinson agreed, noting that changes were needed in order to protect "the worthy against the licentious."[22]

James Madison had similar concerns. In 1787 he reported to Jefferson that America was displaying "symptoms . . . truly alarming, which have tainted the faith of the most orthodox republicans." People were stretching the meaning of liberty far beyond the intent of the Revolutionary fathers, taking the law and other people's property into their own hands. "Neither moral nor religious motives," he insisted, "can be relied on as an adequate control." Madison shared John Adams's belief that the central government must be strengthened and its role modified to reflect such unexpected developments. Instead of passively serving a people supposedly unified by a classical sense of public virtue and private restraint, it must now become an active mediator and enforcer, governing a factious people torn by conflicting economic and political interests. In his celebrated defense of the new Constitution in *Federalist 10*, Madison turned classical theory on its head, arguing that the American republic would succeed not because it remained small and static but because of its expanding physical size and its growing social diversity. The traditional bane of republics—factional self-interest—would no longer represent a mortal threat, since it would be neutralized by the very multiplicity of factions and interests. Moreover, where classical republicanism held that private virtue among a preponderant majority of the citizens was vital to the well-being of the republic, Madison argued that only a relatively few enlightened leaders were actually necessary. The multi-layered constitutional structure would provide a series of electoral filters that would sort out and elevate the men "who possess the most attractive merit and the most diffusive and established characters." Thus, America did not have to have the virtuous *public* deemed necessary by classical theorists. It only needed a system of checks and balances that would ensure that a meritocracy of talent and virtue held power. And every nation, he promised his readers, had at least a few such virtuous men. The new American nation after 1787, as Philip Greven has written, was in this sense "to be a republic of laws and of institutions rather than a republic of virtue."[23]

It was also to be a republic of commerce and manufacturing. At least that was the hope of Alexander Hamilton and other early capitalist expansionists. The New York patriot had never fallen under the spell of classical republicanism in the first place; nor did he see anything inimical about the modern British system of politics or economy. Where republican idealists were intent upon avoiding the English model of capitalist development, Hamilton was eager to imitate it. If the classical republicans had their way, he warned, the United States would be saddled with a political economy "limited to the maintenance of each family in the simplest manner." Instead of such a stinted program, Hamilton promoted a dynamic, new political economy that would unleash individual economic ambition and the factory system so as to accelerate social "progress" and enhance national power.[24]

Hamilton, the "bastard brat of a Scottish peddler," as John Adams called him, derived much of this modern economic outlook from his reading of the Scottish philosopher David Hume, who during the eighteenth century had developed a theory of political economy quite at variance with classical and Christian simplicity. Far from considering luxurious living and commercial activity necessarily injurious to republics, Hume contended that such practices actually strengthened the body politic by raising the material standard of living and thereby giving a sense of purpose to even the meanest of lives. Besides, Hume argued, acquisitiveness was one of the most basic of human drives. The true statesman must recognize this fact. Since most people were governed mainly by ambition and avarice, these vices should be imaginatively channeled to work toward the public good. Such passions could be controlled only by other passions; to expect virtue to reign was hopelessly naive. It was therefore in the national interest to promote an expansive commercial ethic, since it was "an infallible consequence of all industrious professions to . . . make the love of gain prevail over the love of pleasure."[25]

Hamilton agreed with Hume that material self-interest was the controlling element of human conduct. But unlike John Adams, who came to such a conclusion only regretfully, Hamilton saw nothing to be disappointed about. Rejecting the classical republican concern with how men ought to live, he was satisfied with understanding how man behaves. He seemed to believe that because people *were* naturally selfish they *should* be selfish. Natural acquisitiveness, therefore, was not something to avoid or restrict but to encourage. "We must take man as we find him," he concluded at the Constitutional Convention, "and if we expect him to save the public [we] must interest his passions in doing so." He later argued in *Federalist 12* that commerce was no longer to be feared as destructive of public virtue but rather should be embraced for its political utility: "By multiplying the means of gratification, by promoting the introduction and circulation of the precious metals, *those darling objects of human avarice and enterprise*, it serves to vivify all the channels of industry and to make them flow with greater activity and copiousness." Hamilton therefore sneered at the "whining laments" coming from republican moralists concerned about the dangers of unrestricted commerce and the monied interests. He pitied those like Sam Adams who had harbored "the deceitful dream of a golden age" appearing in the aftermath of the Revolution. Americans must look to the future, not the past. The power of modern republics, Hamilton declared, lay not in public virtue or agrarian simplicity but in public finance. "It is as ridiculous to seek for models in the simple ages of Greece and Rome," he scoffed, "as it would be to go in quest of them among the Hottentots and Laplanders."[26]

In this way, Hamilton and his Federalist supporters aligned themselves with the "Court" party tradition in England and the intellectual world of Mandeville, Hume, and Walpole. It was a world view that saw the encouragement of economic interests and personal aggrandizement, not the cultivation of private restraint, as the best way to promote national power and social stability. The outspoken Hamiltonian William Vans Murray explained that if virtue were "of so delicate a nature, as to suffer extinction by the prevalence of those luxurious habits to which all national improvements lead—it certainly is a principle of too whimsical a nature to be relied upon." Any attempt to impose sumptuary limits, as John Adams had suggested, was therefore fatuous. Such archaic restrictions only stifled the ambition and avarice necessary for modern economic growth. As Hamilton said, "The rich may be extravagant, the poor can be frugal." Again, it seems, simple living was something for the masses to practice; the elite found its strictures too dull and stifling.[27]

In a speech before the New York Ratifying Convention in 1788, Hamilton baldly revealed his modern perspective. "As riches increase and accumulate in few hands; as luxury prevails in society," he predicted, "virtue will be in greater degree considered as only a graceful appendage of wealth, and the tendency of things will be to depart from the republican standard." This was the Protestant ethic boldly displayed in its modern secular guise. Wealth, not grace, was now to be the litmus test of virtue. The "advantage of character," he went on to say, "belongs to the wealthy." In a speech at the Constitutional Convention in Philadelphia, the orthodox republican John Dickinson recognized how far Hamilton had diverged from the classical standard. He reminded his listeners that he "had always understood that a veneration for poverty & virtue were [sic] the objects of republican encouragement" rather than the pursuit of personal enrichment.[28]

The classical republican tradition expressed by Dickinson retained a strong attraction for many American idealists in the era of the Constitution. Richard Henry Lee, for example, rejected the position of Hamilton and the other "American Mandevilles who laugh at virtue, and with vain ostentatious display of words will deduce from vice public good!" So, too, did James and Mercy Warren, Sam Adams, Benjamin Austin, Patrick Henry, and other Antifederalists. Yet most of the founding fathers had come to see by the 1780s that the classical perspective would have to be adapted to fit the demands of the developing new nation. Few of them, however, were willing to go as far as Hamilton in completely dismissing the relevance of republican simplicity.[29]

No sooner had James Madison collaborated with Hamilton in writing the *Federalist Papers* than he began to have sober second thoughts about the direction the nation was taking in its development. Like so many other republican idealists, Madison had originally hoped that America could recreate the classical model of a cohesive, static, agricultural republic. Such an ideal society of independent, self-sufficient farmers and shopkeepers, he felt, would lead to "a greater simplicity of manners, consequently a less consumption of manufactured superfluities, and a less proportion of idle proprietors and domestics." This was all well and good, assuming a relatively stable population. But if the populace continued to grow rapidly, as nearly everyone was predicting, then such a static agrarian society would eventually produce an increasingly large surplus of idle and propertyless citizens, "who will labour under all the hardships of life, and secretly sigh for a more equal distribution of its blessings."[30]

Madison, like Hamilton, had read his Hume, especially the Hume who maintained that standards of taste, decency, and duty rise as a society evolves through the "stages of progress," and luxury arrives at the most advanced stage. But as the ancients had warned and Madison believed, the pervasive love of luxury was fatal to the viability of a republic. The salvation of a progressive, expansive new American nation, therefore, lay in fashioning a new political economy that somehow would freeze societal development in the middle stage, before the onset of widespread luxury and immorality. Consequently, Madison and other like-minded republicans responded to the Hamiltonian program after 1787 by advocating an alternative political economy that would encourage the *controlled* expansion of commerce and *household* manufactures, while at the same time ensuring that agriculture would remain the predominant form of economic endeavor. This would provide a widening base of employment to absorb new generations of American citizens. Thereby the young republic would progress beyond the initial stage of agrarianism to a "middle stage" of development in which commerce, manufacturing, and agriculture would be carefully balanced by statesmen of superior "wisdom and virtue" so as to prevent the excesses of urban-industrial centralization that had corrupted British society. American society would thus "grow prosperous and civilized, but not avaricious."[31]

Thomas Jefferson likewise adjusted his outlook to the changing social and economic conditions of the new nation, without in the process discarding his commitment to the virtues of enlightened self-restraint. His original agrarian version of classical republican simplicity had been based on the assumption that America could remain insulated from the contention and corruption of Old World commercialism and industrialism. To Jefferson, as everyone knows, there was something saintly about the self-sufficient husbandman: "Those who labour in the earth are the chosen people of God, if he ever had a chosen people, whose breasts he had made the peculiar deposit for substantial and genuine virtue." Agriculture, he stressed, was not primarily a way to wealth but a way to goodness. Instead of promoting the creation of more American commercial and manufacturing enterprises, therefore, Jefferson in the early 1780s argued with Hector St. Jean de Crèvecœur, Philip Freneau, John Taylor, and other agrarian republicans that it would be better to let Europe continue to produce necessary items and hope that Americans could be educated to practice conservation at home. That way, the United States could remain a decentralized, agrarian-based republic and thereby avoid the class strife attendant with urbanization. "The mobs of great cities," he claimed, "add just so much support of pure government, as sores do to the strength of the human body."[32]

But Jefferson's agrarian republic had quickly been displaced by the forces of expansive commercialism and the alluring appeal of Hamiltonianism. More and more Americans revealed that they were not content with a simple agrarian way of life. Hence, at the same time that he was completing his paean to husbandry in the *Notes on the State of Virginia*, Jefferson admitted that his purely agrarian philosophy could no longer provide a practical guide to national policy-making. "Were I to indulge my own theory," he observed in 1785, Americans would "practice neither commerce nor navigation, but [would] stand with respect to Europe precisely on the footing of China. We should thus avoid wars, and all our citizens would be husbandmen." Yet he quickly confessed that "this is theory only, and a theory which the servants of America are not at liberty to follow. Our people have a decided taste for navigation and commerce."[33]

As such a servant of the American people himself, Jefferson, first as minister to France and then as Secretary of State and President, concluded that "what is practicable must often control what is pure theory; and the habits of the governed determine in a great degree what is practicable." As early as 1784 he had confided to George Washington that since "all the world is becoming commercial," it would be impossible for the United States to remain uncontaminated. "Our citizens have had too full a taste of the comforts furnished by the arts and manufactures to be debarred the use of them." World developments, he reasoned, required that the nation "endeavor to share as large a portion as we can of this modern source of wealth and power." Jefferson as public official thus gradually modified his earlier aversion to expanding commerce. He heartily endorsed a rising standard of living for ordinary people, since he feared the corruption inherent in the schemes of the Hamiltonians to control and centralize the economy. But in doing so he was careful to insist that such accommodation to changing circumstances did not lessen his commitment to republican simplicity as a personal code of conduct, especially for those "natural aristocrats" in positions of public power. He was willing to promote an industrious and expansive society but not an extravagant or corrupt one.[34]

Hamilton characterized such a Jeffersonian moral economy as the height of folly. The idea of restricting American manufacturing to household necessities, he pointed out, would not enhance public virtue; it would only ensure that the "quantity of every species of industry would be less and the quality much inferior." Such comments convinced Jefferson that Hamilton and his followers had been "bewitched and perverted by the British example" of public corruption and unfettered capitalist expansion. During the 1790s he and Madison decided that Hamilton had become the spokesman for a "mercenary phalanx" of monied men and stock speculators who were conspiring against the virtues of republican simplicity. This was wild exaggeration, but to Jefferson it seemed the sober truth. So, when he and the Republicans took over the reins of power in 1801, they systematically tried to make the tone and policies of government conform to traditional republicanism. President Jefferson symbolically donned a plain wardrobe and adopted an austere fiscal policy in an effort to lead the country back to patterns of frugality and simplicity.[35]

But the most characteristic expression of Jeffersonian political economy in power was the ill-fated embargo. In December 1807, Jefferson revived the self-denying spirit of the earlier nonimportation associations in responding to the continued British infringements of American shipping rights. The embargo was intended not only to end the depredations of the British navy on American ships and sailors but also to help free the United States from its economic dependence on Europe by encouraging consumer restraint and the growth of domestic manufactures. In an address to a workingmen's association in 1808, Jefferson asserted that "there can be no question in a mind truly American whether it is best to send our citizens and property into certain captivity, or to keep them at home and to turn seriously to that policy which plants the manufacturer and husbandman side by side. . . ." Jefferson preferred small-scale domestic manufacturing over unchecked commerce, and in part he saw the embargo as a means of checking a dangerous commercial spirit. New England merchants, he charged, were trying to "convert this great agricultural country into a city of Amsterdam."[36]

But the embargo policy did far more than focus attention on the need for a more diversified and self-sufficient American economy. The controversy with Great Britain over shipping rights helped regenerate the fading saliency of Revolutionary self-sacrifice and republican simplicity. Cutting off trade with England came to represent another redemptive enterprise in the minds of American moralists. "We have been too prosperous and too happy," Secretary of the Treasury Albert Gallatin told his wife in June 1808, "and we consider as great misfortunes some privations and a share in the general calumnies of the world." Gallatin hoped that the sacrifices occasioned by the embargo would demonstrate to Americans that they could live comfortably and peacefully without buying expensive British products. John Quincy Adams likewise pointed to the moral benefits of the trade embargo when he charged that Americans "have grown fat on prosperity." Patriotic austerity was just what was needed to rekindle the spirit of republican virtue.[37]

Yet widespread popular resistance to the embargo quickly revealed how much the economy and the public mood had changed since 1776. Gallatin, charged with the onus of enforcing the trade restrictions, gloomily reported to Jefferson in May 1808: "We have not been properly supported by the people." He went on to explain that "the love of gain & British agency had rendered the stoppage of intercourse so unpopular" that effective enforcement was rapidly becoming impossible. Gallatin was right. As time passed, more and more smugglers evaded detection, and popular demonstrations against the embargo grew more prevalent and excited. Archibald Stuart, one of Jefferson's friends and political advisers, felt compelled to tell the President that material self-restraint and economic sacrifice did not "appear adapted either to the nature of our government or the genius and character of our people." Those opposed to the trade restrictions were so "avaricious, enterprising, and impatient of restraint" that the government would soon be forced "to depart from the prudent measures" it had adopted.[38]

Jefferson, typically, remained stubbornly optimistic. He refused to believe that Americans were as selfish and scheming as such accounts charged. Resistance to the trade ban, he surmised, was occurring only among "the illtempered and rascally part" of the populace. By early 1809, however, it was clear to all that the embargo had failed to achieve its most important objectives. War had been postponed, but the British refused to modify their provocative maritime policies. Yet as Jefferson prepared to turn over the Presidency to James Madison, he pointed out in a letter to his French friend Lafayette that the embargo, "which has been a very trying measure, has produced one very happy and permanent effect. It has set us all on domestic manufacture, & will I verily believe reduce our future demands on England fully one half." Still, he was insistent that such economic expansion must remain limited in purpose and scale. In April 1809 he explained that he was willing to sanction only those manufactures "sufficient for our own consumption, of what we raise the raw material (and no more)" and "commerce sufficient to carry the surplus produce of agriculture, beyond our consumption, to a market, exchanging it for articles we cannot produce (and no more)." Jefferson concluded by calling for an "equilibrium of agriculture, manufactures, and commerce."[39]

The key to understanding this new Jeffersonian political economy is the word "equilibrium." He was careful to distinguish his own progressive vision from that of the Hamiltonian mercantilists, emphasizing that he was not advocating rapid, centralizing industrial and commercial development, but balanced, controlled, decentralized growth. He supported commercial activity only to the extent of exchanging "our superfluities for our wants." Jefferson still shuddered at the thought of the emergence of American "Manchesters" throughout the country, with masses of "starved and rickety paupers and dwarfs" piled one upon another in hovels. Agriculture must remain the nation's "distinguishing feature." Innovations in technology and the abundance of cheap land in America, he hoped with Madison, would facilitate the dispersal of machine production through small-scale household manufactures and thereby avoid the demonstrated evils of urban-industrial concentration in Great Britain. He saw new American manufactures primarily turning out the "coarse articles worn by the laborers & farmers of the family," not luxuries. With this hope etched in his mind, he assured John Adams that America could avoid the corrupt fate of industrial Britain because "here men have choice of their labour, and so may safely and advantageously reserve to themselves a wholesome control over their public affairs, and a degree of freedom."[40]

This nineteenth-century Jeffersonian political economy, therefore, sought to synthesize classical republicanism with a limited commercialism and industrialism, hoping thereby to provide a measure of plain prosperity without promoting either excessive urban growth or a debilitating private extravagance. In 1812 he wrote John Adams that he believed "we shall continue to grow, to multiply and prosper until we exhibit an association, powerful, wise and happy, beyond what has yet been seen by man." Such a program's success depended on enlightened, virtuous public officials maintaining a stable relationship between the commercial and agricultural sectors while ensuring that economic growth be gradual. In this sense, then, the debate between Jeffersonians and Hamiltonians was not so much between agrarianism and capitalism as it was between their differing attitudes toward the pace and extent of capitalist development. Hamilton and his followers sought to use the federal government to bring the United States as rapidly as possible into the new industrial era; the Jeffersonians tried to encourage balanced growth of all sectors of the economy and at the same time reduce governmental involvement.[41]

John Adams was sceptical of such a progressive, decentralized republican vision. Like Jefferson and Madison, he had also come to recognize the necessity of commercial and manufacturing expansion in order to make the nation less dependent upon a corrupt Europe. "The love of poverty," he stressed, was "a fictitious virtue that never existed." But unlike Hamilton and even the Jeffersonians, Adams had serious doubts that the commercial and financial interests, once unleashed, could be expected to restrain themselves without at the same time increasing the control of government over their activities. While Jefferson was calling for less government, Adams demanded more. "I have long been settled in my own opinion," he reported to his Virginia friend, "that neither Philosophy, nor Religion, nor Morality, nor Wisdom, nor Interest, will ever govern nations or Parties, against their Vanity, their Pride, their Resentment or Revenge, or their Avarice or Ambition. Nothing but Force and Power and Strength can restrain them." In expressing such a Puritan view of sumptuary controls, however, Adams found himself in a minority position. He was, it appeared to many observers, a "raspy voice out of the dead past." Growth-minded Americans at the end of the eighteenth century and during the early nineteenth century were in no mood to accept the idea of a permanent aristocracy of intellect or of increased institutional restraints on their economic freedom.[42]

As time passed, and the young nation experienced a dramatic economic boom, Adams grew increasingly disgusted with the uncontrolled selfishness of his countrymen, and he gradually came around to the position of rural isolation espoused earlier by his friend James Warren. After losing the 1800 presidential election, Adams retired to his farm in Quincy. There he took up husbandry and reading, finding as much pleasure in his growing manure pile as in the Stoic philosophers he reread while seated in a chair in his garden. The changes that he saw transforming the new nation only depressed him. "My property is small and the remainder of my life is short," he confided to Benjamin Rush in 1806, "But Oh my country, how I mourn over thy follies and vices." Two years later, when Rush described their young nation as "bedollared," Adams replied that never was a word "better coined or applied."[43]

Adams concluded that republican simplicity had not been enhanced by the educational, governmental, or economic changes promoted by its advocates. The basic difficulty of diverting human energies from material to moral pursuits in a land of seemingly abundant resources and entrepreneurial opportunities remained intractable. In his letters to Jefferson late in life, Adams could not help chiding his New England counterpart for his earlier optimism. "Let me ask you, very seriously, my friend. Where are now . . . the perfection and perfectibility of human nature? Where is the amelioration of society?" Six years later, in 1819, he was even more pointed in presenting his fatalistic view of the future. Like a frustrated Puritan magistrate, he asked: "Will you tell me how to prevent riches from becoming the effects of temperance and industry? Will you tell me how to prevent riches from producing luxury? Will you tell me how to prevent luxury from becoming effeminacy, intoxication, extravagance, Vice and folly?"[44]

Jefferson never responded directly to these agitated queries. And, for the most part, he remained much more confident than Adams in the ability of his countrymen to manage the difficulties inherent in progressive republicanism's social ethic. When compared with the countries in the Old World, he frequently declared, the United States still followed the "middle way" of republican simplicity.

Indeed, most Americans in the early nineteenth century were still plain republicans in their manners. But Jefferson seemed to think that this would always be the case. He never appreciated the disruptive and transforming power of modernity. So long as there was enough cheap land and economic opportunity available for the growing population, he assumed, his temperate, balanced, expansive republic would remain intact. As he boasted to a Frenchman in 1815, "we shall proceed successfully for ages to come, and the larger the extent of the country, the more firm its republican structure. . . ." Thus, big was beautiful for Jefferson, in the sense that an ever-expanding frontier would enable the nation to avoid the social strife and stratification of the Old World. His hopes for the future were "built much on the enlargement of those resources of life, going hand in hand with the enlargement of territory, and the belief that men are disposed to live honestly, if the means of doing so are open to them."[45]

The differences between John Adams and Thomas Jefferson were much like those that divided Puritans from Quakers; the two perspectives revolved fundamentally around their contrasting views of human nature and historical development. Adams consistently held to the more traditional view of classical republicanism and Calvinist social theory that portrayed the decline of public and private virtue as inevitable in the face of territorial and economic expansion. "Human Nature in no form of it," he insisted, "could ever bear Prosperity." History was therefore necessarily cyclical. Just as living organisms go through stages of growth from innocence to decay, so, too, must nations. Consequently, despite the promise of the young American republic, there was no real hope of avoiding eventual public corruption and cultural decline. "Remember," Adams wrote, "democracy never lasts long. It soon wastes, exhausts, and murders itself." In his view of men and history, Adams again reflected his Puritan ancestry. Men "are never good," he maintained, "but through necessity." The Puritans had likewise believed in the power and necessity of institutional controls, but like Adams they saw such mechanical instruments as capable of producing only outward conformity rather than inner virtue. Grace alone could make people truly good, and grace was a gift of God, not of men.[46]

Jefferson initially believed with the ancients in the inevitability of social degeneration. He had warned in 1781 that "the spirit of the times may alter, will alter. Our rulers will become corrupt, our people careless." But an older Jefferson abandoned such fatalism. In his later years he tended to depart from the classical interpretation of history and began to view modern society as being capable of progressive, rather than cyclical, development. With Hutcheson and the Scottish moralists, Jefferson believed that the individual possessed an innate "sense of right and wrong" that was "as much a part of his nature as the sense of hearing, seeing, feeling." To make men good therefore required only that men be set free to follow their naturally benevolent instincts. Likewise, encouraging the democratization of prosperity, he felt, would lessen rather than increase social strains and private ambition. As the standard of living rose, man's baser instincts and passions would gradually be ameliorated and their effects diffused. Man would thereby become an agent of progress rather than a pawn of fate. "I like the dreams of the future," Jefferson stressed, "better than the history of the past." Caught up in the excitement of creating a prosperous republic, he rather ingenuously assumed that public virtue would be enhanced as well. In revising his historical perspective, Jefferson thus also revised republicanism to mean a Quaker-like belief in the "improvability of the conditions of man . . . in opposition to those who consider man as a beast of burden made to be rode by him who has genius enough to get a bridle in his mouth."[47]

Inherent in Jefferson's new republican vision was an abiding faith in technology. He himself loved to tinker with labor-saving devices and was constantly applying them to his own farming operations and household needs. This personal interest led him to sanction the use of applied mechanics throughout the new nation. On the surface, it would seem, the entrance of the machine into the mythic Jeffersonian America of husbandry and innocence would subvert rather than promote republican simplicity. Along with machines, of course, come factories, and factories eventually spawn the urban congestion and social tensions that Jefferson and others deemed inimical to republicanism. But Jefferson was convinced that labor-saving devices, if properly applied and controlled, could in fact enhance the quality of life of the citizenry and facilitate the decentralization of production by bringing machines into the countryside rather than clustering them in cities.

Many other early nineteenth-century proponents of technological innovation similarly portrayed mechanism as an agent of great good to traditional republican values. Horace Bushnell, the Hartford Congregationalist minister, for example, predicted that through mechanization, "the laboring classes will be able to live in comparative leisure and eloquence, and find ample time for self-improvement." This sentiment was echoed by another promoter of the mechanical arts. In 1831 Timothy Walker wrote in the *North American Review* that "if machines could be so improved and multiplied . . . there would be nothing to hinder all mankind from becoming philosophers, poets, and votaries of art."[48]

Such a happy vision of industrial republicanism was reflected in the famous model factory centers established in New England in the early nineteenth century. They appeared first in Waltham in 1815 and quickly spread along riverbanks throughout the interior. The most famous and ambitious of these early planned factory towns was Lowell, Massachusetts. Henry Clay asserted that the Lowell experiment "will tell whether the manufacturing system is compatible with the social virtues." Nathan Appleton, Francis Cabot Lowell, Patrick Tracy Jackson, and many of the other original Lowell investors were members of old Boston commercial families whose Puritan and Revolutionary-era connections combined with their economic success to produce a curiously ambivalent world view that professed simultaneous allegiance to old and new values. On the one hand, these "Boston Associates" were possessed of an acute sense of social responsibility and were committed to the ideals of the original Protestant ethic and republican simplicity. These were the Boston merchants who established over thirty benevolent societies and institutions between 1810 and 1840. Appleton reflected the enlightened moral outlook of the group when he insisted that "my mind has always been devoted to many other things rather than money-making." Yet, at the same time, Appleton and his colleagues were shrewd, far-sighted entrepreneurs who were quick to embrace the new investment opportunities provided by the industrial revolution and applied technology.[49]

At first, the Associates saw no necessary conflict between their economic ambitions and their social and moral philosophy. They believed they could design model factory centers and communities that would enhance rather than corrupt the republican virtue of their laborers. The drab, crowded, and wretched life of the English mill-villages would be avoided by locating the factories in the countryside and then establishing an ambitious program of paternal supervision for the workers. The "manufacturing works," an early promotional pamphlet claimed, are "interspersed with groves and woodlands" so as to "afford a prospect at once sublime and beautiful." The operatives, most of them young women, would be provided with good wages, not very hard work, comfortable housing, moral discipline, and a variety of cultural opportunities. Such a carefully planned and supervised manufacturing system would bring together the benefits of both industrial capitalism and republican simplicity. The "Lowell idea" would produce an enlightened class of female operatives and male mechanics without threatening the survival of the agricultural system deemed essential by Jefferson and others for republican virtue to survive. "Ours is a great novel experiment," the Associates claimed. "Whatever the result, it is our destiny to make it."[50]

Initially the Lowell idea seemed to work according to plan. Observers commented on the well-designed factories with their lecture halls and libraries. The laborers appeared "healthy and happy." Massachusetts Governor Levi Lincoln claimed that mechanical development and moral improvement were coinciding in Lowell. The successful start of the factory community demonstrated that "the richest sources of wealth in this country may be cultivated without danger to the moral habits and chaste manners of a numerous class of our population." One appreciative worker described the Lowell idea as meaning that "corporations should have souls, and should exercise a paternal influence over the lives of their operatives."[51]

The Lowell system was certainly paternalistic. To protect the young women, many of whom were away from home for the first time, each company-owned boardinghouse was staffed by a matronly supervisor. The "high thinking" encouraged by the Lowell owners was obviously not designed to be as profound or learned as that pursued by a Jefferson or an Adams, but it was a program of intellectual and spiritual activity intended to elevate the priorities of the workers above the material and the mundane. Church attendance was mandatory, and temperance regulations and curfews were enforced. Cultural and educational opportunities were also abundant. A lyceum offered free lectures on various subjects, circulating libraries provided access to books, and "improvement circles" promoted creative writing and public discussion. In the early years of the Lowell experiment, the work in the factories seemed no harder than what the women had left behind on the farms. And the pay was much better. Lucy Larcom, whose mother kept one of the Lowell boardinghouses, entered the mills at age thirteen, and she later recalled that the daily routine was for the most part relaxed and pleasant. The girls and women put plants in the mill windows, played games and told stories in between changing bobbins, and found time at night to attend lectures by John Quincy Adams and Ralph Waldo Emerson, as well as to read Shakespeare, Milton, Pope, Mather, and Wordsworth. Harriet Robinson, another early operative, described the community life of Lowell as approaching "almost Arcadian simplicity."[52]

Such working conditions were widely publicized, and Lowell soon began to attract Yankee women from the farms and villages across New England. The rural family economy was then in steady decline, and for many young women, the new factory community offered hope and adventure. Some saw factory labor as a means to social and economic independence, others as a way to help pay off family debts or accumulate a dowry. For whatever reason, they came by the thousands. By 1840 there were thirty-two factories operating in Lowell, and the "Arcadian" village had mushroomed into a bustling city. Other similar factory centers began sprouting up across New England. Between 1820 and 1840 the number of people engaged in manufactures increased eight-fold, and the number of city-dwellers more than doubled.

In the process of such booming growth, however, the experiment in industrial republicanism was transformed. James T. Austin, a Suffolk lawyer and prominent civic leader, expressed the growing fear that the rapid spread of the factory system and urban congestion was proving "decidedly hostile to republican principles, and to the moral character of the community." Some of the workers in Lowell and other emerging factory towns found urban life and a regular income intoxicating, and they discarded their rural frugality in order to indulge in new amenities. Not a week passed, it seemed, without some editor or commentator urging young women not to forsake the simple life of the farm for the sinful life of the factory town. By 1846 a concerned worker told those young girls thinking about taking a job in a factory that they would do well not to leave their "homes in the country. It will be better for you to stay at home on your fathers' farms than to run the risk of being ruined in a manufacturing village."[53]

The degeneration of morals attributed to life in the factory towns was accompanied by the emergence of class consciousness and labor unrest among the supposedly contented workers. Overproduction during the 1830s caused the price of finished cloth to drop, and thereafter relations between workers and management rapidly deteriorated. The original owners, and especially their younger successors, responded to changing market conditions by cutting wages and increasing duties. The machines and their operators were worked at a faster pace. Changes in employer-employee relations occurred as well. By the mid-1840s a new generation of mill managers was in charge, and their outlook differed considerably from the founding group. Profits rather than people seemed their primary, even sole, concern. As one of the new managers admitted, "I regard my workpeople just as I regard my machinery." Absent from his perspective was any sense of paternal responsibility for the moral and intellectual elevation of his operatives. "So long as they can do my work for what I choose to pay them, I keep them, getting out of them all I can." This was not the enlightened industrial republicanism that Jefferson had envisioned and described; rather it was the cynical materialism that Charles Dickens saw at work in England at the time. Visitors to Lowell in the 1830s and 1840s repeatedly noticed the mills' growing similarity to the feared English system and also the discrepancy between the original Lowell ideal and its second-generation reality. "In regard to *intellectual advantages*," one visitor wrote, there was no longer adequate time for the workers to participate. "I asked one of the young operators if they could not take turns in reading aloud while sewing. She replied that they were all either too tired, or they wished a little time to talk, and so they never succeeded when they attempted."[54]

Those workers who had identified with the original moral vision of Lowell's founders felt betrayed by the changing demands of the new industrial system. Shoemakers in Lynn, Massachusetts, for example, complained that their working relations with owners caused frictions "anti-republican in character, which assimilate very nearly to those that exist between the aristocracy and the laboring classes of Europe." In expressing their disillusionment, workers revived the language of Revolutionary republicanism employed by the urban artisans and mechanics. Their owner-protectors, they now claimed, had become greedy tyrants "whose avarice would enslave them" unless the workers took action.[55]

In 1834 and 1836 there were strikes at Lowell protesting wage cuts, and a decade later there was a well-organized petition campaign calling for a reduction in working hours. One mill-girl recommended that her working sisters separate themselves completely from such a vicious wage system. Only by doing so could they salvage their virtue:

> Let it not be said of us here in this land of boasted liberty and equal rights, that thousands are bound down in *ignorance* and worshiping at the altar of the god of mammon! Awake! daughters of America to a realization of the evils which follow in the train of ignorance and selfishness! Awake and arise from the low groveling charms of *dollars* and *cents*, to a knowledge of your own high and holy duties and destinies! Awake and resolve from this time forth to *live*, not merely to gain a bare subsistence, but to live for nobler, worthier objects. *Live*, not to wear out and exhaust your physical energies in obtaining a few more paltry shillings, but to adorn and beautify your minds and intellects which a kind Father hath confered [*sic*] upon you.

But most of the women did not quit. Eventually they swallowed their pride and went back to work in the factories, resigning themselves to the priorities of a new industrial age. A committee called in to investigate working conditions at Lowell lamely concluded its report by stressing the need for more frugal living and more elevated thinking among the workers. The ultimate solution to the festering conflict between management and labor, it said, lay "in the progressive improvement in art and science, in a higher appreciation of man's destiny, in a less love of money, and a more ardent love for social happiness and intellectual superiority."[56]

That such a plea for the operatives to be content with their lot proved less than satisfactory to disgruntled workers illustrates the increasingly anachronistic quality of republican simplicity in an age of egalitarian expectations and industrial advance. How to preserve the best of traditional values and institutions while encouraging new ones remained a frustrating challenge. The factory owners at Waltham, Lowell, Lynn, Lawrence, and elsewhere in New England continued to espouse traditional republican virtues to their workers at the same time that they themselves pursued policies that undermined their rhetoric. As the Lowell example indicates, when the claims of the ledgerbook and republican paternalism conflicted, the owners tended to prefer plain living for the workers and affluent living for themselves.

The Lowell experience was in a larger sense symptomatic of a trend developing throughout American society in the first half of the nineteenth century: the attempt to graft a dynamic, expansive capitalist ideology onto traditional notions of republican simplicity was fraught with unexpected difficulties. An articulate observer of the strains inherent in this new republicanism was Alexis de Tocqueville. During his visit to the United States from France in the 1830s, Tocqueville was quick to distill the shift in American thought from the classical conception of public and private virtue to the more modern emphasis on the virtue of industry and enterprise in an expansive free market society. He shared the hope of Hamiltonians that the strenuous pursuit of private interest in the marketplace could promote the public good. A "sort of selfishness" would make the individual "care for the state." As long as economic opportunities remained plentiful, he continued, the market mechanism would itself impress upon the aspiring that it was in their best interests to regulate their private passions, engage in mutual aid, and participate responsibly in the political process. Tocqueville noted that Americans proudly pointed out to him "how an enlightened self-love continually leads them to help one another and disposes them freely to give part of their time and wealth for the good of the state." This American "principle of self-interest properly understood" ideally would work much more effectively than the traditional classical and Christian emphasis upon suppressing the passions altogether, "for it turns private interest against itself and uses the same goad which excites the direct passions."[57]

At the same time, however, Tocqueville also shared with the Jeffersonians the belief that there were crucial limits to this theory that private vices produce public benefits. He emphasized that he was sanctioning only a "decent kind of materialism" based on the assumption of an *enlightened* egotism propelling public behavior. Such progressive republicanism could work according to plan only as long as each citizen acted as a "virtuous materialist," sacrificing "some of his private interests to save the rest." Thus he saw that the "greatest danger threatening the United States springs from its very prosperity," because when "the taste for physical pleasures has grown more rapidly than either education or experience of free institutions, the time comes when men are carried away and lose control of themselves at sight of the new good things they are ready to snatch."[58]

Tocqueville recognized that the new republicanism was dependent on society maintaining the tenuous Jeffersonian balance between economic growth and political responsibility, private restraint and private ambition. But he and other observers in the early nineteenth century were growing worried that such an equilibrium was already out of joint. Contrary to the ideal limits envisioned by the Jeffersonians, economic expansion after 1820 was rapid and unchecked, and many Americans no longer saw any implied moral limits to material gain. He noticed that an increasing number of farmers, especially those who migrated westward over the Alleghenies, were not content as time passed to remain Jeffersonian yeomen independent of the marketplace; instead they grew enmeshed in land speculation and commercial agriculture. As Tocqueville pointed out, the Americans "carry over into agriculture the spirit of a trading venture, and their passion for industry is manifest there as elsewhere."[59]

American farmers had always produced cash crops for market, but in most cases such surplus production was an incidental rather than a primary activity. By the mid-nineteenth century, however, market-oriented agriculture was firmly established in many parts of the country. In 1852 the president of the New York Agricultural Society contrasted the earlier rural "age of homespun" to the contemporary situation: "At an early period 'production for self consumption' was the leading purpose; now no farmer would find it profitable 'to do everything within himself.' He now sells for money." To be sure, many farmers still resisted the lure of the marketplace and remained loyal to the ideal of contented subsistence. One husbandman, for example, argued in 1852 that generally "it is better that the farmer should produce what he needs for home consumption." Selling a cash crop, of course, would increase one's income, "but taking all things into consideration," he asked, "will he be better off?" This classical plowman, however, was ridiculed by a Hamiltonian farmer for looking to "the past" for his models of rustic simplicity and for failing to appreciate "progress." Another criticized those who disdained the "idea of money-making as a part of good farming." He contended that turning a profit "in our country, at least, is the main point of farming, mechanics, and the sciences in church and state."[60]

Furthermore, where Jefferson, Rush, Madison, and other Revolutionary republicans had typically defined progress to include the growth of public and private virtue, the new breed of economic expansionists and self-made men tended to view it more narrowly in terms of individual well-being. The South Carolina novelist William Gilmore Simms commented that the American love of gain "seems to be the whole amount of our national idea of progress." In the ante-bellum era a doctor from Ohio also expressed his disappointment in his countrymen for viewing their rising standard of living not as an opportunity to engage in high thinking but as an end in itself. "This is decidedly a money making age," he asserted. "All, or nearly all, seem to be struggling for a portion of that wealth which at present is so unequally divided." This in itself was not to be condemned, "provided the ulterior object is a laudable one." But among the majority of Americans "it would seem as though gain was desired for itself alone, or for the facilities it affords for further acquisition, rather than as an instrumentality for augmenting individual or general happiness."[61]

Only too late did Jefferson and other progressive republican idealists perceive the nature of the forces their optimistic boosterism had helped unleash. The rising tide of commerce, manufacturing, and agricultural speculation could not be held back. Economic growth, social mobility, and geographic expansion generated far more selfish and factional behavior among the populace than they had ever envisioned. Albert Gallatin, who as Secretary of the Treasury did so much to facilitate economic and territorial expansion, was in old age dismayed at what he, Jefferson, Madison, and others had earlier encouraged:

> The energy of this nation is not to be controlled; it is at present exclusively applied to the acquisition of wealth and to improvements of stupendous magnitude. . . . The apparent prosperity and progress of cultivation, population, commerce, and improvement are beyond expectation. But it seems to me as if general demoralization was the consequence; I doubt whether general happiness is increased; and I would have preferred a gradual, slower, and more secure progress.

Gallatin, Jefferson, and others had tried to yoke the ideal of republican simplicity with a vibrant industrial, commercial, and agricultural prosperity, hoping that a rising standard of living would help elevate rather than corrupt American character. Yet during the nineteenth century, the age of steam was generating conceptions of life, liberty, and the pursuit of happiness that refused to be bound by the limits they had invoked. America was growing and prospering too much and too fast, and in the midst of the turmoil, republican simplicity was being roughly discarded. "We are all too rich," the *Washington Globe* announced in 1836, "and that is the greatest danger our simple republicans have to contend with."[62]

Thus, like the original Protestant ethic, the progressive republican program linking internal improvements with personal simplicity was a double-edged sword. As manipulated by a new egalitarian-oriented society, it came to serve more as a liberating than a preserving force, unintentionally accentuating the personal vices and social tensions that its original proponents had hoped to curb. Employed initially as a political theory to justify colonial rights within the British empire, republicanism increasingly came to be used after 1800 as a theory of democratic political economy to justify individual rights in the marketplace and political arena.[63] In 1815 Jefferson sounded one of his few pessimistic notes when he confessed that "I fear, from the experience of the last twenty-five years that morals do not of necessity, advance hand in hand with the sciences." Again American moral idealists had been the victims of a cruelly ironic development wherein their plan to spiritualize materialism ended up materializing the spirit.[64]

CHAPTER FIVE

※※●●●◆◆●●●●◆●※

Simplicity Domesticated

As the nineteenth century advanced, the Jeffersonian republican vision of a prosperous but essentially agrarian society led by an aristocracy of character continued to give way to an expansive commercial and urban outlook promoting economic individualism, social mobility, political equality, and material gratification. In the process, the self-limiting assumptions of republican simplicity were brusquely pushed aside by new generations of aspiring Americans. No, the simple life as a national ideal did not disappear during the new century. Old values continued to persist alongside the new, as many Americans retained a strong desire to make their republic a virtuous one by resisting modern trends. But with the demise of the Revolutionary generation of leaders and the subsequent emergence of new and frequently conflicting social and political elites, the ideal of republican simplicity came to be used in different ways for different purposes by different groups.

Sorting out the various strands is a complicated endeavor. Values during the Jacksonian era and after were in a state of rapid flux, and the period witnessed recurring debates over what the republican legacy entailed. Leading politicians and business spokesmen increasingly interpreted republicanism as buttressing a liberal capitalist political economy. Others, however, particularly those aspiring to social and economic success rather than those already enjoying it—struggling farmers, wage laborers, apprentices—stressed a more egalitarian version of republican entrepreneurship. "Free soil and free labor" was their prescription for national happiness. Regardless of whether they were striving for economic success or had already attained it, fewer and fewer Americans during the Jacksonian era associated republicanism primarily with simple living. Judging from the social commentary of the period, material and political opportunities rather than moral restraints or social deference defined American behavior.

Still, even though simplicity was clearly on the defensive after 1820, it remained a prominent subject of social discourse. To generalize, perhaps recklessly so in such brief space, simplicity during the Middle Period (1820–1860) was employed most often as a conservative moral idiom. As state after state eliminated sumptuary laws and other statutory restraints on getting and spending, the concept of simple living gradually retreated from the realm of public policy into the realm of rhetoric, finding its most frequent expression in speeches, sermons, child-rearing manuals, poems, and other forms of expression on the fringe rather than at the center of American social behavior and political power. Most nineteenth-century public figures still periodically proclaimed the virtues of classical or Christian simplicity, although they and their audiences continued to embrace new and frequently contradictory behavior. Especially during periods of economic decline, political crisis, or moral excitement, the familiar appeal for simple living still retained a sentimental and stabilizing attractiveness, both to those Americans being displaced by the forces of social and economic change and to those doing the displacing. In this sense such encomiums to simplicity may not have always represented an endorsement of the ideal as such, but rather were an expression of fears and ambivalence about the pace and nature of social change.

Andrew Jackson and his political lieutenants, for example, repeatedly expressed their regret at the passing of the old agrarian order and preached the virtues of republican simplicity, all the while they and many of their enthusiastic followers pursued economic activities that compromised the sense of self-restraint and high moral purpose that such a social ethic required. They shared the hope of the Jeffersonian expansionists that they could promote both a dynamic free enterprise system *and* a self-limiting republican morality. And they likewise shared a hatred for Hamiltonian centralization. Thus, Jackson, himself a self-made man, advocated the democratization of prosperity, promising that he would "remove every obstacle in the road of wealth, every act of legislation conferring advantages to the *few*, and adding unjustly to the burdens of the *many*." Yet Jackson skillfully coupled such laissez-faire individualism with an appeal for classical simplicity and civic virtue. In defending his famous veto of the charter renewal of the central Bank of the United States (B.U.S.) in 1832, he stressed that his purpose was to "revive and perpetuate those habits of economy and simplicity which are so congenial to the character of republicans." In other public addresses he emphasized that a "middling income" was best for the people, since it did not corrupt private virtue. By abolishing the B.U.S. and thereby encouraging wildcat banking, however, Jackson paradoxically served to expedite the entrepreneurial grasping that his rhetoric opposed.[1]

"Old Hickory," like Jefferson before him, tried to reconcile his sentimental attachment to republican simplicity with his equally strong commitment to economic liberalism, only to see the latter devour the former during the speculative boom of the early 1830s. Many of Jackson's more opportunistic followers enthusiastically endorsed his assault on the "money power," not so much because the B.U.S. threatened their simple way of living but because it served as a restraining influence on their own economic ambitions. In revealing this interesting disparity between political symbolism and citizen behavior, Bray Hammond has argued that the old-fashioned Jeffersonian language of the Jacksonian Democrats "cannot conceal the envy and acquisitiveness that were their real motives." But most of the entrepreneurial Jacksonians were not consciously hypocritical. Instead, they were caught in the paradoxical position of unleashing laissez-faire capitalism while at the same time remaining verbally committed to a chaste personal ethic of republican simplicity. They wanted the best of both visions of the good life and were unable to see that they were trying to harmonize dissonant cultural objectives.[2]

During the 1840s the Democrats' political opponents, the Whigs, were openly supportive of Hamiltonian economic policies. One party loyalist claimed that capitalist enterprise was "the most efficient civilizer of our Barbarous race." And another maintained that America's "virtues are the virtues of merchants." Yet even many Whig spokesmen for industrial and commercial growth, including Abraham Lincoln, Horace Greeley and Daniel Webster, professed a nostalgic personal preference for rustic simplicity as well as a concern that Americans were not using their wealth for noble ends. Some Democrats claimed that this was not ambivalence but chicanery at work. While the Whigs talked sentimentally about the "log cabin days," they were conspiring to get "palaces and champaign [sic]" for themselves.[3]

This was true, to an extent. But many Whigs were genuinely anxious about the too rapid pace of economic growth and social change. New York's William Seward, who would later distinguish himself as that state's governor and as Lincoln's secretary of state, commented in 1837 that "it is a fearful truth, that we are rapidly approximating the maximum of population and maturity of national character, wealth, and power, and yet have made no corresponding advance in moral and intellectual cultivation." The leading Whig journal, the *American Review*, expressed a similar concern. At the same time that it glorified the new industrialism and promoted national economic expansion, it could be remarkably critical of a materialistic outlook. "A man's life with us," one article admitted, "*does* consist of the abundance of the things which he possesseth. To get, and to have the reputation of possessing, is the ruling passion. To it are bent all the energies of nine-tenths of our population." The writer went on to express the hope that it "cannot be many years before the madness of devoting the whole day to the toils of the countinghouse will be acknowledged; before the claim of body and mind to relaxation and cheerful, exhilarating amusement will be seen."[4]

Such simultaneous adherence to contrary values illustrates a culture disoriented by a whirlwind of social, economic, and political changes. The technological and industrial optimists obviously welcomed such change and energetically set about defining the basis for a new society. For others, however, the forces transforming society were more threatening than encouraging, and they earnestly tried to preserve older ways of life. During the Jacksonian era and after, many among the established gentry saw their authority as social and moral spokesmen challenged by the assertiveness of both the *nouveaux riches* and the aspiring masses. Those especially worried about political and social upheavals found a measure of reassurance in a traditional appeal to classical or Puritan ways. Despite the apparent victory of Hamiltonian economic policies and values, many nineteenth-century Americans continued to adhere to eighteenth-century republican conceptions of virtue. "The farther the classical ideal receded from the dynamic reality of the nineteenth-century American economy," one scholar has written, "the more Americans liked to think of themselves in its terms."[5]

In 1837, for instance, a southerner castigated the "inordinate love of money" that distinguished the American from other nationalities. "Every man," he wrote, "seems to think he has been placed in this world to promote the selfish views of himself—alone; and to accomplish but one object—the acquisition of wealth." The writer then tried to define the truly good life, and he looked back to the classical age for his inspiration. It was necessary, he admitted, for a person to have a modest income and access to some of the "comforts and conveniences" of life. But true happiness "shuns the abode of voluptuous wealth, as well as that of squalid poverty. She dwells, most frequently, with contented competency. Peace, cheerfulness, simplicity, and virtue, are the companions who attend upon her. . . . This is the golden mean of happiness!"[6]

Similarly, a Cincinnati writer, in speaking for the new western American, also resurrected the classical ideal when he wrote in 1827: "We avow ourselves passionate admirers of simplicity, in the proper and laudable acceptation of the term. We love it in the arts, in building, in gardening, in dress, in manners, in deportment, in thinking, in conversation, in religion, and in everything that appertains to us, as physical, or intellectual beings." He declared that such an ideal was for everyone to follow. "This simplicity we hold to be not only intimately allied to the high thinking of richly endowed minds, but to virtuous, independent and manly character." Another concerned observer of the social scene highlighted the debilitating effects of luxurious habits and unregulated competition on the national character. Instead of looking back to the golden mean of the Greeks for inspiration, however, he recalled to mind the early Puritans. "If our softness and indulgences, and foreign fashions, must inevitably accomplish our seduction, and lead us away from the simplicity, honesty, sobriety, purity, and manly independence of our forefathers, most readily and fervently would I exclaim, welcome back to the pure old times of the Puritans."[7]

A number of evangelical religious spokesmen during the era also sought to revive the moral code of the early Puritans. Their crusade against material striving and high living reflected in part a traditional elite's typical fears of a disruptive social and political order. Lyman Beecher, the firebrand revivalist from Connecticut, joined other leading evangelicals in bemoaning the urgent preoccupation with money-getting that he saw disrupting family and community ties. The engine of American economic progress was running too fast. He warned that "our Republic is becoming too prosperous, too powerful, too extended." Infidelity and intemperance were spreading like viruses along the frontier and in the immigrant-filled cities. The "greater our prosperity," Beecher claimed, "the shorter its duration, and the more tremendous our downfall." Obviously well versed in the classical republican tradition, Beecher felt that history had demonstrated the eventual effects of the selfish spirit of material gain upon the morals of a people, and the United States was already showing signs of similar decline. "The power of voluntary self-denial is not equal to the temptation . . . and no instance has yet occurred, in which national voluptuousness has not trod hard upon the footsteps of national opulence, destroying moral principles and patriotism, debasing the mind and enervating the body, and preparing men to become, like the descendants of the Romans, effeminate slaves."[8]

Even more disturbing to Beecher was the effect of unrestrained materialism and licentiousness on the established social and political order. He feared that "the power of taxation will come more and more into the hands of men of intemperate habits and desperate fortunes; of course the laws will gradually become subservient to the debtor and less efficacious in protecting the rights of property." In his *Autobiography*, Beecher lamented the passing of the "cocked hats and gold-headed canes" that had symbolized the more stable social order of the previous generation. For him, as well as many other nineteenth-century moralists, simple living was as much a means of maintaining a deferential status quo as it was an ideal mode of living in and of itself. Like many of the colonial Puritans, conservative evangelicals during the Jacksonian era wanted moral reform but not social change.[9]

The evangelicals as well as other religious leaders still considered it part of their social responsibility to impose appropriate forms of moral behavior on the classes below them. Yet how was such moral reform to be effected? How were republican virtue and Christian piety to be restored in the present as well as transmitted to new generations growing up in a dynamic, fluid society? The always vexing problem of discovering effective means to promote and sustain simple and virtuous living stubbornly frustrated the conservators of traditional morality. Attempts to dictate correct moral behavior from the pulpit or at camp meetings were not potent enough to stem the tide of working- and middle-class ambition. And the revivals of the Second Great Awakening, though increasing church membership, nevertheless did little to restore the traditional authority of the churches to enforce moral restraints. Obviously, other measures must be employed.

In searching for more effective ways to revitalize Christian and republican virtues, moral conservatives in the Jacksonian era looked backward rather than forward. They essentially sought to revive and strengthen measures of shaping character that had been tried by earlier generations. In the tradition of the Quaker meetings and Cotton Mather's informal moral and spiritual improvement societies, professional reformers in the early nineteenth century created a spate of voluntary associations intended to help persuade people to believe and behave. Congregationalists, Presbyterians, Unitarians, Methodists, and Baptists organized a diverse array of ecumenical societies designed to restore traditional values and institutional arrangements. There were so many groups serving the cause of social stability and moral reform that a disgruntled observer commented in 1838: "Matters have come to such a pass that a peaceable man can hardly venture to eat or drink, or to go to bed or to get up, to correct his children or to kiss his wife, without obtaining the permission and direction of some . . . society."[10]

Still other concerned traditionalists looked to the arts as a means of elevating republican taste and character and preserving the rural simplicities and folkways of past generations. During the first half of the nineteenth century, New England poets such as Bryant, Whittier, and Longfellow provided Americans with Yankee pastorals that evoked feelings of nostalgia for the days when life seemed less hectic, urban, and crowded. Many of those living in the new, bustling cities had come from the farms and villages of America, and they found such literature warmly reassuring.

This same idealization of the simple and the rustic was a prevalent theme in ante-bellum American painting. Unitarian minister Henry Bellows expressed this conservative interest in aesthetic simplicity when he wrote: "We want some interests that are larger than purse or party, on which men cannot take sides, or breed strifes, or become selfish. Such an interest is Art. And no nation needs its exalting, purifying, calming influences, more than ours. We need it to supplant the mean, utilitarian tastes, which threaten to make us a mere nation of shop-keepers." This open appeal for greater cultivation of the fine arts represented a significant departure from earlier American attitudes. In the aftermath of the Revolution, most republican moralists had associated the fine arts with corruption, since in the Old World high culture was the monopoly of a decadent aristocracy. Yet by the Jacksonian era such attitudes were being challenged by spokesmen arguing that the United States could develop artistic styles that would reinforce rather than corrupt republican simplicity. Art thereby could serve as an instrument of moral uplift and social control.[11]

As society grew more complex, urbanized, mobile, and crowded, artists worried by such trends began recording the corrupting inroads of urban-industrial civilization. The series of gigantic allegorical paintings by Thomas Cole, *The Course of Empire*, completed in 1836, explicitly pondered the problem of retaining rustic simplicity and republican virtue in an age of encroaching urban civilization and expansive prosperity. The final two pictures in the series, "Destruction" and "Desolation," portrayed nature's ultimate triumph over cosmopolitanism, and Cole intended them to serve as "maledictions on the dollar-godded utilitarians." For the most part, however, Cole and other landscape painters chose simply to ignore the corrupting inroads of modernity, and they concentrated on portraying pristine wilderness and rural scenes. The American Art Union, in promoting a lottery sale of its paintings, explained:

> To the inhabitants of cities, as nearly all of the subscribers to the Art Union are, a painted landscape is almost essential to preserve a healthy tone to the spirits, lest they forget in the wilderness of bricks which surrounds them the pure delights of nature and a country life. Those who cannot afford a seat in the country to refresh their wearied spirits, may have at least a country seat in their parlors; a bit of landscape with a green tree, a distant hill, a low-roofed cottage;—some of these simple objects, which all men find so refreshing to their spirits after being long pent up in dismal streets and the haunts of business.

Those promoting such an aesthetic vision "did not wish American art to imitate American life." Instead, "American life was meant to imitate American art."[12]

This idealization of art as an agency of republican simplicity was an especially salient assumption of many of the leading domestic architects of the Jacksonian period. Well-designed houses, one of them claimed, would be an "unfailing barrier against vice, immorality, and bad habits." Another architect suggested that plain, unassuming, functional homes would check "our passions for luxuries of all kinds." Far from being limited to the wealthy, such homes were putatively available to all aspiring Americans. One designer recognized that some objected that "the republican simplicity of America cannot afford the luxury of good architecture." He assured the public, however, that this "was clearly incorrect, for it is knowledge, and not money, that is the chief source of every pleasurable emotion that may be caused by a building. Indeed, a simple, well-planned structure costs less to execute . . . than an ill-planned one."[13]

The most famous of these architects of virtue was Andrew Jackson Downing of New York. Catharine Sedgwick, a leading popular novelist during the Jacksonian era, claimed that no one in America, "whether he be rich or poor, builds a house or lays out a garden without consulting Downing's works." Born in 1815 at Newburgh along the Hudson River, Downing was the son of a struggling nurseryman. As a young man he succeeded his father in the family business, and through sheer effort he at the same time made himself into a scholar and a gentleman. Among his early clients were many of the wealthy, cultured landowners of the Hudson valley region, and he quickly grew enamored with their genteel manners and attitude. His fellow New Yorker James Fenimore Cooper described their outlook when he remarked that a "refined simplicity is the character of all high bred deportment, in every country." Downing was attracted to what he called those "natural conservatives whom Providence has wisely distributed even in the most democratic governments, to steady the otherwise too impetuous and unsteady onward movements of those who, in their love for progress, would obliterate the past." In discussing his moral outlook he listed his values: "the love of order, the obedience to law, the security and repose of society, the love of home, and the partiality to localities endeared by birth or association."[14]

Downing also acquired the distaste felt by the landed gentry for urban and commercial life. He was a Wordsworthian romantic about nature, even though a social conservative. "We rejoice," he once wrote, "much more in the love of country life, the enjoyment of nature, and the taste for rural beauty, which we also inherit from our Anglo-Saxon forefathers, and to which, more than all else, they owe so many of the peculiar virtues of the race." Downing coupled his aristocratic republican temperament and rural tastes with a heartfelt desire to promote a domestic architecture that would enhance the virtues of republican simplicity. "We believe" he wrote, "in the bettering influence of beautiful cottages and country houses—in the improvement in human nature necessarily resulting to all *classes*."[15]

In many ways Downing resembled Jefferson, who had also been a strong believer in the didactic function of the arts and an ardent exponent of tasteful country living. Jefferson's favorite art was architecture, and he had used his considerable influence after the Revolution to help spawn a neoclassical revival in public architecture that sought to replace the "barbarous ornaments" of the Georgian Baroque style with the "chaste and good style" of Roman and Greek buildings. By looking to the ancients for architectural inspiration, Jefferson believed, the United States could end its dependence on decadent British styles and at the same time help inspire its citizens to appreciate classical republican taste and values. In describing the design of the national Capitol, he remarked that it was intended to "exhibit a grandeur of conception, a Republican simplicity, and the true elegance of proportion, which correspond to a tempered freedom excluding Frivolity, the food of little minds."[16]

Downing reiterated Jefferson's belief in the educational and inspirational influence exerted by the arts, asserting that he had a "firm faith in the *moral* effects of the fine arts." And Downing likewise appreciated classical styles. "To the scholar and the man of *refined* and cultivated mind," he noted, "the *associations* connected with Grecian architecture are of the most delightful character." This didactic outlook led him to design country and suburban dwellings intended to serve as instruments of both moral elevation and social order. "We must look for a counterpoise to the great tendency towards constant change, and the restless spirit of emigration, which form part of our national character." When "smiling lawns and tasteful cottages begin to embellish a country," he continued, "we know that order and culture are established." Good landscaping and good housing should provide not only for the physical needs of the residents but also for their "moral, social, and intellectual existence."[17]

Although he shared Jefferson's faith in the uplifting effects of architecture, Downing deplored the application of classical architectural styles to *domestic* living. Americans, he felt, had lost all sense of appropriateness in rushing to apply Greco-Roman forms to their living structures. Classical style had degenerated into democratic fashion. As a visiting British architect reported from New York in 1835: "The Greek mania here is at its height, as you infer from the fact that everything is a Greek temple, from the privies in the back court, through the various grades of prison, church, custom house, and state-house." James Fenimore Cooper likewise noted the way in which the Greek revival had become an expression of conspicuous ornamentation rather than republican simplicity. People preferred it because its bold details and columned porticoes afforded a great deal of display. "One such temple placed in a wood," he wrote, "might be a pleasant object enough, but to see a river lined with them . . . is too much even for a high taste."[18]

Downing recognized that the Grecian and Roman forms had become a ubiquitous fad rather than a vehicle for a unified moral and social vision. Though agreeing with Jefferson that Greek and Roman models were appropriate for America's public buildings, Downing affirmed that a home should be organically related to its natural environment. Domestic architecture, unlike public architecture, "should be less severe, less rigidly scientific, and it should exhibit more of the freedom and play of everyday life." Thus, instead of the stark classicism of a whitewashed Greek temple, he preferred the Gothic or English cottage design for country residences. The Gothic-styled home was to be built of wood and stone and painted tan, green, or russet in order to blend naturally into the landscape. Under "its enchanting influence," he contended, "the too great bustle and excitement of our commercial cities will be happily counterbalanced by the more elegant and quiet enjoyments of country life." Despite his rejection of residential classicism, therefore, Downing was no modernist. His Gothic vision was clearly nostalgic. In discussing the merits of his Gothic homes, he wrote: "The mingled quaintness, beauty and picturesqueness of such a dwelling seem to transport us back to a past age, the domestic habits, the hearty hospitality, the joyous old sports, and the romance and chivalry of which we invest it with a kind of golden glow, in which the shadowy lines of poetry and reality seem strangely interwoven and blended."[19]

In implementing his vision of residential republicanism, Downing brought to his drawing table an eighteenth-century conception of a hierarchical social order, and he designed different homes for the different classes he saw represented in a well-ordered American republic. For the laboring folk of the new factory centers, he offered a plain cottage whose "predominant character is *simplicity*." His ideal farmhouse was similarly plain and utilitarian. As with the cottage, the farm dwelling should "rely on its own honest, straightforward simplicity, and should rather aim to be frank, and genuine, and open-hearted, like its owner, than to wear the borrowed ornaments of any class of different habits and tastes." It was clear that Downing had no sympathy for social pretense. People were to live in homes that reflected their vocational and cultural status and were not to pretend otherwise. As if presenting a sumptuary law for housing, Downing insisted that it "is not fitting that the humble cottage should wear the decorations of a superior dwelling, any more than the plain workingman should wear the same diamonds that represent the superfluous wealth of his neighbor."[20]

Where Downing provided cottages and farmhouses for the common folk, he designed the villa for America's "most leisurely and educated class of citizens." It would be in such patrician republican homes that "we should look for the happiest social and moral development of our people." The villa would be larger than the working-class cottages and farmhouses and more eclectic in style. Yet Downing was quick to note that in comparison with the manors and castles of European aristocrats, his American villa was suitably austere. It would be the "beautiful, unostentatious, moderate home of a country gentleman, large enough to minister to all the wants, necessities, and luxuries of a republican, and not too large or too luxurious to warp the life or manners of his children." Even in designing the villa, he concluded, "we always incline to the simple and chaste." Downing minced no words in condemning those baronial New Yorkers who were building European-styled castles and chateaux along the Hudson, complete with turrets and moats. In discussing "imitations of Gothic castles, with towers and battlements of woods," he maintained that "nothing can well be more paltry and contemptible. The sugar castles of confectioners and pastry cooks are far more admirable as works of art." The "great and glaring mistake of our wealthy men" was the assumption that "only by large places and great expenditure can the problem of rural beauty and enjoyment be solved." Large estates only enslaved their owners. The "true philosophy of living in America," he concluded, "is to be found in moderate desires, a moderate establishment, and moderate expenditures."[21]

Downing's blueprints for simple republican homes were intended to provide the proper physical setting for the moral development of their residents. The actual formation of self-governing republican character, however, required much more than the construction of well-designed dwellings. As larger society was disrupted by new social and economic forces, the family itself was seen by many conservators of republican simplicity as the last bastion of cohesion and order. If anything were to be done about the insidious effects of materialism and social striving, such evils must be addressed in the formative years of childhood. These concerns led to the development of a veritable "cult of domesticity" during the 1820s and 1830s, as concerned traditionalists saw a revitalized home life as the best agency for inculcating republican virtues in the young. Catharine Sedgwick's bestselling novel *Home* (1835) made this theme explicit, as did the popular song "Home, Sweet Home," written by John Howard Payne in 1823. In addition, many of the painters of the era, including William Sidney Mount and Ernst Georg Fischer, were particularly interested in portraying scenes of plain, wholesome family life.[22]

The new emphasis on republican domesticity reflected a shift in attitudes toward youth. Children, who had earlier been viewed by the Puritans as miniature adults, born with the same vices, were now seen in a new light. The impact of Lockean psychology and Rousseau's theories of childhood development, coupled with the general atmosphere of optimistic idealism during the Middle Period, led some American theorists of child-rearing to believe that the young were not necessarily fated to repeat the errors of their elders. One maternal adviser emphasized this change of perspective when he wrote that the "mind of a child may be likened to a piece of unsullied paper, the surface of which, being free from every stain . . . may be made to receive whatever impression we see fit to stamp upon it." Catharine Beecher, one of the leading advocates of domestic morality and the daughter of Lyman Beecher, similarly argued in her influential study, *Elements of Mental and Moral Philosophy* (1831), that human corruption resulted not from predestined depravity but from a temporarily "disordered mind." Such mental dislocation she deemed preventable by careful maternal instruction in religious and moral values. Through a good family environment and parental training, children could be molded into republican citizens. This meant that instead of accelerating the child's assumption of adult behavior, as Puritan divines had stressed, authorities on child nurture during the Jacksonian era encouraged mothers to preserve the child's innocence and simplicity as long as possible.[23]

The training of children thus became the key determinant of social stability for many Americans anxious about the future of republican simplicity. It was an old idea, of course, but during the early nineteenth century the traditional concept of family roles changed to accommodate new circumstances. Earlier, in a much more predominantly agricultural and village America, the father was both worker and household patriarch, serving in theory as primary supervisor of religious and moral instruction. The wife was at most an aide and adjunct. In the new urban setting, however, many husbands now characteristically toiled away from home, ten to twelve hours a day, frequently six days a week. Consequently, it was assumed, they did not have the time or energy to spend on moral education. One writer commented in 1842 that the typical American father "was eager in his pursuit of business, toils early and late, and finds no time to fulfill his duties to his children." Family relations suffered accordingly. The alienation and disintegration so often attributed to the twentieth-century suburban family appeared early in the nineteenth century, as this account suggests:

> How often has the faithful wife to conceal her disappointment . . . while, after toiling to render the only hours of the day that bring her husband and the little ones . . . together—the occasion of happy domestic enjoyment, of mutual improvement, and of a father's instructions and discipline—she finds him full of a restless impatience to have the meal ready even before the appointed time; hurrying through it himself in silence, or if speaking, using only the necessary household words.

The solution to the problem of paternal neglect was self-evident. If men were too busy to provide moral and religious instruction for the children, then mothers must assume those duties.[24]

In this way republican simplicity was to be perpetuated through maternal attention and instruction. The family was to be the repository of moral virtue in the nation, and the mother was to be the curator. As one minister explained to a female audience, "You hold the sceptre in your souls in which, more than the laws of a legislature, now repose the futurity of the nation, the world, and the destinies of the human race." Never was motherhood in America so revered. One symbolic testament to the growing emphasis on maternal influence was the construction of a monument in Fredericksburg, Virginia, not to George Washington, but to his mother.[25]

In part this changing attitude toward women reflected their changing status. Economic developments greatly affected the pattern of domestic living of early nineteenth-century American women, especially among the growing middle class. Many of the household goods that colonial wives had once spent a great deal of time producing were now made better and more cheaply in factories. Moreover, a growing supply of immigrant labor coupled with the rising personal income of middle-class husbands facilitated the increased use of servants to handle many of the household chores. That affluent women were giving birth to fewer children as the nineteenth century progressed also provided them with more time to spend on activities of their own choosing. The increasing predominance of women in benevolent and religious activities reflected this development. Women now composed the majority of active church members. It was therefore only natural for the clergy to expand women's activities within the church and home. In sermon after sermon ministers emphasized the crucial moral and spiritual role played by women and enlisted them as home missionaries, giving over to them much of the responsibility for the training of youth that the church had earlier performed.

Some students of this "cult of domesticity" have seen in it a conscious attempt by American men to "shift the bulk of their moral burden to the shoulders of women." Others have attributed it to the desire of husbands to keep their wives at home rather than see them involved in the emerging women's rights movement. One influential tract on maternal duties, written by a man, insisted that the mother's first responsibility was in the home and not in social reform activities. The author reminded readers that "even if we cannot reform the world in a moment, we can begin work by reforming ourselves and our households—it is woman's mission. Let her not look away from her own little family circle for the means of producing moral or social reforms, but begin at home."[26]

But domesticity was not simply foisted on women by nervous men. To Catharine Beecher the idea that the republic's moral fiber depended upon the quality of maternal devotion represented a glorious challenge:

> The success of democratic institutions, as is conceded by all, depends upon the intellectual and moral character of the mass of the people. If they are intelligent and virtuous, democracy is a blessing; but if they are ignorant and wicked, it is only a curse. . . . It is equally conceded, that the formation of the moral and intellectual character of the young is committed mainly to the female hand. The mother forms the character of the future man.

Women, consequently, were to embrace their new role as domestic redeemers now that men could no longer be counted on to save the nation. "When our land is filled with virtuous and patriotic mothers," one domestic reformer concluded, "then it will be filled with virtuous and patriotic men. The world's redeeming influence must come from a mother's lips."[27]

This was a rather weighty responsibility, and not a few women who took it seriously were understandably intimidated by its mandate. The wife of a minister and mother of five children confessed that she was "so far from discharging the duties of my station or from meeting the high responsibilities which devolve on me as a mother, that the conviction of my deficiencies which sometimes forces itself upon me is sometimes overwhelming." Mothers Associations were formed in many communities in part to assuage such concerns as well as to provide a forum for sharing the "best methods of instilling into our children habits of *Self-Denial*."[28]

Even more important in helping women assume their new domestic duties was the spate of literature on child nurture that appeared during the Jacksonian era. Most of the handbooks shared a common siege mentality and evangelical tone which led them to portray the home as the last haven of traditional republican morality in an increasingly godless and greedy society. The growing passion for speculative gain and ostentatious display, wrote one popular proponent of domesticity, was "draining the very life-blood of our republican integrity and simplicity." A well-ordered home, she continued, provided the best security "for individual integrity, and the surest safeguard for national virtue." According to the child nurture guidebooks, the ideal republican mother was to be chaste, cultured, and unpretentious, devoted both to simplicity of manners and to the elevation of character. In *Uncle*

Tom's Cabin (1852), Harriet Beecher Stowe, Catharine Beecher's sister, portrayed Mrs. Shelby as the model republican woman. She displayed "high moral and religious sensibility and principle, carried out with great energy and ability into practical results." Her husband had no religious character himself, but he quite respected hers, and "he gave her unlimited scope in all her benevolent efforts for the comfort, instruction, and improvement of her servants, though he never took any decided part in them himself." Stowe concluded that Mr. Shelby "seemed somehow to fancy that his wife had piety and benevolence enough for two."[29]

Stowe and other domestic reformers believed that if such an enlightened republican mother could not convert her husband to the principled life, she could at least plant the seed of an enlivened moral sense in her children. As Lydia Sigourney stressed in her *Letters to Mothers* (1838), the republican home was to be a refreshing oasis of idealism in the barren desert of the commercial and industrial world. In speaking to mothers about values to be developed in their children, she wrote: "Let us not inoculate them with the love of money. It is the prevailing evil of our country. It makes us a care-worn people." There would be plenty of opportunities for children to develop their material instincts once they left the home. "Years and intercourse with mankind will soon enough, impress the lesson of pecuniary acquisition."[30]

Another influential popularizer of this "cult of domesticity" was Lydia Maria Child. Her books went through dozens of editions, and her articles appeared in every major periodical. Their persistent theme was that republican simplicity must be implanted in American youth at an early age. In addressing her advice to middle-class mothers, Child told them to teach children "to consider money valuable only for its use" and "that the only purpose of having anything to call their own is that they may use it for the good of others." Poverty and wealth, she advised in *The Mother's Book* (1831), were equally dangerous to public virtue. The wealthy were prone to pride and insolence, the poor to jealousy and envy. "The right path," she emphasized, "is between extremes." Child warned that if children were not taught the goodness of the "middle way," the "inordinate love of wealth and parade" would be "the ruin of our country, as it has been, and will be, the ruin of thousands of individuals." She was candid enough to admit that the republican mother's task was difficult. But what choice did the new nation have? The "care of children requires a great many sacrifices, and a great deal of self-denial, but the woman who is not willing to sacrifice a good deal in such a cause does not deserve to be a mother."[31]

The flood of didactic child-rearing literature during the ante-bellum period was by no means solely concerned with endorsing the simple life. There was much more to the domesticity phenomenon than that. The advice manuals represented a genre that clearly reflected the ambivalence felt by genteel moralists in the face of rapid social change. The objective of many of the reformers was similar to that of Downing and the moral architects: to restore an ordered hierarchical and organic society. Increasingly aware of their isolation and vulnerability, many of the conservative domestic reformers were motivated as much by their fears of the new as by their commitment to simplicity as a fundamental ideal. In the midst of such defensive paternalism, however, there flowered several prominent gentry reformers genuinely dedicated to the simple life as a societal creed. Unlike many supporters of domesticity who seemed concerned primarily with the behavior of those below them on the social scale, two women writers, Sarah Hale and Caroline Kirkland, were equally worried by the extravagance and snobbery of the bourgeoisie, their own kind, and in this sense their espousal of republican simplicity may have been more profound.

Born in New Hampshire in 1788, Sarah Josepha Hale lived the typically domestic life of a New England housewife until the sudden death of her husband in 1822, just before the birth of her fifth child. Thus encumbered with dependents and desperate for a stable and independent source of income, she turned to writing. In 1827 she published her first novel, *Northwood, A Tale of New England*, and it was an immediate success among northern readers, in part because of its explicit condemnation of slavery in the South. A book with little plot but much preaching, *Northwood* tells the highly sentimentalized story of the Romelees, a "middling" family in Northwood, a small New Hampshire village set in the early nineteenth century. The town displayed a "simplicity and purity" in its "manners and morals" and was a community where men were "esteemed more for merit and usefulness, than rank and wealth." But Northwood's simple way of life was being threatened by modern forces and values that were already transforming the eastern seaboard into a society indifferent to the virtues of the founding fathers. An "inordinate thirst for riches" had become the "besetting sin of Americans." And Northwood could not long remain immune to its effects.[32]

To illustrate the changes in American life and values that so troubled her, Hale chose to organize *Northwood* around the rather wooden character, Sidney Romelee. A "sweet-tempered, scholarly" boy, Sidney contentedly grows up in the halcyon atmosphere of Northwood. His father, Squire Romelee, is the epitome of republican simplicity, and he tries to run his household and instruct his children accordingly. For Squire Romelee, personal frugality and enlightened thinking were complementary virtues. "Here was the father of the family," Hale relates, "living in all the simplicity of retirement, inuring his children to habits of prudence and laborious industry; yet cultivating in them a taste for the refinements of literature and the love of science."[33]

Young Sidney learns his lessons well from his father, but while still in his teens, he is uprooted when he goes to live with his rich aunt in Charleston, South Carolina, ostensibly in order to receive a better education. In that bustling, cosmopolitan port city, Sidney experiences a rather exaggerated moral decline. Following a scenario that Charles Brockden Brown had already introduced in *Arthur Mervyn* (1799) and that would become a commonplace literary formula during the nineteenth century, the young lad from the countryside succumbs to the lures of the city—gaming, horse-racing, and beautiful women. "I was in early life," Sidney reflects at one point, "educated to love study and activity; but the tempter came." For the next thirteen years he lives the carefree life of a seaboard aristocrat, ignoring his studies and indulging his passions. "I have seen much, and studied little . . . done nothing at all—nothing, at least, that I can claim any merit for having performed." Later he succinctly pinpoints the problem: "Luxury has undone me."[34]

Good Sidney, however, is not left to waste away in Charleston's high society. Through a fortuitous set of circumstances he finds himself back in Northwood, now a man near thirty. Returning to the house of his youth and the reassuring warmth of his family, he recognizes the errors of his southern experience. As he resettles himself in Northwood as a "plain farmer," he is again convinced of the "superior happiness of a life of simple accomplishment over one of mere amusement." Sidney's transition from aristocrat to yeoman was neither immediate nor easy; his carefree ways still left their imprint. "How often I wish I could," Sidney admits, "with the philosophical serenity of Anaxagoras, at once reconcile myself to the change from luxury to plainness." Yet as time passes, he gradually does shed his debauched ways, thus providing a personal example for the book's readers to identify with and emulate.[35]

Northwood's popularity indicates that at least among some segments of the genteel reading public there remained a powerful attachment to republican simplicity. Yet it would take more than a didactic novel to reform the manners and objectives of Jacksonian society at large. How could the country's values be elevated? Most American fathers, Hale believed, were no longer instilling republican manners in their children. She finally decided that American women held the key to restoring idealism and moderation to a country gone money-mad.

Hale brought this perspective to the editorship of Boston's *Ladies' Magazine*. She was offered the position in 1827, soon after the appearance of *Northwood*, and held it for the next ten years. Her stated purpose as new editor was to discard the traditional emphasis of genteel women's magazines —saccharine love stories, sentimental poetry, and especially fashion plates— and convert the periodical into an organ for "female improvement." Hale took for granted the growing assumption that women were the moral guardians of the new republic, largely because of their detachment from the crass commercial order. And she sharply distinguished between the home and the workplace as human environments. The home was an island of virtue "removed from the area of pecuniary excitement and ambitious competition." Men were supposed to practice republican simplicity, and, according to Hale, most among the Revolutionary generation had done so. But the hectic world of capitalist enterprise in the cities kept the new generation of men too busy and distracted. Daily practicing the ways of trade, they had no inclination to follow the strict standards of the fathers. Consequently, it was left to women to preserve such classical values. "Our men are sufficiently moneymaking. Let.us keep our women and children from the contagion as long as possible." Hale would use her magazine to "remind the dwellers of this 'bank-note world' that there are objects more elevated, more worthy of pursuits than wealth." To attain an appreciation for such "higher" tastes required "the culture of the heart, the discipline of the passions [and] the regeneration of the feelings and affections."[36]

By the early 1830s, Hale had attracted a wide following to her magazine. But she had gone too far and too fast in transforming the publication into an instrument of republican morality, and it did not take long for readers to begin clamoring for a return of the fashion plates displaying the latest European dress styles. In 1830 Hale grudgingly submitted and allowed the illustrations to reappear. She made it clear, however, that the decision did not reflect her own preferences. "There is no part of our duty as editor of a ladies' journal, which we feel so reluctant to perform, as to quote, or exhibit the fashions of dress." At first Hale tried to subvert the appeal of the fashion plates by adding critical or satirical captions, explaining that "we endeavor to make our *plate of fashion* teach a lesson to the heart, as well as the vanity of our fair reader." Yet she came to see that many of her readers cared little for such moralizing, and she eventually ignored the presence of the fashion illustrations in the midst of her many editorials calling for a simple republican style.[37]

In the mid-1830s Louis Godey of Philadelphia suggested to Hale that they merge *Ladies' Magazine* with his own periodical, *Lady's Book*. She accepted in 1837, was made literary editor of the new publication, and for the next forty years remained a dominant figure for middle-class readers. In her first editorial in *Godey's Lady's Book*, Hale vowed to continue to promote republican simplicity through domesticity, promising to "carry onward and upward the spirit of moral and intellectual excellence in our own sex, till their influence shall bless as well as beautify civil society." She urged her predominantly female readers to take the lead in restoring the "plain standards" of an earlier age. This meant abandoning their expensive taste for European fashions and developing their own neat, becoming, and unadorned style of living. "We shall show," she promised, "the various economical and intellectual benefits of a just simplicity." Hale explicitly warned her new readers that simplicity was to be her theme, noting that although "a certain class of political economists prefer to believe that luxury is beneficial to the nation—it is not so."[38]

Caroline Kirkland was as determined as Sarah Hale to promote such a revolution of manners, and she likewise directed most of her efforts at genteel American women. Born Caroline Stansbury into an upper-class family in New York City in 1801, she spent her childhood and adolescence in Manhattan. In 1828 she married William Kirkland, and nine years later they moved to a tract of land deep in the Michigan woods, sixty miles northwest of Detroit. There she began writing thinly disguised autobiographical novels about life on the frontier. In 1843, having received considerable acclaim and attention, Kirkland returned with her family to New York, where she continued to write and also served for a time as editor of the newly founded *Union Magazine.*[39]

The dominant theme of Kirkland's writings was the same as Hale's—the need for a female-led revival of plain republican virtue. In a number of essays, some of which Hale printed in *Godey's*, Kirkland joined in criticizing Americans for continuing to ape the style of living of the England aristocracy. The United States, she wrote in 1846, was dominated by "the deadly strife of emulation, the mad pursuit of wealth, the suspicion engendered by rivalry." Americans needed less aristocratic pretensions and more native republican simplicity, but it must be a "simplicity founded upon principle." The principle she enunciated combined Christian ethics with classical republicanism. To her, simple living meant "moderation in expense for the express purpose of being liberal where liberality is honorable; plainness of dress resulting at once from good taste and from religious self-denial. . . . plainness of living, lest our splendor should separate us and the good to whom God had not seen fit to give riches." Kirkland was not counseling primitivism any more than was Sarah Hale. "We may live liberally, and even elegantly," she assured her readers, "without renouncing the dignified simplicity which draws its maxims and habits from the proprieties of things, and not from the conventionalisms of people in the old world." Kirkland reminded Americans of the "real dignity" of John Adams and asked when "shall we look at the spirit rather than the semblance of things—when give up the shadow for the substance?"[40]

This emphasis on the need for Americans to moderate their acquisitive energies and focus their attention on nobler activities pervaded Kirkland's creative writings. In her novels she adopted the same sermonizing tone as Hale but was a better literary stylist. Poe referred to her in 1846 as "one of our best writers," and William Cullen Bryant noted her "high and almost world-wide reputation." Her first book, *A New Home—Who'll Follow? Glimpses of Western Life*, appeared in 1839 and provided the basic plot scheme that would be repeated in her next two novels, *Forest Life* (1842) and *Western Clearings* (1845). Kirkland, under the pseudonym "Mrs. Mary Clavers, an actual settler," used her own experiences to tell the story of an eastern woman of refined tastes and sensibilities who reluctantly accompanies her husband to a new frontier settlement in Michigan, "on the outskirts of civilization."

Initially Mrs. Clavers's city-bred personality rebels against the homely pioneer mentality and coarse standard of living of backwoods Michigan. "This simplification of life, this bringing down the transactions of daily intercourse to the original principles of society," she finds, "is neither very eagerly adopted, nor very keenly relished, by those who have been accustomed to the politer atmosphere." But gradually she does abandon her haughty eastern gentility in favor of an unassuming western simplicity, rejecting the view then prevailing in the seaboard cities that the "mere possession of property necessarily implies some kind of merit." Mrs. Clavers discovers that what were considered necessities in New York were mere superfluities in Michigan. Several years before *Walden* was published, Kirkland sounded remarkably Thoreauvian when she wrote that after living in Michigan, "simplifying our wants and reducing their number, many things which are considered essential to comfort among those who make modes of life a study and a science, appeared to us absolutely cumbersome and harassing." Her own demanding, yet enlightening experience on the frontier leads Mrs. Clavers to "recommend a course of Michigan to the Sybarites, the puny exquisites, the world-worn and sated Epicureans of our cities." Yet Kirkland the author knows that most of her countrymen were not interested in experimenting with such an "outdated" mode of living. They preferred to glorify it from afar. "Republican simplicity," she claimed, "though so evidently the dictate of our real interest and the foundation of our true dignity, is scarcely thought of, except on one day of every year, when it serves to round a period for the orator."[41]

Kirkland's fatalistic observation reflected an obvious fact: the effort to domesticate republican simplicity was not producing the social regeneration envisioned by its advocates. Lydia Child admitted that there "are a few, an honorable few, who late in life, with Roman severity of resolution, learn the long-neglected lesson of economy. But how small is the number, compared with the whole mass of the population!" Judging by Hale's experience with the fashion plate controversy, many women seemed more interested in accumulating superfluous finery and in breaking into "high society" than in practicing and teaching republican simplicity. As an editorial in the *Ladies' Repository* reported in 1845: "Many a husband and father is being made bankrupt by female extravagance." Instead of assuming the responsibility of chaste republican mothers, some "ladies even boast ignorance of domestic science."[42]

An equally disturbing development was that many mothers who were diligently instructing their children in moral behavior were apparently not teaching either classical republican simplicity or the original Protestant ethic, but instead were emphasizing traits that would promote social mobility and material gain. "If we look around us on every side," one writer remarked, "we behold numerous examples of women, who are practicing self-denial and enduring privation, not in reality to train their children for the stations to which God has appointed them, but to educate them above the place which they will be probably called on to fill." An article in *Harper's New Monthly Magazine* in 1853 echoed this point in noting that the "idea instilled into the minds of most boys, from early life, is that of 'getting on.' The parents test themselves by their own success in this respect; and they impart the same notion to their children." In some cases, it was noted, the mothers themselves were practicing traditional republican moderation, but the children they were supposed to have trained were not. In 1857 a foreign traveler observed: "The simplicity, the frugality of the parents, contrasts often disagreeably with the prodigality, the assumption, self-assertion, and conceit of the children."[43]

The failure of American mothers to mold their progeny into republican saints is not hard to understand. Huck Finn was undoubtedly typical of many American boys who resisted the imperatives of maternal domesticity. It would have taken a truly exceptional person to have accomplished all that was being asked of republican women. In noting the "prevailing neglect of household duty," a mother observed in 1841 that "comparatively few women at the present day are content to be simply useful, and to shine in the domestic circle alone." Genteel women were preoccupied with "high society" life. Working-class wives, on the other hand, were increasingly working women, and, as the Lowell example indicated, they had little leisure to devote either to self-culture or domestic management.[44]

Finally, there was an even more basic conceptual flaw inherent in the idea of republican domesticity. Even if the home could be made into a haven of republican virtue, it was but a haven. Eventually, of course, children grow up, leave the maternal sanctuary, and enter the world of material striving and status seeking that Hale, Kirkland, and others had deemed inimical to republicanism. And it was naïve to think that in the midst of such a worldly "contagion," most young Americans would have had instilled in them enough moral stamina to avoid infection. Thus, in essence, the idea of relegating republican morality to the home was but another example of the simple life as a societal ideal being shunted aside by the forces of modernity and social change. As with the Puritans, Quakers, and old republicans, the domestic redeemers of the Jacksonian era found themselves advocating a static set of values in the face of a dynamic new culture.

Perhaps the most striking indication of the failure of republican domesticity was the proliferation of reformatories, orphanages, and prisons during the Jacksonian era. One social historian, in fact, has called the period the "age of the asylum."[45] By the 1830s, many social and political leaders had already given up on the family as the primary socializing agency and were promoting new ways to provide the paternal guidance and external controls so obviously missing from large segments of an increasingly diverse population. The most ambitious of these new institutional approaches was the burgeoning movement for state-supported public schools. At the same time that the "cult of domesticity" was reaching its peak, a new class of professional educators was vigorously promoting the substitution of the common school for the home as the best agency for ensuring the survival of republican virtue and national prosperity. The earlier emphasis of Revolutionary leaders such as Jefferson and Rush on education as the best preserver of republican values was revived and expanded in the Jacksonian era. It was also significantly modified.

A prevailing theme running through the literature promoting public school systems in the 1830s was that the family alone could not be counted on to carry out the necessary process of socialization. Parents, especially those among the Irish and German immigrants, were portrayed as either too indifferent or too lenient in their attitude toward moral instruction in the household. In "the present state of society," wrote one school advocate, "a vast majority of parents are unable, either on account of their own deficient education, or from want of time, to attend, in person, to the discharge of this duty." Nor did the combination of private academies, charity schools, and church schools come close to meeting the need for the moral instruction of youth. A universal system of compulsory public schools, therefore, must assume the responsibilities of moral instruction for the nation's children.[46]

Some reformers supported both republican domesticity and the new common school idea, seeing maternal care and public schooling as complementary means to achieve the same goal. In fact, most of the public school advocates accepted the assumptions about feminine virtues that lay behind the "cult of domesticity." Many of them coupled their advocacy of state-supported common schools with a call for women to displace men as classroom instructors. "Females," Horace Mann argued, "govern with less resort to physical force, and exert a more kindly, humanizing and refining influence upon the dispositions and manners of their pupils." Mann and other school reformers also shared many of the ideas about child development that had guided the supporters of domesticity. They viewed schools as fulfilling the same shaping function as the homes were supposed to have done. Public schools would similarly be outposts of virtue, built away from the centers of commercial and industrial activity. The school, like the ideal republican home, would provide "an asylum for the preservation of childhood."[47]

Like most of the advocates of republican domesticity, the leaders of the public school movement were activated by a number of intertwined and frequently ambivalent motives. That several of the most prominent educators such as Mann and Henry Barnard were Whigs who had been raised on New England family farms has led some scholars to attribute their intensity to a sense of nervousness felt by a declining ruling gentry being rapidly displaced by the forces of industrialism, immigration, and democratization. The state school was in this sense intended to be a civilizing agency impressing the values of republican simplicity on the untutored masses. Barnard, the conservative Connecticut reformer, for example, told the Rhode Island legislature in 1845 that it was the responsibility of civilized men to decide for the urban poor how best to raise them from barbarism. Catharine Beecher similarly saw an army of new women teachers marching into newly built frontier schoolrooms "to civilize the barbarous immigrants and lower classes of the West."[48]

Horace Mann (1796–1859), the most prominent spokesman for state-supported common schools in the ante-bellum period, reflected in his own career the confusion of motives and goals that characterized most of the educational reformers. Born in the small town of Franklin, Massachusetts, in 1796, Mann grew up in the midst of poverty, hardship, and self-denial. As a youth he developed a voracious appetite for reading, and through his self-education he was able to gain admission to Brown University in 1816. There he performed so well that he was hired as a tutor after graduation. Like so many of the founding fathers before him, he became, first, a lawyer, then a public official, serving in the state legislature as a champion of conservative social reform. Mann led the fight for the creation of a state hospital for the insane and was also an energetic participant in the temperance movement. But public education was his real interest, and in 1837 he resigned his post as president of the state senate and gave up his law practice in order to accept the secretaryship of the state's first Board of Education. "I have abandoned jurisprudence," he joyfully announced, "and betaken myself to the larger sphere of mind and morals."[49]

As a former lawyer and Whig politician, as well as a convert to Unitarianism, Mann brought to his campaign for school reform rather typical bourgois concerns about the social changes transforming the pace and tenor of American life—immigration, urbanization, industrialization, migration. In a society like the United States, marked by a growing emphasis on individual liberty, something must be done, he believed, to encourage the development of natural virtues and discourage the growth of natural vices. But he declared that neither the law nor the church was the effective moral force it once was. And "pernicious family and social influences" were undermining rather than enhancing the moral development of youth. Mann, therefore, searched for new means to restore order, harmony, and moderation to a society torn loose from its moorings. "Again, then, I ask, with unmitigated anxiety," he said in a lecture, "what institutions we now possess, that can furnish defense or barriers against the actions of those [selfish] propensities, which each generation brings into the world as part of its being?" He answered his own question. There were no such stabilizing institutions. Mann concluded, however, that there was a "way by which these nobler faculties can be elevated into dominion and supremacy over the appetites and passions. But if this is ever done, it must be mainly done during the docile and teachable years of childhood."[50]

Mann began his campaign for public schools by focusing primarily on the *moral* benefits that universal education would provide for the young nation. Through the new model schools, he argued, "we shall teach mankind to moderate their passions and develop their virtues." Unlike the hierarchical plans put forward earlier by the founding fathers, his system would be open to all children regardless of material standing, social status, or intellectual ability. Education must be made universal, he contended, because the social problems were universal. His faith in the school as the best instrument for indoctrinating republican morality and civic virtue in an increasingly diverse populace was boundless. The common school, he claimed, "is the greatest discovery ever made by man. . . . Other social organizations are curative and remedial: this is a preventative and antidote."[51]

Yet as time passed and Mann encountered stiff resistance from the middle- and upper-class property holders who would be forced to pay for such a system of public education, he shifted his emphasis from the *moral* benefits of common schooling to the *economic* and *class* benefits. Most of his 1841 annual report as commissioner of the Massachusetts Board of Education was devoted to "showing the effects of education upon the worldly fortunes and estates of men." Education, he assured the respectable citizenry, is "not only the most honorable, but the surest means of amassing wealth." Mann tried to demonstrate that "education has a market value; that it is so far an article of merchandise, that it may be turned to a pecuniary account: it may be minted, and will yield a larger amount of suitable coin than common bullion."[52]

At the same time that Mann stressed to the prosperous that education would ensure their children economic success and increase worker productivity, he also argued on behalf of its social benefits. "Would not the payment of a sufficient tax to make such education and training universal," he asked, "be the cheapest means of self-protection and influence?" Otherwise, a mad social scramble would soon disrupt all traditional distinctions. If "besotting vices and false knowledge bear sway, then will every wealthy, and every educated, and every refined individual and family, stand in the same relation to society, in which game stands to the sportsman!" Such arguments appealed to the bourgeoisie, judging by the success of Mann's proposals and the support he received from the affluent. On one occasion thirty-four Boston businessmen sent him a letter commending his efforts: "You have demonstrated that the arm of industry is served, and the wealth of the country is augmented, in proportion to the diffusion of knowledge, so that each humble school-house is to be regarded, not only as a nursery of souls, but a mine of riches."[53]

Had Mann succumbed to the materialist ethos of the age? Was public education for him primarily a means for improving the economic development of the nation? His rhetoric has led many to interpret him in this light. Certainly Mann had a pronounced middle-class bias that helped shape his outlook on social and economic issues. Yet, like so many other republican reformers in the ante-bellum period, he was motivated by a mixture of prejudices, fears, hopes, and idealism. That he obviously felt uncomfortable in so baldly stressing the economic advantages of his educational proposals was evinced by his agonized disclaimer: "However deserving of attention may be the *economical* view of the subject which I have endeavored to present, yet it is one that dwindles into insignificance when compared to those loftier and more sacred attributes of the cause which have the power of converting material wealth into spiritual well-being, and of giving its possessor lordship and sovereignty alike over . . . the dangerous seducements of prosperity."[54]

Personally, Mann was a sincere advocate of plain republican virtues. He was known among his friends as a man of simple tastes who did not want or need much money. Like Sam Adams he could also be an unremitting critic of ostentatious finery. In a letter to the wife of his friend Josiah Quincy, Jr., Mann wrote: "You have bantered me not very infrequently on my want of appreciation for elegance, and adornments; and I readily confess that I have often spoken disparagingly of those things that perish with the using compared with those treasures, of which heaven consents to be the banker." Mann was suspended between tradition and modernity, privately eager to retain old virtues yet, in his public role, he was also aware of new social and economic factors.[55]

Such confused loyalties led Mann and other educational reformers to promise everything to the citizenry. The affluent were told that state-supported schools would increase their wealth, stabilize society, prevent revolution, and train the poor for the factories, while the working classes were assured that education would catapult their children out of their inherited social and economic status. The middle classes were promised economic advance, social order, and moral development. As time passed and state after state (outside the South) adopted public school systems, however, it became evident that education was not the panacea the reformers had envisioned. Just as the spokesmen for republican domesticity had exaggerated the power of maternal care in the home, so, too, did Mann and his fellow educators overstate the effectiveness of the school as teacher and preserver of republican simplicity. The classroom was little better equipped than the parlor to compete effectively with the entrepreneurial values of the workplace and marketplace.

In practice, the public schools, like many early Victorian mothers, tended to promote values that bore more resemblance to the vocational utilitarianism of Benjamin Franklin's Poor Richard than to the enlightened republicanism advocated by a Thomas Jefferson or an Abigail Adams. Despite the concerted efforts of the evangelical, domestic, and school reformers, the preoccupation with material values and mundane affairs that the Revolutionary leaders had feared would come to smother republican simplicity seemed to be in the ascendant by mid-century. Art critic Henry Tuckerman observed in 1855 that the "ideal of success had totally changed with the blandishments of prosperity from the resources of character to the artifices of wealth."[56]

Three years later, a contributor to the *Atlantic Monthly* noted this same development in discussing the continuing degradation of the Protestant work ethic in the face of the secularization and atomization of society:

> The maxims of Franklin have been literally received and adopted as divine truth. We have believed that to labor is to be thrifty, that to be thrifty is to be respectable, that to be respectable is to afford facilities for being still more thrifty; and our experience is, that with increased thrift comes increased labor. This is the circle of our ambitions and rewards. All begins and ends in labor. The natural and inevitable result of this is both physical and mental deterioration.

Ideally, the writer continued, Americans should resurrect the spirit of their colonial ancestors and live for something nobler than their work and its monetary rewards. They should "rise from every period of labor into an atmosphere of intellectual and social activity, or into some form of refined family enjoyment." This was the same ideal that many of the advocates of child nurture and educational reform had also professed. But by combining such an elevated vision of work with the cultivation of other traits deemed essential to the practical needs of urban-industrial society, the conservative reformers, most of them unwittingly so, helped steer republican simplicity aground on the shoals of economic democracy. Perhaps Mann recognized this development when he admitted that it "may be an easy thing to make a republic, but it is a very laborious thing to make republicans."[57]

CHAPTER SIX

Transcendental Simplicity

Not all advocates of simple living during the first half of the nineteenth century were intent upon institutionalizing traditional moral and social values. As Ralph Waldo Emerson observed in 1844, there "was in all the practical activities of New England for the last quarter of a century, a gradual withdrawal of tender consciences from the social organizations." These "tender consciences," imbued with a romantic emphasis on naturalism, immediatism, individualism, and perfectionism, espoused a more spontaneous and liberating version of the simple life than that promoted by conservative moralists such as Horace Mann, Andrew Jackson Downing, and Lyman and Catharine Beecher. The romantics viewed simplicity as a personally chosen, rather than a socially imposed, way of living. Full of burning enthusiasm and millennialist expectations, these visionary nonconformists were more interested in perfecting individuals than in perfecting institutions, and they insisted on the sufficiency of their own standards of happiness and virtue. In practice this meant that romantic simplicity was less a societal ethic than a spiritual ethic, and many of its excited practitioners were deemed eccentric, naïve, or utopian by their peers.[1]

The romantics were indeed more extreme and diverse in their interpretation of simplicity than their Puritan, Quaker, or Revolutionary era predecessors. They inclined toward the party of rebellion and innovation rather than of preservation. Some followed the advice of Sylvester Graham, a charismatic minister and self-taught nutritionist who advocated sexual moderation, chaste reading, meatlessness, and a bran bread diet as the prescription for moral improvement and physical health. Others promoted the simplification of clothing, favoring Byron collars, loose, flowing garments, and gaily colored blouses. A few professed a sweeping disavowal of the cash nexus and the factory system or assailed particular professions such as law and commerce. Many joined utopian communities designed to avoid the snares and temptations of laissez-faire individualism and cosmopolitan living.[2]

Such attitudes and practices proved quite disconcerting to defenders of the status quo. In 1841 William Ellery Channing, the inspiring Unitarian minister and social activist, noted the fears expressed by many public spokesmen upon learning that there were "enthusiastic romantic reformers" preaching the virtues of "quaker plainness of dress" in a nation devoted to superfluous finery. Channing, however, was not worried by such activities:

> What! Danger from romance and enthusiasm in this money-getting, self-seeking, self-indulging, self-displaying land? I confess that to me it is a comfort to see some outbreak of enthusiasm, whether transcendental, philanthropic, or religious, as a proof that the human spirit is not wholly engulfed in matter and business, that it can lift up a little the mountains of worldliness and sense with which it is so borne down.

Channing saw great potential in a romantic movement dedicated to simplicity, spirituality, and societal change. There is "an element—spiritual, moral, and tending towards perfection—in the present movement; and that is my great hope." He was overjoyed that there were young Americans moved not by dreams of material success but by "ideas, by principles, by the conception of a better state of society."[3]

Among the many romantic "enthusiasts" preaching the virtues of simple living in the Middle Period, the most articulate were the Transcendentalists, that colorful group of inspired poets and philosophers centered in Concord. While other Americans were clamoring for internal improvements in the form of canals, railroads, and harbors, the Transcendentalists wanted internal improvements in man himself. Emerson, Thoreau, Theodore Parker, Frederic Hedge, Bronson Alcott, George Ripley, Margaret Fuller, Elizabeth Peabody, Orestes Brownson, and other like-minded thinkers literally sought to *transcend* the limitations of Lockean rationalism and penetrate the inner recesses of the self. To them, intuitive truths were ultimately more meaningful than empirical facts or entrenched conventions. The Transcendentalist, Emerson explained, "believes in miracle, in the perpetual openness of the human mind to new influx of light and power; he believes in inspiration, and in ecstasy." Religious freethinkers, philosophic idealists, and literary romantics, they sought to experience the same felt spirituality that had energized the early Quakers. This mystical emphasis led them to promote the ideal of self-culture already being so eloquently espoused by the Reverend Dr. Channing. In seeking the good life, Channing had argued, one must begin with the conviction that "there is something greater within him than in the whole material creation, than in all the worlds which press on the eye and ear; and that inward improvements have a worth and dignity in themselves."[4]

As interpreted by the Transcendentalists, Channing's ethic of self-culture entailed a Pythagorean simple life of material self-control and intellectual exertion. It also implied a reverential attitude toward the natural world. Where Enlightenment simplicity found its guiding impulse primarily in classical philosophy and Protestant simplicity looked to Jesus' example, the romantic sensibility saw nature as the source of aesthetic pleasure, moral goodness, and spiritual inspiration. Jefferson, Crèvecœur, Philip Freneau, William Bartram, and other eighteenth-century agrarians had foreshadowed such an attitude. For them, however, nature primarily represented earth to be worked and planted. The farmer's labor was itself an ennobling enterprise. During the nineteenth century, however, farming was frequently a life of "quiet desperation" rather than Homeric or Jeffersonian contemplation, and thus the romantics tended to view nature more in pastoral than agrarian terms. They found in the woods both a retreat from modern complexity and an opportunity for soul-searching introspection. The divine energies at work in the countryside had an ecstatic effect on them, elevating and expanding their vision of the possible and clarifying their understanding of themselves. For the romantic naturalists, therefore, the path to the good life began with self-discovery and then led to an organic synthesis of that self with the natural world surrounding it.[5]

This ideal, of course, had been commonly espoused by Old World romantics for years. But the American Transcendentalists differed from their European counterparts in that they grafted a romantic naturalism onto the tough and springy root of Puritan moralism. "The moral law," Emerson wrote, "lies at the center of nature and radiates to the circumference." He and other like-minded Transcendentalists translated that nature-inspired moral law into a personal ethic of material restraint and profound thinking. With Wordsworth they believed that "there is no real happiness in life but in intellect and virtue." But with Winthrop and Edwards they insisted that the moral life entailed a spartan-like control of the baser instincts.[6]

The Transcendentalist appeal for a more enlightened and spiritual approach to getting and spending, however, evoked little sympathy among the New England social and economic elite. "The view taken of Transcendentalism in State Street," Emerson remarked in his journal in 1841, "is that it threatens to invalidate contracts." To many members of the New England business and religious establishment, the Transcendentalist outlook smacked of antinomianism, and most commentators declared its reformist message subversive; it challenged both social stability and economic progress. Consequently, the Transcendentalists, like the Quaker enthusiasts of the mid-eighteenth century who had also found their ideas rebuffed by the larger society, were forced to turn back on themselves for fellowship and support. It was a "sign of our times," Emerson observed, that ". . . many intellectual and religious persons withdrew" from the "market and the caucus" in order to find something "worthy to do."[7]

Since the Transcendentalists were convinced that life was too precious to waste on the mere pursuit and enjoyment of things, their common goal was to develop modes of living that reduced their material and institutional needs to a minimum so that they could more easily pursue spiritual truths, moral ideals, and aesthetic impulses. William Henry Channing, the nephew of the Reverend Dr. Channing, succinctly expressed their credo: "To live content with small means; to seek elegance rather than luxury, and refinement rather than fashion; to be worthy, not respectable, and wealthy, not rich; to study hard, think quietly, talk gently, act frankly. . . . This is my symphony." The Transcendentalist symphony included many variations on this theme, ranging from the communal experiments in simple living at Brook Farm and Fruitlands to the more individual and reclusive patterns of living practiced respectively by Emerson and Thoreau. Whatever the arrangement, it was a difficult symphony to play. The Congregationalist minister Horace Bushnell pointed out in 1843 that only "a few towering trunks alone" were successfully practicing such a romantic simplicity. In the Transcendental forest, the two most "towering trunks" were Emerson and Thoreau, one a majestic oak, the other an aloof elm.[8]

"Life is a selection, no more." So wrote Emerson in 1846. It was one of those deceptively simple pronouncements that he was a master at composing. In those six words he captured the essence of his own moral outlook and that of the Transcendentalists. The selections Emerson made during his life were almost always intended to reduce the complexity of his life and to enhance his ability to engage in contemplation. "Great men," he once maintained, "are they that see that [the] spiritual is stronger than any material force; that thoughts rule the world." Thoughts certainly ruled Emerson's universe, and the sources of his thinking were numerous and diverse, ranging from Greek and Roman philosophy to German idealism and English romanticism to Quaker and Oriental mysticism. Often overlooked but equally influential in shaping his moral philosophy was the combined influence of his difficult childhood and his Puritan heritage.[9]

In 1811, when Emerson was only eight, his minister father died of tuberculosis, leaving the family destitute and dependent on charity. The congregation provided widower Ruth Haskins Emerson with a $500 annual pension and the privilege of living in the parish house for a time. Still, to meet expenses, she was forced to sell the family library at auction and to take in boarders over the years. Growing up in such "deprived" circumstances taught young Emerson the necessity of hard work, cooperation, frugality, and charity. He and his four brothers helped with the housework, performed odd jobs, and shared overcoats in winter. With few frills to distract him, Waldo, as he was called, developed during his youth a preoccupation with reading and thinking. He later credited the "iron band of poverty, of necessity, of austerity" with steering him and his brothers away from the purely sensual and "into safe and right channels," making them, "despite themselves, reverers of the grand, the beautiful, and the good."[10]

Learning was the one commodity in plentiful supply in the Emerson household, thanks largely to the commanding presence of Aunt Mary Moody Emerson. Aunt Mary moved in soon after the Reverend William Emerson died, and she exerted a powerful influence over the boys. Her domineering personality was a volatile combination of Puritan rigor and intellectual curiosity. It was said that she wanted everyone to be a Calvinist but herself, and this antinomian conservatism guided her eccentricity. "I love to be a vessel of cumbersomeness to society," she boasted. Raised herself in a household of "deep poverty," Mary Moody Emerson developed a fervent impatience with any false adornment. She despised the "feverish lust of notice" plaguing New England society. When Thoreau's mother, Cynthia, arrived for a visit wearing a bonnet highlighted with pink ribbons, Miss Emerson shut her eyes in disgust while they talked. After waiting several minutes for her guest to ask for an explanation, Mary Emerson finally grew exasperated and explained: "I don't like to see a person your age guilty of such laxity in dress."[11]

An avid reader of Milton, Plato, Coleridge, Byron, and Channing, Aunt Mary took it upon herself to instill both knowledge and ethics into her nephews. As she told a friend, "They were born to be educated." Aunt Mary introduced young Emerson to Oriental literature and classical philosophy, speculated with him about John Donne, and laughed at his riddles and puns in Greek. She also implanted in him a preference for the thoughtful life over the acquisitive life. In writing about her colonial Emerson ancestors, she reported: "They all believed in poverty and would have nothing to do with Uncle John of Topsfield who was very rich." One of their forebears "prayed every night that none of his descendants might ever be rich." Aunt Mary followed in this tradition and was forever counseling the boys to "Lift your aims" and "scorn trifles." When Emerson bought a cheap popular novel with six of his few pennies, she scolded him for his extravagance: "How insipid is fiction to a mind touched with immortal views." In a classic bit of understatement, he later said that Aunt Mary "gave high counsels."[12]

Once, when Waldo and his brother Edward supposedly gave their only loaf of bread to a pauper, Aunt Mary helped assuage their hunger by telling them of similarly benevolent sacrifices made by their "heroic" Puritan ancestors. Perhaps it was such experiences and such stories that led Emerson later in life to acknowledge "the debt of myself and my brothers to that old religion . . . which taught privation, self-denial & sorrow. A man was born not for prosperity, but to suffer for the benefit of others, like the noble rock-maple-tree which all around the villages bleeds for the service of man." Calvinist theology repelled Emerson, but the grandeur and virility of the early Puritans, their hardihood and total commitment to high spiritual and moral purposes, inspired him. The early colonists, he said, thought "life had something worth contending for. They lived and died for sentiments & not for bread alone." Puritanism, Emerson felt, in this way served as "an antidote to the spirit of commerce and economy." His reverential image of his spiritual ancestors taught him to elevate his sights and to use his time wisely. How "to spend a day nobly," he emphasized, "is the problem to be solved." If Emerson could not in good conscience sanction a revival of Puritan theology, he could recommend an updated version of the original Puritan ethic. "Let us shame the fathers," he pleaded, "by superior virtue in the sons."[13]

Family tradition initially led Emerson into the ministry, but by 1832 he had come to find the formalisms of the "cold and cheerless" Unitarian faith too confining. The tragic death of his young wife in 1831 heightened his disillusionment, and he resigned his pastorate at twenty-nine. After an excursion to Europe that included visits with Wordsworth and Carlyle, Emerson settled with his mother in Concord in 1834, living in the "Manse" that his grandfather had built before the Revolution. The next year he and his new wife, Lidian Jackson, relocated to a house on the Lexington road. There he was soon "imparadised." The house was nestled among two acres of stately pine and fir trees near the Concord River. It was also surrounded by an inviting countryside, and there Emerson found both solitude and solace. "In the woods," he discovered, "is perpetual youth."[14]

Emerson took walks almost daily. From his house he strolled down the river to Peter's Field or sauntered to Walden Pond, where he would sit on the bank for enchanted hours reading Goethe. The meadows, streams, hemlocks, and pines around Concord filled him with a sense of Providential immanence. All nature was metaphor to him, freighted with meaning and mystery. The countryside was indeed the poet's province, and in its beauty and wonder Emerson surmounted his melancholy and achieved the organic unity between the mental and the spiritual, the human and the universal, that characterized the romantic temperament. He thus rejected the Puritan idea that nature was "a howling wilderness," inhabited by the unredeemed, and therefore a force to be fought and subdued. Instead, he came to see the woods as a source of inner harmony and moral strength, a place suffused with divinity and beauty, waiting to enlighten and enliven all visitors. To Emerson, who always valued the seeing eye over the shaping hand, nature was to be contemplated, not conquered. By communing with nature, he wrote, man became "part and parcel with God," thereby approaching the ultimate simplification of life. Having discovered himself through nature, Emerson would now be the spokesman for young America, exchanging the gown of pastor for the frock coat of lecturer, ministering to "all who would live in the spirit."[15]

Thanks largely to the $1200 a year he received from a legacy provided by his first wife, Emerson developed in Concord the scholarly routine of intro-spection, writing, community service, occasional preaching, and frequent lecturing, for which he quickly became famous. Occasionally he felt some uneasiness about his unexpected source of income. "I please myself," he reassured his conscience in one of his journal entries, "with the thought that my accidental freedom by means of a permanent income is no wise essential to my habits." Emerson's Puritan strain ensured that he led a life of enlightened material restraint. His wife Lidian once said: "No one should take any more than his own share, let him be even so rich," and he later labeled this the "true doctrine." Inured to simple pleasures as a youth, he was easily contented as an adult. Emerson compensated for his own good fortune by sharing it with others, frequently inviting needy friends such as the Alcotts or Henry Thoreau to share his house and his beneficence.[16]

The moral philosophy that Emerson formulated in Concord was based on the same duality of man and hierarchy of values developed by the Greeks and later modified by the Puritans and Quakers. Like Aristotle, Winthrop, and Woolman, he believed that there were two selves—inner and outer, spiritual and material, imaginative and physical. Each is an essential aspect of human experience, but Emerson insisted that the inner self was ultimately superior. The care and culture of man's spirit was far more important than satisfying the political economy of his senses. This is not to say that he dismissed the material side of life lightly. At times in his essays, in fact, Emerson could be rhapsodic about the benefits of prosperity and technology, leading some readers over the years to label him a bourgeois apologist. In one of his most exuberant moods, Emerson found "money in its effects and laws, as beautiful as roses." He often heaped praise on the nation's entrepreneurial and engineering achievements, noting that American technology promised to "make the world plastic and to lift human life out of its beggary to a god-like ease and power."[17]

But this was the aesthetic, not the moralistic, side of Emerson speaking. He always maintained that money and technology were to be valued only for their *instrumental* qualities, for what they could contribute to the more noble pursuits of self-culture. "Trade was one instrument," he wrote in "The Young American," but "Trade is also but for a time, and must give way to somewhat broader and better, whose signs are already dawning in the sky." Though recognizing that the world of business was not intrinsically evil, he noted that it was too often considered an end in itself. The "general system of our trade . . . is a system of selfishness; is not dictated by the high sentiments of human nature; is not measured by the exact law of reciprocity; much less by the sentiments of love and heroism, but is a system of distrust, of concealment, of superior keenness, not of giving but of taking advantage." The "true thrift," he cautioned, "is always to spend on the higher plane; to invest and invest, with keener avarice, that he may spend in spiritual creation and not in augmenting animal existence."[18]

Emerson called this his "gradational ethic." In an essay on Plato he wrote that all "things are in a scale, and begin where we will, ascend and ascend." Emerson repeatedly explained to his listeners and readers that in stressing the primacy of thoughts over things he was not asking them to abandon their coarse labors and flee to the woods like Rousseau's "noble savage." The good life, he stressed, required more than "the crust of bread and the roof." It should include "the freedom of the city, freedom of the earth, traveling, machinery, the benefits of science, music and fine arts, the best culture and the best company." Emerson clearly recognized the benefits of a capitalist economy. The "end of culture," he explained, "is not to destroy this, God forbid!" Americans needed not to overthrow the economic order but to redress the imbalance that had developed between materialism and idealism in their pursuit of happiness. This meant instituting a thoroughgoing reform of domestic habits that "must correct the whole system of our social living." And such reform must "come with plain living and high thinking." By placing work and its rewards in the proper perspective, subordinating the material to the spiritual, man could achieve the higher level of being advocated earlier by Puritans, Quakers, and classical republicans.[19]

Emerson therefore shared Woolman's belief that leading the good life required neither external legislation nor institutional reforms but inner self-control, the ability to live within one's means in order to afford the luxury of contemplation and creativity. In his "Lecture on the Times" (1841), he praised the conservative reformers for their objectives but criticized them for their methods. They were relying too much on institutions, legislation, peer pressure, and other external "circumstances" to promote republican simplicity. Most of the self-appointed improvers of society, Emerson felt, apparently forgetting his own sermonizing tendencies, were so busy pointing out the faults of others that they neglected their own moral deficiencies. He referred to most reformers as "narrow, self-pleasing, conceited men, [who] affect us as the insane do. They bite us, and we run mad also."[20]

Emerson was especially sceptical of the many educational reformers dotting the New England landscape. "A treatise on education, a lecture, a system," he wrote, "affects us with a slight paralysis and a certain yawning of jaws." Nor was he enamored of those moral guardians advocating the domestication of manners and mores. "I suffer whenever I see that common sight of a parent or a senior imposing his opinion and way of thinking on a young soul to which they are totally unfit." His own family had taught him how to think rather than what to think, and this was Emerson's preferred approach, for his ideal of self-culture required the freedom of self-discovery. The domestication of culture "in the high sense does not consist in polishing and varnishing," but in "liberating oneself from acquired habits." He himself refused to specify any precise code of conduct that could be used as a universal standard in American homes and classrooms. Since to him intuition was the fount of truth, man needed to free himself as much as possible from external restraints in order to allow "new infusions" of the spirit of God to transform him."[21]

Here Emerson was obviously parting company with his Puritan forebears and reflecting the individualism so visible in his Aunt Mary. Moral instruction was done best, he argued, by benign example rather than by coercive dogmatism. "Cannot we let people be themselves and enjoy life in their own way?" While the conservators of culture were demanding conformity to their version of republican simplicity, Emerson was urging that "Whoso would be a man, must be a nonconformist." In a land of abundant opportunities and social diversity, the American, Emerson assumed, had the luxury of freedom of choice. If he wanted to engage in a life devoted to pursuits higher than the merely material, it was his choice to make. He "may fix his inventories of necessities and enjoyments on what scale he pleases, but if he wishes the power and privilege of thought, the chalking out of his own career and having society on his own terms, he must bring his wants within his proper power to satisfy."[22]

The self-reliance Emerson preached was in this sense quite distinct from tooth-and-claw individualism, for the thoughtful individual in his scheme must place clearly defined limits on economic activity where the latter did not. "It is better to go without," he asserted, "than to have them [possessions] at too great a cost. Let us learn the meaning of Economy." For him, frugality was merely a means to a noble end. Plain living was designed to lead to high thinking of one sort or another—intellectual, moral, spiritual. "Economy is a high, humane office, a sacrament, when its aim is grand; when it is the prudence of simple tastes, when it is practiced for freedom, or love, or devotion."[23]

Despite his frequent criticism of professional reformers, Emerson, like so many other spokesmen for simple living, could be interpreted as a social conservative preaching to those below him to be content with their material lot. He once advised, "If we will take the good we find, asking no questions, we shall have heaping measures." He never could identify with the intense practical problems of those who were literally hungry or physically mistreated by callous foremen. Yet to interpret Emerson as merely reflecting class bias is to ignore the fact that he spent much of his time lecturing those already successful on their need for simpler living. His experience dealing with Boston's social and cultural elite, for example, convinced him that possessions held in excess tended to become barriers to honest human relationships. People of means too often preferred to show visitors what they owned rather than what they thought. Emerson once imagined in his journal that if "Socrates were here, we could go and walk with him; but Longfellow, we cannot talk with; there is a palace, and servants, and a row of bottles of different colored wines, and fine coats."[24]

As he viewed American society in the 1830s and 1840s, Emerson saw far too many Longfellows cluttering their lives with the trappings of wealth. "It is a sufficient accusation of our way of living," he maintained, ". . . that our idea of domestic well-being now needs wealth to execute it." He agreed with those foreign observers who highlighted the excessive materialism of Americans: "We . . . set a higher value on wealth, victory and coarse superiority of all kinds, than other men, have less tranquility of mind, are less easily contented." A "vulgar prosperity" was corrupting the nation's moral vision, and it was largely to help remedy such a situation that Emerson directed much of his oratory and prose. In an early issue of the Transcendentalist journal, the *Dial*, he promised that the new magazine would serve as a forum for promoting "the new heroic life of man, the now unbelieved possibility of simple living, and of clean and noble relations with men."[25]

Emerson was an eloquent spokesman for contemplative simple living, and his words helped inspire a wide array of individual and group efforts to put into practice the ethic he preached. Like Channing, he took great pleasure in the "few hermits" who were expressing "thoughts and principles" that went against the grain of larger society's materialist conformity. But he was somewhat taken aback by the explosive manifestations of romantic simplicity. In a letter to Thomas Carlyle in 1840 he reported: "We are all a little wild here with numberless projects of social reform. Not a reading man but has a draft of a new community in his waistcoat pocket. George Ripley is talking up a colony of agriculturalists & scholars with whom he threatens to take the field & the book. One man renounces the use of animal food; and another of coin; and another of domestic hired service, and another of the State." Emerson himself retreated from such extremes and panaceas. "I do not wish to be absurd and pedantic in reform. I do not wish to push my criticism on the state of things around me to that extravagant mark, that shall compel me to suicide or to absolute isolation from the advantages of civil society."[26]

Emerson revealed his consternation at the eclectic applications of Transcendental simplicity in his response to the communal experiments at Brook Farm and Fruitlands. Brook Farm, founded in 1841 in West Roxbury, was ostensibly designed to put into practice the ideals that Emerson had promoted. Its residents were determined, as one of them wrote, "to secure as many hours as possible from necessary toil" in order to spend more leisure time "for the production of intellectual goods." The Brook Farmers were not countenancing primitivism, but hoped to provide "all the elegances desirable for bodily and spiritual health: books, apparatus, collections for science, works of art, means of beautiful amusements." Brook Farm's organizer, George Ripley, declared that the community was not intended to be a pastoral retreat but a revived "city on a hill." If "wisely executed," he promised Emerson, Brook Farm "will be a light over this country and age. If not the sunrise, it will be the morning star." Genuinely convinced that such enlightened communalism was the wave of the future, Ripley saw Brook Farm as providing a practical alternative for Americans oppressed by competitive capitalism and eager to pursue self-culture within a community of like-minded souls. Brook Farm, one visitor wrote, "aims to be rich, not in the metallic representation of wealth, but in wealth itself, which money should represent, namely, *leisure to live in all the faculties of the soul*."[27]

Certainly Emerson could not find fault with such elevated aspirations. He sympathized with Ripley's "noble and humane" intentions and initially was tempted to participate if he could be "sure of compeers of the right stamp." But when Ripley refused to give him such assurances and stressed his intention to promote a diverse group of settlers, Emerson balked. "I wish to break all prisons," he pointed out, and to him the eclectic collectivism of Brook Farm promised to be a "larger prison than his present domestic life." Moreover, Emerson disliked the idea of living in a community intentionally isolated from society. In Concord he already lived "in an agreeable neighborhood, in a town which I have many reasons to love."[28]

Utopian reformers such as Ripley, Emerson felt, failed to recognize that "we do not make a world of our own but fall into institutions already made & have to accommodate ourselves to be useful at all." He then admitted that such accommodation represented "a loss of so much integrity & of course of so much power." Obviously, Emerson's earlier praise of nonconformity had its limits. He did not intend to be taken so literally. Practically speaking, he asked, how "shall the world get on if all its *beaux esprits* recalcitrate upon its approved forms & accepted institutions & quit them all in order to be singleminded?" He feared that such perfectionist communities would inevitably become asylums. Emerson concluded that instead of turning their backs on the world, Ripley and his followers should disperse "and so leaven the whole clump of society."[29]

Perhaps Emerson was right. Or maybe he was being hypocritical. Whatever the case, Brook Farm was a significant expression of the romantic desire to pursue simplicity as an actual way of life, and the efforts of its residents should not be lightly dismissed. Most of them found considerable happiness and improvement there. Work was shared, compensation was equalized, and leisure time was devoted to contemplation and artistic creation. Although Nathaniel Hawthorne left the community because he felt overworked shoveling manure and found little time or energy to write, he was the exception. A Brook Farmer expressed the view of most of the residents when he wrote: "We were happy, contented, well-off and carefree; doing a great work in the world, enthusiastic and faithful, we enjoyed every moment of every day, dominated every moment of every day by the spirit of Brook Farm." Even Hawthorne later spoke of his "old and affectionately remembered home at Brook Farm" as being "certainly the most romantic episode in his life." Posterity, he predicted, "may dig it up and profit by it." Indeed, even though the Brook Farm experiment officially ended in 1849, it served thereafter as an inspiration for many later idealists interested in practicing communal simplicity.[30]

In his own household Emerson tried to "accommodate" the virtues of the Brook Farm experiment in greater self-sufficiency by cultivating a garden and by simplifying his domestic life. He reported in a letter to his brother in 1840 that he was "quite intent on trying the experiment in manual labor to some considerable extent & of abolishing or ameliorating the domestic service in my household." But neither Emerson's temperament nor his physical constitution was suited for such work. "God has given me the seeing eye," he was soon forced to admit, "but not the working hand." He finally decided that the ideal of agrarian self-sufficiency was a "whimsy . . . which infects us all like an influenza," but, alas, only a few hardy souls were capable of carrying it out. So he hired Henry Thoreau as his gardener and handyman. He also quickly abandoned his attempt at a vegetarian diet. Too bland, he said. And although Emerson claimed that he could do without domestic servants, his mother and his wife insisted that they could not.[31]

Emerson was supportive of Brook Farm's aims and enjoyed his visits to the community, despite his unwillingness to participate himself. But he was more disapproving of the Transcendentalist settlement at Fruitlands, a ninety-acre utopian farm community organized by the tirelessly quixotic Bronson Alcott.[32] Emerson considered Alcott one of his closest friends, but always prone to extremes. He could be a "tedious archangel." Alcott had moved to Concord from Boston in 1840 and had initially taken up farming in order to dissociate himself from the sins of urban commercial life. Unfortunately for Alcott and his family, however, he was a poor farmer. So he next tried manual labor as a woodchopper, but he soon decided that such menial work was essentially wage slavery, and he abandoned it as well. Meanwhile, his principled economic stance drew him deeper into debt and into the pockets of sympathetic friends, relatives, and neighbors. In a typically splendid rationalization, Alcott concluded that economic failure was in fact a virtue. As he explained, "transcendent excellence is purchased through the obloquy of contemporaries; and shame is the gate of the temple of the renown." When his wife Abigail pointed out to him that by repeatedly borrowing money from others, he, too, was engaging in a form of capitalist exploitation, Alcott quickly dismissed her logic, arguing instead that he was doing his benefactors a favor by drawing out their sympathies.[33]

Alcott's eventual solution to his vocational quest was to form a communal brotherhood that would cultivate a divine economy, laboring only enough to satisfy basic needs so as to devote most of their time to self-culture and group discussion. During a visit to England in 1842, Alcott suggested the founding of such a moral community to Charles Lane, an English journalist, reformer, and educator. Lane was enthusiastic about the idea, so much so that he agreed to finance the venture, and in 1843 Fruitlands was established outside the village of Harvard, Massachusetts. It was to be a community whose residents were not "so active to do, as sincere TO BE." This meant completely disavowing the market economy and engaging in subsistence farming and bartering. Thus, unlike the Brook Farmers, the Fruitlanders promoted ascetic, not simple, living. Alcott declared that Brook Farm was not "sufficiently ideal." Likewise, Lane declared that abstinence, not merely moderation, was the key to spiritual freedom and physical health. He and Alcott were, said William Henry Channing, the "Essenes of New England."

So, too, were most of the early residents of Fruitlands. Lane, his son William, and the Alcotts were joined by a handful of courageous, well-intentioned, but rather bizarre idealists, most of whom were fanatical purists about the body. Samuel Bower, for example, was a nocturnal nudist from England, who found moonbathing in the buff stimulating to the tactile senses. Another settler, Samuel Larned, a Rhode Island intellectual, was famous for having subsisted a whole year on a diet of crackers. He had also exhibited his eccentricity by traveling around New England swearing at everyone he met, since he believed that such indiscriminate profanity was not vulgar but liberating. Other members of the community included Joseph Palmer of No Town, Massachusetts, and a man named Abram Wood, who preferred to be called Wood Abram. There was also a character who had been "imprisoned in a mad house" by his relatives.[34]

This motley assortment of a dozen or so communal experimentalists refused to wear clothes made of cotton or wool because the former was the product of slave labor and the latter was forcibly taken from sheep. Hence they wore linen. The Fruitlanders also disdained "contaminated" foods such as root vegetables and all animal and dairy products. Salt was considered a dangerous luxury. Fruit was to be the staple crop, but there was never enough to go around, so cornmeal mush became the standard fare. Those violating the prescribed dietary rules were quickly disciplined. Anna Page, a young teacher and aspiring poet, was summarily dismissed from the community after it was learned she had eaten some fish while visiting a neighboring farm. "But I only ate a bite of the tail!" she tried to explain. "The entire fish had to suffer and die that you might eat its tail!" the fastidious Lane replied, and she was sent packing.[35]

The daily routine at Fruitlands was carefully structured. Each day was to begin at dawn with a plunge in the cold pond, followed by a music lesson and a breakfast of nuts and grains. The residents would then work at some "occupation" until noon, when they ate another vegetarian meal and followed it with some "interesting and deep-searching conversation" that "gave rest to the body and development to the mind." Late afternoon would bring more outside work, and the day was to end with supper and more discussion before the residents went to sleep on pallets. But this schedule was quickly discarded. The male Fruitlanders tended to spend more time cultivating their conversations than their crops. And Alcott's wife, Abigail, soon discovered that she and her daughters were doing the bulk of the work. "There was only one slave at Fruitlands," she recalled, "and that was a woman." Her daughter Louisa May remembered that the men of Fruitlands "were so busy discussing and defining great duties that they forgot to perform the small ones." That male spokesmen for the simple life too often forgot to acknowledge the crucial role played by womenfolk in making such an ethic possible was quite apparent to Abigail Alcott. "Miss Page made a good remark, and as true as good," she recorded in her journal, "that a woman may live a whole life of sacrifice, and at her death meekly says 'I die a woman.' But a man passes a few years in experiments of self-denial and simple life, and he says, 'Behold I am a God.'"[36]

Emerson was suspicious of an intellectual colony that was making the women do most of the work so the men could spend the day philosophizing. Alcott and Lane, he confided in his journal, "are always feeling of their shoulders to find if their wings are sprouting; but next best to wings are cowhide boots, which society is always advising them to put on." Emerson also disliked being periodically solicited to provide financial support for Fruitlands. He remarked that Alcott and Lane assumed that their "whole doctrine is spiritual, but they always end with saying, Give us much land and money."[37]

Although Emerson admired the singleness of purpose of the many scholarly and spiritual ascetics in the Western tradition, he could not advocate such a stringent code of conduct for American society at large. As he had concluded years before, "Ascetic mortification and unremitting martyrdom of all the sensual appetites, although far more innocent than the contrary extreme, is nevertheless unwise because it fails of the intended effect." Asceticism, he believed, too often became a fad or an eccentricity, rather than a self-effacing credo. And its practitioners too often developed an irritating hubris and intolerance. The last straw for Emerson was when Charles Lane arrived at his house, clad entirely in white linen, including even the lining in his shoes. After their principled guest left, Emerson told his wife that they must somehow rescue the Alcotts from such a madman. But the harsh New England winter saved the Emersons the effort. As the cold Canadian winds began to sweep across Fruitlands, the residents found themselves without adequate food or shelter. Lane thereupon sought refuge with the Shakers. Alcott was so depressed by the disintegration of his communal dream that he fasted for three days. Then, as if the recipient of a vision, he rose and led his family back to Concord.[38]

Enthusiasts such as Lane and Alcott prompted Emerson to declare that Transcendentalism in practice often gave him a headache. It "is the Saturnalia of Faith. It is faith run mad." Emerson also recognized the intellectual elitism inherent in Transcendentalism. He and his friends, he admitted, had little patience with the uneducated man in the street. They were suspicious of Catholics and snide toward the Irish. As Emerson confessed, "I like people who like Plato." But he realized that such a scholarly perspective could become too callous and insular. He described the limitations of the Transcendental outlook in an essay:

> See this wide society of laboring men and women. We allow ourselves to be served by them, we live apart from them, and meet them without a salute in the streets. We do not greet their talents, nor rejoice in their good fortune, nor

foster their hopes, nor in the assembly of people vote for what is dear to them. Thus we enact the part of the selfish noble and king detached from the foundation of the world.

By separating themselves from society in antiseptic philosophical and ascetic communities, the utopians, he felt, were turning their backs on society and evading their civic responsibilities. "Let our affection flow out to our fellows," he advised; "it would operate in a day the greatest of all revolutions."[39]

Brook Farm, Fruitlands, and the many other individual expressions of Transcendental ethics revealed the continuing ambiguity and power of the simple life. Plain living and high thinking encompassed a wide spectrum of behavior, and it was only a slight step from misplaced simplicity to mere eccentricity. One man's self-restraint was another's asceticism; one man's self-reliance was another's isolationism. Emerson's observations of such eclectic forms of the good life only reinforced his belief that his own version of temperate self-reliance was best. "Everything runs to excess," he contended, and a "sweet and sound life" required adopting the golden mean of the Greeks as the standard to follow. "The mid-world is best."[40]

Yet Emerson concluded that such a middle way could not be imposed effectively by legislative statute or public decree. Since we "boil at different degrees," each person must establish priorities and boundaries for himself. If that meant the creation of Brook Farms and Fruitlands and the emergence of dogmatic enthusiasts such as Charles Lane, Emerson was willing to accept such diversity. Thus, in speaking of Brook Farm, he remarked: "Let it live. Its merit is that it is a new life. Why should we have only two or three ways of life & not thousands and millions." He still preferred idealistic radicalism to materialist conformity. The impulse motivating such utopians, Emerson correctly recognized, was quite admirable, even though they occasionally expressed themselves in destructive ways. All the "forms of ultraism, blind and headlong as they seem, have yet a meaning which, if it cannot command assent, must at least preclude contempt."[41]

It was this attitude of respectful criticism that Emerson adopted in his relationship with Henry Thoreau. Initially, he thought that Thoreau had the potential to personify his ideal of a balanced life of self-sustaining work and self-examining thought. Emerson, the sedentary seer, was always inspired by men of practical abilities. "I like people who can do things," he said, and young Henry Thoreau, fifteen years his junior, could do a lot of things well—carpentry, masonry, painting, surveying, gardening. Short, lean, inwardly frail but outwardly tough and sinewy, he was a master of the woodland arts. Emerson admired his "muscle," his determination, and his simplicity. "My good Henry Thoreau made this else solitary afternoon," he noted in his journal, "sunny with his simplicity and clear perception." Emerson realized early on that despite Thoreau's "peculiarities," he "gives me in flesh & blood & pertinacious Saxon belief, my own ethics. He is far more real, & daily practically obeying them, than I." Indeed it was the growing disparity between Emerson's profession of Transcendental simplicity and Thoreau's pertinacious practice of it that eventually contributed to the growing rift between them during the 1850s. The two Concord philosophers agreed that the goal of life was to subordinate lower impulses to higher purposes; how best to do so was another matter.[42]

"Simplicity, simplicity, simplicity." This was Thoreau's repeated advice to his society. But he himself was by no means a simple man. From the pronunciation of his name to the enunciation of his beliefs, the author of *Walden* bequeathed a confusing legacy. Even Emerson never truly understood him. Over the years scholars have authoritatively portrayed Thoreau as a skulking misanthropist and a lover of humanity; as an individualist, collectivist, activist, recluse, pacifist, militant, stoic, epicurean.[43] Thoreau encouraged such contrasting interpretations. "Use me," he wrote, ". . . if by any means ye may find me serviceable." The dramatic, yet elusive quality of Thoreau's prose was accentuated by his consciously extravagant use of hyperbole and paradox. In a letter to a friend he once confessed: "I trust that you realize what an exaggerator I am.—that I lay myself out to exaggerate whenever I have an opportunity." In part Thoreau used artful exaggeration and contradiction to mask his own uncertainties. But he also employed such dramatic effects to get the attention of his reader, since "you must speak loud to those who are hard of hearing."[44]

Thoreau's intentionally provocative and contradictory mode of expression makes using him as an example of simple living somewhat treacherous. Several of his more extreme statements in his journal, lectures, and published writings do make him sound at times like a hermit and an ascetic rather than a prophet of the "middle way." Understanding Thoreau requires taking his words seriously but not always literally. As he once confessed, "Those things I say, others I do." By looking at what he *did* as well as what he *said*, one can see that his moral philosophy had more in common with the tradition of Protestant and republican simplicity than with the tradition of ascetic fanaticism.[45]

Admittedly, Thoreau did have a reclusive, iconoclastic temperament; he relished solitude far more than Emerson. That he showed no ambition for public accomplishment was always a distinct disappointment to Emerson, as was his lack of compassion. Unlike John Woolman, Thoreau was prickly as a hedgehog. His nature was acidic, and he had little patience with those who did not share his outlook. Thoreau's rugged idiosyncrasies and demanding personality made it hard, even for his friends, to feel comfortably close to him. As Emerson once said, many loved Henry, but few liked him.[46]

Yet with all his waywardness and dogmatism, exaggeration and contradiction, Thoreau remains the most conspicuous and persuasive exponent of simple living in the American experience. Why? Certainly the dramatic nature of his experience at Walden Pond has contributed greatly to his reputation. Perhaps even more important in explaining Thoreau's sustained influence is that he was a man who acted on his ideals rather than passively submit to social convention. Where Emerson spoke of self-reliance while surviving on a legacy, Thoreau earned his way by using his practical skills and by controlling his desires. "To be a philosopher," he argued in *Walden*, "is not merely to found a school, but to love wisdom so as to live according to its dictates a life of simplicity, independence, magnanimity, and trust. It is to solve some of the problems of life, not only theoretically, but practically."[47]

The living philosophy that Thoreau fastened upon as a young man grew out of the same basic sources that had shaped Emerson's outlook. His family circumstances and his Protestant heritage provided the raw ore for a moral ethic that would later be refined by his reading of Greek philosophy, Oriental religion, and Romantic literature. He grew up in a family whose economic straits were as pinched as Emerson's. His father, John Thoreau, began his career as a successful shopkeeper but went bankrupt in 1817. The "poor and hard pressed" Thoreau family then moved to Concord in 1823, where John began anew as a pencil-maker, sign painter, and jack-of-all-trades. But it was not until the 1840s that he enjoyed a stable and comfortable income. Henry remembered that his father had "pecuniary difficulties to contend with the greater part of his life."[48]

It may have been John Thoreau's life of "quiet desperation" in search of vocational success and financial solvency that in part influenced Henry to cut a different path. Unlike so many of his countrymen in similar circumstances, young Thoreau did not develop a consuming passion to work his way above his given condition. Instead, he came to appreciate how free and satisfying a life could be led with a minimum of money and status. In middle age he recalled that his greatest skill since childhood had been "to want but little." He was able early on to find pleasure in simple things and activities. He loved to hunt and fish and while away the afternoons in dreamy reverie. "I love to see anything," he later wrote, "that implies a simpler mode of life and a greater nearness to the earth."[49]

Thoreau's preference for rustic simplicity was in part the result of his complex relationship with his parents. Without pressing the psychological point too much, there does seem to be a connection between Thoreau's adult behavior and his ambivalent relationships with his father and mother. Cynthia Thoreau often expressed her desire that Henry become the social success his father was not. Assertive, outspoken, and conventionally ambitious for her children, Mrs. Thoreau apparently wanted them to achieve the stature of her father, Asa Dunbar, a Harvard graduate, lawyer, and civic leader. Henry was clearly dependent on his mother for attention and love, but at the same time he resisted her efforts to steer him toward a "respectable" career. By keeping his economic desires to a minimum and adopting a plain and frugal ethic, he could chart an independent course while at the same time avoiding his father's crippling indebtedness. And, by withdrawing to nature, he perhaps could find in Mother Earth the tender consolation and approval that he so much desired from Cynthia Thoreau.[50]

But other sources, of course, also contributed to the making of Thoreau's philosophy of living. As a young man, he immersed himself in Greek and Oriental writings, discovering in the process that the great exemplars of simple living were the "ancient philosophers, Chinese, Hindoo, Persian, and Greek." For such contemplative saints, he noted, virtue was "an intellectual exercise, not a social and practical one. It is a knowing, not a doing." Yet, at the same time that he came to admire such a contemplative simplicity, Thoreau, like Emerson, was also attracted to the strenuous piety of the Puritans. He was a hungry reader of William Bradford's history of Plymouth and other accounts of New England life, and he developed an intense admiration for the Puritans as a people of "simple . . . straightforward, prayerful" habits. Although he could not abide the institutional church, and quickly discarded the Calvinist emphasis on original sin, predestination, and Biblical sufficiency, Thoreau remained nonetheless deeply influenced by the Puritan conscience. "Our whole life is startlingly moral," he once asserted. Like the early colonists, he believed that body and soul were in a perpetual struggle for man's heart. True virtue resided with those who successfully resisted needless material and sensual temptations in order to concentrate on spiritual or inward development. The distinctive quality of a man's life "consists not in his obedience, but in his opposition, to his instincts." More than anything else, it was this Puritan strain of moral toughness leading to self-control that differentiated Thoreau, and, to a lesser extent Emerson, from most European romantics and later American "hippies" who preached instinctual liberation.[51]

Imbued with this Transcendental version of the Puritan ethic, Thoreau surveyed American life and concluded that the nation's fundamental problem was a loss of moral identity and proportion. While still a student at Harvard in the 1830s, he described the "commercial spirit" as a virus infecting his age. The United States was tragically becoming a society without moral distinction or unity, bent only on the "blind and unmanly pursuit of wealth." Thoreau sharply criticized those material optimists whose sole aim was to "secure the greatest degrees of gross comfort and pleasure merely." Cultural progress, he felt, was not keeping pace with mechanical progress. He could no longer even buy a blank note pad; all of them had lines for ledgerbooks. He was determined himself to avoid such short-sighted materialism, for he had a "desire to soar."[52]

Instead of seeking more wealth and more machines, man would do better, Thoreau contended, if he elevated his moral character. Doing so required an individual decision to revive the sense of "Puritan toughness" and higher purpose that he found so inspiring among his colonial ancestors. Yet it also required modifying the glorification of work itself. The emphasis of the founding generation on the duty of diligent work at one's calling may have been necessary during the starving time of the first settlements or the critical decades after the Revolution, but not in the midst of a thriving young America. Thoreau believed that national prosperity now offered Americans an ideal opportunity to work less in order to spend more time on the "things of the intellect and the soul."

This was a significant alteration of the traditional role played by work in both Protestant and republican simplicity. In a Class Day conference at Harvard in 1837 Thoreau indicated how different his perspective was from that of earlier American prophets of the simple life when he suggested that the "order of things should be somewhat reversed, the seventh should be man's day of toil, wherein to earn his living by the sweat of his brow; and the other six his Sabbath of the affections and the soul,—in which to range this widespread garden." Several years later, he repeated his theme: "Work, work, work. It would be glorious to see mankind at leisure for once."[53]

Young Thoreau was bent on devoting most of his time to his thoughts rather than his labors, but he had to subsist on something, and gaining even a little income required work of some sort. Thus he, too, confronted the vexing problem of choosing a vocation. When he graduated from Harvard in 1837, religion and business were the two prevailing career options. Unfortunately, he sighed, "neither the New Testament nor Poor Richard speaks to our condition." For him, the vocational dilemma was "how to make the getting of our living poetic! If it is not poetic it is not life but death we get." His father and too many others among his Concord townsmen, he had observed, were making themselves virtual slaves to the acquisition of money and things.[54]

Thoreau was determined not to follow the same worn path. But how? According to his close friend Ellery Channing, Thoreau asked his mother what profession he should choose. Always eager to shape his ambitions, she replied, "You can buckle on your knapsack, and roam about and seek your fortune." It was not what he wanted to hear. Tears welled up in his eyes, causing his sister Helen, who was standing nearby, to embrace him and say, "No, Henry, you shall not go! You shall stay at home and live with us." Henry had come to depend a great deal on his mother and sisters and the familiar community of Concord. It was his home, and he saw no reason to live elsewhere, despite his mother's advice. To this end he returned to Concord from Cambridge, and after a short stint as a public school teacher, he, along with his brother John, started a private academy. Thoreau took his students walking, rowing, and swimming, demonstrating in the process that learning was as much an experiential as intellectual activity. In 1841, however, his brother's failing health forced the closing of the school.[55]

It was just as well, for Thoreau had already grown tired of the mundane tasks of formal education. "I have thoroughly tried school-keeping," he reported, "but as I did not teach for the good of my fellow-men, but simply

for a livelihood, this was a failure." The New England schools designed by
Horace Mann and others, he believed, were intended more for vocational
and disciplinary training than for true self-enlightenment. As he later said,
"How vain to try to teach youth, or anybody, truths! They can only learn
them after their own fashion, and when they get ready. I do not mean this to
condemn our system of education, but to show what it amounts to." How
much better than the standardized curriculum was "a constant intercourse
with nature and the contemplation of natural phenomena." His own intuitive
experience in the huckleberry-field "was some of the best schooling I got,
and paid for itself."[56]

Yet if Thoreau was not satisfied with being an educator, what could he do
to make a living? At this point Emerson intervened. He had come to know
Thoreau very well since his return from college and was quite impressed by
his thoughtful, yet spartan personality. "I delight much in my young friend,"
Emerson wrote in his journal, "who seems to have as free and erect a mind as
any I have ever met." He invited Thoreau to participate in the Transcendental
Club meetings in his home, and their relationship deepened as the years
passed. By the early 1840s Emerson was lecturing so much out of town that
he found his household chores too taxing. He was also worried about leaving
his family alone for extended periods. So he offered Thoreau "his board &c
for what work he chooses to do," and in April 1841 Henry moved in with the
Emersons. There he occupied a small room at the head of the stairs, tended
the garden, took frequent walks with his host, played with little Waldo,
helped edit the *Dial*, and sampled widely in Emerson's large library.[57]

Still, Thoreau was not completely comfortable in the midst of such genteel
domesticity. In the fall of 1841 he wrote to a friend that he was "living with
Mr. Emerson in very dangerous prosperity." The problem of discovering a
self-sustaining, yet liberating vocation remained acute for Thoreau, and after
a short stint in New York trying to make a living as a writer, he began to
consider a life of simple sufficiency in the woods as a temporary option. His
Harvard classmate Stearns Wheeler had earlier built a shanty at Flint's
Pond, and Ellery Channing, even more daringly, had gone to live on the
Illinois prairie for a time. Although Thoreau had been invited to join Brook
Farm and Fruitlands, he, like Emerson, had declined. Thoreau admired
Alcott, calling him the "best-natured man" he had ever met, but he had no
interest in joining the settlers at Fruitlands. "I had rather keep bachelor's hall
in hell than go to board in heaven." He recognized the value of working
together to achieve common goals, but he was suspicious of the value of
living together in such corporate, regimented fashion.[58]

Since communal living in nature was not for him, Thoreau began looking
for a small farm to buy, only to discover that his meager capital was
insufficient. Then, in October 1844, when Emerson bought fourteen acres of

woodland sweeping down to the north shore of Walden Pond, Thoreau saw his chance. Although sceptical of Thoreau's experiment in isolated simplicity, Emerson eventually agreed that Henry could "squat" on the property in exchange for clearing part of it. Thus believing that a "man is rich in proportion to the number of things he can do without," Thoreau began building his cabin in the woods in March 1845 and moved in on Independence Day. Nature would now provide his path to an ideal world and an inner discovery. In this sense his Walden episode entailed an honest introspection that earlier prophets of simple living—Oriental, classical, Puritan, Quaker, republican—had repeatedly deemed necessary. The Revolutionary poet Philip Freneau, for instance, had written in 1782 that such self-reflection was essential to the maintenance of republican virtue. "Every rational man, let his business or station in life be what it may, should . . . at least once a year withdraw himself from the numerous connections and allurements that are apt to give us a too great a fondness for life; he should take time to reflect, as a rational being ought to do, and consider well the end of his being." Thoreau saw his Walden experience as accomplishing the same purpose. In the woods he could "live deep and suck out the marrow of life."[59]

Those who know *Walden* only by reputation too often assume that Thoreau lived at Walden Pond the life of a hermit bent on returning to the isolated condition of Adam. Yet it is important to remember that his famous hut was only a mile or so from town, within earshot of Concord church bells and the Fitchburg railroad, and so close to the Lincoln highway that he could smell the pipe smoke of passing travelers. By his own account he had "more visitors while I lived in the woods than any other period of my life." His little cabin rang "with boisterous mirth" on many an occasion. Almost every Saturday his mother and sisters made a special trip out to the pond to bring him something to eat. Thoreau kept up with life in Concord by reading the newspaper and by making trips to the town himself. "Every day or two," he remembered, "I strolled to the village to hear some of the gossip which is incessantly going on there. . . . I was even accustomed to make an irruption into some houses, where I was well entertained." Thoreau may have been a deliberately singular character, but he was not an anchorite.[60]

Nor was Thoreau's life in the woods as primitive as its popular image might suggest. He did not go to the Pond to "live cheaply nor to live dearly there, but to transact some private business with the fewest obstacles." The "private business" was initially the writing of his first book, *A Week on the Concord and Merrimack Rivers*. His broader purpose was to discover how many of the so-called necessities of life he could do without in order to experience the wonders of nature and the joys of self-culture. By setting out on his own and stripping away all pretense and superfluity, he could "first learn what are the gross necessaries of life and what methods have been taken to obtain them." Then he could begin to "entertain the true problems of life." If some mechanical aids or modern conveniences contributed to this goal, he saw nothing wrong with using them, as long as one did not become used by them. "Though we are not so degenerate but that we might possibly live in a cave or a wigwam or wear skins to-day," he wrote, "it is certainly better to accept the advantages, though so dearly bought, which the invention and industry of mankind offer." Since he had no desire to be truly primitive, he decided to make "the most of what means were already got." So, he borrowed Alcott's axe—which he conscientiously returned with a sharper edge—cleared his site, and then he built a cozy cabin of milled boards and brick, inserted two glass windows, shingled the roof and walls, and stocked the interior with a bed, desk, and books.[61]

Before moving to Walden Pond, Thoreau, like so many of the Transcendentalists, had often praised the simple life close to nature without specifying its practical meaning or appreciating its practical difficulties. In his journal he used the terms "poverty," "simplicity," "savagery," and "primitive" interchangeably. During his two-year bivouac, however, he learned that many of his preconceptions about life in nature were in fact misconceptions. Savagery and poverty and primitivism were not necessarily the conditions most conducive to virtuous living or elevated thinking. The Indians he met during his 1846 excursion in the Maine woods, for instance, were hardly the model examples of the good life he had once supposed. Earlier he had referred to the Indians' life as representing "practical poetry." They stood "free and unconstrained in Nature." That may have been the case centuries before, but the Indians he saw in Maine were "sinister and slouching fellows" who made but a "coarse and imperfect use . . . of Nature." He found them generally to be unreliable and slovenly characters. The savage, Thoreau admitted, was not the "child of Nature" he had pictured. "The fact is, the history of the white man is a history of improvement, that of the red man a history of fixed habits of stagnation." For all their simplicity, the Maine Indians lacked imagination and nobility.[62]

Nor did Thoreau find much nobility in the white woodsmen he met while at Walden. As he was walking across Baker Farm one day, a sudden rainstorm led him to take cover in a ramshackle hut rented by the Irish immigrant John Field and his family. Thoreau was shocked at the condition of Field's residence. The roof leaked, and chickens roamed freely about the hut's filthy interior. Field and his perspiring wife apparently worked hard but for nought. According to their own testimony, they remained constantly on the bare edge of survival. Thoreau took the opportunity of his unexpected visit to lecture Field "as if he were a philosopher, or desired to be one." He suggested that his Irish host could build his own hut for much less than he paid in rent. Moreover, by recognizing that coffee, butter, milk, fresh meat, and other expensive foods were not daily necessities, they would not have to work so hard and lead such a grueling life. "If he and his family would live simply," Thoreau felt, "they might all go a-huckleberrying in the summer for their amusement." Yet Field and his wife were not philosophers, and they could not see the advantages of the life Thoreau suggested. The simple life "was dead reckoning to them, and they saw not clearly how to make their port so." Thoreau finally decided that the Fields were born and bred for such myopic poverty, and there was little chance of broadening their vision. "Through want of enterprise and faith men are what they are, buying and selling, and spending their lives like serfs."[63]

Thoreau initially had a much higher opinion of Alek Therien, the French Canadian woodchopper and post-maker. The two met in the woods shortly after Thoreau finished his cabin. Therien was a skilled woodsman who, unlike John Field, could do without tea and coffee—even money itself—and still lead a genuinely joyful, self-sustaining existence. A man of "unalloyed mirth," he displayed a childlike exuberance for nature and a true satisfaction with his livelihood. "A more simple and natural man it would be hard to find," Thoreau remarked. Therien seemed to be the ideal Homeric peasant. And he was literate. If "it were not for books," he told Thoreau, he "would not know what to do [on] rainy days." The Canadian was unaffected in his manner and simple in his tastes, and Thoreau greatly enjoyed his company.[64]

Yet the longer Thoreau observed Therien, the more he came to realize that his new friend's aspirations were not much more elevated than Field's. The animal in him was not truly counterbalanced by an intellectual or spiritual side. His only books turned out to be an "almanac and an arithmetic," and the Canadian was ignorant of every major social issue, from the factory system to monetary reform to antislavery. Thoreau commented that "I never, by any maneuvering, could get him to take the spiritual view of things; the highest that he appeared to conceive of was a simple expediency such as you might expect an animal to appreciate." And, he concluded, such "is true of most men."[65]

This was a frustrating realization for Thoreau. The Transcendental outlook saw a moral or spiritual sentiment inherent in all people, regardless of station or circumstance. If such "low and primitive" men, he pined, would only "feel the influence of the spring of springs arousing them, they would of necessity rise to a higher and more ethical life." Heretofore, he had tended to interpret such untapped sensibilities as the result of materialism's smothering spiritualism. But Field and Therien demonstrated that even people leading simple lives could lack an enlivened moral sense and intellectual curiosity. Simplicity could mean barrenness; plain living did not necessarily lead to high thinking.[66]

Thoreau's observations of Indian life and his encounters with Field and Therien helped him begin to recognize the complexity of the simple life as an actual way of living. After leaving Walden in 1847, he gradually decided that there was indeed more to simplicity than living a spartan existence in the woods. "There are two kinds of simplicity," he explained; "one that is akin to foolishness, the other to wisdom. The philosopher's style of living is outwardly simple, but inwardly complex. The savage's style of living is both outwardly and inwardly simple." The savage, he went on to say, "lives simply through ignorance and idleness or laziness, but the philosopher lives simply through wisdom." Thoreau clearly preferred the philosopher's version. The truly "heroic spirit" could never be satisfied *merely* with the "innocent pleasures of country life."[67]

Thus, like Rousseau before him, Thoreau concluded that the wilderness and the primitive life it afforded were periodically necessary but not permanently sufficient conditions for the good life. This revelation in part led him to return to Concord. The wilds provided inspiration and physical challenge, but a "civilized man must at length pine there, like a cultivated plant, which clasps its fibres about a crude and undissolved mass of peat." Thoreau still found in himself "an instinct toward a higher, or, as it is named, spiritual life, and another toward a primitive rank and savage one, and I reverence them both." Satisfying both instincts, however, required that he live not in permanent isolation at Walden Pond but in what he called a "border life" between primitivism and civilization. That way he could "combine the hardiness of the savages with the intellectualness of the civilized man."[68]

Ideally, then, the simple life could best be led not in the wild or in the city, but in "partially cultivated country" like Concord. Periodic excursions into the wilderness would provide necessary raw materials for the soul, and civilization would provide necessary finished products. Total immersion in either, however, was dangerous. In this way, Thoreau approached the golden mean of the Greeks. The "temperate zone," he wrote, "is found to be most favorable to the growth and ripening of men." Until his death in 1862, Thoreau would live a simple life in Concord, helping manage the family business during his father's illness, and earning his own income as a part-time surveyor, all the while saving most of his time for sauntering, writing, and reading. He had found, he told Horace Greeley, that six weeks of manual labor would support him for a year.[69]

Thoreau's twenty-six months of camping, hiking, gardening, and thinking at Walden Pond had given him a more profound appreciation of himself, the simple life, and Concord. His town and family provided him with much needed emotional warmth. "Here are all the friends I ever had or shall have, and as friendly as ever," he wrote in his journal. "A man dwells in his native valley like a corolla in its calyx, like an acorn in its cup. *Here*, of course, is all that you love, all that you expect, all that you are." Though he still needed the "tonic of wildness," he now recognized that civilization did represent "a real advance in the condition of man. . . . though only the wise improve their advantages." As long as he could keep his wants under control and thereby keep his workday requirements to a minimum, he would be satisfied living in larger society. "I am grateful for what I am and have," he acknowledged to a friend in 1856. "My thanksgiving is perpetual. . . . O how I laugh when I think of my vague indefinite riches. No run on my bank can drain it—for my wealth is not possession but enjoyment."[70]

Thoreau still believed that a person would be better off "raising what you eat, making what you wear, building what you inhabit, burning what you cut or dig." And it was this spartan strenuosity that made him increasingly impatient with Emerson's genteel simplicity, just as Emerson in turn had been critical of Longfellow's affluence. But Thoreau had come to see by the 1850s that most Americans no longer had the luxury of pursuing his version of self-sufficiency, even if they were so inclined. Modern mass society constantly warred against pure simplicity. "Those to whom you are allied insanely want and will have a thousand other things which neither you nor they can raise and nobody else, perchance, will pay for." Hence he published *Walden* in 1854 not in order to convince everyone to abandon their factory jobs and city homes and build isolated cabins in the forest. Too many reformers, he believed, were intent on imposing their prescription for moral reformation on others. "Alas! this is the crying sin of the age, this want of faith in the prevalence of a man. Nothing can be effected but by one man."[71]

Although in his dealings with others, Thoreau frequently appeared sanctimonious, in *Walden* he explicitly denied having any single program for simple living that could be universally applied. "I would not have anyone adopt *my* mode of living on my account. . . . I would have each one be very careful to find out and pursue *his own* way, and not his father's or mother's or neighbor's instead." His expressed purpose was not so much the specification of means as it was the elevation of ends. As he had learned from watching John Field and Alek Therien, the standard of living was not nearly as important as the object of living. Responding to a young disciple's request to "*teach* men in detail how to live a simpler life," Thoreau again emphasized that he had "no scheme about it,—no designs on men at all; and, if I had, my mode would be to tempt them with fruit, and not with the manure." In elaborating on this point, he observed:

> To what end do I lead a simple life at all, pray? That I may teach others to simplify their lives?—and so all our lives may be *simplified* merely, like an algebraic formula? Or not, rather, that I may make use of the ground I have cleared, to live more worthily and profitably? I would fain lay the most stress forever on that which is most important—imports the most to me,—though it were only (what it is likely to be) a vibration in the air. As a preacher, I should be prompted to tell men, not so much how to get their wheat bread cheaper, as of the bread of life compared to which *that* is bran.

In *Walden*, therefore, Thoreau was fundamentally preaching the advantages of self-culture, not writing a how-to book. Simplify your life, yes, he said over and over again, but do it in your own way.[72]

Thoreau knew, however, that most Americans would not follow his advice. They were far more interested in high living than in high thinking. "We see mankind generally either (from ignorance or avarice) toiling too hard and becoming mere machines in order to acquire wealth." The mature Thoreau had no illusions about contemplative simple living being taken up by the masses or by the wealthy classes. He shared Emerson's opinion that it "is hard to be simple enough to be good." As Thoreau stressed, "there never was and is not likely soon to be a nation of philosophers, nor am I certain it is desirable that there should be."[73]

Yet such an appreciation of the difficulty of the simple life as a societal ethic did not deter Thoreau, Emerson, and many other Transcendentalists from greeting the outbreak of the Civil War with tempered optimism. They were, after all, idealists at heart, and they could not help succumbing to the promise of societal regeneration provided by such a national crisis. In the same way that colonial spokesmen had viewed the Revolutionary struggle with Great Britain as a stimulant to public and private virtue, the romantics saw the Civil War producing a moral revival in the process of resolving the sectional dispute and the tragedy of slavery. As William Henry Channing predicted in 1861, it would serve as the "Providential method of national redemption," a "holy war" tempering the public soul with the noble virtues of sacrifice and honor. The southern abolitionist and Transcendentalist Moncure Conway reported after visiting Concord in the summer of 1861 that Thoreau was "in a state of exultation about the moral regeneration of the nation" that would undoubtedly accompany the sacrifices on the battlefield.[74]

Emerson was even more excited about the prospects of a war-induced moral awakening. He had long believed that American character was growing flabby in the midst of economic prosperity and personal liberty. In 1843 he had written that "Americans have too much freedom, need an austerity, need some iron girth." Twenty years later he saw the Civil War as providing such a disciplining event. The sacrifices required by the conflict would revive a self-denying spirit and elevate the priorities of the American people above crass economic gain. The "moral aspect" of life would again become important. He saw the struggle as a means to "restore intellectual & moral power to these languid & dissipated populations." Martial conflict on such a vast scale would produce a new generation of spartan philosopher-heroes who would help renew the virtues of the Puritans and Quakers: "A new Socrates, or Zeno, or Swedenborg, or Pascal, or a crop of new geniuses, like those of the Elizabethan age, may be born in this age, & . . . bring asceticism & duty & magnanimity into vogue again."[75]

Interestingly enough, many of the conservative spokesmen for simple living adopted the same outlook toward the war, despite their ardent opposition to the "eccentric" social philosophy of the Transcendentalists. In the wake of the disaster at Bull Run, the New England Brahmin Charles Eliot Norton saw in the military crisis a formidable new instrument to foster a patrician version of simple living:

> It is well to face up to the fact at once, that this generation is to be compelled to frugality, and that luxurious expenses upon trifles and superfluities must be changed for the large and liberal costliness of a noble cause. We are not to expect or hope for a speedy return of what is called prosperity; but we are greatly and abundantly prosperous, if we succeed in extending and establishing the principles which alone can give dignity and value to national or individual life, and without which, material abundance, success in trade, and increase in wealth are evidences of the decline rather than of the progress of the state.

Similarly, the editors of *Harper's Monthly* insisted in December 1861 that the experience of military struggle was one of the best means of instilling in the common man the age-old virtues of frugality and self-discipline. The "boasted cure for an age of luxury is war, and we are ready to allow that the discipline of the camp is a wonderful check upon effeminacy and self-indulgence."[76]

With the outbreak of fighting, many orthodox Yankee ministers revived the old Puritan technique of interpreting such social crises as evidence of moral and spiritual decay. The editor of the *American Presbyterian and Theological Review* maintained that in abandoning the "republican simplicity" of the fathers in favor of "style and luxury and extravagance," Americans had provoked God to bring down upon them his judgment in the form of the ultimate national calamity—civil war. Yet if such excesses had helped cause the conflict, the martial struggle itself might help remove them. A Philadelphia minister suggested as much in 1861: "This war promises to arrest in a measure the extravagance and parade, the epicureanism and effeminacy into which we are so fast running. It puts our young men upon a training which will nourish their manly virtues. It inculcates, as no moralist could, lessons of economy, of moderation, of patience, of self-control." For such patriots, the Civil War was not so much about slavery in the South as it was about degeneracy in the nation as a whole.[77]

Even in the South, where high living had become by the 1850s the expressed ideal among the planter-merchant elite, the needs of war produced a rather striking revival of classical simplicity. George Fitzhugh, the outspoken apologist for the slave system, explained to his regional confederates that the social benefits of superfluous consumption during peacetime became vices during periods of war:

> We have shown that luxury promotes civilization; but economy and frugality must also be practiced, even by the rich, else there will be no fund laid up for future contingencies. . . . In this life we are always steering between Scylla and Charybdis. Our virtues daily degenerate into vices by being pursued too far; for

> vice is but virtue in excess. Just at this time our duty is plain enough. Self-denial, economy, frugality, and parsimony should be practiced. . . . The rich set the fashions. In times of peace and plenty, it is mean in them not to live sumptuously; they encourage industry and skill, and promote civilization by doing so. But now, a different duty devolves on them. Let them show the example of self-abnegation, of cheap and simple living. Let them dress in homespun and encourage home industry. . . . Let them imitate Roman simplicity, Roman courage, and Roman patriotism.

The editor of the *Southern Literary Messenger* likewise welcomed the ennobling effects of war. He expressed the hope, however, that the classical simplicity promoted by the conflict would represent not a temporary but a permanent refining of character. Through the suffering and "chastening of which we stand so much in need," a "higher, purer standard of manliness would be substituted in place of the commercial estimate of virtue now existing."[78]

Thus, both northerners and southerners, conservatives and romantics, saw the Civil War as a purifying and strengthening event. But as the Revolution had shown, wars maim ideals as well as people. Just as the struggle for independence had failed to produce a prolonged societal commitment to republican simplicity, the Civil War also dashed the hopes of those Americans who expected the conflict to promote a sustained moral revival. Their dreams of social purification were proven illusory long before Appomattox. After the firing on Fort Sumter, many northerners rushed not to join the ranks but to bid on the many contracts for supplies and equipment issued by the government. Judge Thomas Mellon observed in 1863 that such "opportunities for making money had never existed before in all my former experience." That same year, when his son James, then a young lawyer in Milwaukee, asked his father's permission to enlist, Judge Mellon replied: "Don't do it. It is only greenhorns who enlist. Those who are able to pay for substitutes do so and no discredit attaches. I had hoped my boy was going to make a smart, intelligent business man and was not such a goose as to be seduced from his duty by the declamations of buncombed speeches."[79]

Such economic opportunism led the editor of the *Princeton Review* to note in 1864 that, while many citizens were making real sacrifices for the war effort, there was little evidence of such public spiritedness among the affluent. "Our opulent classes, and those who have profited largely by the war . . . have not generally curtailed their expenditures or their luxuries. Many who have become suddenly rich, have outrun all precedent in voluptuous self-indulgence, vulgar extravagance, and ostentatious expenditure." Edward Everett, one of the most popular political orators of the mid-nineteenth century, was similarly disappointed in the conduct of his fellow citizens. He reported that extravagance, "as tasteless as it is otherwise reprehensible—is growing upon us, and consuming . . . the substance of the country." To win the war, he concluded, a "reform is needed, on the part of both sexes, and in many things beside foreign luxury."[80]

The North won the war, of course, but the nation emerged from the conflict with no viable commitment either to republican or romantic simplicity. The "energy of the nation," Emerson commented, "seems to have expended itself in the war, and every interest is found as sectional & timorous as before." In a letter to Carlyle in early 1866, he repeated his disillusionment: "We were proud of the people, and believed they would not go down from this height. But peace came, and every one ran back into his shop again." Instead of the war producing a Socrates or a Pascal, it spawned a Jay Cooke and a Jay Gould. Peace ushered in not a golden era of renewed social restraint and individual morality but a gilded age of entrepreneurial scrambling and political corruption. In the process, the simple life as a societal ethic was pushed even farther from the realm of practice into the realm of memory.[81]

CHAPTER SEVEN

Patrician Simplicity—At Bay

After the Civil War the United States was one nation again, but within the next half-century it was a nation transformed. No sooner had the fighting ended than the forces of modernity recovered their momentum, and the country resumed its transition from a predominantly rural society and agrarian economy to a highly structured urban-industrial civilization. The scope, pace, and complexity of American life increased dramatically during the second half of the nineteenth century, and the decentralized Jeffersonian republic of small farmers, mechanics, and merchants faded into American mythology. Technological innovations greatly enhanced industrial productivity and personal mobility, migration westward expanded the scale of social activity, and the influx of immigrants from southern and eastern Europe brought growing ethnic, racial, and cultural tensions. By the end of World War I, modern metropolitan America had arrived. "We cannot all live in cities," Horace Greeley argued, "yet nearly all seem determined to do so."[1]

The Gilded Age, as the decades after the Civil War came to be known, was an era of large affairs and large imaginings. In 1866 Senator John Sherman told his brother William Tecumseh that the war gave "a scope to the idea of leading capitalists, far higher than anything ever undertaken in this country before. They talk of millions now as confidently as formerly of thousands." Everything about postwar American life, in fact, seemed to be getting larger and more impersonal. A manufacturing sector of small, owner-operated workshops and factories still primarily dependent on skilled workers evolved after the Civil War into a system of mass production utilizing large numbers of unskilled laborers and dominated by huge trusts under the control of a handful of finance capitalists. Big business, big labor, big cities, big farms— all were quickly becoming the norm rather than the exception. During a visit to his native America in 1905, the expatriate novelist Henry James saw the "will to grow . . . everywhere written large, and to grow at no matter what or whose expense."[2]

What in large measure accelerated such growth was the lure of wealth. Opportunities for making easy money seemingly abounded in the postwar era. Mark Twain, who himself was often lured into speculative ventures, asked in 1871: "What is the chief end of man?—to get rich. In what way? dishonestly if he can; honestly if he must. Who is God, the one only and true? Money is God." A beneficent God, he might have added, since national and per capita wealth increased significantly during the Gilded Age, despite the periodic depressions endemic to modern industrial capitalist societies. The maturation of the economy also spawned a growing new middle class— clerks, salesmen, managers, government employees, technicians, salaried professionals—as well as a sharp rise in the number of very rich. In 1861 there were only a few dozen millionaires in the country; by 1900 there were more than four thousand. The vast fortunes accumulated by such titans of industry and finance stirred both the ire and envy of large segments of the public. American boys were told in countless success manuals and school texts that they, too, could rise to such heights through hard work, sobriety, and pluck. By the end of the nineteenth century, a student of such literature has written, "the dominant concept of success was one of opulent materialism competitively won."[3]

The popularity of such a success myth as well as the onset of modern urban-industrial society served to challenge even further the relevance of the simple life as either a societal or personal ethic, and during the Gilded Age the earlier pious and civic standards of virtue were more than ever displaced by entrepreneurial valuations of the good life. "The character of our nation is highly complex," William Dean Howells confessed in 1878. After the war, he explained, "new wants were invented, prudence and simplicity of life went out of fashion, and habits were formed and sentiments adopted which have wrought most important changes" in American life and aspirations. Indeed. Throughout the second half of the nineteenth century, the efforts of republican moralists to use the home and school to preserve traditional values failed to keep increasing numbers of farmers, villagers, and immigrants from flocking to factories and cities in search of higher wages and higher living.[4]

At the same time, Transcendentalism, as one of its proponents observed in 1876, was "manifestly on the decline." As early as 1859 Emerson had lamented the fading of the movement. "I have been writing & speaking what were once called novelties, for twenty five or thirty years, & have now but one disciple." It is hard to be a Transcendentalist all the time, as Santayana once observed, and by the 1860s the apostles of Transcendental simplicity had begun to die off or turn to other interests. After the Civil War, Emerson increasingly suffered from aphasia, Orestes Brownson and Sophia Ripley converted to Catholicism, while Brook Farm's George Ripley became a wealthy journalist, famous for his lavish champagne parties. Bronson Alcott was one of the few original Transcendentalists who persisted in his Platonic ways. Throughout the postwar era, supported by his wife and children, he continued to lead a life of contemplation and conversation. Clearly, the Transcendental temper was out of place in the Gilded Age. The carnage of the Civil War and the collapse of Radical Reconstruction dismayed sensitive consciences. Likewise, the rise of Darwinian naturalism cast serious doubts about the romantic vision of nature. Octavius Frothingham recalled the transition that took place in his own thinking: "The scientific view . . . succeeded to the transcendental, and I began to walk by knowledge, steadily and surely, but not buoyantly any more." No longer preoccupied with promoting social change, he and other aging romantics longed for social stability and the "quiet ways of culture" as the nineteenth century progressed.[5]

Yet despite the fact of modern complexity and the fading of Transcendental optimism and romantic naturalism, determined proponents of simple living and traditional folkways remained persistent throughout the Gilded Age and after. The trauma of modernization generated not only the well-known organized political responses of farmers, laborers, socialists, and anarchists, but also a wide array of individual reactions and alternative programs, some of which held in common a desire to promote simple living. As with their ante-bellum predecessors, proponents of enlightened restraint during the second half of the nineteenth century remained quite diverse in both their motives and their methods. Some continued to reflect a paternal conservatism in looking to institutions to impose republican simplicity upon American youth. Frederick Law Olmsted, for example, sustained the emphasis of Jefferson and Downing on moral architecture and landscaping with his urban parks. And the cult of domesticity also remained a prominent feature of Victorian culture.

At the same time, a few spokesmen for simplicity, such as Walt Whitman, retained a transcendental naturalism coupled with a democratic idealism, putting their faith in the moral sentiments and noble aspirations of the American people. As Whitman said in 1871, "Singleness and normal simplicity and separation, amid this more and more complex, more and more artificialized state of society—how pensively we yearn for them! how we would welcome their return!" For them to return required that the powerful forces of materialism be "met by at least an equally subtle and tremendous force-infusion for purposes of spiritualization, for the pure conscience, for genuine esthetics. . . ." Otherwise, modern civilization, "with all its improvements, is in vain, and we are on the road to a destiny, a status, equivalent, in its real world, to that of the fabled damned."[6]

One prominent group of patrician intellectuals, centered in Boston but represented in other parts of the country as well, practiced a refined simplicity that combined attributes of both conservatism and romanticism. Self-consciously identifying with the outlook of the Revolutionary generation of

Augustan statesmen-philosophers, these "best men" considered themselves a natural aristocracy of virtue and culture. Henry and Brooks Adams, George William Curtis, Richard Watson Gilder, E. L. Godkin, Thomas Wentworth Higginson, Oliver Wendell Holmes, William Dean Howells, William James, James Russell Lowell, Charles Eliot Norton, Barrett Wendell, and other like-minded intellectuals saw their role as that of a saving remnant, imbued with an abiding sense of public duty and a presumptive sense of moral and intellectual superiority.

Curtis, the former Brook Farmer turned editor of *Harper's Weekly*, explained that the patrician intellectuals were "visionaries who hold that morality is stronger than a majority." Men of classical learning and aesthetic sensibility, mostly Harvard or Yale graduates and products of old-line New England families, the "Brahmin" intellectuals were a fraternal band of cultivated gentlemen who took seriously the ideal of pursuing the good, the true, and the beautiful. Henry Adams expressed the sense of brotherhood felt by the members of the group when he commented in a letter to his brother Charles in 1862 that "what we want is a *school*. We want a national set of young men like ourselves or better, to start new influences not only in politics, but in literature, in law, in society, and throughout the whole social organism of the country—a national school of our own generation."[7]

These custodians of culture, much like their counterparts in England—Matthew Arnold, Thomas Carlyle, and John Ruskin—were intent upon asserting their authority as moral spokesmen for the nation. As Henry Adams admitted, "he thought himself a rather superior person," and most of his intellectual friends exhibited a similarly exalted notion of themselves. Adams and the others considered it their responsibility as decent, intelligent, and tasteful men to teach culture, manners, and probity to the nation's middle and upper classes. In politics they were Liberal Republicans and, later, independent Mugwumps, preoccupied with promoting civil service reform and electing their kind to public office. Although some of them had been abolitionists, they were not active social reformers during the Gilded Age. Their goal was to promote political honesty and high culture, not proletarian causes; they had little interest in, or understanding of, the untutored masses. Charles Francis Adams, Jr., once observed that "I don't associate with the laborers on my place." Doing so, he added, "would not be agreeable to either of us." Throughout the Gilded Age, most of these intellectuals remained thoroughly contemptuous of both agrarian and worker protests. They usually combined support for a public policy of economic liberalism with a personal ethic of cosmopolitan simplicity. Through the uncorrupted operation of the marketplace, they assumed, the economy would prosper, and through their cultural guidance as leading editors, writers, lawyers, and professors, such prosperity could be used to elevate the taste and morals of the nation. They would be, as William James said, the "yeast-cake for democracy's dough."[8]

This new generation of northeastern patricians took for granted their role as a secular priesthood ministering to the moral and cultural needs of the public. The common folk, Charles Eliot Norton contended, could not set their own moral standards because they "sit in the dark night of ignorance and know little of the light of love and faith." The masses must have their moral vision "stimulated by the few who have been blessed with the opportunities, and the rare genius fitting them to lead." Norton and his circle clearly wanted to lead the populace back to the enlightened values of the eighteenth century. When a Frenchman asked Lowell how long the United States would endure, he replied: "So long as the ideas of its founders remain dominant."[9]

Yet if these Brahmin intellectuals were conservative elitists in their social outlook and political gentility, preferring the security of tradition over the idealism of revolt, they were romantic individualists in their stress on the desirability of personal freedom (within prescribed bounds) and in their fondness for country life. They reflected a transcendental distaste for organizations and institutions. William James spoke for many of his peers when he declared: "My bed is made; I am against bigness and greatness in all their forms, and with the invisible molecular moral forces that work from individual to individual." In their methods of moral improvement, then, the patricians preferred exhortation and example over legislative means. Republican virtue depended not "upon forms and institutions of government," Norton insisted, "but upon the moral dispositions of the individuals who compose a nation." And it was up to the "best men" to assume the responsibility of helping the people elevate those moral dispositions. "You must not legislate," Godkin stressed, "but *teach*." An older and in some respects more conservative Emerson, to whom several of these "gentle reformers" looked for inspiration, referred to the group in 1867 as the "few superior and attractive men" who must "calm and guide" a "barbarous age."[10]

In the aftermath of the Civil War, this fastidious New England intellectual elite eagerly took up the mantle of cultural guardianship bestowed upon them by Emerson. Initially, they exuded a Jeffersonian and Emersonian confidence that they could use their influence to see that the nation's growing prosperity was put to good and noble uses. They believed it possible to make real the republic of virtue dreamed about in 1776. The newly reunited America, Godkin wrote, was to be a "promised land." Curtis was equally buoyant, emphasizing after the war that "materially and morally, the country was never more hopeful, never fuller of promise, than now." Many of them repeated Jefferson's dream that it was possible to join a dignified affluence with high thinking in an expanding America without necessarily bringing about the social degeneracy that both theologians and moralists had deemed an inevitable result of prolonged prosperity.[11]

America in the aftermath of the Civil War thus seemed to offer a further opportunity to elevate the material basis of the ideal of self-culture. The patricians felt that high thinking in the form of intellectual inquiry and artistic creativity could be pursued without resorting to pinched austerity. The refined Massachusetts politician George Frisbie Hoar, after proudly noting that he had been raised in the "pure, noble and simple society" of Concord, explained that modern Americans had the luxury of choosing genteel simplicity over austere simplicity: "Plain living and high thinking are doubtless the best conditions of human life. But if the living be too plain, the thinking will not be high. The soul and body will not often hunger or thirst at the same time. Mean and base surroundings without the refinements of taste, are apt to degrade alike the intellect and the moral nature." Hoar and the other patrician intellectuals were proposing a conservative Emersonian simplicity of the drawing room and library rather than of the garret or hut.[12]

The assumption of Woolman and Thoreau that the freedom for high thinking could be gained best by scrupulously plain living seemed an unnecessary burden to such spokesmen, most of whom enjoyed the security of inherited wealth. Oliver Wendell Holmes spoke frequently of the contributions to enlightened simplicity that money could make. In his masterpiece of urbane wit and wisdom, The Autocrat of the Breakfast-Table (1858), he referred to himself and his group of New England intellectuals as forming a natural aristocracy. "Of course money is its corner-stone," he admitted. "But now observe this. . . . Money buys air and sunshine, in which children grow up more kindly, of course, than in close back streets; it buys country places to give them happy and healthy summers, good nursing, good doctoring, and the best cuts of beef and mutton." At the same time he recognized with his Puritan ancestors that money had its negative side as well. Too often, young people succumbed to the "intoxicating vision of gold and glory" and strayed from the virtuous path of high thinking. Yet the dangerous lure of wealth and splendor was no reason to sanction asceticism or even a Thoreauvian simplicity. "Beware of making your moral staple consist of the negative virtues," Holmes advised. "It is good to abstain, and teach others to abstain, from all that is sinful or hurtful. But making a business of it leads to an emaciation of character, unless one feeds largely also on the more nutritious diet of active sympathetic benevolence."[13]

James Russell Lowell, the poet, editor, and professor of modern literature at Harvard, agreed with Holmes that simplicity need not mean primitivism. Lowell, who clearly never understood Thoreau, argued that there was no reason to go "back to the age of flint and steel" portrayed in Walden. All "which is most admirable in the primitive simplicity of an heroic age is quite capable of being reproduced in a modern and highly cultivated state of society." E. L. Godkin, the outspoken editor of the Nation, likewise maintained that the old classical republican fear of national prosperity was no longer relevant. No other nation, he said, was as historically committed to the "virtues of frugality and simplicity" as was the United States. Yet Godkin now emphasized the possibility of "constructive luxury," provided that it was governed by refinement and "within the limits prescribed by religion and morality." He envisioned a national future of great material abundance "controlled and directed to a very high order of cultivation, both intellectual and aesthetic, and perhaps richer, more varied, and more original in many of its manifestations than any that had been seen in modern times." Still, Godkin wryly commented in paying tribute to the old ideal, every congregation and every community ought to have "at least one model of Christian simplicity."[14]

The patrician intellectuals were cheered by the way in which several of their newly rich countrymen demonstrated the positive effects of wealth on culture and society. Of these patrons of culture none was more visible in asserting nor more generous in supporting the material basis of high thinking in the late nineteenth century than Andrew Carnegie. The classic example of the rags-to-riches myth, he had risen by force of will and shrewdness from immigrant bobbin boy to become the richest man in the world by the turn of the century. Yet the successful Carnegie was a man both driven and repelled by his acquisitive desires. No religionist he, the Scottish weaver's son nevertheless brought with him to the United States a spiritual discomfort about money. His business success plagued his conscience so much in December 1868 that he underwent a rather remarkable self-examination. While staying at the fancy Hotel St. Nicholas in New York, he spent an evening alone in his suite reflecting on his economic and personal progress. The year had been a quite prosperous one for him. "Thirty-three and an income of 50,000 per annum." But he pledged that his good fortune would thereafter be directed not toward further accumulation but toward promoting the good of society. In language reminiscent of a Winthrop, Mather, or a Woolman, he vowed: "Beyond this never earn—make no effort to increase fortune, but spend the surplus each year for benevolent purposes. Cast aside business forever, except for others."[15]

A princely income now within his grasp, Carnegie promised that he would henceforth devote his time to self-culture and public service. He wrote in his journal that in two years he would resign his business affairs, move to Oxford, receive a "thorough education," and then settle in London and spend the rest of his years as a journalist writing on behalf of pressing social issues such as illiteracy and poverty. Carnegie's language was earnestly serious and morally orthodox:

> Man must have an idol—the amassing of wealth is one of the worst species of idolatry—no idol is more debasing than the worship of money. Whatever I engage in I must push inordinately; therefore I should be careful to choose that life which will be the most elevating in its character. To continue much longer overwhelmed by business cares and with most of my thoughts wholly upon the way to make more money in the shortest time, must degrade me beyond hope of permanent recovery.

Carnegie was aware of the historical pitfalls of "long-continued prosperity," the chief of which was "the reign of luxury and vice it breeds." And he struggled with the same troubling question that John Adams had asked Jefferson: how could a society that offered such abundant opportunities for the acquisition of wealth avoid encouraging a purely materialistic cast of mind? Carnegie, however, thought he had discovered the answer. Through creative public philanthropy and private self-culture, the wealthy could make their riches serve rather than subvert republican values.[16]

Carnegie, of course, never went to Oxford, nor did he call a halt to his business operations in two years. On the contrary, he grew ever more enmeshed in managing the growth of his business empire. Instead of allowing his personal income to level off, he saw it increase geometrically as the years passed. By 1900 Carnegie's annual income was estimated at $40,000,000. The process of empire-building and the accumulation of personal wealth were intoxicating stimulants that the steel baron found irresistible. Nevertheless, Carnegie in his more reflective moments still felt there was much more to the good life than the making of money. Although he did not live up to his resolves of 1868, he never completely abandoned his ideal of self-culture and public benevolence. By the late 1880s, as social tensions and labor violence mounted around the country, he found himself dwelling more and more on the social role of the millionaire in modern society.[17]

The result of such ruminations was his famous essay, "Wealth," published in the *North American Review* in 1889. It is a fascinating document, presenting at once a defense of the new industrial order and a plea for a new form of simple living for the wealthy. Carnegie began by defining the issue at hand: "The problem of our age is the proper administration of wealth, so that the ties of brotherhood may still bind together the rich and poor in harmonious relationship." In this way he restated the puzzle of prosperity that had long troubled both Christian and republican moralists. As he recognized, however, the dramatic gap between the very rich and the very poor that had developed in the modern industrial era added special gravity to the issue. But Carnegie was quick to point out that any sentimental longing for a pre-capitalist society was no answer. In referring to the unequal distribution of wealth in the United States, he asserted: "Much better this great irregularity than universal squalor. The 'good old times' were not good old times. Neither master nor servant was as well situated then as today." The capitalist system, for all its unfortunate aspects, he argued, remained the best program for promoting the material welfare and individual liberty of all. "We accept and welcome, therefore, as conditions to which we must accommodate ourselves, great inequality of environment; the concentration of business . . . as being not only beneficial, but essential to the future progress of the race."[18]

After upholding the sanctity of the prevailing socio-economic order, Carnegie then went on to develop what he thought was a new version of the simple life, one specifically directed at the very wealthy. The older Christian and classical ideal, he observed, was no longer applicable to living conditions in modern America. Instead of imitating heroic figures such as Christ, Woolman, Thoreau, or Tolstoy, affluent Americans needed to adopt "modes of expressing this spirit suitable to the changed conditions under which we live." The entrepreneur should feel free to make his fortune, Carnegie maintained, but only under certain conditions. The man of wealth must take care to "set an example of modest, unostentatious living, shunning display or extravagance; to provide moderately for the legitimate wants of those dependent upon him; and, after doing so, to consider all surplus revenues which come to him simply as trust funds which he is called upon to administer." Such a statement would have pleased John Winthrop, Cotton Mather, and William Penn, each of whom had insisted that wealth itself was not evil, only the love of wealth. They had also stressed a similar ethic for the man of riches to follow, making sure that his surplus wealth was used to serve the community rather than himself alone.[19]

Yet there were elements of Carnegie's program that many Christians, then and since, have found less commendable. When Carnegie went on to specify the types of charitable giving deemed worthy of the philanthropist, he disavowed any sympathy for those at the bottom of the social scale. The "pauper is a social leper," he declared, without initiative or ability, and, as Herbert Spencer had demonstrated, the "rotten apple must be removed." The primary consideration of the benevolent millionaire, therefore, "should be to help those who will help themselves." This dictum he translated into aid for free libraries, universities, public parks, hospitals, and other similar institutions.[20]

Through his "gospel of wealth," Carnegie transformed the crass pursuit of private gain into a magnanimous enterprise on behalf of the "better" public. The businessman's moral duty under Carnegie's new concept, therefore, was not to limit his entrepreneurial instincts but "to increase his revenues. The struggle for more is completely freed from selfish or ambitious taint and becomes a noble pursuit. Then he labors not for self, but for others; not to hoard, but to spend. The more he makes the more the public gets." In large measure Carnegie fastened on such a philanthropic work ethic as a means of solving his increasingly worried conscience. He later explained that by living simply and giving generously, the rich "can, perhaps, also find refuge from self-questioning in the thought of much greater portion of their means which is being spent upon others."[21]

Carnegie's essay understandably attracted much attention. Most commentators praised him for his generosity and sense of public spiritedness, but a few questioned the paternalism inherent in such a gospel of wealth. Others raised a more pointed objection. Carnegie's scheme was narrowly focused on the dispensing of the surplus wealth of a few; it took for granted the original maldistribution of wealth that occasioned such philanthropy. "The ethical question of today centres, I am sure," one theologian asserted, "in the distribution rather than the redistribution of wealth." Still, most critics were willing to admit that if every rich man followed Carnegie's prescription of simple living and generous giving, then indeed society would be much improved.[22]

Yet such a pristine "gospel of wealth" was in fact practiced by only a relatively few enlightened entrepreneurs. Carnegie himself began a concerted program of philanthropy and self-culture as he was increasingly withdrawing from active participation in business affairs. He eventually distributed over $300,000,000 in America and Scotland. At the same time, he established cordial friendships with many of the world's leading intellectuals and artists, including Kipling, Matthew Arnold, and Paderewski. A journalist who visited Carnegie in Scotland found him to be "at bottom a man of great simplicity, not only in his tastes and pleasures, but in his instinctive attitude toward things." From what the reporter gathered during his two-day visit, Carnegie had not worn his soul in piling up his millions nor had he hardened his heart toward others. In this respect, he seemed "the precise antithesis of the conventional 'moneyed man.' Wealth so far from having spoiled him seems hardly to have affected him; he wears it as lightly as a flower."[23]

But some might wonder about such characterizations of Carnegie's "simple" and "unostentatious" life. Although he dressed modestly and avoided gaudy entertainments, Carnegie did feel the need for a Fifth Avenue mansion, a private yacht, and a huge castle in Scotland surrounded by 32,000 acres, complete with a golf course, fish hatcheries, and a glass-enclosed swimming pool. Even the King of England came to tour Carnegie's much publicized feudal domain. Despite his repeated assertion that it was a disgrace for a man to die rich, Carnegie at his death still controlled an estate worth almost $30,000,000. Carnegie made no statement more fanciful than when he asserted that the "modern millionaire is generally a man of simple tastes and even miserly habits," spending "little upon himself." Perhaps this was true in the case of a Peter Cooper, an Abram Hewitt, or a George Peabody, but for the vast majority of *nouveaux riches*, flagrantly luxurious living was the norm. One writer observed that "where one rich man appreciates the true use of wealth, a hundred regard it only as an instrument for luxurious indulgence and vulgar display." For all his good intentions and good deeds, Carnegie the self-cultured philanthropist was an eccentric. His peers among the financial and industrial titans tended to be gaudy plutocrats narrowly intent upon spending their wealth on themselves. J. P. Morgan baldly announced that he "owed the public nothing."[24]

As Thorstein Veblen and others demonstrated, the conspicuous consumption of the affluent during the late nineteenth century bordered on the ridiculous. The behavior of new urban economic elites during the Gilded Age seemed to bear out the age-old predictions of republican moralists that excessive wealth brings excessive degradation. The parvenu barbarians had arrived. Lacking any sense of patrician taste and viewing the city more as a marketplace than a commonweal, the industrial and commercial barons sought to buy prestige and dignity. Examples abound of their social excesses and reckless spending. One tycoon gave a lavish dinner in honor of his dog and presented the mutt with a diamond collar worth $15,000. At a party at Delmonico's restaurant in New York the guests smoked cigarettes wrapped in $100 bills. Mrs. William K. Vanderbilt spent $250,000 for a dress ball held in her Fifth Avenue chateau. Then there was the notorious Bradley Martin gala at the Waldorf Astoria in 1897, so extravagant in its imitation of the court at Versailles that accounts of it "dazed the entire Western world."[25]

If the rich were not attending such parties, they were relaxing in monumental mansions overlooking the cliffs at Newport, atop the hills of San Francisco, along Chicago's Lake Shore Drive, on New York's Fifth Avenue, and down the "Main Line" in Philadelphia, mansions that were a far cry from Andrew Downing's "tasteful" villas. The owners of such homes spared no expense in producing palatial estates as magnificently vulgar as those owned by the barons and crowned heads of Europe. The prevailing architectural style among the rich was neither the chaste simplicity of Greek classicism nor the picturesqueness of the English Gothic. Instead, wealthy Americans embraced a gaudy eclecticism. Plain mid-Victorian homes were rejected in favor of "gingerbread" houses, overladen with ornamental scrollwork, fluted and carved windows, door frames, and lintels. Cupolas, corner towers, and conical turrets sprouted above the cityscape.

The colossally self-indulgent behavior of the "robber barons" served to symbolize for many distressed observers of the social scene all that was wrong with modern urban-industrial America. The "gospel of grab" rather than the "gospel of wealth" ruled the day, and in the midst of the self-congratulatory optimism of the economic boosters, there emerged a rising chorus of discontent during the last quarter of the nineteenth century. Disgruntled farmers and factory workers struggled to form cooperatives, and proposals to regulate railroads and control trusts flooded state legislatures and Congress. The journalist-turned-social-prophet Henry George proposed that the disparity between rich and poor could be eased by placing a "single tax" on the increase in land values. Equally popular was the utopian scheme outlined by the novelist Edward Bellamy whereby selfishness would be replaced by cooperation, and the state would control the means of production. Other diagnoses and programs of action were put forward by anarchists, socialists, and communists.[26]

The Mugwump intellectuals were equally dismayed at the growing division of the classes and the rising power of ruthless businessmen. A few of them, in fact, were transformed by the stark contrast between rich and poor in the new industrial order and began openly sympathizing with the working classes. William Dean Howells, for example, was a transplanted Ohioan who, as an editor of the *Atlantic Monthly* and as a novelist of growing repute, mixed comfortably with Godkin, Norton, Lowell, and the cultural elite of Cambridge and Boston. Like Samuel Clemens, his close friend, Howells made a lot of money, and also like Clemens he remained preoccupied with its meaning, as the satirization of money-lust in the writings of both men exhibits. The violent Haymarket riot in Chicago in 1886 served as a turning point in Howells's career, for he was so shocked by the event and the kangaroo trial of the anarchists that he was galvanized into active criticism of the prevailing social order.[27]

In clarifying his own attitudes in the face of the growing class strife in the country, Howells was directly influenced by his reading of the Russian novelist and humanitarian Leo Tolstoy, and he, too, came to advocate a form of Christian socialism and simplicity. A newly enlightened Howells agreed with Tolstoy that Christ "really meant the young man of great possessions to give up his worldly goods when he said so, and that He taught a political economy in no wise impossible or mistaken." Thereafter he steadfastly believed that "most of the good things come from the mean of life which is rightly praised as the golden mean." Yet at the same time that he embraced the Tolstoyan ideal, Howells struggled vainly with the implications of such a creed for his own genteel life. "Words, words, words! How to make them deeds. . . . With me they only breed more words." Since, as Howells freely admitted, he could provide through his own way of living neither "an example of nor an incentive" to Christian simplicity, he would try to do so through characters in his novels. In the process, he departed from Brahminism and joined the social activists of the younger literary generation.[28]

The patrician intellectuals shared Howells's disgust at the crass materialism pervading the Gilded Age, but they did not join him in becoming "fur-lined socialists." Lowell was filled "with doubt and dismay" at the "degradation of the moral tone" in American life, and he found himself wrestling with the same self-doubts as Howells. Actually, it was his reading of Howells's *A Hazard of New Fortunes* (1890), in which the elder Dryfoos appears as a man of the soil and simple tastes whose Pennsylvania Dutch virtues are corrupted by the sudden acquisition of wealth, that led Lowell to reassess his own social conservatism. Speaking of the novel to a friend, he wrote that a "noble sentiment pervades it, and it made my inherited comforts here at Elmwood discomforting to me in a very salutary way." Yes, the clue to solving the social crisis must be in some form of social cooperation, but Lowell doubted its appearance in the face of a rapidly growing, ethnically diverse population. Nor was he willing to put any faith into the socialist schemes "of which I have looked, for I should be bored to death by the everlasting Dutch landscape. Nothing but the guillotine will ever make men equal on compulsion."[29]

Most of the other Brahmins adopted Lowell's perspective. They had little sympathy for either the agrarian or proletarian movements, nor did they approve of much of the regulatory legislation put forward by "mistaken humanitarians." Yet, in a pattern remarkably similar to that of Albert Gallatin and the disillusioned republican expansionists of the early nineteenth century, they did find themselves disavowing their original postwar assumption that a flowering of culture and virtue would automatically accompany rapid economic growth. The same E. L. Godkin who in 1865 had noted the cultural benefits of luxury was within a few years bemoaning the excesses of the rich. New York City, he wrote in the *Nation*, was being flooded by a "gaudy stream of bespangled, belaced, and beruffled barbarians. . . . Who knows how to be rich in America? Plenty of people know how to get money; but . . . to be rich properly is, indeed, a fine art. It requires culture, imagination, and character."[30]

Unfortunately, Godkin admitted, most of the men of new wealth he had encountered lacked the "restraints of culture, experience, the pride, or even the inherited caution of class or rank." He found further evidence for such a generalization as early as 1869, when Commodore Vanderbilt, who loved to boast that he had read only one book, erected a hugh bronze statue of himself in his New York Central Freight Depot. To the *Nation*'s editor, this was the height of arrogance. There, "in the glory of brass, are portrayed . . . the trophies of a lineal successor of the medieval baron that we read about, who may have been illiterate indeed; and who was not humanitarian; and not finished in his morals." Godkin regretted that more of his countrymen did not make "sufficient objection to [such] a display of unmitigated and unmitigable selfishness." He had no grievance against men being wealthy, but too often, as in the case of Vanderbilt, they were illiterate and unrefined men, devoid of artistic taste. Our "modern rich men," he concluded, "know little of the possibilities of luxury."[31]

Godkin admired the Peter Coopers and Andrew Carnegies among the wealthy, but he quickly came to see that they were truly exceptional. Most self-made men were not self-cultured men. A "very large proportion" of businessmen "know no more, read no more, and have no more to say than the bricklayer and the plumber." If the subjects of stocks and strikes were ruled out, he wondered, what would the captains of industry and finance have to say at dinner? "Would there be much to talk about except the size of the host's fortune, and that of some of the others present?" Equally irritating to Godkin was the tendency among the monied and rising middle classes to presume a veneer of culture. He coined the term "chromo-civilization" to describe the American emphasis on purchasing culture rather than cultivating a discriminating aesthetic sense. In his jaundiced view, the public's artistic standards never rose above the level of Currier and Ives prints.[32]

Godkin's growing distaste for the new rich reflected his old-fashioned belief that money must always be viewed as an instrument of culture and civic service rather than merely as a means of self-gratification or social grandstanding. In 1865, before being offered the post at the *Nation*, he had told a friend that he felt the "need to make money, so as to secure me at an early period what I have always longed for—leisure and liberty to choose my own work." Editing the *Nation* fortunately provided him with his wish—a stable income, a challenging job, and the chance to exercise his mind on behalf of the public good. In 1870, when Charles Eliot offered him a professorship at Harvard, he declined, observing that "I don't think my value to the community would be as great, as a professor as an editor." But Godkin the editor worried that the lavish style of living of the wealthy was making it harder for gentry intellectuals to sustain their own accustomed comforts. The feisty Irishman could get quite exercised about such matters. In his notebook he scribbled a verse from Wordsworth:

> Rapine, avarice, expense
> This is idolatry; and these we adore;
> Plain living and high thinking are no more;
> The homely beauty of the good old cause
> Is gone.

Godkin especially criticized the wealthy for paying such high wages to their servants, thus forcing the people of middling income to pay their help the same.[33]

That the newly affluent were too often illiterate and unrefined ruffians who spent money both lavishly and garishly caused Godkin and many other patrician intellectuals to revive the old fears of materialism corrupting virtue in a republic. "We have learned, by sharp experience," Curtis declared in 1876, "that prosperity is girt with peril." During their frequent conversations about the behavior of the monied classes, Curtis and his fellows reinforced each other's prejudices and dismay. Godkin, in a letter to Norton in 1871, reported that "Howells has just breakfasted with us. . . . He talks despondently like everybody else about the conditions of morals and manners." Godkin told an English friend a few years later that "Norton and I used at one time to have such gloomy talks over the future of modern society late at night in his library that the story got about Cambridge that the dogs used to howl in sympathy with us." Heightening their anxieties was the growing social unrest during the last quarter of the century. The increasingly vociferous laboring classes and city poor, especially the frightful growth of "alien" immigrants from southern and eastern Europe, threatened not only the social but cultural order. The Brahmins felt that the intemperate behavior of the masses showed the same deplorable sensual indulgence and lack of refinement exhibited by the wealthy and middle classes.[34]

These developments were of great moment to the discreetly elegant and increasingly gloomy Charles Eliot Norton, who edited the *North American Review* before becoming the first professor of fine arts at Harvard. Like his close friend Godkin, Norton was a prominent spokesman for refined taste and genteel moral standards who at the time of the Civil War and just after still felt a patrician obligation to serve and improve humanity and had entertained modest hopes for American democracy. The people had demonstrated their capacity during the war for sacrificing selfish interests on behalf of a noble cause, and the "example of a strong, rich, prosperous republic" initially excited him. Rather quickly, however, he came to share his friends' deepening pessimism about the possibilities for cultural greatness in a nation grown too rich, too corrupt, and too democratic. In 1869 he questioned "whether our period of economical enterprise, unlimited competition and unrestrained individualism is the highest stage of human progress."[35]

A trip abroad soon thereafter confirmed Norton's doubts, as he compared the cultural achievements of pre-modern Europe with those of modern America. His friendships with Arnold, Carlyle, and Ruskin reinforced Norton's belief that urban-industrial mass society was fast smothering high culture. "Of all the civilized nations," he decided, the United States was "the most deficient in the higher culture of the mind." American abundance had "offered the most splendid opportunities to human energies," but the people were either too busy or too dull-witted to focus on the serious cultivation of the arts. Wealth was now being sought "not only as a means to other ends, but as itself an end." The "prevalence of vulgarity," he concluded, "is a national disgrace."[36]

Norton's colleague at Harvard, the philosopher William James, was another member of this cultured elite disgusted by the vulgarity and callousness of the American rich. In a letter to his brother Henry, he described a potential donor to the university as a "real Balzackian figure—a regular porker, coarse, vulgar, vain, cunning, mendacious, etc., etc." James considered the lust for money as such, without any moral, useful, or tasteful purpose to direct its use, invariably degrading. Its conspicuous display in the mansions of Newport was "repulsive." Equally he deplored "the moral flabbiness born of the exclusive worship of the bitch-goddess SUCCESS. That—with the squalid cash interpretation put on the word success—is our national disease." Americans, James lamented, had come to "despise any one who elects to be poor in order to simplify and save his inner life."[37]

When comparing the rich and the poor, James was much concerned with the attitudes of men toward their own economic conditions. He discussed this question at length in *The Varieties of Religious Experience*, remarking that a basic theme in human affairs had always been the opposition "between the men who *have* and the men who *are*." The gentleman "in the old-fashioned sense," James asserted, had always been a man of property, but "he never has identified his essence with . . . possessions but rather with the personal superiority, the courage, generosity and pride supposed to be his birthright." The poor, on the other hand, had their own kind of heroism, a dogged devotion to daily toil for necessary ends devoid of ulterior motives. The patrician James emphasized his moral by saying that "lives based on having are less free than lives based either on doing or on being." A laborer of James's time might have found such remarks patronizing; one of the late twentieth century would probably find them simply absurd.[38]

James, though an alert and concerned observer of American life, clearly lacked any sophisticated appreciation of modern complexity, especially the economic realities which underlay the class antagonisms and social problems. In this sense he resembled his hero Emerson. Once, after chastising Godkin for being too critical of the Knights of Labor, he quickly retracted his remark, explaining that "I never dare to trust myself now when you're agin me." Like that of most others in his circle, James's diagnosis of contemporary social ills was myopic. He and the patrician intellectuals never saw clearly the hard social facts that critics such as Henry George and Karl Marx fixed upon with such clarity. Where Howells recognized in the Haymarket riot the explosiveness of the "labor question," James dismissed the event as the lawlessness of "a lot of pathological Germans and Poles." He labeled the typical social reformer a "plebeian cad," whose proper "sphere is with the masses struggling into the light, not with us at Harvard."[39]

Still, James was much more sympathetic to the plight of the working class than most of his fellow Mugwumps. Like Jefferson, who once said that the nation needed a little revolutionary ferment from time to time, he saw in the increasing rebelliousness of the workers "a most healthy phase of evolution, a little costly, but normal, and sure to do lots of good to all hands in the end." James similarly glorified the constructive energies and enthusiasms in all men. He shared Jefferson's belief that everyone possessed an innate moral sense. The "feeling of the innate dignity of certain spiritual attitudes and of the essential vulgarity of others is quite inexplicable except by an innate preference of the more ideal attitude for its own pure sake. The nobler thing *tastes* better, and that is all we can say." His own discovery of the power of the individual will in lifting himself out of a prolonged bout of melancholia during his twenties and early thirties convinced him that man was a morally free agent capable of determining his own fate. Circumstances, he innocently claimed, posed no insurmountable obstacle to human aspirations. James thus concluded that the "labor question" was at base an issue of individual motivation rather than a reflection of systemic flaws or environmental determinism. People who consciously accepted and surmounted deprivation, toil, and pain, he argued, achieved a higher level of humanity than others.[40]

James therefore sympathized with the views of Tolstoy on the dignity and sanctification of manual labor. But, at the same time, he insisted with Thoreau that labor itself was not ennobling; the spirit in which the labor was done determined one's quality of being. No rational person would want to be condemned permanently to "hard, barren, hopeless lives," without some redeeming grace, some ideal or "inner springs" to move the spirit. "The backache, the long hours, the dangers," he wrote, "are patiently endured—for what? To gain a quid of tobacco, a glass of beer, a cup of coffee, a meal, and a bed, and to begin again the next day and shirk as much as one can."

Monuments were built for soldiers, James contended, not for laborers, because the soldiers had died for ideals, whereas "laborers are supposed to have followed none." Marxists and trade unionists would bristle at such ivory-towered candor. And others might question James's own commitment to the simple life he advocated. Like Emerson, James lived a life of genteel simplicity. "It is true," he stressed, "that so far as wealth gives time for ideal ends and exercises to ideal energies, wealth is better than poverty and ought to be chosen." An inheritance from his father along with a substantial income from lecturing and teaching enabled James to buy a spacious home in Cambridge, a summer retreat in New Hampshire, and a rustic camp in the Adirondacks. His affluence also enabled him to take frequent excursions to Europe, entertain often and graciously, and send his children to expensive private schools. Still, he felt that in most cases wealth endangered rather than enhanced moral character. The "desire to gain wealth and the fear to lose it," he contended, "are our chief breeders of cowardice and propagators of corruption." James thus counseled the classic "middle way" to Americans, urging them to "abstain from both extremes, excessive mortification being as unreal and unworthy as mere desire and pleasure." Wisdom, he concluded, was in "knowing what to overlook."[41]

This was also the message that Charles Eliot Norton tried to present in his Harvard classroom. During the Gilded Age he decided that America's colleges and universities represented the main defense "against the ever-rising tide of ignorance and materialism." As he told Godkin, "the Nation & Harvard & Yale College seem to me almost the only solid barriers against the invasion of modern barbarism & vulgarity." Professors, Norton decided, must train young Americans to "seek for wisdom as better than wealth," and to his own students he presented models from the past for them to emulate. One student recalled that Professor Norton "tells us it were better for us had we never been born in this degenerate and unlovely age." Greek culture, Norton said, offered a clear "lesson of moderation, of self-control, of sweet, simple, temperate living, of which we stand in need in these days of eager haste, of complex interests, of restlessness of spirit, of nervous over-excitement." But "this football generation" of students, he sighed, was incapable of appreciating the merits of such past cultures. Narrowly utilitarian and sensual in their outlook, the younger generation were intent on pursuing the tempting economic opportunities modernity offered them.[42]

Disillusioned with his students and his society, Norton increasingly retreated to his summer home at Ashfield, a small rural village nestled among the hills of northwestern Massachusetts. "I am a farmer up here," he beamed, "and like it better than being a professor." In a letter to Charles Darwin, Norton observed that his farmer neighbors in Ashfield had somehow been able to retain the old virtues of classical republicanism—"the simplicity of manners, the vigor of character, and the general intelligence which were characteristic of early New England, before the flood of Irish immigration set in, and before the gold in California and Australia had begun to corrupt and vulgarize the world." The isolated town represented the ideal republican community envisioned earlier by Jefferson. It was homogeneous, orderly, stable, and beautiful. Norton wrote Ruskin that it "is pleasant to live where everyone has self-respect, where there are no differences of condition."[43]

Ashfield had thus escaped the perils of modernity. It suffered neither a class of paupers nor a ruling plutocracy. Most residents were farmers and shopkeepers, and nearly all were landowners. "One could write Massachusetts idylls or a New England 'Arcadia' in this happy tranquil region of the world," Norton reported to George Curtis. "Ashfield has neither telegraph nor railroad, and but one mail a day. . . . The scenery all around is delightful, with the mingled charms of fresh wild nature and cultivation of cheerful farms." In Ashfield, Norton found the serenity and beauty he felt were absent in metropolitan America. John Jay Chapman described Norton's idyllic life in Ashfield as constituting "that rarest of all phenomena in America, the relation of the man of intellect to the soil." Another friend characterized Norton's country simplicity as a "moderate ideal—indeed, the old classical ideal of a pleasant home in a smiling country, with books, friends, children, dogs, horses, fields, and a garden and trees. He remembered such a one in his youth, and attained it in his old age." So Norton was able to make his nostalgia for a latter-day Concord come true. In a pattern reminiscent of Emerson and the Transcendentalists, he would devote his mornings to reading and writing in his study and his afternoons to sauntering across the fields and hills or tending his garden. As he told the English writer Leslie Stephen, the "gardens, and the hills, and the woods, solicit one to leave books and desk,—and I often yield."[44]

Norton's patrician friends also found life simpler and more fulfilling in the country. The corrupt alliance of politicos and plutocrats, the vulgarity of the rich and the philistinism of the bourgeoisie, the boorishness of the urban masses, and the tensions of city living all combined to create concerns and stresses that traumatized many in Norton's circle. One by one, most of them likewise sought to create a pastoral sanctuary for themselves along the lines of Horace's Sabine farm. George Curtis bought a summer home in Ashfield, near the Nortons, and others summered in cottages scattered throughout New England or relocated their permanent residences far from the city. Heirs of the Revolution, they remind one of John Adams retiring to Quincy or of Jefferson to Monticello. "The simple life," Van Wyck Brooks wrote in his study of the New England literary intellectuals, "had been everybody's heritage." Now they retreated to it.[45]

Although William James relished his Cambridge routine of entertaining, teaching, and intellectual discourse, the timid decorum of urban life wore on his always fragile nerves, and he often retreated to the country. "Simplification of life and consciousness I find to be the great thing," he wrote a friend, "but a hard thing when one lives in city conditions." This was especially true for cloistered academics. James noted that "we of the highly educated classes (so called) have most of us got far, far away from Nature. We are trained to seek the choice, the rare, the exquisite exclusively, and to overlook the common. . . . We grow stoneblind and insensible to life's more elementary goods and joys." To combat such urbane artificiality, the James family summered in Chocorua, New Hampshire. There they remodeled a spacious old farmhouse wonderfully suited to James's penchant for fresh air and free thinking. As he bragged to his sister Alice, it had fourteen doors, all opening to the outdoors. Like Norton's Ashfield retreat, the place was his realized dream of rural, domestic simplicity. He told brother Henry that "if you want some real, roomy, rustic happiness, you had better spend summers with us." James relished his leisurely walks through the pines and laurel, and he lingered over the beautiful surroundings. After a few days in the country he felt "washed clean, without and within, by the light and the tender air." In the summer of 1903, back home after two years in Europe, he exulted again to Henry: "We have been here for ten days; the physical luxury of the simplification is something money can't buy. Every breath is a pleasure." He went on to report that "we have a first-rate hired man, a good cow, nice horse, dog, cook, second-girl, etc."[46]

James quickly learned to distinguish between rural poverty and enlightened simplicity. Once, during a trip through the western North Carolina mountains, he commented on the "simple life" of Appalachian mountain folk. "The impression on my mind was of unmitigated squalor. . . . Talk about going back to nature!" Upon reflection, however, he decided that the people living in such conditions were probably perfectly happy with their way of living. But he made it clear that he required for himself a considerably more refined version of simple living. Plainness was not sufficient. "Never thus, with nothing but the bare ground and one's bare hands to fight the battle! Never, without the best spoils of culture woven in!"[47]

James also shared Thoreau's appreciation for the tonic provided by occasional contact with the true wilderness. "I need to lead a purely animal life for at least two months to carry me through the teaching year," he informed the French philosopher Charles Renouvier in a letter written from Keene Valley in the Adirondacks. There James and several friends had established a rustic camp on an abandoned farm surrounded by the heavily wooded mountains. This was perhaps his favorite retreat, and he returned for a few weeks each year most of his mature life. There he could "get a little health in me, a little simplification and purification and sanctification" surrounded by the "smell of spruce," or standing before a "divine outlook from the cliff."[48]

James clearly loved nature, as did Norton, Curtis, and most of the others, but their patrician sense of duty initially kept bringing them back to society to tilt with the windmills of modernity. They could not be satisfied as year-round hermits. And yet the modern world they kept returning to seemed ever more indifferent to their ideals and opinions. Modern American democracy was a continuing disappointment. "Like Horace Walpole," Norton told an English friend, "I should love my country exceedingly if it were not for my countrymen." In his last years, Norton found himself repeatedly dreaming of life in an earlier, ideal America, that of "eighty years ago" when the "habits of life were simpler; the interests of men less mixed and varied; there were more common sympathies, more common and controlling traditions and associations."[49]

He and his friends thus grew ever more estranged from their society and their age as the century came to a close. The nation no sooner survived the catastrophic depression of the 1890s and staved off both proletarian uprisings and agrarian radicalism than it took an imperialistic swim in the Caribbean and the Pacific. For most of the Mugwumps, America's colonial adventure spawned by the Spanish-American War was the last straw. "America has rejected her old ideals," Norton wrote, "turned her back on her past, and chosen the path of barbarism." A dynamic industrial culture had become decadent, and the American intellectual elite joined with their counterparts in Europe in bemoaning the fate of Western civilization in the face of the rise of mass society and industrial imperialism.[50]

In their letters the now elderly Norton and Godkin struck a despondent tone of almost unbroken fault-finding remarkably similar to that of John Adams in his correspondence with Jefferson. Their failure to stem the tide of economic imperialism and to promote a revival of the republican simplicity of the founding fathers, Norton decided, was "the worst blow that modern civilization had had, perhaps a mortal blow." Their machine age society had no use for their sensitive minds and scrupulous consciences. Americans, Henry Adams concluded, "cared little for simplicity and much for complexity."[51]

Now that their hopes had proven illusory, however, the disheartened patricians did not, for the most part, join Howells in blaming industrial capitalism and align themselves with one of the many protest groups so prevalent at the turn of the century. They had too much at stake to sanction radicalism and too much disdain to embrace radicals. Rather, they blamed themselves for placing such unwarranted faith in their countrymen to put prosperity to noble uses. "I have been too much of an idealist about America," Norton confessed. Like the disillusioned Jeffersonian republicans earlier in the century, he admitted: "We gave too much credit to the influence of material things in securing a better order of society. . . . The Democracy has been a disappointment in its capacity to rise morally in proportion to its rise in material welfare and power." He and the others "had not rightly considered the lessons of history." Godkin agreed with his friend. "When I think of what I hoped for America forty years ago, and see what is coming, I see that we all expected far too much of the human race. What stuff we used to talk!" Godkin retired "from the active elevation of mankind" and sailed to England in 1901, convinced, as he said, that he could not prepare for Heaven in America.[52]

Of this group of patrician intellectuals, William James was distinctive for his ability to sustain a sense of involvement and optimism in modern life. As his friends basked in morbidity, he relished the notion that despite the world's problems, personal security could be achieved by a sheer exercise of positive will. James had long before decided that he could not afford the luxury of perpetual anxiety, and he spent his mature years full of enthusiasms and hopes, a man of spontaneous high spirits, adored by his wife, his children, and his students. In a veiled reference to the gloomy perspective of his patrician friends, James wrote: "Too much questioning and too little active responsibility lead, almost as often as too much sensualism does, to the edge of the slope, at the bottom of which lie pessimism and the nightmare or suicidal view of life." He had long felt that the people deserving of admiration were those who "courted the arduous," who suffered hardships gladly, who refused the easy way, who resisted fatalism and conquered great physical and mental obstacles. This attitude more than anything else conditioned his view of modern social problems. So instead of giving up on America in the aftermath of the Spanish-American War, he, like Howells, placed his faith in "the gradual advent of some socialist equilibrium," an equilibrium which he never chose to define. Such dreams, although illdefined, he believed, were far preferable to the despair of his friends, for hopeful alternatives "help to break the edge of the general reign of hardness and are slow leavens of a better order."[53]

Perhaps. But most of James's friends remained embittered and withdrawn at the start of the new century. That the Mugwump intellectuals were neither statesmen in the mold of Jefferson and John Adams nor humanitarian saints like Woolman or Tolstoy should not, however, negate the value of their example of patrician simplicity. Men of refined sensibilities, they gave material concerns their due regard, but no more, so that they might engage in their genteel version of high thinking. In the process they not only exerted a profound influence on those immediately around them but also bequeathed a rich collection of cultural artifacts—books, editorials, essays, and letters—all of which combine to express in poignant fashion the tensions and aspirations of men of good taste struggling to elevate the priorities of a gilded society.

CHAPTER EIGHT

Progressive Simplicity

The prospects for cultural and personal regeneration at the turn of the century were not as gloomy as the New England patricians believed. The same specter of modernization that led Godkin, Norton, Adams, and other elderly Brahmins to despair provoked many younger and less genteel moralists to action. This acceptance of the challenge of modernity, goaded in part by the memories of the social turbulence of the 1890s, helped give the period from about 1900 to 1920 its distinctive flavor, its self-conscious "progressivism." The era was one of reforms and reformers, as activists energetically set about reining in a runaway urban-industrial society. The dynamic free enterprise system so innocently promoted by Jefferson and other early republicans continued to produce unintended results. As Theodore Roosevelt noted in 1913, the industrial and financial revolutions had provoked a "riot of individualistic materialism, under which complete freedom for the individual . . . turned out in practice to mean perfect freedom for the strong to wrong the weak."[1]

Roosevelt and other reformers had come to view slums, sweatshops, child labor, and trusts as symptoms of a growing cancer infecting the commonweal, and they vigorously searched for antidotes. Governments were reorganized for greater efficiency, purged of corruption, and made more responsive to popular rule. Corporations were regulated in the "public" interest, laborers and consumers were protected, and natural resources were more scientifically managed and conserved. In addition, clergymen and social workers provided a "social gospel" ministering to the needs of the urban poor and working classes.

One frequently ignored thread moving in and out of the complexly woven fabric of social thought during the Progressive era was a renewed interest in simpler ways of living. Social reformers drew upon the combined heritage of the Christian social ethic and Jeffersonian republicanism in revitalizing the old dream of a prosperous, yet virtuous American commonwealth in which most of the citizenry enjoyed a comfortable standard of living but at the same time possessed a high degree of civic involvement and personal sobriety. The "tyranny of things," one reformer asserted, must be attacked along with the tyrannies of trusts and boss rule. Thus, at the same time that progressives were busily improving the political and economic environment through institutional and legislative means, the personal ethic of simple living enjoyed quite a revival at the turn of the century, a revival so widespread that it assumed the status of both a cult and a fad.[2]

The simple life advocated by progressives was much more democratic and energetic than that professed by the New England Brahmins. It included a cluster of practices and values that have since remained associated with the concept: discriminating consumption, uncluttered living, personal contentment, aesthetic simplicity (including an emphasis on handicrafts), civic virtue, social service, and renewed contact with nature in one form or another. Enthusiasts varied in the respective emphasis they placed on these components of the good life, but they all shared a belief that Jeffersonian simplicity could be made relevant to modern urban industrial life; old and new means could be employed to make it a "progressive" ethic. "Nowadays," as one advocate of such an updated form of republican simplicity declared in 1910, "we label our most progressive movements with a contradictory word of retrogression. We have come to realize that 'back to the land' means a step forward; that 'back to the simple life' expresses a wish to advance" to a higher, nobler stage of civilized living.[3]

The thrust behind this revival of simplicity was provided primarily by civic-minded members of the new middle classes. Unwilling to reject modernity outright, they saw the rise of modern America as both a formidable reality and a mixed blessing. Much about metropolitan life was attractive, especially the economic, educational, and cultural opportunities found in the city. But there were serious drawbacks as well. City life was increasingly secular life, and the fading of felt religion and conventional Protestant morality left many sensitive urbanites caste adrift in a sea of anonymity and purposelessness. Likewise, the clutter, corruption, and hectic pace of urban life were producing enervating consequences for adults and especially for children. In 1895 the New York Health Commissioner declared that "in no nation at any time have the demands on the nervous forces been as great as in these United States." Symptoms of nervous disorder, popularly called neurasthenia during the nineteenth century, plagued the genteel and the bourgeoisie. Norton, Henry Adams, and William James had each experienced such "nervousness." In their case the malady most often reflected varied personal traumas as well as a sense of displacement by the forces of modernity, and it usually manifested itself in an almost morbid introspection. For the typical middle-class man or woman, however, neurasthenia resulted not so much from a sense of lost prestige and influence as it did from overwork, crowdedness, ennui, and the other tensions associated with metropolitan living.[4]

To combat the effects of such nervous tension, many men and women among the growing professional class—doctors, lawyers, professors, teachers, social workers, bureaucrats, mid-level managers, journalists—embraced simple living at the turn of the century primarily for its therapeutic effects. These "harried" Americans, much like millions of their descendants today, were especially eager to learn how to relax and at the same time to engage in forms of constructive recreation and social service. "A feature of the simple, natural life that is to be long and happy," said one writer, "must consist in a husbanding of vital resources during and after times of critical strain." Progressive simplicity thus represented a combination of productive occupations and civic involvement coupled with careful control of material desires and physical and mental energies. "If the high thinking of the Pilgrims is to be kept," a writer in the *Century* argued, "their plain living must not be altogether dropped." One could live plainly yet well in modern America, but this meant developing a carefully considered taste for the essential, the beautiful, and the good. Simple living—spending time and money wisely, tastefully, and moderately—was an ethic of self-conscious discrimination and limitation, of modest but comfortable circumstances for those with adequate but not swollen financial resources. As an editorial in the *Independent* contended, simpler living provided "the only possible relief from the nerve destroying complexity of modern civilization," and it therefore made both good economic and psychological sense to many among the "overpressured" bourgeoisie.[5]

In fact, it made good sense for all classes. At least that was the message of many reformers who saw in simple living not just a therapeutic balm but a means of provoking meaningful social change. Henry Demarest Lloyd, whose dramatic exposé of the monopolistic chicanery of the Standard Oil Company gave rise to a popular assault on corporate concentration, stressed that any solution to the ills of modern America must begin with the transformation of individual hearts and minds. "A thorough, stalwart resimplification of life governed by simple needs and loves," he maintained in 1894, "is the imperative want of the world." Likewise, the leading spokesman for the Social Gospel, the Reverend Washington Gladden, preached to the rich and the poor about the need for greater personal simplicity and social harmony. Money, Gladden insisted, must always be earned and spent carefully, with due consideration given to the consequences to the spender as well as to society. Self-indulgence and waste, regardless of their larger economic effects, were dangerous practices for any true Christian.[6]

This plea for conscientious consumption was given added justification by the publication of Thorstein Veblen's *Theory of the Leisure Class* in 1899. An iconoclastic social scientist who led the simple life of a disheveled academic, indifferent about his dress and domestic comforts, Veblen subjected the "conspicuous consumption" and "pecuniary waste" of the affluent to a devastating sociological and anthropological analysis. His conclusions confirmed what John Adams and Tocqueville had said years before: in a capitalist democracy such as the United States, people tend to derive self-esteem and social status from parading their wealth and leisure before others. This "ostentatious display" was motivated by "the stimulus of an invidious comparison which prompts us to outdo those with whom we are in the habit of classing ourselves." But, Veblen emphasized, conspicuous consumption was not limited in its effects to the wealthy. It eventually became a "prescriptive canon of conduct for the rest of society." The middle and working classes also found themselves caught up in a ceaseless pecuniary competition for prestige. As he concluded, the "standard of living of any class, so far as it concerns the element of conspicuous waste, is commonly as high as the earning capacity of the class will permit—with a constant tendency to go higher."[7]

Veblen steadfastly denied harboring any intention to pass judgment on the spending habits of the well-to-do. He was, he claimed, a dispassionate observer of social phenomena, not a propagandist for social reform. But the pungency of his prose spoke otherwise, and his *Theory of the Leisure Class* was widely interpreted as a convincing indictment of the callous wastefulness and social snobbery of the affluent. Charlotte Perkins Gilman, the prominent crusader for women's rights and child labor reform, described the book as a "clear and impressive" treatise "illuminated by the most penetrating satire I ever saw."[8]

The practical lesson that Gilman and other progressives took from Veblen's *Theory of the Leisure Class* was that the vicious cycle of pecuniary emulation and conspicuous consumption must be broken through the promotion of simpler, more sincere habits of living. Professor Irene Sargent, an art critic and moral reformer at Syracuse University, asserted in 1902 that "simplicity in private life is at once the first essential and the source of public strength, morality and art." Reading Veblen left her with a clear moral: "the ostentatious extravagance and display of the individual are the agents of rapid degeneration and decay in all that stands for good government and civilization." This was no isolated assessment. Rather, it was a common theme among progressives. Lloyd and Gladden preached it, as did political leaders such as "Golden Rule" Jones, Brand Whitlock, and Teddy Roosevelt. John Spargo, who was instrumental in promoting the cause of child labor reform, likewise claimed that the remedy for the "disease of civilization, the way to attain unity and brotherhood, that wholeness of the body social . . . is simplicity of living and abundant friendship. . . . For society and for the individual, then, the simplification of life becomes a matter of vital significance."[9]

Ray Stannard Baker, the investigative journalist who became the confidant and biographer of Woodrow Wilson, also promoted progressive plain living. Under the pen name "David Grayson," Baker wrote a series of popular novels in which the contentment provided by simple living was a common theme. Grayson, an obviously literate farmer, who reads Marcus Aurelius, William Penn, Emerson, and Thoreau, represented for Baker the good life personified. "I have a cow and a horse, and a few pigs," Grayson explains in *Adventures in Contentment* (1906). "I have a comfortable home. . . . Inside the house I have the best books ever written and I have time in the evening to read them—I mean really read them." His was a progressive rather than a primitive simplicity. It "does not necessarily . . . consist in doing without things, but rather in the proper use of things." David Grayson, Baker stresses, does "not believe in Diogenes and his tub. . . . I am no reactionary." He neglects "no tool of progress," but rather ensures that mechanical things do not enslave him.[10]

Baker's novels and short stories detailing David Grayson's contented simplicity had a profound impact on many readers. One of them reported that he and his wife had become "David Graysonized." They lived simply, but were happy with their "moderate income and enjoyed life to the full." This they attributed to their acquiring the "habit of contentment" and to their small-town life. "If we had lived in a large city, or among the selfishly fashionable, we might have been discontented and miserable, but we have lived in towns of a few thousand, where people have not been extravagant and who prize a friend for what he can contribute to the general good." This fan of David Grayson emphasized what a full and happy life could be led with an annual income of $1000. He and his family enjoyed "a home, our home, heated, lighted with electricity, bathrooms, cases filled with the best books, tables covered with the best magazines. . . . Here we continue to live and enjoy our friends, books, and children until the time of our earthly life is done."[11]

Most progressives, however, did not limit their advocacy of simple living to the rural or village context. Concerns similar to those motivating Baker prompted other progressives such as Florence Kelley, Maud Nathan, Julia Lathrop, Louis Brandeis, and John R. Commons to form the National Consumers League. Although primarily intended to promote better working conditions for women and children by mobilizing consumer pressure, the organization also repeatedly criticized the showy spending habits of the urban well-to-do. One spokesman argued that the Consumers League rejected the "prevailing idea" that "it is an evidence of superiority to buy without questioning whatever is shown." Affluent women were urged to be more conscientious about their expenditures so as not to demoralize the lower classes by breezing into stores and ordering items with no thought to their cost or utility. "We must learn to be better choosers," stressed a League supporter. Consumers, she and others maintained, should be encouraged to govern their purchases "by excellence rather than by expense; to prefer simplicity; to make use serve beauty; and beauty usefulness." Adopting such scrupulous habits would also not only ease social tensions but provide more money to be spent on "education and the other spiritual values of life."[12]

The reformers involved in the growing settlement house movement advocated a similar consumption ethic. Hull House, America's most famous social settlement, was founded in Chicago in 1889 by Jane Addams and

Ellen Gates Starr, both of whom also served on the board of the Consumers League. In their enclave of beauty and concern settled within the harsh ugliness of the ghetto, they sought to create a sense of community among all classes. Doing so, they hoped, might help avoid more radical attempts to solve the growing "social problem" that so worried and alienated the New England patricians. By bringing the immigrant poor together with bourgeois staff members, both groups would benefit from contact with each other. Young middle-class women considering joining the Hull House staff were told that interacting with the "other half" would "beget a broader philanthropy and a tenderer sympathy, and leave less time and inclination for selfish ambition, or for real or fancied invalidism."[13]

This last point referred to the rash of neurasthenia among single middle-class women, particularly those college graduates who were no longer content to accept the imperatives of Victorian domesticity or the detachment of gentility. Jane Addams recalled that she had been "smothered and sickened with advantages." Social work, she told applicants, had lifted her out of a debilitating nervousness and given her a sense of purpose and hope. Like one of her heroes, William James, Addams was bent on making strenuous contact with the "reality of life." In the process, she and the other genteel women at Hull House learned to appreciate simple virtues through their contact with the working poor. The age-old customs of the immigrants revealed the organic vitality inherent in traditional cultures, thus giving the overcultivated and overindulged social workers "a touch of the refinement which adheres to simple things." Starr expressed a similar sentiment in a letter to her sister. The female settlement workers, she wrote, would "learn to know the people & understand them and their ways of life: to give them what they have out of their culture & leisure & overindulgence, & to receive the culture which comes of self-denial, poverty & failure, which these people have always known."[14]

But Addams, Starr, and the other social workers were careful to sanction only "a touch of the refinement" associated with proletarian simplicity. Addams, herself the product of a well-do-do Illinois family, saw no need for the bourgeoisie to adopt a Franciscan vow of poverty. During a visit with Leo Tolstoy in 1896, she was much impressed by his adopting the simple life and hard labor of the Russian peasant. She recalled being gently chided by him for the amount of material in the sleeve of her dress and not so gently reproved for living off the income of her Illinois farm as an "absentee landlord." Stung by Tolstoy's gibes, Addams resolved after returning to Chicago to spend two hours a day baking bread in order to experience more directly the life of the working poor. But she soon decided that such sympathetic labor was "utterly preposterous. . . . The half dozen people invariably waiting to see me after breakfast, the piles of letters to be opened and answered, the demand of actual and pressing human wants,—were these all to be pushed aside and asked to wait while I saved my soul by two hours' work at baking bread?" Tolstoyan simplicity was "more logical than [modern] life warrants," she concluded.[15]

Hence, Addams, like Thoreau before her, rejected the idea that everyone should live and work in poverty. Simplicity, she decided, had as much to do with one's intentions as it did with one's possessions or vocation. She thereafter preferred spending her time promoting the settlement house ideal rather than becoming an urban proletarian herself. Perhaps Jane Addams's ambivalence about simple living places the middle-class rhetoric on the subject into perspective. When one was comfortable, one could and should worry about the bad taste of excess and the tensions of modern complexity; when one was poor and living on the edge of bare survival, simplicity was a self-limiting fact of existence, hardly a voluntary ideal by which to live.

In practice this distinction meant that moral reformers promoting simple living at the turn of the century increasingly directed their appeals to the well-to-do rather than the struggling. The need for simpler living among the fortunate was the subject of repeated discussion in middle-class periodicals. A writer in the *Outlook*, edited by the Social Gospeler Lyman Abbott, reminded readers that the United States "is a young country, and it has many things to learn; among them the truth that the charm of life lies very largely in small things. Satisfaction does not consist in getting rich, it consists largely in what one gets day by day." The editors of the *North American Review* also focused on the therapeutic effects of what they called "gentler living." They urged their middle-class subscribers to avoid extremes, to restore "sanity and even poise" through greater self-control, and to revive "modesty and living within one's means and station." If people would learn "that simplicity of life may bring us more real comfort than elaborateness," one contributor claimed, then much of the tension plaguing modern Americans would be eased.[16]

The most persistent voice promoting simple living for the middle-class millions at the start of the new century was Edward Bok, the intense young editor of the *Ladies' Home Journal*. Bok is best known today as an example of the "rags-to-riches" success story, an immigrant youth who made good in America and then became a public benefactor and inveterate booster, telling others how to do the same. Yet Bok was far more than a typical success specialist. He was at heart an ardent moral conservative who found in simple living the key to personal happiness and social improvement. In 1900 Bok proclaimed that from "every class in American life, there comes the same cry for a simpler, more rational way of living," and he was determined to promote such a changed lifestyle in his flourishing magazine. Between 1889 and 1919, when he resigned his editorship, Bok probably exerted more influence on middle-class American values than any other editorial spokesman. In the process, the *Ladies' Home Journal* developed into an uplifting practical guidebook for middle-class simplicity.[17]

Bok's career remarkably paralleled that of Andrew Carnegie. A Dutch immigrant, he arrived in Brooklyn with his destitute family in 1870 at age six. Seven years later Bok quit school in order to help support his struggling parents. Energetic and ambitious, he eventually became a stenographer for a publishing firm and began editing a small Brooklyn church magazine at night. At the same time he embarked on a rigorous program of self-education. By 1886 his magazine had grown quite successful, and Bok sold it in order to start a syndicated newspaper feature. Realizing that most women were not regular newspaper readers, he sought to attract their attention by providing articles of interest to them, and soon the "Bok page" blossomed into a profitable enterprise with 137 subscriber newspapers across the country.

Such success caught the eye of Cyrus Curtis, the owner of the *Ladies' Home Journal*, and he offered Bok the post of editor in 1889. Thus, at the tender age of twenty-six, bachelor Edward Bok assumed control of the nation's leading periodical for women, then boasting 400,000 subscribers. He later remembered the irony of his selection: "No man could have been chosen who had less intimate knowledge of women. Bok had no sister, no women confidantes. He had lived with and for his mother. His boyhood days had been too full of poverty and struggle to permit him to mingle with the opposite sex." Although Bok had little experience with women, he nevertheless felt confident in his understanding of the American home and what it needed in the way of improvement. With this curious mixture of innocence and dogmatism, he plunged wholeheartedly into his new venture.[18]

Bok arrived at *Ladies' Home Journal* at a time when the idea of a mass-circulation, general-interest magazine was just coming to fruition. The already large but rapidly growing urban middle class was eager for a cultural outlet relevant to its needs and interests. Bok recognized this fact, and he self-consciously directed his magazine at the "middlebrow" readers, the "intelligent American woman rather than the intellectual type." He was interested neither in the patrician nor parvenu classes but in those families with annual incomes from $1200 to $2500. The "class with incomes of perhaps from $3000 to $5000," Bok explained, "would receive supplementary attention, but the other classes above were not large enough in number to warrant specific appeal." The new editor promised that the *Journal* would provide "a great clearing house of information" for its audience, and he quickly revised its format accordingly. After soliciting suggestions from his readers, Bok created a number of new departments covering such topics as infant and child care, sewing, cooking, religion, and civic beautification. He also published short stories by Howells, Mark Twain, Bret Harte, Hamlin Garland, Sarah Orne Jewett, and Kipling, and political discussion by Presidents Cleveland, Harrison, Roosevelt, Taft, and Wilson.[19]

In presenting such varied fare, Bok was careful to highlight his own clearly articulated vision of American values. The *Journal* to him must "be more than a mere assemblage of stories and articles." It must stand for ideals.

Bok's own rapid success in his new country gave him a heady optimism about the nation's distinctive moral mission, and his avid reading of Emerson as a youth had impressed upon him the virtues of plain living and high thinking. He frequently quoted Emerson's assertion that, "Great men are they who see that the spiritual is stronger than any material force." And like Emerson, he believed that the best way to reform society was not through the manipulation of institutions but through the promotion of enlightened self-improvement. Consequently, unlike *McClure's* and other muckraking periodicals, Bok's magazine was intended not to attack "all the evils of the day" but to reveal "the tremendous influence of personal power" in correcting social problems. He was bent upon using the *Ladies' Home Journal* as a stimulant for self-culture. As he told George Bernard Shaw, the *Journal's* editorial pages constituted the world's "largest possible pulpit."[20]

Much like Sarah Hale and other earlier advocates of republican domesticity, Bok saw the middle-class American woman as the crucial "steadying influence" between the "unrest among the lower classes and rottenness among the upper classes." For him the ideal woman was one who led a simple life in the home and conscientiously passed on such a perspective to her spouse and children. She was inherently "better, purer, conscientious and morally stronger than man." Bok was no feminist. "My idea," he wrote, ". . . is to keep women in the home, especially as there are enough writers who are trying to take her out of it." Perhaps because he appealed to what many traditional women wanted to be, Bok's new *Ladies' Home Journal* was an amazing success. By 1892 the number of subscribers had increased to 700,000; by 1910 they numbered 1,950,000, thus giving the magazine the largest circulation of any in the world.[21]

Bok used his editorial pulpit to promote a variety of "progressive" causes—city beautification, billboard removal, wilderness preservation, sex education, American-designed fashions, and pure food and drug legislation. The most consistent subject of his avuncular preaching, however, was the personal satisfaction provided by simpler living. Like many Americans at the turn of the century, Bok was inspired by the writings of Charles Wagner, a French Protestant clergyman noted for his emphasis on Christian simplicity. Wagner's book, *The Simple Life* (1901), was widely reviewed and quoted in the American press, so much so, in fact, that President Roosevelt invited him to the United States in 1904. In speaking of *The Simple Life*, Roosevelt claimed that he knew of "no other book . . . which contains so much that we of America ought to take to our hearts."[22]

Wagner's explicitly religious perspective coupled with his reverence for a traditional republican morality rooted in a well-ordered family life struck a responsive chord among American advocates of simplicity. Bok was especially taken with Wagner's message. He told his readers that *The Simple Life* was the "sanest little book" on the subject yet published, and "in its words there are health and salvation for thousands of American women." By emphasizing that simplicity had to do more with one's perspective than one's income, the French minister had implicitly sanctioned the prevailing capitalist system, thereby reassuring Bok and middle-class Americans that leading a simple life required a spiritual revitalization, not a social revolution. In the aftermath of Wagner's American lecture tour and with the growing popularity of his ideas, Bok noted that the phrase "simple life" had become quite fashionable among American journalists. "We read about the 'simple life' and love to talk about it, but we refuse to live it." He attributed this failure in part to the widespread confusion about the concept's practical meaning. Too often it was associated with "a barren abode and crude living." On the contrary, he emphasized, simplicity was not a fruit-and-nuts primitivism. There was a need for a basic sufficiency, "a healthful diet, simple, serviceable clothing, a clean, healthy dwelling-place, open-air exercise and good reading." The more one added to these essentials, however, the more complex living became. As possessions increase, so do desires, and a person must therefore work harder, worry more, and communicate less with his family and friends.[23]

At base, Bok affirmed, the simple life was a personal state of being dependent neither "upon our condition nor our station in life." Like Wagner's message, his recipe for simplicity was delectably plain and reassuring: "Make home happy; hold loved ones first in your heart; leave off fussing over fashionable ways of living, be natural, and you will be living the simple life though you ride in a motor-car, clean house by electricity, entertain at the country club, and have every convenience known to man. The quality of the individual is what determines the simple life, never his surroundings." Yet while assuring the well-to-do that they could simplify their lives without spartanizing them, Bok advised that to have "small means makes the problem of simple living really easier." The key to simplicity was self-confident contentment. He reflected his reading of Veblen when he stressed: "There must be no imitation of others, no reaching of fancied heights to outdo someone else: no thought of how our mode of living will be judged by others." When Americans learned the difference between the accessories and the essentials of life, they would begin to experience better physical and mental health. "There are no nervous breakdowns in the simple life," he counseled his careworn readers. Contentment, discrimination, sincerity—that, Bok concluded, "is the genuine simple life—according to Charles Wagner, if you will, or according to those everlasting precepts and principles that were lovingly laid down for all mankind some nineteen hundred years ago."[24]

In this way, Bok retrieved the traditional concept of Christian simplicity and made it relevant to his middle-class American audience. Some may see in his rather broad definition of simple living a rationalization for the status quo. He certainly was not calling into question the free enterprise system or the sanctity of private property. Like most progressives, he was a moral reformer, not a social radical. But he clearly did intend his editorial sermons to result in changed patterns of living and thinking. To this end he created a department entitled "How Much Can Be Done with Little," devoted solely to providing practical tips for simpler living. Bok also pioneered the "how-to" journalistic technique. Articles such as "How We Can Lead a Simple Life, by an American Mother," "How We Live on $1000 a Year or Less," "How To Live Cheaply," "A Lesson in Plain Sewing," "What Nervous People Should Eat," and "A Spartan Mother" were intended to demonstrate that simpler living was an applied ideal accessible to all. In addition, Bok solicited prominent Americans to express to his readers the virtues and joys of simplicity. His greatest coup in this respect was in getting President Roosevelt to participate in a series of interviews on the subject of better living habits.

To say that Theodore Roosevelt was himself a consistent practitioner of simple living would stretch the concept beyond any clear meaning, as variously as it has been applied in American history. Roosevelt defies any simple classification. A bundle of nervous energy, he could be a conspicuous dandy in spending his inherited money. He rode to hounds, played polo, loved big houses, fast horses, pearl-handled revolvers, gold-plated rifles, and fine clothes for indoors and out, despite his boasting about getting by with a buckskin shirt. But Roosevelt was a patrician determined not to be genteel. He despised fastidious intellectuals such as Norton and Godkin, asserting that they and other Mugwumps were debilitated by "a love of ease and luxury." This was unfair, but Roosevelt frequently let his prejudices get in the way of his reason. Whatever the case, Roosevelt claimed repeatedly to lead a life of "dignified simplicity." In a letter to William Howard Taft in 1903, he described his way of life in the White House: "We have two maids and live as any family of gentlefolk of small means should live. When I leave the Presidency I shall not mind in the least going back to the utmost simplicity of life and I wish to live simply as President." He later told an English friend that from "the standpoint of real pleasure, I should selfishly prefer my old-time ranch on the Little Missouri to anything in Newport."[25]

Roosevelt thus fervently supported Bok's moral program, declaring that excessive materialism was the greatest danger threatening the country. And he agreed that the most effective antidote was a revival of republican simplicity in modern form. "The evils that have come," the Rough Rider argued, "need not corrupt the world, if the old watchwords of the simpler life—virtue, loyalty, courage, cheerfulness—are made part of each individual's life." Roosevelt maintained that a "sane charity and simplicity" should again be taught in the home so that young Americans would learn that the "sinews of virtue" rest in the realization that "the moral must permeate the material or the best in life decays." The American raised in such a moral household would find that his "good plain sense will prevent him from securing luxuries he cannot pay for, and his courage will save him from imagining that such luxuries are necessaries."[26]

The popular Roosevelt undoubtedly had a strong influence on the readers of the *Ladies' Home Journal*. But it was Edward Bok himself who was the magazine's most rousing voice on behalf of simple living. In his editorials he repeatedly expressed the virtues of enlightened restraint in a didactic, intimate, homely way that drew its effect from his intense sincerity. "It is a hard thing," he wrote in one typical Christmas message, "for those who have little to believe that the greatest happiness of life is with them: that it is not with those who have abundance." Nevertheless, he insisted, the "more we have the less we actually enjoy it." As Emerson had pointed out, there is a "law of compensation" at work in life. Those of great wealth must bear the constant burden of greater complexity and concern. "The woman of simplest means," Bok contended, "is the happiest woman on earth, if she only knew it."[27]

To enlighten his women readers to this assertion, Bok cited the example of a family he knew who enjoyed an affluent income but conscientiously organized their lives and their purchases around the principles of utility and simplicity. Their furniture was of high-quality wood but of plain design, no servants were hired, an automobile was rented for specific trips rather than bought to sit outside, and toys for the children were "fewer and simpler" than those of the neighbors. A large portion of the family's discretionary income went to charities. It was a family, Bok stressed, where pleasures remained real and appetites were neither clogged nor jaded. The result was a mental contentment with the joy of life itself.[28]

To Bok the need for such familial simplicity assumed the proportions of a crusade, and he was determined to make the middle-class household his battleground. "We have drifted away from simple living," he charged, "and our children are suffering from it." Reminiscent of Andrew Jackson Downing, Bok led a highly publicized campaign for a simplified domestic architecture. He found most late Victorian homes to be "repellently ornate." Money was "wasted on useless turrets, filigree work or machine-made ornamentation." As a result, all sense of style and proportion was lost. To remedy the situation, the *Journal* in 1895 began publishing plans for plain, more functional, and attractive houses that could be built for $1500 to $5000. Many leading architects submitted designs, including Ralph Adams Cram, Frank Lloyd Wright, and Stanford White. Bok offered complete blueprints for five dollars, and soon thousands of "*Journal* houses" began going up across the country. White maintained that "Edward Bok has more completely influenced American domestic architecture for the better than any other man of his generation." These "*Journal* houses" eliminated the Victorian parlor, made the kitchen more compact, substituted built-in cupboards for pantries, and discarded all cupolas, scrollwork, and balconies. Cram explained that his design was an "attempt to restore something of the simplicity characteristic of good colonial work." Its effect depended "solely on simple lines and quiet detail."[29]

Frank Lloyd Wright had a similar perspective. "Radical though it may be," he observed, his work was "dedicated to a cause conservative." This quality of "innovative nostalgia" was a persistent thread running through much of progressive culture. Many of the aesthetic and moral reformers were intent upon using new means to achieve traditional objectives. Certainly this was true for Wright. At the turn of the century he was emerging as both a seminal figure in modern architecture and a fervent spokesman for traditional republican virtues through a union of simplicity and an organic aesthetic as guiding concepts of design. Like Bok, he was thoroughly disgusted with the "General Grant Gothic" style prevailing in late Victorian America. "My first feeling," he recalled, "had been a yearning for simplicity. A new sense of simplicity as organic."[30]

A highly articulate and inspired champion of the social role of architecture, Wright sometimes expressed his ideas more clearly in his buildings than in his prose. His principle of organic simplicity was derived initially from his association with Louis Sullivan, who once announced that "the intellectual trend of the hour is toward simplification." For Wright this trend meant that a building's interior and exterior should blend into a harmonious whole and, in turn, blend into the natural environment. Function and beauty would thereby be intertwined, and superfluity banned. As employed in the design of homes, such a principle would "help the people to feel that architecture is a destroyer of vulgarity, sham, and pretense, a benefactor of tired nerves and jaded souls, an educator in the high ideals of yesterday, to-day, and to-morrow." In presenting one of his "prairie house" designs to the readers of *Ladies' Home Journal*, Wright introduced it as a "simple mode of living" in "keeping with a high ideal of family life together."[31]

While promoting a plain, functional, affordable architectural style, Bok also led a campaign for simplified home interiors. "The curse of the American home to-day," he wrote in 1900, "is useless bric-a-brac." The tasteless overfurnishing in the Queen Anne style then so popular among the urban middle class, he had decided, was contributing directly to the rising nervousness of American women, for they were becoming harried slaves to the "useless rubbish" filling their parlors. Moreover, such homes were not conducive to the development of good moral character in the young. "No child," he said, "can develop a true simplicity of nature when the home of his parents was stifled by shams." Useless gimcracks, he insisted with Thoreau-like reasoning, only gather dust and offend the eye. "Simplicity is the only thing that ornaments." In fact it does more than that, he continued, "it dignifies." The most aesthetically pleasing rooms were determined not by what they contained but by what they disdained. Nothing should be bought for a home that did not perform a useful or aesthetic function. To show what he meant, Bok regularly published illustrations of home interiors that included examples of simple and gaudy furniture and furnishings placed side by side. Underneath each picture he would provide terse evaluations such as "This chair is ugly" or "This table is beautiful." Yet Bok was convinced that simplicity transcended such aesthetic considerations. "More simplicity in our homes," he argued, "would make our lives simpler." If women developed a plain, functional domestic taste, they would have more time and more money to spend on things that really mattered. "It is only because we have got away from the simple and the natural that so many of our homes are cluttered up as they are, and our lives full of little things that are not worth the while."[32]

Bok's assault on the needless stuffiness of Victorian home decoration and clothing provoked a considerable response from his readers. Many of them revealed a desire for such simpler living, yet remained hesitant. As one correspondent confided, "We women want simpler lives. There's no doubt about that. But we are dismayed by the difficulties confronting the woman who essays to 'come out and be separate.'" She went on to describe the problem of finding "simple" clothes at reasonable prices. An even more worrisome issue for her was the fear of social ostracism. If she and her family modeled their domestic life according to the simplicity Bok advocated, they would be "dropped from visiting lists." This was a poignant reflection of the way in which middle-class citizens had become culturally intimidated to engage in conspicuous consumption and pecuniary display. In concluding her pained response to the editor's "admirable" program, the concerned subscriber raised a dilemma that has since become commonplace: "Thousands of women see clearly the force of the needs you point out, and see them with an intensity born of defeated hopes and thwarted lives. But they find themselves helpless against the ever-increasing tide of complex and artificial standards of living. Woman knows and feels it a difficult task to hold her way in the swift currents of prevailing customs. But they are forced upon her."[33]

Like a stern father, Bok took up such objections one by one, parrying them with the skill of a fencer. He characterized the reader's fear of being deemed eccentric a "false notion." The woman who simplifies her life "will find herself of a sisterhood that numbers more votaries than she has ever dreamed of." Besides, he asked, is not being true to one's own values far more important than satisfying the jaded standards of society? That some friends might drop a "simple-living" couple from their "visiting list" was an indication that they were not true friends; the loss of their good graces should not be an issue of concern. "I repeat," Bok emphasized, "our lives are what we make of them ourselves. If we are weak and accept the artificial our lives will be so. And just in proportion as we make our lives artificial we make them profitless and unhappy." When enough Americans displayed the courage of conviction to act on their own rather than wait for simplicity to become socially acceptable, then the country might begin to approach its original spiritual and ethical ideal. America might indeed become a nation of "real people, where each man and woman is measured by his or her own true worth, where friendships are honest and where laughs are hearty and tears are real: where lives are happiest because they are lived simplest: where the air is clear and where people look you in the eye, and where the clothes you wear do not signify."[34]

Bok and the contributors to *Ladies' Home Journal* voiced a concept of aesthetic simplicity much in accord with that being espoused by participants in what was known as the Arts and Crafts Movement. Emerging in the United States at the end of the nineteenth century after first appearing in England, this crusade on behalf of good taste protested against the ugliness and superficiality of modern urban life. It also decried the conditions of modern factory production which separated the worker from his creation and rendered him merely an automaton. In England the proponents of the Arts and Crafts revival thus sought not only to improve the taste of society but also to improve the living and laboring conditions of working people by reviving the handicraft tradition. The movement's most important English prophets were the art critic and historian John Ruskin and his many talented disciple William Morris. Joining social criticism and aesthetic ideals, the two judged the moral worth of a nation by the quality of its art and architecture. Where the Puritans and Quakers saw rectitude and piety as primary, and were suspicious of the arts, Ruskin, Morris, and other artistic reformers saw beauty and refinement as central human values. "What we *like*," Ruskin asserted, "determines what we *are*, and is the sign of what we are; and to teach taste is inevitably to form character." He later added that the "ideal of human life is a union of Spartan simplicity of manners with Athenian sensibility and imagination."[35]

Unlike patrician or Tory proponents of refined simplicity, however, Morris and his supporters self-consciously oriented their ethic of taste toward the working classes, especially the artisans and skilled craftsmen. They were determined to promote a simple art and architecture for all rather than for the advantaged few. Morris saw this ideal most admirably expressed in the handicraft tradition, and he maintained that the guild community of the Middle Ages was the positive standard against which to measure the aesthetically meaningless and exploitative labor under which most modern factory workers suffered. Medieval crafts, he observed, promoted quality, not quantity, in the lives of workmen as well as in their products. But such an ideal working environment had been gradually superseded by the factory system. As a result, the artisans and craftsmen were displaced by the specialized laborer, and the worker became no more than a wage slave and machine-tender. Morris was an artistic but not a scientific socialist, blending Marx's critique of bourgeois capitalism with his own joyful aestheticism. Associations of artist-craftsmen, he hoped, would be a counter-force against the dehumanizing effects of industrial capitalism. He once confessed that besides wanting to make beautiful things, "the leading passion of my life has been and is hatred of modern civilization." To remedy the ills of that civilization, Morris urged the "simplification of life, and the curbing of luxury and the desires for tyranny and mastery."[36]

By the turn of the century, Americans were becoming avid supporters of Morris and the Arts and Crafts idea. Bok observed in the *Ladies' Home Journal* that a "William Morris craze has been developing, and it is a fad that we cannot push with too much vigor." Bok claimed that Morris lived the "gospel of healthy need and not of fancied want." He designed and made furniture, tapestry, wallpaper, books and other things with an eye for their use rather than their gaudiness. Thank goodness, Bok concluded, that American artisans and craftsmen were beginning to follow his lead and produce their own native furnishings that represented a moral principle rather than a badge of social rank. Bok conspicuously avoided any mention of Morris's critique of the factory system or his advocacy of a communal socialism. For him, Morris was important for his aesthetic simplicity, not for his social radicalism. In America simplicity as an aesthetic norm had almost always been the possession of educated, reflective minds who sought to impose their sense of correct design, which they often saw in moral terms, on the rest of society. This was certainly the case with the Puritans, Quakers, Jefferson, and Downing—and Bok fit well into this tradition.[37]

So, too, did most of the participants in the Arts and Crafts movement in the United States at the turn of the century. Actually, it was not a unified movement as much as it was an aesthetic impulse that manifested itself in a variety of different approaches. Some enthusiasts were primarily interested in producing quality handcrafted goods to be purchased by the affluent. Others wanted to develop among the working and middle classes an appreciation for tasteful simplicity so as to free them from the lures of the mass production marketplace. By 1904 there were twenty-five organized Arts and Crafts societies, mostly in the Northeast and Midwest. An elderly Charles Eliot Norton was a leading member of the Boston Arts and Crafts Society, which tended to be dominated by like-minded aesthetic elitists. The Chicago Society, on the other hand, was closely connected with Jane Addams's Hull House and was much more sympathetic to the "working-class" problem. There were also about a dozen rural Arts and Crafts colonies scattered across the country, the most famous of which was Elbert Hubbard's Roycroft in New York state. Intended to attract disaffected artisans and craftsmen from the cities, they usually combined subsistence agriculture with cottage industries to provide for their basic needs. What unified these diverse adherents was a belief in the traditional ideal of classical republican virtue and a rejection of vulgar Victorian materialism.[38]

In the United States, the leading organ for the Arts and Crafts ideas of Morris and Ruskin was *The Craftsman: An Illustrated Monthly Magazine for the Simplification of Life*. The magazine was founded in 1901 by Gustav Stickley, a Wisconsin-born stonemason turned woodworker. During a visit to the 1876 Centennial exhibition at Philadelphia, Stickley was struck by the functional severity of Shaker furniture. Soon thereafter, he and two of his brothers established a furniture shop in Binghamton, New York. By 1900 Stickley had visited Europe, become a committed follower of Ruskin and Morris, and moved his workshop to Syracuse. There he produced what became known as "mission" furniture—massive, simple oak pieces that were quite popular among the middle classes. He named his company "United Crafts" and organized his workshops according to the guild ideas of Morris, providing a profit-sharing plan for his workers.[39]

Stickley started the *Craftsman* with the objective of promoting both simple living and the Arts and Crafts aesthetic. Devoting its first issue to Morris, its second to Ruskin, the magazine began by combining the aesthetic and social reform impulses of the English theorists. In an early editorial commentary, Stickley challenged his fellow craftsmen to follow the model of Ruskin and Morris, Tolstoy and Thoreau, for these were saintly "men of simple ways" who have

> asked little and given much, who have freed their shoulders from the burdens of luxury, who have stripped off from their lives the tight inflexible bondages of unnecessary formalities, and who thus have been left free for those great essentials of honest existence, for courage, for unselfishness, for heroic purpose, and, above all, for the clear vision which means the acceptance of that final good, honesty of purpose, without which there can be no real meaning in life.

Such "right living and clear thinking" would require being contented with plain clothing and functional accommodations as well as a recognition that work and rest were complementary activities. Stickley was quick to disavow those who took either a superficial or extreme approach to the subject. "By simplicity here is not meant any foolish whimsical eccentricity of dress or manner or architecture . . . for eccentricity is but an expression of individual egotism and as such must inevitably be short-lived." America needed less "posing for mere picturesque reform" and more "actual simplicity of heart."[40]

Stickley and most other proponents of the Arts and Crafts program in the United States believed that elevating the taste of craftsmen and their bourgeois customers would provide both therapeutic personal and regenerative social benefits. Making and owning beautiful objects, they asserted, would relieve some of the tensions and boredom afflicting the middle-class city man and his wife. Although "the age of handicraft is gone beyond recall," Stickley admitted in 1904, "the value of handicrafts for the numberless thousands of men and women who are leading ill-balanced, abnormal lives" was incalculable. In addition, the crafts reformers also stressed the cultural and moral importance of simple, functional housing and close-knit families. One advocate of the Arts and Crafts revival promised that "simple living is one of the first methods of escape" from the "machine of commercial tyranny." By living simply, he stressed, "we do not say cheap and mean living, but rather rational living," keeping eating, dressing, and recreation "in proportion to the great things in life."[41]

These crafts reformers, like Edward Bok and other progressive moralists, saw in good taste and simple living the means for the middle classes to turn away from the artificialities and decadence of modern civilization, while leaving the basic capitalist structure intact. Most of the American followers of Morris never felt comfortable with the Englishman's brand of utopian socialism, nor did many of them have much sympathy for the unskilled proletariat. The president of the Boston Arts and Crafts Society, for example, in referring to Morris's socialism and his critique of the factory system, congratulated the membership in 1903 for "keeping those questions entirely out of our midst . . . and in attending to our proper concerns." He went on to add that it was "not only futile but wrong to attempt to carry on a crusade against those great systems [of production] which have made the best that there is in the modern world."[42]

In Edwardian England and in the United States, Arts and Crafts houses, decorations, jewelry, furnishings and the like became high fashion for the very wealthy. One commentator noted that "millionaires are through good intentions and fine desires placing such works of art in their palaces that American artists are making names as decorators and designers." Wealthy patrons such as Astor and Rockefeller hired Stickley to furnish their Hudson Valley country estates with "mission" furniture, and Henry Ford filled his Manhattan apartment with it. Charles Greene, a California craftsman, when asked why his architecture was so good, explained that "it was because he had rich clients."[43]

Arts and Crafts simplicity was in this sense in danger of becoming a restricted aesthetic movement catering only to those who could afford such chaste handicrafts. Frank Lloyd Wright's "prairie houses" may have embodied the principle of organic simplicity but only the affluent could afford to build them. Thorstein Veblen saw that when simplicity was equated primarily with good taste, it ran the risk of becoming merely chic. Along with others he suggested that the Arts and Crafts movement was being manipulated in the United States by the "arty" and the "crafty." In speaking of the British origins of the Arts and Crafts revival, Veblen recognized that a consumer taste for the irregularities of hand-made objects and the "lure of the rough edge" was becoming just another form of conspicuous consumption.[44]

A more friendly critic than Veblen tried to evaluate the American Arts and Crafts movement in all its aspects. Writing in the *Forum*, Alvan F. Sanborn noted the growing number of craft colonies and societies founded to promote the simple life, but he had to admit that their example was not doing "very much as yet toward curing the numerous ills that society is heir to." The working classes in the United States, Sanborn acknowledged, were not rushing to support either the radical socialism of Marx or the aesthetic socialism of Morris. Instead, they continued to align themselves with the promises of industrial capitalism. When asked what his objective was as head of organized skilled labor in the United States, Samuel Gompers replied: "More!" For him and other American labor leaders, then and since, the simplicity espoused by the Arts and Crafts spokesmen represented an anachronism. Why should the working classes limit themselves to plain living when through organization and protest they could gain a larger slice of the capitalist pie? This "bread-and-butter" unionist philosophy was a far cry from the contented republicanism expressed by many artisans and craftsmen during the Revolutionary era, and it showed just how deeply the dream of universal prosperity offered by mass production had penetrated into the national consciousness.

Still, Sanborn insisted, at least some Americans were elevating their vocational and artistic priorities, and he noted that the Arts and Crafts movement had a beneficial effect on many members of the bourgeoisie. It gave vital work to "resourceless society women who were trembling on the verge of ennui and provided over-worked, nerve-wracked men with an avocation that has restored their tone." Yet Sanborn concluded by echoing Veblen's criticism that a movement ostensibly intended to elevate the labors of the working class and the taste of the middle class could not depend on handcrafted objects available only to the well-to-do. Most Arts and Crafts ideologues, however, ignored such warnings. For them, it seems, personal salvation was far more important than public salvation, and they were fast becoming subsidized artists rather than truly independent craftsmen. "It is a proof of the growth of artsmanship to be able to make a living making things for use," one of them admitted, "even if only the few can afford to buy them."[45]

That the aesthetic simplicity embodied in the American Arts and Crafts movement was frequently a salve for overindulged and overworked members of the urban middle and upper clases rather than a profoundly transforming ethic was clearly evident in the sentimental idealization of country life that accompanied the revival of handicrafts. One leading publicist of the Arts and Crafts point of view claimed that the renewed interest in rural life at the turn of the century, joined to a newly found respect for honest craftsmanship, would simplify human existence and "preserve it from the sordid qualities . . . and make it cheerful and replete with manifold interest." Country living, in the "free spaces of nature," would provide psychic and physical release for modern Americans oppressed by city life. Moving to nature meant an "escape from the blighting tyranny of wealth and lust."[46]

The return to nature advocated by most Arts and Crafts spokesmen was not that of a Thoreau or a Tolstoy but that of an Emerson, Downing, or Norton—a comfortable home and vegetable garden in the country, within commuting distance of the city, and blessed with the amenities of civilized living. Stickley, for example, preached the need for building houses "which will simplify the work of home life and add to it its wholesome joy and comfort." In order for these houses to serve as agencies for republican simplicity, however, they must be "either in the open country or in a small village or town," for "we firmly believe that the country is the only place to live in." The city was a useful place for doing business and enjoying the public arts, but the "better" people must have their residence "in some place where there is peace and quiet, plenty of room and the chance to establish a sense of intimate relationship with the hills and valleys, trees and brooks and all the things that tend to lessen the strain and worry of modern life by reminding us that after all we are one with Nature." To aid those interested in taking up country living in a more practical way, Stickley organized "Craftsman Farms" in New Jersey, a training center for young urbanites interested in learning about farming, landscape gardening, and handicrafts. "Just as I said that everyone should live in the country at least part of the year," he explained, "so I saw that every boy should receive part of his education on a farm."[47]

In advocating such commuter pastoralism, Stickley bore witness to a veritable nature craze that seized the middle classes of America and Europe at the turn of the century. In the United States, country life had proven soothing to the patrician intellectuals for years, and now, thanks to rising incomes and improved transportation, the middle classes could partake of it as well. Thousands of frazzled urban dwellers were swept up in a wave of outdoor enthusiasm, determined to recapture the nutrients deemed vital to the soul that contact with nature supposedly provided. Like the Transcendentalists they found spiritual nourishment more satisfying in nature than in churches. "Country life," one journalist observed, "is fortunately winning its way into the affections of all classes. The longing for fresh air and sweet odors and fresh fruit and a simple life all go together."[48]

The turn-of-the-century nature revival took on several different forms, some superficial, some serious, all of which shared many overlapping ideas and emotions. At least three main elements in the general phenomenon are discernible: a back-to-the-land movement, which sought both to revitalize rural life for those already on the land and to encourage city dwellers to take up homesteading; a wilderness movement, designed to preserve and experience life in the wild; and, finally, what might be termed an outdoor fresh air movement, which was frequently related to the other two activities yet for the most part was more urbane and superficial in its contact with nature, typified most often by country vacations and summer camps.

Although the means for experiencing the benefits of country life were diverse, enthusiasts for each of these movements were united in their objection to the curses of year-round urban living, with its menaces to health and morals, its hectic pace, its ugliness and cancerous materialism. An article in the *Independent* in 1905, entitled "Suburbanism for the Professions," noted that with the increasing ownership of automobiles and telephones, urban professionals were destined to follow the artisans and craftsmen to the country. "The continuous racket of city life," the writer added, "pulls down the physical structure, disturbs and disorders the mental faculties, and has no slight bearing upon the *morale* of the human being." In such an urban environment, the "professional man is especially in need of rest and recuperation. Only the strong can endure the strain of city life for any length of time."[49]

Contact with nature, whether the virgin wilderness, the plowed field, or the Arcadian retreat, meant turning away from the artificiality of modern civilization to more abiding realities. God and goodness always seemed more accessible in the woods than in the city. Moreover, the countryside offered fresh air and a stimulus to strenuous activity. Physical exertion, it was widely assumed during the Progressive era, was vital both to moral vitality and mental alertness. And excursions into the countryside or wilderness were to be preferred over urban forms of recreation.

This was the persistent message of two charismatic figures who inspired and guided nature enthusiasts at the turn of the century. John Muir and John Burroughs were both articulate, impassioned naturalists who immersed themselves in nature and practiced a genuine version of outdoor plain living and high thinking. In the process they helped promote both the wilderness conservation movement and the more general interest in outdoor recreation and relaxation among urbanites. At the same time, their examples gave added impetus to the progressive crusade for simpler living.

Muir was a feisty Scot who at age eleven had emigrated with his family to Wisconsin in 1849. There he and his siblings labored long hours under their father's stern direction, struggling to make their small farm self-sustaining. Young John developed a consuming passion for reading, but his father prohibited his doing so at night, so the determined son would rise before dawn and doggedly educate and entertain himself through books. As a result of such efforts, Muir grew quite knowledgeable and was able to gain admission to the University of Wisconsin in 1860. Although he took no degree, he did discover a keen interest in botany, chemistry, and geology.[50]

In 1867, while working in an Indiana wagon factory, Muir suffered an eye injury that led him to "bid adieu to mechanical inventions" and spend the rest of his life studying "the inventions of God." His resolution made, Muir set off on foot on a thousand-mile trek across the country, carefully recording his observations of plant, animal, and human life in his journal. In 1868, his itch for travel still unrelieved, he boarded a steamer in New York and arrived in California two months later. Soon Muir made his way to the Yosemite Valley, where he worked at a variety of part-time jobs—breaking horses, shearing sheep, and milling lumber—that allowed him to spend much of his time hiking and living in the Valley. In 1880 he married, and for the next decade he and his wife lived on his father-in-law's farm in Martinez, fifteen miles north of Oakland. Muir helped make the farm a quite profitable enterprise, but his heart was always in the woods. By 1891 he had saved "more money than I thought I would ever need for my family or for all expenses of travel and study." So he sold part of his share of the farm and leased the remainder in order "to devote the rest of my life, as carefree as possible, to travel and study." He recalled later that "I might have become a millionaire, but I chose to become a tramp." Thereafter most of his life was spent in the woods.[51]

By the turn of the century Muir had become the nation's foremost spokesman for wilderness preservation. He published numerous articles on western forests and landscapes in magazines such as the *Atlantic Monthly*, *Harper's*, *Scribner's*, and *Century*, articles that proved instrumental in educating the eastern public about the need for protecting the West's wilderness areas. Muir promoted his cause with the passion of a zealot, for to him nature was a sacred reservoir that must be preserved for future generations. A latter-day Transcendentalist in his view of nature, he found in the woods a "window opening into heaven, a mirror reflecting the Creator." To him, natural objects were "sparks of the Divine Soul." Thus he believed with Emerson and Thoreau that by shedding the artificialities of civilized society and penetrating the *wild* one could experience the rapture of Divine presence. "The clearest way into the Universe," he maintained, "is through a forest wilderness."[52]

Muir was—and is—the ultimate hero of the wilderness cult, and rightfully so. He was a hardy, dominating man, convinced of the righteousness of his cause and the rightness of his philosophy of living. "The impression of his personality," wrote David Starr Jordan, the naturalist president of Stanford University, "was so strong on those who knew him, that all words seem cheap beside it." Muir made such a strong impression on Emerson during a visit to Yosemite in the early 1870s that the aging Concord sage supposedly wrote to a friend: "This is a more wonderful man than Thoreau."[53]

Muir was far more committed to a sustained life in the wild than was Thoreau. Although discovering much in Thoreau to admire, he ultimately found him too tame. After all, Muir loved to point out, the cabin at Walden was only a "mere saunter" from Concord. Muir's kind of rugged plain living placed him on the primitive end of the simple life spectrum. He once asserted that he lived more simply than the hated sheep he saw devouring the vegetation covering California's high Sierra mountain slopes. When hiking and camping, which he did for extended periods every year of his adult life, Muir slept under the stars on a bed of ferns and sequoia plumes. He ate crumbled bread and oatmeal, washed down with a little tea or water from a mountain stream.[54]

Muir was aware that his wilderness primitivism was eccentric, and he never expected that the mass of Americans would or should follow his example. But he was absolutely convinced that his citified countrymen, caught up in the "gobble gobble school" of capitalist endeavor and "benumbed with care," could benefit from contact with "the deep green woods," however short in duration. "Our crude civilization," he declared, "engenders a multitude of wants" that smother and harass the average American. "Yet few think of pure rest or the healing power of Nature." Wilderness was the best potion for sick lives "bound by clocks, almanacs . . . and dust and din." In the mountains, he assured the urban weary, "Nature's peace will flow into you as the sunshine into the trees. The winds will blow their freshness into you, and the storms their energy, while cares will drop off like autumn leaves." In promoting such revivifying contact with nature, Muir envisioned himself as a modern-day John the Baptist. "I care to live only to entice people to look at Nature's loveliness."[55]

To aid him in his crusade, Muir helped found the Sierra Club in 1892, an organization designed to promote the cause of wilderness preservation and to provide a sense of group fellowship for urban dwellers desirous of common experiences in nature. The Club, wrote one early member, "has come to mean an ideal to us. It means comradeship and chivalry, simplicity and joyousness, and the care-free life of the open." That many middle-class progressives were among the Sierra Club's most avid members indicates again the "soft" side of that larger reform impulse. While "hard," efficiency-minded progressives such as Gifford Pinchot were primarily interested in managing nature for productive use and economic growth, "soft" progressives, romantic enthusiasts such as Muir and members of the Sierra Club, were intent upon preserving wilderness areas both for their own sake and because they offered therapeutic experiential opportunities for harried urbanites. There was a simplicity and calmness in nature—as well as exhilaration—that acted as a soothing poultice on the psychic sores of overcivilized Americans.[56]

Muir was quite encouraged by the rapid growth of the Sierra Club and the popularity of the nature movement in general at the turn of the century. In an essay on the wilderness parks which President Roosevelt had been so instrumental in creating, he noted:

> The tendency nowadays to wander in wilderness is delightful to see. Thousands of tired, nerve-shaken, over-civilized people are beginning to find out that going to the mountains is going home; that wilderness is a necessity. . . . Awakening from the stupefying effects of the vice of over-industry and the deadly apathy of luxury, they are trying . . . to mix and enrich their own little ongoings with those of Nature, and to get rid of rust and disease. . . . Some are getting in touch with the nerves of Mother Earth.

If Muir's own style of wilderness living was too demanding for most middle-class enthusiasts, his actions and writings clearly inspired many of them to look to nature as a vital means of renewed vitality and temporary solace.[57]

Muir's friend and eastern counterpart, John Burroughs, had the same effect. Burroughs was not the scientific naturalist that Muir was, but he was much the better writer, and he published far more. He was the favorite nature essayist of Edward Bok and his literary editor Hamilton Mabie, and their admiration for the "hardy grey poet of things rural" was almost universally shared by the middle-class reading public. From the last few years of the nineteenth century almost until his death in 1921, Burroughs's rustic cabin and study, "Slabsides," a retreat he built a mile from his stone house, "Riverby," situated on seventeen acres about eighty miles above New York City on the Hudson, complete with a "Morris chair" and "Craftsman rocker," was the object of a pilgrimage for thousands—writers and journalists, Vassar students and professors, bird-watchers, wildflower enthusiasts, business magnates, and politicians. Theodore Roosevelt came, like the rest, seeking Burroughs's genial wisdom, warmth, and nature lore. A description in the *Outlook* of the mellow, white-bearded prophet of nature attests to his popularity: "The simplicity of Mr. Burroughs's nature and the simplicity of his spirit, as well as his innate kindliness, have made him the companion and neighbor of the whole country." Another journalist claimed that Burroughs, more than any other American, was the "man who has taught the simple life and sent his visitors away with an increasing perspective for the things that really count."[58]

Although Burroughs began his writing career in the early 1860s, it was not until the 1890s that he actually emerged as the nation's foremost embodiment of the love of nature and the virtues of simple living. Many found in Burroughs's writing certain qualities lacking in Thoreau—a congenial normality, a ripe and comfortable domesticity, a warmth for other human beings. Burroughs "brings us home for tea," wrote one literary critic, while "Thoreau leaves us tangled up in the briars." Hamilton Mabie considered Burroughs "riper and saner" than Thoreau. Where Thoreau loved to startle and sting readers by issuing sweeping indictments against modern civilization, Burroughs "is not a schismatic; he is a harmonizer." Burroughs was typically humble in the face of such repeated comparisons with Thoreau. "Why compare me to the disadvantage of Thoreau? Thoreau is my master in many ways—much nearer the stars than I am—less human, maybe, but more divine—more heroic." He observed that Thoreau "gave us an example of plain living and high thinking that is always in season, and he took upon himself that kind of noble poverty that carries the suggestion of wealth in soul."[59]

Readers and acquaintances also seemed to appreciate that Burroughs was a true man of the soil. One admirer observed that he was "a thorough-going countryman," who made his "living by tilling the soil, rather than by literature. . . . Money is a small temptation to him . . . and he is not in pursuit of either riches or fame." At Riverby, Burroughs tended a vineyard and a berry farm. At the same time, he consciously followed Thoreau's advice and limited his material needs in order to have greater control over his own time. As he grew older, Burroughs later explained,

> I am more and more inclined to reduce my baggage, to lop off superfluities. I become more and more in love with simple things and simple folk—a small house, a hut in the woods, a tent on the shore. The show and splendor of great houses, elaborate furnishings, stately halls, oppress me, impose upon me. They fix the attention on false values, they set up a false standard of beauty; they stand between me and the real feeders of character and thought.

Once, when Burroughs asked a farmer neighbor for an apple and some cabbage leaves for his resident rabbit, who lived under his study, he revealed that simple living was as good for animals as for humans. When the neighbor brought the food, Burroughs handed some back, observing with a chuckle that he did not want "to corrupt the rabbit" with such a lavish meal.[60]

The consensus portrait that emerges from the dozens of essays on Burroughs that appeared in turn-of-the-century magazines is that of a genial and tender saint, renowned for his rustic sincerity and friendliness. He loved old clothes and old books, old paths and old friends. Burroughs was no patrician elitist scolding the country for its ineptitude but rather a modern John Woolman of the fields, more Quaker than Puritan in his instincts, possessed of warm human sympathies and deep humane interests. "I am not a fighter," he admitted in 1907. "I dislike any sort of contest, or squabble, or competition, or storm. My strength is in my calm, my serenity, my sunshine." When Edward Carpenter, the English socialist writer and advocate of simple living, visited Burroughs, he described his American host as having a "tough, reserved farmer-like exterior." Burroughs resembled "some old root out of the woods, one might say, obdurate to wind and weather, but [he was] a keen quick observer, close to nature and the human heart, and worth a good many Holmeses and Lowells."[61]

Burroughs's most complete statement about his own preference for simple living was published in *Cosmopolitan* in 1906, some fifteen years before his death. The essay, "What Life Means to Me," received the most reader response of any he ever wrote. It taught patience and acceptance, the joy to be found in small pleasures and simple moments. As such the essay represented an eloquent objection to the dominant trends of the time, especially the mad scramble for money and the sharp class divisions of modern urban-industrial society. Burroughs believed the blind pursuit of wealth to be "one of the most lamentable spectacles the world has ever seen." In 1896, while reading Henry Demarest Lloyd's *Wealth Against Commonwealth*, he had told a friend that the book "makes me so mad that I can't read it long at a time. It tells how the people are robbed by trusts and combines." Thereafter he continued to be angered by the "greed of monopolies, the insolence and tyranny of railroads." In "What Life Means to Me," Burroughs asserted that "very many" of the great fortunes had been amassed by diverting "all the streams into . . . [one's] own private reservoir." A lot of people were thereby deprived of access to water. But socialism or other "isms" provided no answer to social inequalities and tensions. Differences in wealth and power, even if unjust, reflected stubborn differences in natural human abilities. Burroughs thus fell back on the concept of Christian simplicity advocated by John Woolman, urging the rich to live simply and devote their excess income to the "common good" in order to "bring to the masses increased comfort and refinement."[62]

For himself, Burroughs was willing to forgo economic ambition. "I have never sought wealth," he said. "I have been too much absorbed in enjoying the world about me." He accepted the good each day brought, usually unexpected, and in his case considerable—in "friends, travel, and opportunity." What he wanted, and implied all people should want, was a "moderate competency." Beyond that, wealth was a burden: "A man may possess a competency; great wealth possesses him. He is the victim." Only a few men, such as the Stoic Roman emperor Marcus Aurelius, he noted, could remain pure and simple while living in a palace. Consequently, when his son expressed a hint of avaricious ambition, Burroughs came down hard. "I think you are too strenuous and ambitious on the money side," he lectured. "Do not dream of wealth. . . . You are sure of $2000 a year, and that is enough."[63]

In concluding his essay in *Cosmopolitan*, Burroughs presented a paean to the simple life representing a mixture of generalization and detail that demonstrates the compelling effect his crisp prose and crackerbarrel philosophy had on his devoted readers. He wrote:

> I am bound to praise the simple life, because I have lived it and found it good. When I depart from it, evil results follow. I love a small house, plain clothes, simple living. Many persons know the luxury of a skin bath—a plunge in the pool or the wave unhampered by clothing. That is the simple life—direct and immediate contact with things, life with the false trappings torn away—the fine house, fine equipage, the expensive habits, all cut off. . . . To see the fire that warms you, or better yet, to cut the wood that feeds the fire that warms you; to see the spring where the water bubbles up that slakes your thirst, and to dip your pail into it; . . . to be in direct and personal contact with the sources of your material life; to want no extras, no shields; to find the universal elements enough . . . to be thrilled by the stars at night; to be elated over a bird's nest, or over a wild flower in spring—these are some of the rewards of the simple life.

It was an Emersonian wisdom that Burroughs preached and a Thoreauvian hardihood he practiced. And his sane simplicity proved remarkably soothing to careworn urbanites. A writer in *Cosmopolitan* in 1910 declared that "there is no man among us to-day whose message, if heeded, could bring more real contentment to the thousands of nerve-wracked business men in the country."[64]

As noted earlier, however, national as well as personal purposes helped generate both Progressivism and the nature cult at the turn of the century. In 1893 historian Frederick Jackson Turner had declared that the frontier had been the most positive force in shaping the national character. Among other things, it had been responsible for forcing Americans to discard "complex European life" in favor of the "simplicity of primitive conditions." The wilderness, Turner said, in language reminiscent of a Fenimore Cooper, Caroline Kirkland, or John Muir, "masters the colonist. . . . It strips off the garments of civilization and arrays him in the hunting shirt and the moccasin." Yet now, he contended, the frontier was fast receding. The continent had been colonized and civilized, and Turner wondered if American ideals and institutions "have acquired sufficient momentum to sustain themselves under conditions so radically unlike those in the days of their origin?"[65]

Theodore Roosevelt shared Turner's emphasis on the key role played by the frontier experience in shaping American character. In his numerous histories and biographies dealing with the West and westerners, Roosevelt had likewise focused on the pioneer experience as crucial to American development. Contact with nature, he argued, had stimulated "that vigorous manliness for the lack of which in a nation, as in an individual, the possession of no other qualities can atone." And, like Turner, he, too, was anxious about what the closing of the frontier and the urbanization of life would mean to national virility and traditional values. Throughout the 1880s and 1890s, Roosevelt worried that the metropolitan American was fast becoming an "overcivilized man, who has lost the great, fighting, masterful virtues." Roosevelt believed that Americans needed to adopt what he called "the doctrine of the strenuous life, the life of toil and effort, of labor and strife," which he deemed necessary as an antidote both to the "mere money-getting American" and to "the over-civilized man," the patrician intellectual and businessman leading a "cloistered life which saps the hardy virtues in a nation."[66]

William James echoed Roosevelt's critique of an overcivilized and sedentary America, but he was incensed at his former student's passion for war. Roosevelt, he groused, "gushes over war as the ideal of human society, for the manly strenuousness which it involves, and treats peace as a condition of blubberlike and swollen ignobility, fit only for huckstering weaklings, dwelling in gray twilight and needless of the higher life." James lashed out at Roosevelt for so narrowly equating strenuosity with militarism. "May not voluntarily accepted poverty," the philosopher asked, be "'the strenuous life,' without the need of crushing weaker peoples?" Of course it could, he answered in his famous essay, "The Moral Equivalent of War." James agreed with Roosevelt that Americans, in pursuing a narrow materialism and leading citified lives, were compromising their spiritual heritage and sapping their physical hardihood. But he proposed an alternative solution to military endeavor: organizing civic armies in which American youth would perform hard and invigorating work in nature for public benefit, reclaiming swamps, fighting fires, improving roads, planting trees. After such a rugged, but not combative experience, the "gilded youths" would return to metropolitan life, "the childishness of society knocked out of them . . . with healthier sympathies and soberer ideas." James suggested that through such a program, "hardihood and discipline would be wrought into the growing fibre of the people; no one would remain blind as the luxurious classes are now blind."[67]

Though never abandoning his glorification of martial combat as the supreme agency of manly virtue, Roosevelt as President saw considerable merit in the back-to-nature emphasis of Jamesian strenuosity. He himself had long before developed an acute enthusiasm for almost any outdoor activity—sports, hunting, bird-watching, hiking, horsemanship. "There are no words," he stressed, "that can tell of the hidden spirit of the wilderness, that can reveal its mystery, its melancholy, and its charm. There is delight in the hardy life in the open, in long rides rifle in hand, in the thrill of the fight with dangerous game." As a nationalist, sportsman, and naturalist, Roosevelt valued America's natural resources as necessary for her material greatness, and he valued contact with the wilderness or outdoor work such as farming or ranching as necessary for the moral and physical development of the citizenry. A friend of both Muir and Burroughs, Roosevelt came to acknowledge the possibility of enhancing American character without resorting to war. In discussing the merits of wilderness parks, for instance, he announced that "no nation facing the unhealthy softening and relaxation of fibre that tends to accompany civilization can afford to neglect anything that will develop hardihood, resolution, and the scorn of discomfort and danger." Thus, he concluded, "as our civilization grows older and more complex, we need a greater and not less development of the frontier virtues."[68]

It was this cluster of national and personal concerns that led Roosevelt in 1908 to convene the first national Country Life Conference, appointing the noted Cornell University horticulturist Liberty Hyde Bailey as its chairman. The Country Life Movement, as it came to be known, was an example of the moral and utilitarian tendencies of Progressivism coming together. Avowedly unromantic, it was a practical uplift effort on the part of idealistic, well-educated middle-class professors, social critics, and government officials, most of whom were born on farms or raised in small towns in the Midwest. In part the program was scientific and educational, intended to improve agricultural production, and in part its purpose was social, to make the simplicities of rural life more attractive to disaffected urbanites as well as struggling farmers and alienated villagers. In addition, there was the hope that farm youth could be kept at home, where they could learn traditional American values and avoid the temptations of the metropolis. After all, it was widely assumed, farming was the principal occupation of the nation's purer republican youth; the founding fathers had for the most part been men close to both the soil and the frontier. Therefore, it seemed to progressive participants in the Country Life Movement, some experience in growing things in the midst of the simplicity and freshness of the countryside could not only make people more self-reliant but in some cases actually help solve the pressing social and economic problems associated with modern urban living.[69]

This was the abiding hope not only of prominent progressives such as Roosevelt and Bailey, but of lesser known figures such as Bolton Hall, a New York lawyer and follower of Henry George, whose books *Three Acres and Liberty* (1907) and *A Little Land and a Living* (1908) belonged to a long tradition of agrarian self-sufficiency "how-to" manuals and truck-garden success stories. Hall was convinced that a partial solution to the crowded and expensive life of the cities, too often overlooked by many "conservative" urban reformers, was to encourage people to move back to the land and take up homesteading, either as a full-time vocation or as an invigorating form of recreation that would also provide a partial sufficiency. Commuter pastoralism, he claimed, had long been a "healthy and beautifying diversion" for the wealthy, and now commuter agrarianism was readily available to the middle classes as well. "With the improvements in steam and electricity, the revolutionizing of transportation, the cheapening of the telephone, it is becoming possible to live at a distance from our place of business." But Hall emphasized that country living was not merely therapeutic. To him, gardening was more than a relaxing hobby for the affluent; it was a means to self-sufficiency and self-respect for the disadvantaged as well. It provided a way out of the straitjacket of modern urban-industrial capitalism. The times demanded that "we improve the conditions surrounding our lower classes." To enable some of the poor to escape the degrading life of the tenements, he helped organize the "Little Land League," a philanthropic effort designed to raise money to buy up farm land surrounding the cities and then offer it to the working poor at reduced prices. Its object was "to minimize the danger from overcongestion in the large city and to encourage those who are neither successful nor happy in it to find means of livelihood in the country." Hall assured his readers that it was "easier to live in comfort on the outskirts of the city as producers, than in the slums as paupers."[70]

To urban dwellers who complained of the drudgery and long hours of farm labor that had initially led many of them and their parents to move to the city, Hall responded that dramatic innovations in applied technology had greatly improved the quality of farm life. His vision of the modern farmhouse was much like that of David Grayson. It would include labor-

saving appliances and implements, a piano, books and magazines, and a
much more comfortable pace of living than that of commercial or traditional
farm life. As he explained:

> Those who extol the simple life as the ideal condition of happiness do not mean
> that want and deprivation of necessities is the ideal condition. . . . Both
> extremes of wealth and of poverty are burdens and retard mental and moral
> progress. The ideal condition is to be found on a farm where the land is paid for
> and ample means are at hand to supply the necessities for physical demands,
> with leisure to learn and enjoy those pleasures of the mind, which come with
> Nature's laws and wisdom, to live in harmony with them, and in a measure
> comprehend the purposes of creation.

Hall knew that he was fighting against the trend of the times in encouraging
people to leave the city for the countryside. The amusements, excitement,
and mythic economic opportunities afforded by the city remained alluring.
Yet he believed he could prove that with a little work and imagination, a
three-acre plot of land could yield enough produce to sustain any family. To
this end, he wrote *Three Acres and Liberty*, as well as later books, in order to
demonstrate in precise detail how to go about buying land and establishing a
working homestead.[71]

Edward Bok wholeheartedly agreed with Hall and the Country Life
Commission that contact with nature was essential to the simplification of
life he continually espoused for his middle-class readers, and in his many
editorials on the subject he reflected the wide range of motives and practices
making up the phenomenon. But he drew back from Hall's vision of a nation
of homesteaders liberated from the corporate culture. That was perhaps
desirable but unrealistic. Yet he did agree that country living was the ideal
environment for progressive simplicity. It was vital, he believed, that the
modern businessman and professional have some leisure and repose, and
this was only possible "when a man lives in the country—in some suburban
place, away from the actual scene of the daily grind." He was encouraged
by the growing suburban trend and argued that "there would be a far
smaller percentage of nervous women in America today if suburban life
had been in vogue ten years ago as much as it is today." As the transplanted city housewife "sees the simplicity with which Nature works, unconsciously will the lesson be forced upon her and enter into her own methods."
Nature's "restful ways" would allow tense and tired husbands and wives to
relax, and outdoor activity and sports would promote more "robust constitutions." In addition, Bok suggested, "Healthy morals are more easily instilled
into a child's mind where the air is healthy. Wholesome ideas come from a
clear intimacy with Nature."[72]

Although Bok preferred year-round country or suburban living for everyone, he realized that many people would remain in the cities. For them he

proposed a variety of options intended to provide at least some of the enrichment and simplicity that contact with nature had to offer. If full-time living among farmers and villagers was impossible, then at least one should "go to the country in the summertime and live with them, and extract some of the wholesome lessons of simple living which their lives can teach us." Hence, just as Jane Addams and Lillian Wald stressed to their middle-class social workers the benefits of contact with the immigrant poor, Bok saw great merit in the urban bourgeoisie rubbing elbows with rural folk. In an effort to entice his readers into the country, Bok published a series of pictorial essays entitled the "Prettiest Country Houses in America," and he regularly published inexpensive plans for summer cottages. One of the contributing architects noted that a summer cottage was a luxury, but one "that may be had at little cost," if the builder took advantage of the cheapness of land and constructed a plain, functional dwelling.[73]

For those unable to afford even a rustic cottage, Bok insisted upon the necessity of a vacation in the woods. Every woman, he stressed, "should occasionally have a respite from the thousand and one perplexities of housekeeping. That respite may be brief or long, but a respite there should be." But Bok decried the fashionable practice of summering in resort hotels. Such places were too often islands of urban socializing in the midst of Arcady. He maintained that whatever benefit vacationing children and mothers received by being in the country was counteracted in such luxury hotels by "the innutritious food that is eaten, the irregular hours that are kept, the air of artificiality that is charged into their lives, and, above all, the cosmopolitan acquaintances that they make." It would be better for families to rent a cottage in one of the "hundreds of quiet rural nooks" than to engage in the urbane and shallow social life of the resorts.[74]

Bok was particularly concerned that the nation's children have access to the revitalizing effects of nature, and he joined Bolton Hall and other progressive moralists in vigorously championing both the urban playground and youth camping movements that began to flourish during the late nineteenth century. Bok was one of the early supporters of Fresh Air Funds that were organized in many eastern cities to subsidize country vacations for disadvantaged urban children. In such youth camps, as well as those sponsored by Boys' Clubs, the YMCA, and other municipal and church groups, sporting activities and handicrafts were integrated with cooperative living in what one writer called the "simplicity and sincerity of nature." The counselors were supposed to provide ideal role models, endowed with "manly" physical strength and high moral values, especially courage, honesty, and devotion to an ideal. One of the most important ideals was the capacity to accept and surmount challenges, a theme of particular importance to Bok, the self-made immigrant. Young bodies hardened by the rigors of outdoor camp life, he felt, would help overcome the weaknesses of effete city youth.[75]

The similarity of such a camping ideal to William James's "moral equivalent of war" proposal is clear. Strenuosity, simplicity, and nature would combine to form the basis for a rejuvenated American character, and the nation was bound to benefit. In this sense, much of the anxiety felt by Bok, James, Addams, Roosevelt, and other middle-class moralists about a loss of virility and hardihood was occasioned by the growing feeling that modern urban life, with its enervating material comforts, pervasive filth, wearying working conditions, moral temptations, and sedentary leisure was sapping children of all classes of their virtue, self-reliance, and physical vigor.

Equally disconcerting to some was the growing feminization of American culture. The cult of domesticity had gone too far. Overprotective Victorian mothers and female schoolteachers now dominated the formative years of boyhood and threatened to produce a generation of passive and dependent men. As one concerned reformer observed in 1911, the American boy in the past "could ride, swim, hunt, and skate; he was handy with tools; he knew nature's secrets in field and wood; had chores to do. He was self-reliant and well developed in body and brain. Because of a careful rearing in a *real home* he was respectful and obedient, the right material from which to build a nation." Now, he charged, too many American boys were coddled and pampered "sissies." The summer camp, however, would help make up for such deficiencies. In the camp, one enthusiast claimed, "boys are taught self-reliance, self-respect and to respect the rights of others." A Baptist minister likewise saw in the summer camp an environment where coddled city boys could learn the joys of living a "life as simple and unostentatious, as benevolent and unselfish, as our Lord." In such rustic outposts of muscular morality and simplicity, modern temptations such as "fashion and display and dissipation" would be eliminated, and boys would develop an appreciation for self-control and collective endeavor.[76]

So the values of youth camping—fostering healthy bodies, self-confidence, civic virtue, simplicity, and a love for and knowledge of nature—were preached to much the same middle-class audience that was devouring literature about the out-of-doors at the turn of the century. The message was an appealing one to parents anxious about the degenerative effects of city life upon fragile youth. Their own supine dependence on specialists, financiers, middlemen, technicians, and servants convinced many of the need to expose their offspring to the salutary effects of summer camps and other forms of outdoor activity, and the camping movement mushroomed into a major middle-class activity. For those "who cannot afford yachting trips and the like, and whose ideas of summer recreation are not attuned to the string band of a 'summer hotel,'" promised one camping advocate, "there is nothing that returns so much for the expenditure of strength and money as plain American camping. It's a very simple matter."[77]

A founding figure in the youth camping movement in the United States was Ernest Thompson Seton, one of the most popular nature writers. Born in England in 1860, Seton migrated to Canada with his family six years later, settling on a farm in Ontario. There he developed a passionate interest in outdoor life. After studying to be a painter in London, he returned to Canada and spent five years in rural Manitoba, sketching wildlife, exploring, hunting, and collecting specimens of plant and animal life. In the 1890s Seton relocated to New Mexico, where he worked as a wolf killer on a cattle ranch before embarking on numerous personal expeditions throughout the American West. All the while, Seton was producing exciting wildlife stories and colorful illustrations for major American periodicals. Like Muir and Burroughs, he became a propagandist for outdoor life, arguing that it "is not enough to take men out of doors; we must also teach them to enjoy it."[78]

Seton shared with Bok and many other progressive moral reformers the belief that city children especially needed to be taught the ways of nature and exposed to its beauties. At the same time, he harbored a romantic preference for simple living and a patrician desire to revive Anglo-Saxon folk traditions. To promote such values, he transformed a group of abandoned Connecticut farms into a naturelore training center, and in 1902 he started his first "band" of Woodcraft Indians, of which he was "Head Chief." His image of the Indian was highly idealized, much like the early impression Thoreau had developed and that James Fenimore Cooper had portrayed in his novels. For Seton the Indian was the "great prophet of outdoor life," who revered beauty in all creation and was untouched by avarice. Indeed, the Indian was a natural "socialist" who solved the "great economic problem that vexes" modern civilization—"abject poverty and monstrous wealth"—by "nationalization of all natural resources and national interests." Such a plain living communal society, marked by dignity, simplicity, and cooperation, tucked away in nature, was the vision Seton held out to those who would join him in the Woodcraft camping adventure.[79]

Seton intended to make his Woodcraft Indian organization serve as a "school for mankind" whose curriculum would be based "on the simple life of primitive times, divested, however, of the evils that ignorance in those times begot." His purposes were explicitly moral. As he wrote: "We know all too well that many Americans . . . have become arrogant, ignorant and, consequently, degenerate. We know money grubbing, mundane politics, degrading sports, cigarettes, town life of the worst kind, false ideals, moral laxity and lessening, in a word 'city rot' has worked evil in the nation." Now youth living in an "over-busy world" would be cleansed of such impurities by learning the naturelore that their forefathers had taken for granted. Seton's program and vision inspired Bok to invite him to start a new department in the *Ladies' Home Journal*, entitled "American Woodcraft for Boys," in which the "Woodcraft Indians" idea was first introduced. Seton explained that boys joining his new organization would find "something to do, something to think about, and something to enjoy in the woods, with a view always to character building, for manhood, not scholarship, is the first aim of education." Members would be taught crafts and skills but also democratic values,

since the boys would organize their own self-governing tribes. Such a partici-
patory and egalitarian system would inculcate a constructive, yet critical
frame of mind, rather than promote a doctrinaire conformity.[80]

Soon, Woodcraft Indian tribes were being formed throughout New
England. In 1906 John Burroughs visited one of the "Woodcraft" camps,
and afterwards wrote President Roosevelt that Seton had "a big thing in his
boys Indian camp. . . . All the boy's wild energy and love of devilry are
turned into new channels, and he is taught woodcraft and natural history
and Indian-lore in a most fascinating way. I really think it is worthy of your
attention and encouragement." Within a few years, other youth groups
similar to the Woodcraft Indians, including Daniel Beard's Sons of Daniel
Boone and the Camp Fire Girls, also appeared.[81]

The youth camping movement was by no means a uniquely American
phenomenon. Throughout western Europe at the turn of the century, similar
groups were being formed to expose city children to the aesthetic delights
and enriching vitality of outdoor life. In Germany the *Wandervogel* was the
youthful expression of a widespread anti-urban and anti-industrial sentiment
that had developed among the bourgeoisie. Loosely organized in small
groups, the urban German naturists had a penchant for hiking and camping,
singing folk songs, and learning about outdoor life. In the countryside they
found an outlet for their romantic exuberance and their adolescent desire for
autonomy. "Their return to nature was romantic," one student of the *Wandervogel* has written, "as were their attempts to get away from a materialistic
civilization, their stress on the simple life, their rediscovery of old folk songs
and folklore, their adoption of medieval names and customs."[82]

In England the outdoor youth movement at the turn of the century took
on a quite different cast. The Boy Scouts, founded by Lieutenant General Sir
Robert Baden-Powell, the hero of the siege of Mafeking, was an organization
for building character rather than picking flowers. Baden-Powell's boys were
not to be romantic rebels but sturdy citizens—patriotic, courageous, industrious. An English Teddy Roosevelt in his enthusiasm for the martial
virtues and in his glorification of outdoor strenuosity, Baden-Powell had
been dismayed to find in Africa that the typical British army recruit lacked
mental toughness, physical stamina, and outdoor experience. To remedy
such a situation, he began planning upon his return to England a new youth
organization, and in doing so he borrowed heavily from Seton's Woodcraft
Indians and Daniel Beard's Sons of Daniel Boone. His research done,
Baden-Powell announced the creation of the new organization in 1908,
outlining his intention to place "on a positive footing the development, moral
and physical, of boys of all creeds and classes, by a means which should
appeal to them while offending as little as possible the susceptibilities of their
elders."[83]

There was an electric response to the Scouting idea. The organization
enjoyed immediate popularity in England, and by 1910 it had spread to

France, Denmark, Greece, Russia, and a score of other countries, including the United States. Scouting was brought to America by a Chicago publisher, William D. Boyce, who first learned of the movement when he was rescued from a London fog by a Boy Scout. After returning to the United States, Boyce met with representatives from the YMCA, the Camp Fire Girls, various church and municipal groups, as well as Seton and Beard, to discuss the creation of an American Scouting organization. They all responded enthusiastically to his plans, and in 1910 the Boy Scouts of America (BSA) was founded. It, too, experienced remarkable growth. By 1920 there were 350,000 scouts and 15,000 scoutmasters.[84]

Ernest Thompson Seton and Daniel Beard initially had high hopes for the Boy Scouts, and the two veteran woodsmen energetically supported the movement. Both received honorific positions, Seton serving as Chief Scout of America, and Beard as Chief Scout Commissioner. But their most important contribution was as publicists. In numerous articles and speeches, Beard portrayed the Boy Scouts as the crucial agency for sustaining traditional American values in the twentieth century. In Turnerian prose he explained that the "Wilderness is gone, the Buckskin Man is gone, the painted Indian has hit the trail over the Great Divide, the hardships and privations of pioneer life which did so much to develop sterling manhood are now but a legend in history, and we must depend upon the Boy Scout Movement to produce the MEN of the future." Seton likewise emphasized the strenuous simplicity that Scouting would evoke in American youth. He promised that the Boy Scouts would inject some "robust, manly, self-reliant boyhood into a lot of flat-chested cigarette smokers with shaky nerves and doubtful vitality." In the first Scout *Handbook*, Seton declared that camping "is the simple life reduced to actual practice." Yet, he and Beard were careful to emphasize that American Scouting was not to be tainted by militarism. In essence, it seems, they wanted to combine the youthful spontaneity of Germany's *Wandervogel* with the moral discipline of British Scouting to forge a distinctively American youth organization.[85]

Like Seton and Beard, a number of the early proponents of Scouting endorsed its promotion of a hardier, simpler, yet peaceful and humane way of living. Gustav Stickley, in announcing the creation of the Boy Scouts to his Arts and Crafts supporters, explained that the outdoor youth movement was "heartily in accord with the Craftsman point of view." Others noted the organization's resemblance to William James's proposed civic army. "To some extent," a writer reported in the *Chautauquan*, the self-professed organ of enlightened middle-class thinking, "the boy scout movement is a moral equivalent of war." Religious spokesmen and Victorian moralists particularly welcomed a youth organization whose stated purpose was "to unite culture and restraint" in American boys. Rugged outdoor recreation would provide a much-needed balm for urban children caught up in the dizzying whirl of metropolitan life. "Scouting, if successfully and universally applied," said one church spokesman, "will remove from American life much of its present industrial and social feverishness. The intensely 'practical' and selfish interests will be supplemented by those that are aesthetic, social, religious, or, in other words, natural and comprehensive." Like the Indian, the ideal Scout lives "a simple life. His food is simple and it satisfies a natural appetite. His habits are not controlled by a passion for hoarding up vast sums of money. . . . When his immediate wants are satisfied he is content."[86]

It was an arresting image—but one that was only rarely translated into practice. The emergence of the Boy Scouts as a powerful middle-class American institution during the Progressive era provides a striking example of the way in which the simple life and the nature movement became intertwined with conflicting values and methods that served to dilute and compromise their original ideals. It soon became evident that the rustic simplicity advocated by Seton and others was not of paramount importance to the Boy Scout executive board. The early administrators, many of whom were former city social workers with the YMCA, reflected a bureaucratic orientation that was characteristic of many reform organizations during the Progressive era. Urban reformers with little if any woodcraft experience themselves, they tended to place a higher priority on promoting mental discipline and social responsibility in the scouts than on pioneering. Forging an efficient, well-managed national organization became their guiding objective, and the BSA quickly began to take on the appearance of a highly structured corporation. Like the Lowell mills, the organization was no longer an ideal; it was an administration. In 1911 the central staff formed a public relations bureau and a Scout Supply Service to sell standardized uniforms and equipment. Attendance at centralized "official" Scout camps was more and more emphasized at the expense of local troop outings. And by 1915 much of the organization's stress was on vocational preparation rather than nature recreation. The tension between personal and national objectives so characteristic of Progressivism in general was illustrated in the Boy Scouts by an editorial statement in the organization's official magazine, *Boy's Life*: "Scouting aims to make boys good citizens partly for their own benefit, partly for the benefit of the country." Maintaining the right balance between such objectives, however, proved extremely difficult.[87]

Seton, Beard, and other outdoorsmen connected with the Boy Scouts observed such developments with consternation. In a letter to the Scout Treasurer, Beard bemoaned the institutionalization of the movement: "All the enthusiasm, all the picturesqueness and all those things which make it interesting are gradually being squeezed out and the whole thing made dry as dust and Academic." Seton was also disheartened by the emergence of what he called "city scouting." Scouts now commonly spent less time on the trail than in commodious shelters. Even more disturbing to Seton was the corporate tone that had come to pervade the Boy Scouts. The administrative "Philistines" had efficiently removed from Scouting its "spirituality, the power of ceremony, the charm of romance and the importance of the beautiful." Where his Woodcraft Indians had been a decentralized group loosely organized into "tribes" designed to encourage individual self-expression and self-realization, the Boy Scouts had become a complex hierarchical organization—highly centralized, standardized, and homogenized. The *Wandervogel*-like spontaneity of boys learning in nature about flora, fauna, and woodcraft was being replaced by Baden-Powell's utilitarian program of managerial discipline and military regimentation. In expressing similar concerns, Beard characterized himself and Seton as being "the last of the original dreamers, men of artistic and literary education." If the Boy Scouts continued to alienate such figures, he predicted, the movement would "lose its soul and become a machine which only runs from the momentum of its original impulse."[88]

For several years, Seton kept such reservations mostly to himself, hoping that the disturbing trends would somehow reverse themselves. Then, with the outbreak of war in Europe in 1914, his worst fears were realized. The taint of militarism and jingoistic nationalism that he and other Scout spokesmen had long resisted seemed finally to have contaminated the movement. He had earlier complained that too many of the men applying to be scoutmasters displayed the personality of aspiring drill sergeants whose "entire notion of Scout activity is military evolution." And with the outbreak of the Great War the situation was growing worse, not better. Seton had originally supported the Boy Scouts in order to provide a message of "conservation and brotherhood." But now, to the professional administrators, he argued, "conservation is a meaningless wind and brotherhood is giving way to jingoism."[89]

Seton's persistent criticism of the intrusion of martial chauvinism into the Boy Scouts created much resentment among the executive board, and James West, the Executive Secretary, began looking for a discreet way to remove the cantankerous Chief Scout. It did not take him long to act. Early in 1915, West and other Board members used the flimsy pretext of Seton's English birth and Canadian citizenship to declare him ineligible for any Scout post. Seton thereupon resigned, noting, however, that "the question of my British birth has [no] bearing on the case whatever." Seton correctly realized that it was his anti-institutional and anti-military views that had caused his ouster.[90]

The BSA was also coming under increasing pressure to follow Baden-Powell's policy in England of removing pacifists from its ranks. Theodore Roosevelt, an original member of the Boy Scout National Council, wrote a letter in 1915 to his friend West, reporting that he had learned from General Leonard Wood that the organization was harboring "certain leaders . . . [who] have used the Boy Scout organization as a medium for the dissemination of pacifist literature and . . . as a propaganda [*sic*] for interfering with the training of our boys to a standard of military efficiency." He then threatened to resign his post and withdraw his public support if such individuals were not rooted out. In concluding his ultimatum, Roosevelt maintained that a Boy Scout "who is not trained actively and affirmatively that it is his duty to bear arms for the country in time of need is at least negatively trained to be a sissy."[91]

The Rough Rider's message carried much weight with the Republican patriots who dominated the executive board. Where earlier Scout spokesmen had explicitly disavowed any military objectives or inclinations, they now reversed such a policy, clumsily announcing in 1915 that the organization was not "unmilitary." Soon thereafter, Roosevelt stressed in the Boy Scout *Yearbook* that Scouting had "no use for timid boys." Seton found such bullying discrimination a travesty. In a *New York Times* interview explaining his resignation, he revealed that he had been "out of sympathy with the Boy Scout organization for a number of years," and had "endeavored to combat its growing materialism. The movement as originally launched . . . was an organized attempt to give *all* our young people the advantages of out-of-door life and training." Seton heatedly objected to the attempts by Roosevelt and others to indoctrinate the boys in a lock-step nationalism. Instead, children should be taught to support the national policies they believed in and to oppose those they felt were wrong-headed.[92]

After leaving the BSA, Seton busily set about reviving his Woodcraft Indians, emphasizing that his rejuvenated youth group was for all children. It "fits both sexes and all ages, the weak and the strong; for none is too young or too old to enjoy it. It avoids the dangerous military and autocratic form of domination from the top, and shows equally the dangerous pitfall of unguided self-government by the young; it combines the best elements of both." In its attempt to combine democratic idealism and romantic naturalism, Seton's Woodcraft program was intended to counter the forces of modernity—urbanism, commercialism, imperialism, militarism—by instilling in children an appreciation for the communal ecology of an idealized Indian life. That it eventually lost out to the bureaucratic Boy Scout model was a pathetically ironic re-enactment of the earlier conquest of Indian culture by white civilization and its "progressive" ways.[93]

The displacement of Seton's Woodcraft Indians by the Boy Scouts reflected tensions within the scouting movement similar to those in the Arts and Crafts and back-to-nature movements. The conflicting motives and methods inherent in each of the groups illustrate some of the difficulties facing the broader crusades for simpler living and social justice during the Progressive era. The tensions between romantic individualists and authoritarian bureaucrats helped complicate many progressive attempts to elevate the tastes and priorities of the nation. True, those who replaced a romantic faith in ameliorating individual behavior with reliance on an organization run by efficiency-minded administrators often achieved beneficial and more widespread results. But too often the emphasis on the use of bureaucratic methods and scientific management to promote traditional ideals ended up smothering, compromising, or co-opting the old values to be restored.

Even more impeding to the crusade for simple living was the accumulated momentum of modern urban industrial life. As early as 1906 a writer in the *Outlook* predicted that there "is small chance that this revolt against wealth as the supreme aim of life will go too far; the tendencies in the other direction are far too powerful, the opportunities too tempting." Corporate life and values had come to dominate middle-class aspirations by the early twentieth century, and much of the attention given the simple life and the nature movement was superficial and fleeting. A movement intended to provide a meaningful antidote to the ills of urban commercial culture was transformed by many into merely a popular supplementary activity. One nature writer commented that the Arcadian ideal was being trampled by "the fashionable, the idle, the curious, the faddish." What many urban Americans wanted to experience in nature was not rural simplicity but stylish rusticity. "Living in the country without being of it," announced one bourgeois commuter, meant "allowing the charms of nature to gratify and illumine, but not to disturb one's cosmopolitan sense."[94]

Suburban garden homes and country clubs, restored farmhouses, cottages at the mountains or the shore, summer camps, scouting, boarding schools for the children, and Arts and Crafts furnishings—all rather quickly became standard aspects of affluent cosmopolitan life. Simple living in the American experience had always displayed cruel ironies. The Protestant ethic had become simply a work ethic, Jeffersonian republicanism was transformed into laissez-faire individualism, and Transcendentalism gave way in old age to Brahminism. Likewise, simple living during the Progressive era was being used by some as a placebo to calm frayed nerves before plunging back into the maelstrom of metropolitan life and by others as a means of imposing Victorian moral standards on the rising millions. A movement ostensibly dedicated to pristine aesthetic and normative ideals thus ran the risk of being itself exploited and made to serve the status quo.

This creeping *embourgeoisement* of simplicity and the back-to-nature movement was clearly evident when the Boy Scouts began offering merit badges in such "outdoor" subjects as automobiling, business, salesmanship, engineering, accounting, and mechanical drawing. By the 1920s, critics complained that Scouting had changed from being an organization dedicated to promoting a robust simplicity in nature to a "parlor game" catering to the needs of well-heeled middle-class urbanites. "Hiking today," one disaffected Scouting executive contended in 1930, "is almost a lost art. . . . The boys ride to the appointed place in automobiles or a truck. . . . They take along chicken salad sandwiches, cookies, lady-fingers, canned goods, thermos bottles, paper napkins—and a change of underwear." The movement, he charged, "was irretrievably in the hands of American businessmen." Even those who defended the organization confessed a longing "for the old days when there was more hiking and camping, less organization, more real scouting spirit, when all the men backing the movement were in it for the joy of service rather than self-aggrandizement."[95]

Still, if progressive simplicity in its various forms did not provoke a dramatic shift from the status quo of conventional urban life, it was a significant departure for many and a genuine transformation for a few. True, much of its real meaning was diluted and distorted by organizational conflicts and by the mixed motives of powerful individuals such as Theodore Roosevelt. But even in its most superficial forms, turn-of-the-century simplicity did reflect a yearning for more lasting values and enriching experiences than orthodox middle-class corporate and community life had to offer. "Say your worst for it," the literary critic Henry Seidel Canby noted in 1917, "the fact remains that more Americans go back to nature for one reason or another, annually, than any civilized men before them." If Addams, Bok, Stickley, Hall, Seton, Burroughs, Muir, and other propagandists succeeded in luring even a few indulgent urbanites out of their cluttered houses and "nervous" frame of mind and into the countryside or the settlement house and a more enlightened approach to getting and spending, they considered it an important first step in restoring balance and sanity to the American way of life. "We can never make life simple," Bok confessed, "but we can make it simpler than we do."[96]

CHAPTER NINE

Prosperity, Depression, and Simplicity

Imminent American entry into World War I not only caused tensions within the Boy Scouts; it also served to split much of the Progressive movement. Social reformers such as Jane Addams, Lillian Wald, Florence Kelley, and Frederic Howe reluctantly parted company with President Woodrow Wilson over the preparedness issue. They believed, as Wald explained, that war "was inevitably disastrous to the humane instincts which had been asserting themselves in the social order." Yet most reformers eventually endorsed Wilson's great crusade. They did so not only to help rid the world of tyranny but also to help revive among the American people a sense of sacrifice and community involvement. Like the Transcendental idealists and conservative moralists after the firing on Fort Sumter, they hoped that the war effort would exercise a positive influence on American character. Progressives, claimed one enthusiast, "may come to understand why the war is a blessing in disguise if it will check the extravagance against which they have impotently protested." He assured his countrymen that "every one of us should be better for eating less, walking more, and having fewer clothes to worry about and choose from." Another progressive predicted a similar result: "Out of the turmoil and sacrifice will come discipline and orderly living and thinking."[1]

President Wilson likewise recognized the moral benefits of war. In a speech delivered shortly after Congress approved the war declaration in April 1917, he challenged the public to revive old virtues: "This is the time for America to correct her unpardonable fault of wastefulness and extravagance. Let every man and every woman assume the duty of careful, provident use and expenditure as a public duty." Herbert Hoover, whom Wilson appointed as food administrator, similarly appealed for the "elimination of waste and actual and rigorous self-sacrifice on the part of the American people." To encourage such frugality, the Department of Agriculture sponsored Wheatless Mondays, Meatless Tuesdays, and Porkless Thursdays and

215

Saturdays. Edith Bolling Wilson, the President's second wife, convinced the cabinet members' wives to pledge with her to "reduce living to its simplest form and to deny ourselves luxuries in order to free those who produce them for the cultivation of necessities." Much of the public followed the Administration's example. Thrift campaigns, victory gardens, and conservation efforts contributed greatly to the military effort.[2]

But such patriotic simplicity was typically short-lived. As early as December 1917 a writer in the *New Republic*, after acknowledging the real sacrifices made by millions of citizens, nevertheless claimed that "as a people we have not responded with sufficient vigor to the requirements of thrift. We are still lavish with ourselves, for the most part." No sooner was the war over than the mood of patriotic self-sacrifice quickly dissipated. "During the war we accustomed ourselves to doing without, to buying carefully, to using economically," one reformer noted in 1920. "But with the close of the war came reaction. A veritable orgy of extravagant buying is going on. Reckless spending takes the place of saving, waste replaces conservation."[3]

Such assessments have a familiar ring and a familiar hyperbole. Yet what differentiated the postwar buying binge from its predecessors was its scale and the vigorous and imaginative support it received from public figures and business spokesmen. "There is a widespread idea energetically fostered of late," reported the *Outlook* in July 1919, "that national prosperity is increased by liberal spending." A few months later, a writer in the *Independent* recognized a similar attitude at work. "Extravagance and pretentiousness," he wrote, were being "energetically encouraged . . . by the admonitions of our social mentors." Shortly after the war ended, a group of business representatives formed the National Prosperity Bureau to convince the public to abandon its war-induced simplicity. The agency distributed posters showing Uncle Sam sitting at the throttle of a locomotive. Above him was the inscription: "Full speed ahead! Clear the track for prosperity! Buy what you need now!"[4]

The quick transition from public conservation to public prodigality was a stunning disappointment to progressive idealists. The editors of the *Nation* argued in vain against the publicity campaign organized by the Prosperity Bureau. "Civilization," they maintained, "needs to be simplified" rather than made more complex and cluttered by indiscriminate economic expansion. "We need to reduce our wants, to cut down our standard of living, to buy less, to make less, to work less, to consume less of our lives in the machinery of living." But alas, they recognized, the country was hurriedly rushing in the other direction. Even the naturally optimistic John Burroughs was crestfallen at the course of events. In his journal of 1920 he observed: "For the first time in my life I am ashamed to be an American. . . . I knew in advance that it would be impossible to hold the people of this country up to a sense of high moral obligation, yet the concrete reality has cut me deeper than I thought it could. I am shocked." Similarly, in the aftermath of the landslide Republican victory in 1920, the defeated Democratic vice-presidential candidate, Franklin Delano Roosevelt, concluded that the nation's self-denying energies had been spent in the war against Germany and in the battle over the League of Nations. "Every war," he said, "brings after it a period of materialism and conservatism; people tire quickly of ideals and we are now repeating history."[5]

Roosevelt was right. The ideals of simple living and social justice, so often intertwined at the turn of the century, did lose much of their appeal in the aftermath of the Great War. The electorate clamored for what President Harding ambiguously called a return to "normalcy," which apparently meant going back to the tried and true values of the Gilded Age—laissez-faire individualism, limited government, isolationism, and, above all, material prosperity. "This is essentially a business country," Harding reminded his critics, and he, along with his Secretary of the Treasury, Andrew Mellon, shaped federal policies so as to promote a resurgence of corporate capitalism.[6]

Their efforts soon bore fruit. When Harding died in August 1923, Calvin Coolidge inherited an unprecedented economic boom that would continue to expand throughout the decade, thus giving the 1920s its popular, albeit distorted, image as a period of pervasive prosperity and carefree living. Greater mechanization and more efficient techniques of industrial management resulted in dramatic increases in productivity and lower retail prices. Consequently, the "democracy of things" that nineteenth-century economic boosters had promised to the public finally began to appear during the 1920s. Goods and services once available only to the affluent were now made more accessible to the lower classes through mail-order houses or in huge department stores. This raised standard of living for the millions was an achievement that even the sharpest critics of capitalism came to recognize. One such appreciative critic was Lincoln Steffens, the influential progressive journalist, who in 1928 reversed his long-standing opposition to corporate America when he wrote: "Big business in America is producing what the Socialists held up as their goal: food, shelter, and clothing for all."[7]

What Steffens and others found worrisome, however, was the age-old fear that materialism would come to be a god. President Coolidge fueled such fears with his terse assertion that brains "are wealth and wealth *is the chief end of man*." The nation's political leader went on to make the connection between business and religion explicit. The "man who builds a factory," he commented, "builds a temple, the man who works there worships there, and each is due . . . reverence and praise." For Coolidge, as well as many other Americans in the 1920s, the "business of America was business."[8]

Edward Bok discovered the strength of such economic orthodoxy as he tried to carry his campaign for simpler living into the postwar era. Bok had resolved soon after taking control of the *Ladies' Home Journal* in 1889 that he would retire from his post after twenty-five years. The outbreak of the Great War in Europe and eventual American involvement in the conflict had caused him to postpone his departure, but once the war ended, he announced his retirement in December 1919. Bok was fifty-six years old, wealthy, and in the full flush of intellectual and physical vigor. The magazine was also flourishing. Its October 1919 issue sold more than 2,000,000 copies. Nevertheless, Bok wanted out. It was time to leave business and devote his money to philanthropy and his time to social service.

As he began his new career, Bok wrote several articles promoting his gospel of retired activism and bemoaning the crass preoccupation with material pursuits that seemed to pervade Jazz Age America. "Money is King," he declared in 1924. "Business is our God. Commerce rules." After acknowledging the many benefits resulting from economic growth, he reminded readers that "years of unexampled industrial productivity and of the accumulation of great wealth are not bringing, and have not brought, happiness to mankind." Poverty, crime, tension, anonymity, and despair remained prevalent in the midst of unparalleled prosperity. Bok warned the businessmen of the country that "bliss in possession does not last" and that "the fundamental things which really matter are outside the pale of the banking-house." His advice for the well-to-do was to follow his own example. Those who had worked diligently enough to earn a comfortable income should "abandon the harness of business" and devote their energies to "higher" causes. "Where all a man's thought has been centered on himself, now he turns and thinks of others."[9]

Although religious spokesmen and social activists praised Bok's outlook, many among the business community were aggressively critical. His idea of early retirement coupled with public service struck Glenn Frank, editor of *Century* magazine, as "a dangerous and essentially anti-social doctrine" that threatened the "American tradition of sticking to business until one drops in the harness." Bok, he claimed, "was advocating a new asceticism, which consists in running away from business in order to be useful to society." Instead of being praised for such a stance, the successful editor should be "morally court-martialed for deserting his post in the midst of the battle." Another apologist for the modern work ethic, William Feather, was even more caustic in his criticism of Bok's promotion of "simplicity and service." Writing in the *Nation's Business*, he charged:

> Mr. Bok is un-American. In proof of this I cite that he has quit work and is now attempting to Do Good, and conducting a vigorous propaganda to induce other business men to do likewise. Bok is ashamed to work. He is ashamed of profits. He regards trade as inferior. Doing Good, patronizing the stupid and weak, giving the people something they don't want, is his idea of a worthwhile life. I contend that no 100 per cent American subscribes to such a doctrine. The 100 per cent American dies in harness.

At first glance, Feather's comments could be taken as a witty satire of Ben Franklin's work ethic gone out of control. But he was not joking. His ideal "100 per cent American" unashamedly believed "in the doctrine of selfishness" and was proudly "rich, fat, arrogant, superior."[10]

Such a brazen materialism was heard often during the 1920s. A capitalist evangelical claimed that the *summum bonum* of life was the accumulation of material goods and pleasures through hard work. "Man's nature could realize its loftiest aspirations only in a materialistic heaven on earth," he said. Bok's promotion of the Thoreauvian idea that prosperity offered a unique opportunity for Americans to devote more of their time and attention to "higher" pursuits seemed lost on those inebriated by the promise of wealth. "You know the quality of the lads that come to this school," Harvard law professor Felix Frankfurter wrote in 1924—"the best there are in the country. And yet, on the whole, a pretty crass materialism is their dominating ambition."[11]

The glorification of work and wealth during the 1920s was in part stimulated by the changing nature of the economy. A new consumption ethic was rapidly displacing the production ethic of the nineteenth century. Dramatic increases in productive efficiency flooded the country with a welter of consumer delights that threatened to cause economic havoc unless the populace accelerated its spending. Hence, business leaders, salesmen, and public relations experts began a concerted effort to eradicate what was left of the original Protestant ethic's emphasis on frugal living. Americans were now told that traditional Christian or republican simplicity was a luxury an advanced capitalist country like the United States could no longer afford. "People may ruin themselves by saving instead of spending," one economist maintained. Plain living, he predicted, could be "economically disastrous" if practiced on a large scale. A newspaper editorial reflected this growing assumption when it concluded that the American's "first importance to his country is no longer that of citizen but that of consumer. Consumption is a new necessity."[12]

Henry Ford and other industrialists recognized that, in order to expedite this mass consumption ethic, employers must provide higher wages as well as shorter working hours and vacations so that employees and their families would have the money and time to consume the products that were being turned out in record numbers. The average industrial work week did decline throughout the decade, and real wages rose significantly, although not in proportion to corporate profits—a fact of ominous portent. Purchasing power was enhanced even more by the dramatic increase in installment buying. It was no longer necessary to save in order to buy; instant credit promised instant gratification, and the working classes were now offered an enticing avenue into the luxury marketplace. Paying for purchases with cash and staying out of debt came to be considered needlessly "old-fashioned" practices.

Still, putting more money in workers' pockets and giving them time to spend it did not necessarily get them to the department store or automobile dealership. The public had to be taught the joys of consumerism and the ease of buying on credit. The springs of impulse must be uncoiled. Enter Madison Avenue. During the 1920s and after, manufacturers increasingly found in mass advertising a powerful instrument for counteracting the abstemious "customs of the ages." One ad-man claimed that his industry was the most effective force working "against puritanism in consumption." It was. The revelations of behavorist psychology convinced advertisers during the 1920s that they could manipulate as well as inform the public mind. Copywriters and lay-out designers were now encouraged to appeal more to the "instincts" of the consumer than to his logic, especially the instinct of envy that John Adams, Tocqueville, Veblen, and others had already recognized as peculiarly potent in a capitalist democracy where material display was the primary determinant of social status. Through the cultivation of what they called "fancied need," advertisers were confident that they could greatly expand consumer tastes and desires. Robert and Helen Lynd, in their famous sociological study of Muncie, Indiana, *Middletown* (1929), remarked that the ads of the 1920s were "concentrating increasingly upon a type of copy aiming to make the reader emotionally uneasy, to bludgeon him with the fact that decent people don't live the way *he* does: *decent* people ride on balloon tires, have a second bathroom, and so on." The owner of Middletown's leading clothing store testified to the effect of such advertising when he explained that his customers were "no longer content with plain, substantial low-priced goods, but demand 'nifty' suits that look like those everyone else buys."[13]

Yet advertising executives argued that they were not trying to create consumer dissatisfaction but relieve it. Where Edward Bok had prescribed simplifying one's life as an antidote to middle-class nervousness and frustration, Helen Woodward, the leading female copywriter of the decade, contended that frivolous buying was the salvation of the bored middle-class housewife. "To those who cannot change their whole lives or occupations," she explained, "even a new line in a dress is often a relief. The woman who is tired of her husband or her home or a job feels some lifting of the weight of life from seeing a straight line change into a bouffant, or a gray pass into beige." By portraying impulse buying as a therapeutic measure to improve self-esteem, the advertising industry shrewdly helped undermine the conscientious frugality that progressives had helped revive at the turn of the century.[14]

For many literary intellectuals critical of the values of postwar American society, advertising served as the perfect symbol of the mundane business mentality, standardized mass culture, and spiritual vacuity that they felt permeated the age. In a number of his novels, particularly *Main Street* and *Babbitt*, Sinclair Lewis condemned advertising for distorting reality and creating false needs. George Babbitt, the frustrated real-estate salesman, centers his life and that of his family on the consumption of mass-produced and nationally advertised products. His primary goal as head of the family is not to inculcate traditional republican virtues or generate respect but to practice outward conformity, to ensure that his household possesses the same products and participates in the same activities as other families in the neighborhood. Thus "did the large advertisers fix the surface of his life," Lewis observes, "fix what he believed his individuality. These standard advertised wares—toothpastes, socks, tires, cameras, instantaneous hot-water heaters—were the symbols and proofs of excellence." Babbitt was thus representative of what David Riesman would later call the other-directed personality that grew out of the shifting corporate and cultural priorities of advanced capitalist society. The Protestant work ethic of the eighteenth century, with its emphasis on industry, thrift, and an inner-directed sense of self-worth, as Tocqueville had feared, continued to be displaced by an ethic of impulsive gratification coupled with an anxious desire to be accepted and envied by others.[15]

Thousands of American intellectuals and college students chuckled with Lewis at the banality of George Babbitt, but millions of those caught up in the self-enchantment generated by the consumer culture undoubtedly would have seen little humor in the caricature. To them, Babbitt was everything an American was supposed to be, and they enthusiastically participated in the expanding mass culture. In an editorial entitled "Dare To Be a Babbitt," *Nation's Business* asserted that the world would be far "better for more Babbitts and fewer of those who cry 'Babbitt.'" Another defender of middle-class consumerism provided a tribute to Babbittry in verse:

> Babbitts—though we jeer and flout them—
> We could never do without them.
> Artists all—we would be beggars
> Were it not for Butter 'n Eggers. . . .
>
> Babbitts great and Babbitts small,
> Speaking frankly, "Aren't we all?"

Such was the message pounded time and again into the American consciousness during the 1920s: the growth of the economy and the psychic health of the citizenry depended upon ever-increasing consumerism and the cultivation of at least the appearance of success.[16]

And, for a few glorious years the blueprint seemed to work according to plan. During the height of the "Coolidge prosperity," the industrial horn of plenty overflowed with new consumer delights. By 1928 almost two out of three families owned an automobile; one out of three had a radio. More and more homes were stocked with new electrical appliances such as washing machines, refrigerators, and vacuum cleaners. Moreover, expenditures on education, the arts, medical and scientific research, and social charities reached record levels. Hence, when President Coolidge addressed Congress in December 1928 he was understandably buoyant. "No Congress of the United States ever assembled on surveying the state of the Union," he boasted, "has met with a more pleasing prospect than that which appears at the present time." There was peace abroad, while at home there was "tranquility and contentment, harmonious relations between management and the wage earner, freedom from industrial strife, and the highest record of years of prosperity." All in all, he concluded, the country "can regard the present with satisfaction and anticipate the future with optimism."[17]

In the midst of such an atmosphere of self-congratulatory materialism, many prominent public figures such as Coolidge, Hoover, and Ford still paid verbal homage to the creed of simple living and professed the joys of contact with nature at the same time that they pursued policies promoting modern urban complexity. In 1928, Hoover, the millionaire mining engineer and Secretary of Commerce, described himself in a campaign speech as a "boy from a country village, without inheritance or influential friends." Fishing, he remarked, was "good for the soul of man." Much of the popular literature of the period likewise played to the nostalgic sentiments of the urban reading public. Best-selling novelists such as Gene Stratton Porter, Zane Grey, and Harold Bell Wright consciously evoked the Arcadian myth by setting their plots in the countryside or out West. And Americans by the millions continued to enjoy the invigorating benefits of periodic contact with nature in the form of camping, scouting, hiking, and so forth.[18]

But those advocating simple living as an alternative to modern urban industrial life rather than merely a recreational activity, political strategy, or nostalgic sentiment were few and far between. The sense of social urgency that had energized turn-of-the-century enthusiasts had dissipated by the 1920s. The leading journalist and social commentator of the decade, Walter Lippmann, observed in 1929 that the ethic of plain living and high thinking embodied in the lives of "Socrates and Buddha, Jesus and St. Paul, Plotinus and Spinoza" was "clearly out of favor" among the American people. Charles Stokes, writing in the *New Republic* the same year, agreed with Lippmann's assessment. Stokes confessed that he and others were "sick and tired of this present complicated life, and yearn for a simpler one." But, he continued, to "arise and preach it now, when every day in every way life is getting speedier, jazzier, and more and more delighted with its own cleverness, seems to be harder than ever. Who wants to go back to the Simple Life when the Dizzy Life is so much more fascinating?" Stokes then facetiously suggested that, in order to make simple living more attractive to a hedonistic public caught up in the era's soaring prosperity, advocates should turn to advertising. "Why not harness its enormous force to sell simplicity? It would do it. And you and I could enjoy a traitor's revenge, in using advertising to bring back what it has been most instrumental in destroying—the Simple Life."[19]

Yet there were a few hardy idealists during the 1920s who promoted simpler living along with Edward Bok. The homesteading ideal of Bolton Hall and other earlier back-to-the-land proponents was especially persistent in the face of the urban-industrial boom. Wilsonian progressives such as Franklin K. Lane, Ellwood Mead, and Frederic Howe had proposed during World War I that the federal government sponsor a homesteading program for returning soldiers. Lane was Secretary of Interior under Wilson, and Mead was his assistant. Together they helped draft legislation for a soldier settlement program while Howe, a prominent journalist and municipal reformer, served as the idea's most effective spokesman. In part, they saw their homesteading plan as a means of easing unemployment. Even more important was their Jeffersonian hope that the small family farm could be restored as the seedbed of republican virtue and simplicity. Howe stressed that the purpose of the soldier settlement plan was to create communities whose residents shared "a wide-spread interest in something other than wealth, or getting more and more land, or monopolizing more and more property." In Lane's view, such farms were intended to promote a simple life close to the soil. The veterans' homesteads would "not be large, but large enough to support a man, his wife, and three or four children, but not large enough to make a basis of speculation—small farms, intensely cultivated, sufficient for a man and his family."[20]

President Wilson endorsed the soldier settlement plan in December 1918, and during 1919 and 1920 over a dozen versions of the scheme were introduced into Congress. But strong opposition from commercial farm groups helped defeat each bill. Equally significant was the indifferent interest among soldiers themselves. As one supporter confessed, "The city bred veteran, who could not tell clover from alfalfa, simply did not respond." When a land settlement package finally passed as a rider to the Bonus Bill in 1923, President Harding vetoed it. The back-to-the-land advocates then turned their attention to the South, where political support for such programs was more enthusiastic. Mead, who remained in the Department of Interior during the 1920s, met with a delegation of southern congressmen in 1927 and helped them draft several bills intended to fund a series of experimental farm colonies in the agriculturally depressed region. But President Coolidge's ardent opposition to such schemes kept them from ever coming to a vote.[21]

This was quite a disappointment to an articulate group of southern intellectuals clustered at Vanderbilt University. The Nashville Agrarians, as they were called, had grown increasingly disillusioned with modern American society as the 1920s progressed. They especially resented the intrusion of northern urban-industrial culture into their own region. To Allen Tate, John Crowe Ransom, Donald Davidson, Frank Owsley, Robert Penn Warren, Andrew Lytle, and others among the Vanderbilt group of literary critics, poets, economists, and historians, it was imperative that the South sustain a culture of meaning rather than succumb to the North's culture of indiscriminate production and consumption. This was the theme of their manifesto *I'll Take My Stand* (1930), in which they portrayed the Old South as a regional society based on subsistence agriculture, the fellowship of family, a sense of belonging to an historical and regional tradition, and a deeply felt belief in a stern God—all bound together in an organic sense of community.[22]

In defending the virtues of their region and its traditions, the Agrarians created a dreamy, idyllic southern past in order to accentuate their disgust at the inroads being made by the forces of urbanism, industrialism, and secularism. As Ransom explained, they sought in their regional heritage a "certain terrain, a certain history, a certain inherited way of living" that would serve as a counterforce to the cult of Progress. "The past," Warren argued, "is always a rebuke to the present . . . it's a better rebuke than any dream of the future." But the usable past that he and the others portrayed was highly idealized by the haze of time and the needs of the present.[23]

The sentimentalized picture of the Old South that emerges from *I'll Take My Stand* is that of an organic, hierarchical agrarian social order made up of a compatible mixture of subsistence farmers, planter aristocrats, and slaves. But the Agrarians repeatedly tended to blur the distinction between the pre-Civil War small farmer and the stately planter, melding the virtues of the two into one composite portrait. They attached the refinements of the country gentleman—familiarity with the classics, Shakespeare, and Wordsworth—to the ennobling manual labor exercised by the yeoman farmer, seemingly oblivious to the fact that such physical and mental activities were rarely joined in one person. Hence, Ransom claimed that the southern farmer had been able to "develop his work and his play with a leisure which permitted the maximum of activity of intelligence." Reading the Agrarians, one almost forgets that most southern farmers rarely had the means or motivation to practice the kind of high thinking they attributed to them. In unconsciously shifting their admiration back and forth between the virtuous yeoman and the gentleman planter, the Agrarians reflected the old tension between the desire to translate classical simplicity into a societal ideal for the masses and the practical reality of its being primarily the possession of an educated elite.[24]

There is considerable impressionistic evidence supporting the Agrarians' contention that many southerners were less enamored of the acquisitive ethic than their counterparts in the North. A southerner, for instance, told a northern journalist traveling in the South in 1831 that most of the common people in his region "lived as well as they wanted to. They didn't want to make slaves of themselves; they were contented with living as their fathers lived before them." Similarly, a generation later, Frederick Law Olmsted found the Homeric ethic alive and well in the South. "The Southerner," he wrote, "has no pleasure in labor. . . . He enjoys life itself. He is content with being. Here is the grand distinction between him and the Northerner; for the Northerner always enjoys progress in itself. He finds happiness in doing." But however much the plain folk of the Old South rejected the anxious spirit of gain that they felt motivated northern society, few were the enlightened

Jeffersonian yeomen that the Agrarians portrayed. Their leisure was most often occupied with tobacco, liquor, horse racing, cock fights, and salty fellowship—not classical literature.[25]

By highlighting the best aspects of both planter and yeoman life and making a synthesis of the two their prescription for the good life, the Agrarians greatly undermined the effectiveness of their cause. Though many readers and reviewers sympathized with such an ideal Jeffersonian society of small, middle-class, independent farmers who appreciated simple pleasures, spiritual values, and the graces of unhurried life, few believed that such a society ever existed. The Old South evoked by the Vanderbilt group was simply too good to be true; it had no seamy or scheming characters such as Flem Snopes, Jeeter Lester, or Thomas Sutpen. It had no pellagra, hookworm, or illiteracy. Instead it was a Golden Age, a mythic pastoral scene of thoughtful herdsmen and cultivators like that depicted by Horace and Virgil. One critic understandably complained that the Agrarian manifesto "dwells only on the felicities of the patriarchal farmer, as if the small farmer regularly secured a dependable living from the rude forces of nature: as if nature were beneficent, and cared for his wants; and his children were never ill; and his wife were never overburdened with bearing and raising children."[26]

Despite its historical distortions, however, *I'll Take My Stand* did provide an incisive critique of the dangers posed by excessive industrial growth in contemporary society. The book in this sense was more than a chauvinistic reaction on the part of southern intellectuals. It was an articulate response to the same intrusion of modernity that had so perplexed the New England patrician intellectuals during the Gilded Age. Convinced as they were that the industrial commercialism being so assiduously courted by "New South" boosters represented a "foreign invasion of Southern soil, which is capable of doing more devastation than was wrought when Sherman marched to the sea," the Agrarians intended their book to serve as a clarion call, warning the South of what it stood to lose by blindly embracing modern ways.[27]

When the Agrarians moved from the realm of stylized history to contemporary social commentary and analysis, they strode onto firmer ground. There was much truth, for instance, in Ransom's characterization of the South in 1930 as a region still devoted primarily to rural and village ways and relatively more stable, orderly, pious, and plain than other areas of the country. Few disagreed with his assertion that "it is the character of our urbanized, anti-provincial, and mobile American life that it is a condition of eternal flux." The Agrarians also displayed a prescient clarity in their recognition of the vicious cycle inherent in the modern consumer culture. Though reduced working hours and improved industrial efficiency gave people "more time in which to consume, and many more products to be consumed," the hidden penalty for such advances would be endlessly rising expectations and expanding appetites. The modern cult of Progress, Ransom perceived, "never defines its ultimate objectives, but thrusts its victims at once into an infinite series. Our vast industrial machine . . . is like a Prussianized state which is organized strictly for war and can never consent to peace."[28]

In so pungently rebuking the Madison Avenue purveyors of such secular materialism, the Agrarians spoke eloquently to the spiritual crisis of the twentieth century. Similarly, when they dropped their polemical tone and cast their glance at the future rather than toward the past, they displayed considerable realism and moderation. Poet Allen Tate emphasized at one point that the Agrarians' true intention was to help the South resist the negative aspects of modernity without retreating into a "nostalgic anti-quarianism." Similarly, Robert Penn Warren admitted that the rural life he advocated for the twentieth-century South must be attended by improvements in the living and educational standards of blacks and poor whites. And Stark Young confessed in his concluding essay that "we can never go back" and that neither he nor the others truly desired a "literal restoration of the old Southern life, even if it were possible; dead days are gone, and if by chance they should return, we should find them intolerable."[29]

Hidden among the wistful nostalgia in *I'll Take My Stand* was a statement of principles that called not for a return to the mint-julep days of the planter nabobs but for a modern realization of the balanced economic and social system that Jefferson had envisioned long before. The "agrarian society" the twelve southerners espoused in their introductory statement was, they wrote, "hardly one that has no use at all for industries, for professional vocations, for scholars and artists and for the life of cities." Their utopia would include machines, factories, electricity, and profits. But ideally it would not tolerate "superfluous" industries or a leviathan central government. The southern intellectuals would accept industrialism into their region with "bad grace," viewing it is a necessary evil and sharing Jefferson's hope that manufacturing in the South could somehow be kept small, local, humane, and limited to producing articles for immediate household use. At the same time, agriculture would continue to "enlist the maximum number of workers" and be given preferential treatment by the government so that commoners would again have access to the ownership of land. All this, they added, must be achieved without creating the political centralization endemic to both communism and fascism.[30]

Perhaps because of their consummate literary skills, the Agrarians have received more attention than Ralph Borsodi, a New York social critic, decentralist, and homesteader, who emerged in the late 1920s as a prominent practicing spokesman for small family farming as an alternative for city dwellers oppressed by the psychological and economic tensions of metropolitan life. The Vanderbilt critics were aware of such northern sympathizers, and they expressed their willingness to join with all those who wanted "a simpler economy to live by." Both groups resisted the dominant trends of history, but where the Agrarians were literary and mainly metaphorical in their paeans to husbandry, Borsodi and his supporters put their neo-Jeffersonian philosophy to the practical test. As a columnist in the *New Republic* observed, the Tennessee Agrarians wrote about rural simplicity with great verve and imagination. But "only one man in America seems bent on moving mountains to get there. That man is Mr. Ralph Borsodi, a consulting economist who has an almost anarchic prejudice against the institution of the State."[31]

Borsodi's career as a social critic extended from about 1920 until his death in 1977, but his reputation was established in the decades between the two world wars. He was born in New York in 1888 to Hungarian immigrant parents. Most of his education was informal and private, but both books and ideas abounded in his household. He especially loved reading American history. Jefferson, he later remembered, "was my teen-age idol. He was much more profound than his laudators realize. He was the apostle of freedom and education, not of the demos and democracy." Young Borsodi was also influenced by the writings of Schopenhauer and Nietzsche. Although he followed neither "to their ultimate conclusions," he agreed with them that leading the good life required "sharp intellects, disciplined wills, and vigorous bodies."[32]

Borsodi's father, William, introduced Ralph to some of the New York followers of Henry George. Among them was Bolton Hall, with whom William Borsodi cooperated in promoting subsistence homesteading at the turn of the century. Young Borsodi soon adopted George's and Hall's ideas as his own. Throughout his life, he would insist that legitimate private property values were those derived from improvements made upon land rather than from speculative profits. As a young man, while working at Macy's as a marketing consultant, Borsodi took an active role in New York Single Tax organizations and for a time edited *The Single Taxer*. He also dreamed of one day acquiring his own homestead.

In 1911 Borsodi, the young urbanite who made his living within the business establishment but was attracted to simplicity, agrarianism, and land reform, married a woman from the midwestern plains. Myrtle Mae Borsodi thereafter became the heroine of the kitchen, loom, and sewing room in her husband's writings and at the same time was a publishing home-economist in her own right. In 1920 the Borsodis decided to flee the inflated prices and unwholesome atmosphere of Manhattan. As he explained, "I got fed up with helping big corporations get bigger as we became over-urbanized, over-centralized, over-industrialized, and indifferent to the Jeffersonian vision of an agrarian nation." So, he and his wife moved with their two sons into the countryside near Suffern, New York. There, on seven acres, they built a stone house, raised chickens, rabbits, and goats, grew their food, and made their own cloth and furniture. In the process, Borsodi claimed, they found economic security and independence, family unity, healthful and varied work and recreation, a better education for the boys (including practical experiences as well as traditional learning), and the aesthetic and spiritual satisfactions of rural life.[33]

Borsodi described their lifestyle and adventure in his two best-known books, whose subtitles reflect his lifelong motives: *This Ugly Civilization: A Study of the Quest for Comfort* (1929), and *Flight from the City: An Experiment in Creative Living on the Land* (1933). *This Ugly Civilization* represented a strident assault on the dominant consumer culture. Borsodi charged that the "idea that mankind's comfort is dependent upon an unending increase in production is a fallacy." The two most precious commodities at man's disposal, he contended, were the natural resources of land and time. To waste either was to damage directly the quality of life. When a person "produces more things than are necessary to good living, he wastes . . . time and he wastes material, both of which should be used to make the world a more beautiful place to live." By the creative use of land and machinery, people could lead the good life, the essential aspect of which was control of one's own time in pursuit of creative leisure and reflection.[34]

This Ugly Civilization was very much an elitist book, addressed to an elitist audience, as the many quotations Borsodi cited from Nietzsche's *Thus Spake Zarathustra* made obvious. "Men are not equal," he bluntly asserted. "Their inequality is inexorable. And that they should be equal is undesirable." Borsodi divided mankind into the "herd-minded" 97 percent, the "quantity-minded" 2 percent, and the "quality-minded," the group to whom he directed his message, only 1 percent. These "quality-minded" types were notable not "for their ability ruthlessly to sate their appetites, but for their sensitivity to what is desirable to do with life." They could be writers, educators, professionals, mechanics, or farmers—their vocation was irrelevant. But with William James, Borsodi believed that the person aspiring to lead a good life must have a conscious sense of elevated purpose. "It is not what he does so much as how and why he does it that makes it clear that this is really the superior life. He extracts beauty, truth, and goodness from the common stuff of life . . . much as a miner extracts gold from crude ore."[35]

Only such "quality-minded" individuals could and would overcome the barriers to simple living that the factory and conformist social institutions erected. Borsodi admitted that the factory system had shortened the average work week, raised wages, lowered prices, produced many necessary items, and elevated the political and social status of the worker. But there were many disadvantages to industrial capitalism that the public too often overlooked. In prose reminiscent of William Morris, Borsodi charged that the factory system's ravenous appetite for raw materials plundered the landscape, encouraged class conflict, destroyed the self-expression of skilled craftsmen, intensified tensions between workers and owners, and condemned the "natural-born robots" of the herd to perform monotonous jobs throughout their wretched lives. In addition, the quality-minded were prostituted by the system to earn money to pay for the necessities of life.

The means to liberation from such ugly and degrading effects of the factory and city were clear to Borsodi. The "quality-minded" must seek a measure of self-sufficiency on small family farms, or organic homesteads, "mastering" the machine by the use of small-scale tools and appliances, producing goods for use and exchange, not for sale. In such homes, art and the religion of the hearth would flourish. The "quality-minded" still might obtain some income by working in the establishment, but their independence from exploitation by the factory economy would be ensured by their ability to provide most of their own basic needs on "little islands of intelligence and beauty amidst the chaotic seas of human stupidity and ugliness." Borsodi believed that those leading such lives would be the Jeffersonian "natural aristocrats" of the twentieth century, serving as "a sort of leavening in the lump of mankind. They produce ideas, create beauty, promote understanding." But by admitting that such natural aristocrats would always remain few in number, Borsodi reflected the continuing transformation of the simple life from a societal ethic to a minority ethic.[36]

Borsodi's agrarian condemnation of mass-scale mechanization, the city, and modern culture in general for their dehumanizing and standardizing effects was characterized by one critic as a romantic pipedream "got up by sentimentalists who hadn't any idea what they are talking about." Certainly Borsodi's views fit into the mainstream of romanticism, with its distaste for industrial squalor, hatred of a brutalizing economic system, and fondness for pastoral versions of nature. But where the achievements of most nineteenth-century romantics were primarily artistic, their efforts directed at taking the pastoral myth out of history and restoring it to its traditional place in culture, as a vision of art and literature, Borsodi's purpose was to make the pastoral vision come alive. "I recommend country life," he stressed, "not because it is *merely* romantic; not merely because it involves a return to nature, but because it is a satisfying life; because I believe the evidence indicates that it is the normal life of man." He did not consider himself a dreamy romantic but rather a practical reformer—hard-headed, inventive, involved. Borsodi did not spend his time writing artistic raptures over the early morning dew but preferred to talk about compost and canning. Those seeking to lead a simple life, he advised, must first understand that the "acquisition of food, clothing and shelter is prerequisite to the pursuit of the good, the true and the beautiful." Careful planning and hard work, therefore, were essential to the good life he described, just as they had been to that practical romantic, Henry Thoreau.[37]

Borsodi's analysis of the homesteading family's needs and values was guided by the same middle-class outlook that had generated the turn-of-the-century crusade for simpler living. The main difference between the Borsodis and earlier advocates of commuter simplicity was in their Thoreauvian willingness to produce their own food and much of their clothing, and to construct their housing and furnishings. But Borsodi's most original idea was his desire to "domesticate" the machine and mechanize the homestead, to synthesize the pastoral urge and the technological fact in a literal sense. If bringing the machine into the garden could enable the "quality-minded" to enjoy greater economic independence, satisfying and varied work, and a life of beauty, then doing so posed no necessary threat to one's dignity or freedom. Electrical appliances and gasoline motors were thus essential to the success of Borsodi's experiment and argument. His first purchases for the homestead were, in fact, a Merryway mixer and a pressure cooker. Unlike the more famous socialist homesteaders, Scott and Helen Nearing, who began their primitive life in the Vermont woods in 1932, the Borsodis saw no need to give up any of the basic comforts in their quest for control of their own time, for economic self-sufficiency, and for physical and emotional health. Indeed, they were determined to combine the best of both country and city life. Borsodi's insistence that this was possible, along with his repeated praise of the virtues of small machinery, home appliances, and electrical power, underscores how urbanized and domesticated that portion of the middle class he addressed had become by the 1920s, and how new and captivating labor-saving appliances were at the time.

Not all those promoting simplicity during the 1920s insisted on the necessity of living on a farm or a homestead. Lewis Mumford, for instance, believed that a simple life could be lived in cities as well as in the countryside. An articulate generalist in an age of increasing specialization, Mumford distinguished himself during the 1920s and after as a literary critic, cultural historian, social philosopher, and urban planner. He has also been an outspoken critic of the consumer culture and an ardent advocate of simple living. A spiritual descendant of Emerson and Thoreau, Morris and Ruskin, Mumford joined other intellectuals during the 1920s in criticizing what he called a "blankness, a sterility, a boredom, a despair" generated by modern urban industrial life. Standardization, regimentation, and efficiency had become the bywords of American society, and in the process of conforming to the materialist ethos of the "New Era," people neglected the aesthetic and spiritual aspects of life. Everyone seemed to think that a mere abundance of goods would guarantee a better living. He emphasized, however, that material organization was no substitute for moral order. The "opulence of carefully packaged emptiness" was a faulty prescription for the good life.[38]

What was required to restore meaning to the American experience, Mumford observed, was neither liberalism nor socialism nor any other ideological program that focused primarily on changing the external social structure. Instead it was time for a transcendental reformation of man himself. The American must rein in the work and consumption ethic and adopt an organic approach to life that would develop the inner person as well as the outer garments of material necessity. "How many men," he charged, "sweat in their offices so that they may give their wives a private car, a house with multiple bathrooms, or expensive furs! How many men whose wives would be far more happy, far more richly satisfied, with a little more of their husband's time and a little more of a lover's attentions!" His advice to his machine age society was quite traditional: strip away needless superfluities, try to make work more satisfying and less stifling, concentrate on developing more sincere personal and familial relations, and strive to reach the synthesis of practicality and spirituality, mechanism and humanism, that idealists had for so long prescribed. "We begin again," he concluded in 1926, "to dream Thoreau's dream—of what it means to live a whole human life."[39]

Mumford's diagnosis of modern America's spiritual and cultural degeneration thus closely paralleied that of the Nashville Agrarians and Borsodi. He sympathized with their homesickness for rustic simplicity, and he shared their desire to "cut loose from an environment in which the day is announced by the alarm clock, instead of the birds, and finished by the blare of the radio, instead of by the crickets and the katydids." He also agreed that the modern city created not "a common bond but a common repulsion." Yet Mumford criticized their prescriptions for cultural renewal. He saw too much escapism and elitism inherent in the homesteading and agrarian perspectives. Borsodi, the Agrarians, and other neo-Jeffersonians were trying to create "an environment into which people may escape from a sordid workaday world, whereas the real problem . . . is to remake the workaday world so that people will not wish to escape from it!"[40]

This desire to domesticate and humanize the cityscape rather than simply flee from it led Mumford during the 1920s to join other like-minded architects, social theorists, and urban planners in forming the Regional Planning Association of America (RPAA). The group included Clarence Stein, Stuart Chase, and Benton Mackaye, designer of the Appalachian Trail. Together they advocated a series of regionally planned communities modeled after the New Town movement in Great Britain. Drawing upon the ideas of the turn-of-the-century British urban planners and social reformers Patrick Geddes, Victor Branford, and Ebenezer Howard, Mumford and the others espoused a new living environment that would combine the best features of town and country, farm and factory, and thereby establish a habitat in equilibrium with nature and civilization. These garden cities would be limited in both spatial and population size, surrounded by a "greenbelt" of farmland and forests, and interspersed with small-scale manufacturing enterprises designed to provide satisfying work and a basic material self-sufficiency for the community, thus differentiating them from mere commuter suburbs. Land would be owned by the community and leased to individuals in order to control speculation and ensure widespread access to property. Common greens, open courtyards, bicycle and pedestrian paths, playgrounds and parks, trees and gardens would help naturalize the townscape, as well as help overcome the anomie inherent in mass urban living.[41]

Where Mumford differed from his associates in the RPAA was in his emphasis on the cultural implications of such garden cities. It was, he said, the role of the "artist, the poet, the philosopher to make these aims clear and comprehensible and, above all, desirable." Mumford saw his role as being such a humanistic spokesman. In his view, everything about the new planned communities would be designed for life, and "one uses the word life in no vague sense," Mumford stressed. "One means the birth and nurture of children, the preservation of human health and well-being, the culture of the human personality, and the perfection of the natural and civic environment as the theater of all of these activities." Life in his planned communities would be a richly integrated and cooperative social experience in which people, regardless of their economic circumstances, would enjoy a sense of belonging with each other, with nature, and with their work. Such regional settlements, Mumford was convinced, would do far more than Borsodi's subsistence homesteads to help "eliminate our enormous economic wastes, give a new life to stable agriculture, set down fresh communities planned on a human scale, and above all, restore a little happiness and freedom in those places where things have been pretty well wrung out."[42]

Guided by such a vision, Mumford enthusiastically supported the RPAA's attempt in 1929 to put the garden city idea into practice with the construction of Radburn, New Jersey. After locating a 1200-acre site seventeen miles from Manhattan, they designed a planned community for 25,000 people. Liberally sprinkled with parks, curvilinear streets, and separate roadways and pedestrian ways, Radburn was intended to develop into a self-sufficient, fully integrated rural and urban community whose very design would help promote a renewed sense of togetherness, an "organic simplicity," as Mumford called it. But the depression struck before the town was completed, and the development corporation was forced into receivership in 1931. At that time Radburn's population was only 1500. The greenbelt was never purchased, and the small industries and businesses intended for the community never appeared. As a result, Radburn during the 1930s evolved into simply an attractive commuter suburb for white-collar workers.[43]

Though the onset of the Great Depression undermined Mumford's ideal community experiment at Radburn, the social and economic crisis did offer a silver lining, for it served to revitalize the almost dormant ethic of simple living. The devastating effects of the depression called into question the whole ethos of the consumer culture. For millions of Americans, the dream of unlimited prosperity based on eternal credit had proven illusory, and they searched frantically for new leadership and new ideals. The desperate conditions created by the economic crisis called for desperate solutions, and there was no lack of proposals and panaceas.

Among the responses to the depression was a concerted effort to restore Jeffersonian simplicity as a goal of national social policy. Franklin Roosevelt and many of his advisers initially saw in the economic calamity a means of promoting the republic of virtue envisioned by the Revolutionary generation. In his acceptance speech at the Democratic convention in July 1932, Roosevelt explained in sermonic tones the root cause of the economic collapse. "Let us," he remarked, "be frank in acknowledgment of the truth that many amongst us have made obeisance to Mammon, that the profits of speculation, the easy road without toil, have lured us from the old barricades. To return to higher standards of living we must abandon the false prophets and seek new leaders of our own choosing." He was to be a presidential Moses, leading the people out of a period "of loose thinking, descending morals, [and] an era of selfishness" into a new dawn of public spiritedness and private sacrifice. He thus pleaded for a "concert of action, based on a fair and just concert of interests." Cooperation, Roosevelt and his followers hoped, would replace cutthroat competition and selfish individualism. The social crisis would inspire Americans to band together for mutual aid and comfort. "The keynote of the new frontier," said Henry Wallace, Roosevelt's farm expert, "is cooperation, just as that of the old frontier was individualistic competition. Power and wealth were worshiped in the old days. Beauty and justice and joy of spirit must be worshiped in the new."[44]

Roosevelt repeated this theme in his first inaugural address. Happiness, he told the expectant nation, "lies not in the mere possession of money; it lies in the joy of achievement, in the thrill of creative effort." Work must again come to be viewed as a spiritual calling rather than merely a money-making enterprise. The "joy and moral stimulation of work no longer must be forgotten in the mad chase of evanescent profits." The business of America might be business, as the Republicans had been saying, but Roosevelt insisted that the true mission of America was to be measured in its collective goodness rather than by its accumulated goods. The "generation of self-seekers" must be cast out from the temple of public responsibility, and the new order must "apply social values more noble than mere monetary profit." One of those ennobling social values was simplicity. Later, in dedicating the birthplace of Woodrow Wilson in Staunton, Virginia, Roosevelt expressed with evident sincerity his admiration for the simple life. "I like the old phrase that this home was a home of plain living and high thinking and wherever the family moved . . . they carried with them ideals which put faith in spiritual values above every material consideration."[45]

Roosevelt's verbal praise of cooperation and simplicity was soon accompanied by legislative action. Although primarily concerned with handling the immediate problem of reviving the economy and providing relief for the unemployed, the President and many of his advisers harbored a desire to use Hamiltonian means (centralized planning and public financing) to encourage a revival of Jeffersonian values. Roosevelt told a Kansas City audience in 1936: "In all our plans we are guided, and will continue to be guided by the

fundamental belief that the American farmer, living on his own land, remains our ideal of self-reliance and of spiritual balance—the source from
which the reservoirs of the nation's strength are constantly renewed." The
urbane New Deal administrator Rexford Tugwell, a former student of
Thorstein Veblen, later remembered that this rural nostalgia was widespread among many of the intellectuals serving in the Roosevelt Administration. "There was a kind of homesickness—historic homesickness, Veblen
called it—for the simple days of the past when such terrible troubles were
still unknown. This was largely imaginary . . . but it had reality in people's
wishes."[46]

It also had reality in several of the early New Deal programs. Just as his
cousin Theodore had sought to revivify country life, Franklin Roosevelt
dreamed that he could engineer a massive back-to-the-land movement.
Shortly after his election, he told Louis Brandeis, the progressive jurist and
Wilsonian decentralist, that ten to fifteen million urbanites must be relocated
to rural farms and villages. A few months later, in January 1933, he explained
in a speech: "We have got to restore the balance of population, get them [the
unemployed] out of the big centers of population, so that they will not be
dependent on home relief." But how were indigent city dwellers to become
self-sustaining country folk? "There are hundreds of thousands of boys,"
Roosevelt admitted, "who know only the pavement of cities, and that means
that they can take only those jobs that are directly connected with the
pavements of cities."[47]

Somehow, urban youths must be trained to appreciate the rigors and joys
of rural life. To do so, Roosevelt and his advisers resurrected William
James's idea of a civic army performing public service in nature. The Civilian
Conservation Corps (CCC) would be the New Deal's "moral equivalent of
war." During a visit with some of the first CCC enrollees in 1933, the
President told the young men that their efforts would "conserve our natural
resources and create national wealth" and also be "of moral and spiritual
value, not only to those who are taking part, but to the rest of the country as
well." Questionnaires completed by the young recruits indicated that many
of them shared Roosevelt's moral outlook. Three-quarters of those surveyed
denied that the "best way to be happy is to have lots of money." Instead, they
overwhelmingly affirmed the proposition that "when I work, I am more
interested in the job itself than the money I am making." That had to be true
for those in the CCC, for they were paid only a dollar a day and lived in
conditions of spartan rusticity. Nevertheless, young Americans flocked to
join. By 1935 there were 500,000 enrolled, planting trees, building roads,
parks, and bridges, and carrying out various soil reclamation projects. Not
all of the young men stayed very long, nor did all of them come away with a
new vision of the good life. But many did. And in the process the CCC
emerged as the most successful of all New Deal programs, supported by both
liberals and conservatives, Democrats and Republicans. Even organized

labor quickly ended its initial opposition once it saw the Corps in action. As Tugwell remembered, the CCC was "too popular for criticism."[48]

The CCC was only the first of several New Deal programs intended to restore a Jeffersonian balance to American social and economic life. The legislation creating the Tennessee Valley Authority in 1933 called for a program of regional planning that would encourage the "balanced development of the diverse and rich resources of the region." The TVA was indeed an ambitious attempt to bolster the economy and enhance the standard of living of residents in eastern Tennessee, northern Alabama, Mississippi, and Georgia, southern Kentucky, and western North Carolina and Virginia. Dams were built to provide flood control and hydroelectric power; plants were constructed to manufacture fertilizer; and, various programs were developed to encourage soil conservation and reforestation.[49]

These aspects of the TVA are, of course, well known. Yet Arthur E. Morgan, the agency's first director, had more ambitious goals; he wanted to use the TVA to help restore republican simplicity to the rural region. Morgan was a practical visionary devoted to the simple life. Born in Cincinnati in 1878, but raised in Minnesota, Morgan was the son of Quaker parents, and he inherited their piety and their vocational interests. His father was a surveyor, his mother a schoolteacher, and Arthur Morgan eventually established a national reputation as both a civil engineer and as a progressive educator. He was also widely known as a crusading, uncompromising moralist in the Quaker mold, abstemious in his personal habits and guided by a mystical spirituality. He once wrote his mother: "No job is important enough to hold at the cost of any sacrifice of Christian principle." Such attitudes led one journalist to describe Morgan as the "schoolmaster idealist and engineer" who displayed "a combination of fine, almost saintly enthusiasm, with a hard-headed understanding of ways and means."[50]

Morgan's idealism surfaced early. As a youth he read Edward Bellamy's popular utopian fantasy *Looking Backward* (1888), and he was transfixed by the idea of a cooperative commonwealth displacing the rough-and-tumble competitive strife of laissez-faire capitalism. Technology and social planning, he came to feel, could be employed to recast the nature of modern American social life. Morgan carried this utopian dream with him as he embarked on his successful career as an engineer. By the end of World War I he was president of his own engineering firm and a prominent expert on land reclamation, erosion prevention, and flood control. At the same time, he conducted several experiments in progressive education. In 1917 he started an innovative secondary school in Dayton, Ohio, and three years later he was chosen president of Antioch College in Yellow Springs, Ohio. There he instituted a new curriculum that combined classroom study with actual work experiences in the community. His "Antioch Plan" was adopted by many other colleges and universities around the country.

But it was not simply Morgan's success as an enlightened engineer and educator that convinced Roosevelt to appoint him the first chairman of the TVA. Morgan, the President felt, harbored a similar social vision. He, too, wanted to use public policy to restore traditional cultural practices. Roosevelt referred to Morgan as "an engineer with a social conscience." Indeed, Morgan was one of the first practitioners of what today is called human ecology. He believed with Roosevelt that the economy had grown dangerously imbalanced during the 1920s. The farm sector and the small towns and villages of the nation continued to give way to massive factories and cities. Thus, he shared Roosevelt's hope that the depression might promote a sustained back-to-the-land movement as well as a revival of small businesses and handicrafts. He also dreamed with Lewis Mumford that the competitive free-for-all of unrestrained capitalism could be counterbalanced by a renewed emphasis on mutualism and civic virtue accompanied by an enlightened program of resource management. Such a "community ethic" would harmonize human needs and natural supplies. Morgan, therefore, praised those who "have kept themselves vigorous and tempered to privation, who have achieved poise and have learned to use their energies temperately, who have habitually lived within their means." In the early years of the depression he also encouraged businessmen and public officials to set "examples of simple and modest living."[51]

And, in his role as director of the TVA, Morgan saw the opportunity to create a true new deal for the public. The Tennessee Valley, he asserted, "is the first place in America where we can sit down and design a civilization." For Morgan, the TVA was "not primarily a dam-building program, a fertilizer job or power-transmission job" but instead represented a serious effort to promote a "designed and planned social and economic order" along Jeffersonian lines. The regional development program was to be his "trumpet call for a reawakening of the American spirit, not that aberration known as rugged individualism where selfish traits seemed to foster survival, but the spirit of cooperation, of experimentation, of pragmatism, the antithesis of 'enlightened selfishness.'"[52]

To this end, Morgan used the TVA to stimulate small, handicraft industries, to organize canning, crafts, electrical, and other cooperatives, to provide educational and cultural opportunities for adults, and to warn residents of the evils of tobacco and alcohol. His modern version of Puritan morality and Jeffersonian republicanism, explained writer Dorothy Canfield Fisher, would restore human dignity "without taking us back to the unwashed simplicities of primitive life." Morgan did not believe completely in the agrarian myth; he did not think that everyone could or should move back to the land. But he was convinced that life in the rural regions of the Tennessee Valley could be enlivened and enlightened without compromising its traditional simplicity.[53]

Hence, in constructing the town of Norris, near the site of the first TVA dam, Morgan modeled the community after an English garden city. It was surrounded by woods and carefully laid out in individual homesteads. The residents of Norris, Morgan described in a speech, "have a cooperative bank, cooperative laundry, cooperative shoe repair and clothes pressing service, and will soon have a cooperative dairy, a cooperative store, a cooperative chicken raising plant, and other cooperative efforts." They also had a stringent ethical code, drafted by Morgan, which maintained that "the general good should prevail over personal good" and denounced "deceit, exploitation, favoritism, extravagance, bad personal habits, and selfish personal ambitions." Employees of the TVA, the code suggested, "should live modestly and economically, avoiding competitive expenditures" and disdaining "the expectation of acquiring wealth." By espousing such values, the residents of Norris, Morgan predicted, would provide the "leadership in a great cooperative movement to get those millions of mountain people, now so largely unemployed and rusting away, to produce the things they need for themselves."[54]

For the first few months, at least, Norris appeared to live up to Morgan's perfectionist expectations. The community was, said a visitor, "picturesque. The houses were nicely designed. They were nicely sited. We were living among talented people from all over the country. . . . It was quite an interesting and pleasant experience for all of us who lived there. We had study groups, book review clubs, music clubs and such things." But like the planned factory community at Lowell during the early nineteenth century, Norris failed to sustain its initial sense of community purpose. Within a few years it became known as a "company town," managed by and for TVA employees. Many natives of the Tennessee Valley resented and resisted Morgan's paternalistic efforts to reshape the contours of their social and cultural life. They saw in his attempt to supplant rugged individualism with cooperation the seeds of socialism. Others disliked the idea of northern bureaucrats trying to impose their particular moral philosophy on their regional culture. Jonathan Daniels, a leading southern journalist, remarked after visiting Norris: "Too many of us will prefer a sloppy South to a South planned in perfection by outlanders. We know out of our past that the worst carpetbaggers were the ones who came down here to improve us."[55]

Morgan, the sanctimonious Yankee moralist and mystic, misread not only the southern attitude toward much of his regional plan; he also misread the willingness of other New Dealers to support such an ambitious program of social reconstruction. David Lilienthal and Harcourt Morgan (no relation), the other two directors of the TVA, quickly indicated that they saw the purpose of the program in a different light. For them, the TVA was intended to restore the region's economy, not to create a whole new way of life. As Lilienthal admitted, "I don't have much faith in uplift." Instead of trying to create a government-planned and government-financed cooperative social order and moral economy, Lilienthal preferred to focus more narrowly on the construction of dams and fertilizer plants. Consequently, they rejected Arthur Morgan's ethical code as too regimenting and puritanical.[56]

Such differences of opinion led to a heated dispute between Arthur

Morgan and Lilienthal, a dispute that culminated in 1938 when Roosevelt dismissed Morgan for what he called his "contumacious behavior." Thereafter, Morgan's idea of using comprehensive regional planning to promote cooperative simplicity was gradually displaced in favor of power development, flood control efforts, and fertilizer production. Bureaucratic priorities and personality conflicts had again helped undermine an institutional attempt to revive simple virtues and activities. Still, Morgan's idealistic efforts continued to bear fruit long after he left the TVA and returned to Yellow Springs. Handicrafts and cooperatives of one sort or another continued to exert an important force in the Tennessee Valley's social and economic life, thereby serving as a living monument to Morgan's reforming zeal.

At the same time that Arthur Morgan was trying to use the TVA as an instrument of cooperative simplicity, another New Deal program was pursuing a complementary objective. Much like the Little Land idea advocated by Bolton Hall at the turn of the century, the soldier settlement plans of the 1920s, and Ralph Borsodi's agrarian experiments, the Department of Interior's Division of Subsistence Homesteads was created in 1933 to help ease the degrading unemployment problem by resettling penurious urban and rural families in planned homestead communities. Unemployed workers would thus be transformed into virtuous yeomen. On federally subsidized land, they would help build their own homes, raise subsistence crops, revive domestic handicrafts, and re-create the ideal organic community life envisioned by Jefferson and other early republican visionaries. As Harold Ickes, Secretary of the Interior, commented, the homestead program "can be tremendously potent in building a new America. It opens the door to a more healthful, contented and spiritual well-rounded life. There is nothing quite so soul-satisfying as the joy of seeing things grow through your own labors." In this way, New Deal intellectuals and bureaucrats revived the age-old myth that a man's vine and fig tree would provide a fortress against adversity and a foundation for independence and private virtue.[57]

Milburn L. Wilson, an agricultural economist who during the 1920s had organized a privately financed homesteading settlement in Montana, was appointed director of the Division of Subsistence Homesteads. Like Arthur Morgan, he hoped to use his agency to create a new community life that would replace the competitive materialism and institutional complexity of modern society with a more simple, humane, and socially minded village economy based on "handicrafts, community activities, closer relationships, and cooperative enterprises." Mutualism would thus displace competitive individualism. "Advocates of this pattern of living," he explained, "believe that there are philosophical values which cannot be measured in economic terms and which accrue to the family who, through its own initiative and planning, carries out the enterprise of raising a garden." Though admitting that "we cannot go back to the simple agricultural economy," Wilson insisted with Ralph Borsodi that the mechanical improvements of recent years made possible the creation of "rural industrial communities and partial-subsistence homestead communities adjacent to decentralized industry."[58]

Just as the Boston Associates had placed small industrial plants in the countryside and Arthur Morgan had planned Norris as a garden city, hoping thereby to combine the virtues of both farm and factory work, Wilson envisioned a spate of New Deal communities where factory workers would live on small homesteads, producing much of their own food and clothing, and using their wages to buy necessary commodities. This new type of balanced rural-industrial community would bring together the factory, school, and social services with spacious one to two-acre homesteads. Residents who worked in factories or businesses would then be able to spend part of their leisure time in the cultivation of a kitchen garden, the keeping of poultry, and the raising of fruits, "in this way supplying a portion of the family food needs." They thereby would enjoy "a security and an independence in their modest way of life which we can well envy."[59]

It was an ambitious goal, perhaps the most ambitious of the New Deal. And a few of the government-sponsored homestead communities actually came very close to meeting Wilson's expectations. But, overall, the homestead program was a failure. Trying to re-create eighteenth-century Jeffersonian settlements in twentieth-century America produced an avalanche of unexpected problems. The administrators discovered, as one of them recognized, that they had formulated "ideal plans for ideal people rather than practical plans for real people." About a hundred New Deal communities were eventually established, but almost all of them were short-lived. Many residents found it impossible to shed their engrained individualism and therefore resisted the mutualism encouraged by Wilson and his staff. Others discovered the combination of factory labor and farm labor too demanding, and they returned to the cities they had left or simply came to view the homestead communities as housing projects.[60]

The Austin homesteads in Minnesota, for example, were largely populated by blue-collar workers from the Hormel Packing Company. Many of them worked as much as 54 hours a week, and they had little interest in tilling the soil when they returned home. They preferred, as a report noted, "dancing, card-playing, and drinking beer." Nor did the settlement develop the closely integrated social life the New Dealers had envisioned. The community center was rarely used. One resident told a researcher that the Austin homesteads represented a worthwhile housing project, but he doubted that they had "demonstrated anything in particular with regard to secure and ample life on a small wage." A comprehensive evaluation of the settlement conducted by the Department of Agriculture concluded that many of the people who participated in the project wanted "not to be subsistence homesteaders, but rather to have the security of employment and the adequacy of income which a properly functioning economy could offer them, but which the subsistence homesteads could not." Instead of embracing a Jeffersonian moral economy, they displayed a "fundamental and continuing desire to live according to the dominant tastes of the modern industrial world."[61]

Another problem hampering Wilson's homesteading program was that it proved to be far more expensive than anticipated, and Congress steadily reduced its appropriations. Personal and policy disputes between Wilson and Ickes also served to hurt the program. Wilson wanted the homesteads to be planned and managed as much as possible by local officials and the residents themselves. Ickes, however, was convinced that such decentralized administration was inefficient and subject to graft and corruption. He wanted the program to be directed completely from Washington. Ickes won out. In 1934 he ordered that all of the local homestead projects be federalized. This was a devastating blow to Wilson, who resigned in disgust, just as Ernest Thompson Seton had earlier turned his back on a Scouting movement grown too large and impersonal. Supervision of the homestead communities was thereafter transferred to Rexford Tugwell's Resettlement Administration, where the homesteads were gradually phased out.[62]

The collapse of the government-sponsored homesteading program was quite a disappointment to agrarian idealists who shared Wilson's dream. During the early 1930s a loose coalition of decentralist groups had also called for a revival of Jeffersonian simplicity in the face of the depression. They included the Nashville Agrarians, the Catholic Rural Life movement, followers of the ideas of Henry George such as Frank Lloyd Wright and philosopher Baker Brownell, and homesteading advocates such as Ralph Borsodi, Bernarr McFadden, editor of *Liberty Magazine*, and the historian and journalist Herbert Agar. These and other idealistic traditionalists had initially been quite encouraged by Roosevelt's campaign attacks on Wall Street and Big Business, and they especially liked his talk about revitalizing country life and the farm economy. They supported his homesteading plan, the TVA, and the CCC as constructive measures designed to halt the spread of unfettered urban industrial materialism and restore balance and sanity to the American way of life.[63]

But as the New Deal developed in all its conflicting facets, these decentralists grew more and more disenchanted with the contradictions they discovered in Roosevelt's policies. They saw Arthur Morgan fired, the homestead program taken out of Wilson's hands, its funds slashed, and its emphasis reduced. Even more disturbing was the general trend toward Hamiltonian centralization and corporatism that had developed alongside such Jeffersonian programs as the TVA and the CCC. Columnist Dorothy Thompson, herself a decentralist, pinpointed the dualistic nature of Roosevelt's New Deal philosophy: "Two souls dwell in the bosom of this Administration, as indeed, they do in the bosom of the American people. The one loves the Abundant Life, as expressed in the cheap and plentiful products of large-scale mass production and distribution. . . . The other soul yearns for former simplicities, for decentralization, for the interests of the 'little man,' revolts against high-pressure salesmanship, denounces 'monopoly' and 'economic empires' and seeks the means of breaking them up."[64]

Gradually, these interwoven strands making up the fabric of New Deal social thought began to splay, much to the chagrin of the neo-Jeffersonians. The Nashville Agrarians particularly resented the centralizing tendencies of the New Deal. To them, the philosophy of the massive Agricultural Adjustment Act, which paid farmers not to plant, seemed to contradict the philosophy of the homesteading program. John Crowe Ransom pointedly recognized Roosevelt's inconsistencies: "With one hand he measures acreage out of production, and with the other hand waves city men to the farm." Ransom and the other Agrarians believed that the New Deal should have focused its efforts on promoting the revival of a traditional moral economy based primarily on subsistence agriculture and small business that Roosevelt's early rhetoric had promised. Instead, they saw the New Deal planners energetically fostering a return to large-scale industrial capitalism and commercial farming. Despite his Jeffersonian rhetoric, Roosevelt seemed to them to have accepted the prevailing myth that more production, more cities, more factories, and more jobs would automatically lead the American people to happiness. The President was an "honest man," Allen Tate concluded, "but horribly simple; the best he can do is to think the whole problem will be solved when a little of the big income is restored and all men have enough to eat." Tate and the Agrarians argued instead that the Depression involved far more than an economic decline; it was a symptom of a degenerating culture. As such, it required not contradictory patchwork programs designed to stimulate recovery but a comprehensive effort to recreate a culture of meaning rather than of consumption.[65]

Ralph Borsodi was even more disenchanted with the New Deal as put into practice. In an effort to expand the opportunities for homesteading during the depression, he had served during 1933-34 as a consultant to the Liberty Homestead project in Dayton, Ohio, the first recipient of federal funds under Wilson's Division of Subsistence Homesteads.[66] But almost from the start, the Dayton project fell short of Borsodi's expectations. He quickly became embroiled in disputes involving local personalities, bureaucratic delays, questions of local versus federal control, and even race prejudice on the part of some of Dayton's citizens. After less than a year, the project was a failure, and Borsodi reacted by developing a violent antipathy for federal control of any kind. He was particularly incensed by Ickes's decision to federalize the homestead projects: "Jove had spoken, and Jove would brook no exception to his Jovian orders."[67]

After the Dayton experience Borsodi decided that the homesteading ideal could best be achieved by private initiative rather than by government programs. Near his home in Suffern, he established the School of Living in

1936, a center intended to educate urbanites about homesteading methods. The school taught spinning, weaving, cooking, canning, carpentry, masonry, family economics, animal husbandry, the importance of good household tools and small machines, as well as its own philosophy of living. During the last half of the 1930s, Borsodi and the School of Living continued to promote simple living, and he also started several Georgist homestead communities in the Northeast designed to give urbanites partial security and freedom from bureaucratic government, speculators, and wasteful big industry.

The communities—Bayard Lane at Suffern and Van Houten Fields at West Nyack, New York—were based on leaseholds, with the legal title to the land vested in the community trustees. To help homesteaders with their capital needs, Borsodi formed the Independence Foundation, a nonprofit corporation that borrowed money at 6 percent interest in order to purchase the acreage for the settlements. "The banks were glad to help," Borsodi remembered. "We had the only houses being built in the whole county in 1936." Each homesteader was required to pay his share of the annual taxes, carrying charges, and amortization, but was saved from any high initial capital outlay. At the same time, construction costs were lowered by Borsodi's forming local underemployed carpenters, masons, and plumbers into a guild and guaranteeing them year-round work in exchange for hourly wages lower than the local average. The result was that the workers' annual income rose, so much so in some cases that they too joined the homestead communities. The homesteaders also cut costs by forming cooperative buying associations, car pools, and bartering arrangements. Borsodi once likened the scheme to the "Platonic ideal of a society directed by its teachers and philosophers."[68]

While he was organizing such communities, Borsodi was growing obsessed with what he saw as the New Deal's increasing tendency toward corporatism and the public's growing dependency on state aid. Most urban dwellers still steered a precarious existence between the pay check and the relief check. "While the masses of people are frantically calling upon Washington for old age pensions, unemployment compensation, and other forms of security from the cradle to the grave," he stressed, "we are providing our own as most self-respecting Americans used to do until the gospel of depending on the government for support began to be substituted for the gospel of independence by the proponents of the New Deal." The real basis for economic and social stability, he reiterated, was not Social Security but a population with access to productive land.[69]

That was also the theme of *Free America*, a journal founded by Herbert Agar, Borsodi, and others in January 1937.[70] The magazine's contributors included several of the Nashville Agrarians, various spokesmen for the Catholic Rural Life movement, Bertram Fowler, who was a leading advocate of cooperatives, and Arthur Morgan, who had returned to Yellow Springs and was promoting various private initiatives designed to enhance life in small communities. The contributors to *Free America* were diverse in their activities but unified in their commitment to a restoration of simpler ways of living. Fowler believed that one way out of the treadmill of the consumer culture was through the formation of cooperatives. Consumer and producer cooperatives, he maintained, gave people ownership or control of many of the stores, factories, and services that met their needs and thus contributed to greater individual freedom. Production for use would thereby replace production for profit. As Fowler argued, the cooperative ideal provided the "philosophy by which we can change a warlike and voracious system of profit-making to one of peaceful and cooperative action for the benefit and well-being of all." Buoyed by the enthusiastic reception given *Our Daily Bread* (1934), King Vidor's film glorifying cooperative rural life, and Marquis Childs's study of cooperatives in Sweden, *The Middle Way* (1936), Fowler claimed that a "peaceful revolution is going forward in America today. It is proceeding quietly, without the fanfare of trumpets, without rancor and without confusion. . . . The revolution described is the Consumer's Cooperative Movement that is spreading through this country. It has already enrolled two million families."[71]

The Catholic ruralists shared Fowler's cooperative ideal as well as the agrarian decentralism of Agar, Borsodi, and the Vanderbilt critics. Centered in the Midwest but supported by the urban Catholic Worker organization headed by New Yorker Dorothy Day and the saintly French immigrant Peter Maurin, the Catholic Rural Life movement was led by Fathers Luigi Ligutti and John C. Rawe. They sought to promote economic independence and family unity by encouraging more widespread ownership of farms. Through such self-sufficiency and mutualism on the land, "initiative, prudence, thrift, courage, and other priceless virtues" would be enhanced and a "simple but wholesome and rugged living" would result. Although Ligutti and Rawe helped organize a successful homestead in Iowa under the auspices of Wilson's Division of Subsistence Homesteads, they realized that any widespread back-to-the-land movement must ultimately result from private rather than governmental initiative, so they wholeheartedly supported *Free America* and its decentralist message.[72]

Less certain of the merits of *Free America*'s program was Lewis Mumford. His own advocacy of "organic" simplicity led him to read with interest the early issues of the magazine. Yet though he agreed with the editors' general critique of modern American life, he continued to find their prescription for improvement dangerously narrow. It was "a fundamental mistake," he told them, "to make the notion of domestic production and partial industrial and agricultural self-sufficiency the only possible pattern for future economic change or for urban planning." Mumford admitted that he himself had been practicing home gardening in his small village of Amenia, New York, for several years, and he had reaped both psychic and economic benefits. But he was not willing to dismiss the value or the inevitability of urban culture as readily as the editors of *Free America*. "One does not wish to imitate Mr. Ralph Borsodi's attempts to supplant a mixed economy with a pure household economy—the latter should be a last desperate alternative to starvation." Mumford argued that subsistence homesteading was too often a sentimental cul-de-sac, and it should not be portrayed as the only valid option for those seeking a more meaningful existence. Too many people were arbitrarily left out of such a scheme of salvation. What about bachelors and spinsters, the elderly, poor, and handicapped? How were they to take up homesteading? Instead of being so single-minded about the back-to-the-land alternative, he advised, the *Free America* group should broaden their program so as to reach a larger segment of the population. "It is high time," Mumford concluded, "that the balance was restored between city and country; it is high time that we nurtured people at home in both territories, people capable of living balanced lives."[73]

A first step in this direction would be to recognize the value of well-conceived government projects such as the new "greenbelt" or "garden" cities being constructed by Rexford Tugwell and the Resettlement Administration. A national network of such integrally planned communities, long a favorite idea of Mumford's, represented an effort to transcend the city versus country dichotomy that had so often shaped the outlook of those promoting the simple life. His plea for a more balanced perspective evoked a mixed response among *Free America*'s editors. They acknowledged that there were many routes to simple living, and they welcomed Mumford's future contributions in helping them continue "our imperfect pioneering toward a more rational scheme of living." But Borsodi, Agar, and the other decentralist agrarians remained sceptical that the federal government could do justice to them. As Borsodi emphasized, governments "are the worst instruments for experimenting with fundamental social reforms to which society might turn."[74]

Tugwell and the other idealistic planners in the Resettlement Administration, of course, clearly thought otherwise. Tugwell, as was his bent, had proposed an ambitious program. He envisioned the eventual construction of some 3000 greenbelt communities that would demonstrate "the combined advantages of country and city life for low-income rural and industrial families." Like Milburn Wilson, he hoped to reverse both the demographic and sociological trends of the century. But Tugwell was convinced that his large-scale greenbelt communities would be far more effective than the tiny subsistence homestead settlements. The Resettlement Administration communities would go a long way toward solving chronic urban unemployment and crowdedness as well as improve the life of farmers by bringing new markets and new social and cultural opportunities within reach of country folk. Alas, however, Tugwell's own reach exceeded his grasp—and his budget. By 1937, only three greenbelt cities were under construction—

Greenbelt, Maryland; Greenhills, Ohio; and Greendale, Wisconsin. Although town planners throughout the world hailed the experimental project, many American commentators and politicians were less enthusiastic. One newspaper editor described Greendale as "the first Communist town in America." Many of the early tenants rebelled against the idea of collective ownership and expressed the deeply entrenched American desire to own their individual homes. But the most controversial aspect of the greenbelt community program was its exorbitant cost. Tugwell later admitted: "The people who planned them had no very realistic notion of what they were to build or what the inhabitants were usually to do." Congress balked at the high per unit cost of the planned communities and the subsidized rents, and soon the Resettlement Administration saw its appropriations sharply reduced. The first three planned communities were thus the last three constructed.[75]

The ideal decentralist society of planned garden cities and subsistence homesteads that Tugwell, Mumford, and the neo-Jeffersonians envisioned was certainly an attractive one. Few would deny the desirability of a commonweal where industrial growth and economic policy were planned and regulated according to humane ends and cooperative principles. Ideally, it would also be preferable for most Americans to control more directly their means of subsistence. But, as the New Deal attempts to achieve such goals demonstrated, it was not easy to transform the very nature of American society and individual aspiration by government initiative. Borsodi had predicted as much, but his private homesteading alternative was itself limited in its appeal. By 1940 the Van Houten Fields homestead at West Nyack that Borsodi had founded was the scene of considerable debate about the project's original design. In that year the homesteaders decided to change from leasehold to fee simple ownership. Those at the Bayard Lane community in Suffern did the same. Borsodi the philosopher king could domesticate the machine in his own homestead better than he could preside over a twentieth-century middle-class utopia. Like Henry George, he found it difficult to weaken the deeply embedded American penchant for privately owned property.[76]

The cause of decentralist simplicity was further impeded by the advent of war in Europe, an event which shattered the hopes for a return to a society of small farms, small businesses, and small communities. As always, the exigencies of war produced a powerful centralizing force, and *Free America*'s editors were filled with misgivings about probable American involvement. But after the fall of France, Agar and most of the others writing in *Free America* decided that combating totalitarianism required a massive national effort, even if it proved inimical to their decentralist philosophy. As one editorial concluded: "While *Free America* has never taken kindly to 'national planning' schemes we are ready to scrap any prejudice in war time." Some contributors, in fact, predicted that the military effort might be turned to serve the causes of decentralism and rural and community self-sufficiency. If, as Dorothy Thompson wrote, youth could be taught the virtues of cooperation and agriculture in the Volunteer Land Corps, if people in cities had to be dispersed for their own physical safety and cities were thereby indirectly decentralized—as Lewis Mumford suggested—if small businesses could be revived to produce for the war, and if the virtues of sacrifice and frugality might be restored, then the war's bad tendencies might be turned to good. "No longer," the editors maintained, "are we to buy more, sell more, eat more, wear more."[77]

In many respects the demands of the Second World War did serve to revive habits of simple living and public virtue. Again, millions of Americans patriotically engaged in conscientious consumption and resource conservation. Citizens were urged to "Use it up, wear it out, make it do or do without." The Farm Security Administration sponsored "An Acre for a Soldier" program in rural areas, and soon Victory gardens were sprouting up across the country. By April 1942 there were 6 million new gardeners at work. A housewife who lived in Raleigh, North Carolina, during the war recalled that she and her neighbors formed a Victory garden by plowing up their backyards. They grew and canned vegetables and raised chickens. "The morale was real high in Raleigh," she observed. "Rationing was hard to live with . . . but, you know, you just learned to live without lots of things." The government's slogan was "Give Till It Hurts," and many did just that. By the middle of 1942, it was estimated, 40 percent of the population was involved in some form of voluntary activity in support of the war effort— working in munitions factories, donating blood, selling bonds, saving tin cans and gum wrappers, and scrounging for scrap metal. Stripper Sally Rand even donated fifty of her fifty-two balloons.[78]

Yet after the war ended the same citizens who exhibited such patriotic frugality quickly repeated the familiar cycle and clamored for the emoluments of a consumer culture. The deprivation caused first by the depression and then by the war had resulted in a pent-up consumer demand that exploded in a frenzy of indiscriminate buying. In the face of such developments, *Free America* finally ceased publication in 1947. As Agar and the editorial board admitted, "The American people have not suddenly become converts to the credo that appears at the *Free America* masthead; the editors do not delude themselves by thinking that is likely to happen before the millennium."[79]

The attempt by New Dealers and decentralists to resettle Americans in the countryside either in planned garden communities or on individual home-steads joined one of the oldest American dreams, country simplicity, to the traditional assumption that a good republican society requires that people be economically independent and therefore politically free. Despite their sharp differences over the role of government planning, Roosevelt, M. L. Wilson, Tugwell, Borsodi, Agar, Mumford, Fowler, the Catholic homesteaders, Nashville Agrarians, and others sought to link access to land, dwellings, goods, and jobs so as to produce the moral economy envisioned long before by republican idealists. The urge to return to the land and to humanize the urban landscape thus remained a recurring phenomenon in the modern United States, just as the pastoral image and the agrarian myth remained perennial themes in literature. Yet, however much Borsodi, Roosevelt, Wilson, or the others may have spoken of the restorative virtues of tilling the soil or of producing cooperatively in language similar to purely literary imagery, they obviously believed that some dedicated individuals could realize the goal of partial self-sufficiency. They thus dealt not only in metaphor or symbol; they tried to make the myth a living fact, however small the number of people actually involved. That most of their countrymen were reluctant to share their dream and join in their social experiments, even in the midst of the depression, shows how divorced from actuality the myth of collective simplicity had become by the 1930s.

Whatever can be said about the failings of the neo-Jeffersonians during the inter-war years, they did make an energetic protest on behalf of the assumption that men and women should exert greater control over their livelihood and adopt a higher standard of worth than mere consumerism. Choosing how to live, they zealously demonstrated, is a moral undertaking, entailing the cultivation of certain values and the discouragement of others. Insofar as simple living on homesteads or in garden cities or through cooperative buying and selling arrangements would give some people, admittedly unusual individuals, more control over their time and the making of such daily decisions, it would continue to serve as a compelling vision of the good life.

CHAPTER TEN

Affluence and Anxiety

Prosperity returned with a flourish after World War II, and the corporate and consumer culture again came to shape the contours of American domestic life. *Fortune* magazine claimed in 1946 that "this is a dream era, this is what everyone was waiting through the blackouts for . . . . The Great American Boom is on." During the 1950s, government officials assured the citizenry that they need not fear another economic collapse. "Never again shall we allow a depression in the United States," President Dwight D. Eisenhower promised. This was not just political hyperbole. The leading economists of the postwar era—Paul Samuelson, Walter Heller, and Milton Friedman—were likewise agreed that there need be no more dramatic economic collapses. They and others led the public to believe that perpetual economic growth was possible, desirable, and, in fact, essential, and the expectation of unending plenty thus became the reigning assumption of social thought in the two decades after 1945.[1]

Even those who admitted that the economy's upward spiral might eventually peak and turn downward were caught up in the booster spirit of the age. In 1955 the editors of *U.S. News and World Report* asserted:

> The idea is getting around that there is no end to prosperity. Recessions, wars, other worries of the past seem far away. It's like a "new era." Americans are living high, spending as never before, going into debt for new, fancier homes, cars and gadgets. Where does all this lead? In time, maybe, to excesses, then a correction. But that's some time off. For now, all looks good.

By the 1960s Americans were being told that the dynamo of advanced capitalism was on the verge of eliminating poverty altogether. As President John F. Kennedy maintained, "a rising tide lifts all boats." And Lyndon Johnson explained that his Great Society program "rests on abundance and liberty for all."[2]

248

Native and foreign observers alike marveled at the democratization of goods and services generated by America's prolific industrial plant. In 1950 almost 37 percent of American homes were deemed substandard, in 1970 only 9.5 percent. Weekly visits to beauty parlors and shopping malls became routine activities for housewives, and working-class families owned two cars. Many boasted a boat or camper as well. When he was sworn in as head of the AFL-CIO in 1955, George Meany exclaimed that "American labor never had it so good." Such widespread plentitude was understandably a source of great national pride, especially in the midst of the Cold War. *Life* magazine gleefully reported shoppers filling a "$5 million grocery store, picking from the thousands of items on the high-piled shelves until their carts became cornucopias filled with an abundance that no other country in the world had ever known."[3]

To perpetuate the new prosperity, economists expounded the basic marketing strategy of the 1920s: the public must be taught to consume more and expect more. And more people, both at home and abroad, must be brought into the marketplace. Still, many adults who had undergone the severities of the Depression and the rationing required for the war effort had to be weaned from a decade and a half of imposed frugality in order to nourish the consumer culture. A motivational researcher told a business group that the fundamental challenge facing the modern capitalist economy was to demonstrate to the consumer "that the hedonistic approach to life is a moral, not an immoral one."[4]

Marketing specialists thus accelerated their efforts to eradicate plain living and engineer a revolution of rising expectations and self-gratification. As Vance Packard demonstrated in *The Waste Makers* (1960), packaging emerged as a seductive new art form in the 1950s, and planned obsolescence became a guiding principle for many manufacturers. The "throwaway" psychology was quickly taken up by the masses. "We are notoriously untidy and extravagant people," explained one student of the new prosperity, "but these bad habits may turn out to be unexpected assets. . . . For in this country, at least, it seems that 'Nothing succeeds like a mess.'" Madison Avenue copywriters played a variation on this theme, as they grew more ingenious at teaching Americans that nothing succeeds like excess. Robert Sarnoff, president of the National Broadcasting Company, claimed in 1956 that the primary reason for the postwar prosperity was that "advertising has created an American frame of mind that makes people want more things, better things and newer things." Paying for such "things" was no problem; the age of the credit card had arrived by the 1950s. Between 1945 and 1957, consumer credit skyrocketed 800 percent. Where families in other industrialized nations were typically saving 10 to 20 percent of their income, American families by the 1960s were saving an average of 5 percent. "Never before have so many owed so much to so many," *Newsweek* cheerfully noted. "Time has swept away the Puritan conception of immorality in debt and godliness in thrift." President Eisenhower reflected this attitude when he advised the public during a slight business dip: "Buy anything."[5]

The sanctification of undiscriminating consumerism as a societal virtue seemed to most observers during the 1950s and 1960s a justifiable response to changing economic and social conditions. After all, who would deny that the standard of living for most Americans rose significantly during the period? Life expectancy was greater, living arrangements were more comfortable and sanitary, leisure time was increased, and educational and cultural opportunities were greatly enhanced.

Yet under the surface of such positive advances there were some disturbing developments. The benefits of abundance were by no means equally distributed, and millions of Americans still lived in poverty. Those caught up in the glow of unprecedented national abundance also frequently ignored the social, psychic, and environmental costs of rapid urban-industrial growth. Could a good society be defined by its goods? Could the individual and the national character really find meaning in plastics, chrome, and neon? Richard Nixon certainly believed so when he engaged in his famous "Kitchen Debate" with Nikita Khrushchev, and so did many Americans. But social analysts and creative writers such as Lewis Mumford, Erich Fromm, Allen Ginsberg, Paul Goodman, C. Wright Mills, Reinhold Niebuhr, David Riesman, Daniel Bell, Arthur Miller, Saul Bellow, Edward Albee, and J. D. Salinger earnestly disagreed, and they highlighted in their writings the shallow conformity and mental strains of life in a consumer culture. White-collar workers and suburbanites now led lives of "quiet desperation" much like the farmers and shopkeepers of Thoreau's Concord. Mumford, for example, wrote in 1956 that in modern Western life all but one of the "seven deadly 'sins,' sloth, was transformed into a positive virtue. Greed, avarice, envy, gluttony, luxury, and pride were the driving forces of the new economy." Like a latter-day Jefferson or Emerson, Mumford welcomed the prosperity created by American ingenuity and labor, but he worried that too many people were not using their good fortune wisely. In their pell-mell rush to have more things, they were losing sight of higher aspirations and activities. "What is significant about an economy," he pointed out, "is not the quantity of goods consumed, but the ratio of consumption to creativity." Judging from the assessments of Mumford and the other cultural critics of the period, the postwar era was not only an age of widespread abundance and youthful frivolity; it was also an age of heightened materialism, stress, anxiety, and depression.[6]

For the most part, however, the public paid little heed to such Cassandras. "On however banal a level of human aspiration," one social commentator admitted, "the newly affluent Americans were at home in their own country." The promise of being a people of plenty continued to define the national purpose throughout the 1950s and into the 1960s. In the face of such material expectations, those advocating simple living were deemed more eccentric than ever. And many deserved the label.[7]

Certainly that was the case for the "beat" poets and artists of the 1950s, and it was especially true for the "hippies" of the 1960s, that small, but significant segment of the nation's youth who explicitly rejected the consumer culture and all that it implied. These advocates of the "counter culture" were primarily affluent, well-educated young whites alienated by the Vietnam war, racism, political manipulation, runaway technology, and a crass corporate mentality. With Dustin Hoffman in the popular movie *The Graduate* (1968), they were sceptical that real happiness lay in "plastics" or any other purely money-making opportunity. In their view, conventional urban and suburban life was corrupted by a bland materialism and a smug complacency. Consequently, instead of passively accepting the "absurd" code of conduct and standard of values passed on to them by their well-meaning but "hypocritical" parents, some grew politically radical and others decided to follow the more tantalizing credo outlined so rhythmically by the psychedelic Harvard professor Timothy Leary: "turn on, tune in, drop out." Yippie leader Jerry Rubin was equally direct in his pronouncements. The counter culture, he bellowed, "signifies the total end of the Protestant ethic: screw work, we want to know ourselves."[8]

There were many motives at work among those identified with the counter culture, some silly, some profound, but an especially salient theme was a desire for simpler living. Two of the most influential fellow-traveling adult spokesmen for the youth movement, Charles Reich and Theodore Roszak, saw in the tendency of the disaffected young to abandon the consumer and corporate culture a sign of revolutionary portent. As Roszak, a radical historian teaching at California State University, argued, "for a youngster of seventeen, clearing out of the comfortable bosom of the middle-class family to become a beggar is a formidable gesture of dissent." Likewise, Reich, a transformed Yale law professor, predicted an "impending revolution in consciousness" that would result in "a community bound together by moral-esthetic standards such as prevailed before the Industrial Revolution."[9]

In his best-selling theoretical romance *The Greening of America* (1970), Reich elaborated on this theme and presented an impassioned, if hardly original, critique of modern American culture. Like a disillusioned Puritan divine, he catalogued the sins of his society: disorder, corruption, hypocrisy, war, poverty, technological dependence, environmental degradation, the absence of community, and the loss of self. Over the years, he commented, the United States had turned its back on the innocent dream "shared by the colonists and the immigrants, by Jefferson, Emerson, the Puritan preachers and the western cowboy," a dream of individual dignity, material simplicity, and mutual concern. A corporate mentality that "believed primarily in domination and the necessity for living under domination" had come to pervade American society. "What we have," Reich maintained, "is technology, organization, and administration out of control." Conditioned by advertisers to expect a good life of goods and coerced by the government to participate in an unholy Asian war, the nation's youth were forced to suppress their natural emotions and deny their yearnings for openness, spontaneity, simplicity, and joy.[10]

Roszak presented a similarly comprehensive critique of American social life. In two influential studies, *The Making of a Counter Culture* (1969) and *Where the Wasteland Ends* (1972), he described the United States as comprising a "technocratic" society guided by an excessive scientific rationality that promoted the creation of vast, complex organizational structures and a purely quantitative standard of value. This "myth of objective consciousness," as Roszak called it, served to separate the sensitive person from other people, from the natural environment, and, ultimately, from his or her own self by rigidly divorcing reality from being and denying the possibility of transcendent spiritual truths. "The bourgeoisie is obsessed by greed; its sex life is insipid and prudish; its family patterns are debased; its slavish conformities of dress and grooming are degrading; its mercenary routinization of life is intolerable." In the midst of such an oppressive technocratic state, it was not surprising, Roszak observed, that so many young Americans felt increasingly alienated by the bewildering scale and impersonality of social activity. The "orthodox culture they confront is fatally and contagiously diseased." Roszak expressed only contempt for the consumer culture, asserting that "commercial vulgarization is one of the endemic pests" of twentieth-century Western life, "like the flies that swarm to the sweets in summer."[11]

Like all prophets, Reich and Roszak were not content merely to describe the evils of the status quo. They clearly had in mind a better way, a new version of the simple life based neither on Christian theology nor on classical philosophy but on the visionary ecstasy of Oriental mysticism. Here was their most original contribution to social criticism, for they revived a radical transcendentalism that called for a revolutionary change in consciousness. Political activism and violence, they insisted, were bankrupt. To restore meaning in America required a revolutionary change in individual perception, a dramatic transformation in the way people viewed themselves and the world.

Roszak, for example, proposed a "new culture in which the non-intellectual capacities of the personality—those capacities that take fire from visionary splendor and the experience of human communion—become the arbiters of the good, the true and the beautiful." A mystic influenced by his fondness for William Blake and his attraction to Zen, Roszak contended that America's "science-based industrialism must be disciplined if it is to be made spiritually, even physically livable. There must be a drastic scaling down and decentralizing." He also called for the transformation of the modern work ethic into a "spontaneous celebration of life." The technocratic outlook, he wrote, must be replaced by "a new simplicity of life, a decelerating social pace, [and] a vital leisure." Such a new economics of "low consumption" based on "kinship, friendship, and cooperation" would help infuse Western culture with the "gentle, tranquil, and thoroughly civilized contemplativeness" of

Eastern religions. And in the process, the "visionary commonwealth" of pre-modern times, with its magical and intuitive way of knowing, its affinity for rapture, and its "sacramental awareness" of nature, would spontaneously reappear. Apparently, all that was needed to trigger this revolution in perception and being was for a vanguard of visionaries—"hip artisans," "people's architects," and "dropped-out professionals"—to take the lead in abandoning the consumer culture and the cult of scientific rationalism. "Unless people remain obsessed with acquisitiveness, fixated on their selfish material needs, convinced of their own absolute incompetence and equally convinced of the technocracy's omnipotence, the artificial environment will begin to dissolve like a house of sugar candy in hot water."[12]

Reich's version of the good life, clumsily labeled Consciousness III, was similarly transcendental. He cherished Rousseau's notion that man had been naturally free and contented until corrupted by institutions. With Emerson, he declared that "the individual self is the only true reality." Consequently, the objective for the alienated should be "to gain transcendence." Reich then outlined his prescription for creative autonomy:

> The plan, the program, the grand strategy, is this: resist the State, when you must; avoid it, when you can; but listen to music, dance, seek out nature, laugh, be happy, be beautiful, help others whenever you can . . . love and cherish each other, love and cherish yourselves, stay together.

Reich echoed Roszak in emphasizing that simple living was a necessary prerequisite of such a new consciousness. The practitioner of Consciousness III "must live on a modest scale to retain the freedom that his commitment demands." But he went well beyond Roszak in his insistence that all forms of corporate or industrial life must be abandoned in the quest for the good life. In a fit of ideological assertiveness, he declared: "No person with a strongly developed aesthetic sense, a love of nature, a passion for music, a desire for reflection, or a strongly marked independence, could possibly be happy or contented in a factory or white-collar job." If the affluent American would exchange "wealth, status, and power for love, creativity, and liberation, he would be far happier."[13]

Superficially, at least, Reich's redemptive vision provided a compelling agenda. But as a program for action, his mawkish regimen of all-embracing love coupled with material simplicity was fundamentally shallow, elitist, and, ultimately, unconvincing. His predicted cultural revolution would apparently occur simply by individuals adopting the trappings of a new way of life: "hippie" clothes, long hair, rock music, nature walks, and, of course, drugs. "To blow one's mind," he blithely asserted, "means to become more aware." Reich's most concrete example of how Consciousness III expressed itself in a person's daily life was in the wearing of bell bottoms and blue jeans. Such casual clothing represented a "deliberate rejection of the neon colors and plastic, artificial look of the affluent society. They are inexpensive to buy, inexpensive to maintain." And they were natural. They "don't show dirt, they are good for lying on the ground." Bell bottoms were especially preferred because they "give the ankles a special freedom to invite dancing right on the street. They bring dance back into our sober lives. . . . No one can take himself seriously in bell bottoms."[14]

It was equally hard for most Establishment intellectuals and journalists to take Reich's prophetic program seriously. George Kennan dismissed *The Greening of America* as a reflection of current "romantic-utopian moods, illusions and hysterias of one sort or another." Another reader characterized the book as a "colloidal suspension of William Buckley, William Blake, and Herbert Marcuse in pure applesauce." Reich's psychedelic transcendentalism was obviously much different from the plain living and high thinking ethic promoted by Jefferson and Emerson. He saw no merit in either stoical or Puritan self-control. Moreover, the anti-intellectual bias inherent in his worship of the spontaneous made rational thought appear stuffy and unnecessary. Even Theodore Roszak objected to psychedelic popularizers such as Leary and Reich. He sharply criticized the simplistic syllogism implied in their advocacy of mind-expanding drugs: "Change the prevailing mode of consciousness and you change the world; the use of dope *ex opere operato* changes the prevailing mode of consciousness; therefore, universalize the use of dope and you change the world." There were, he stressed, "minds too small and too young for such psychic adventures." Roszak's concern about the superficiality of much of the counter culture led him to advise the young insurgents to distinguish "between the deep and the shallow, the superstitious and the wise."[15]

This was good advice, for there was both depth and shallowness inherent in the youth movement of the 1960s. The "happy people," as Reich called the dreamy dissenters among the younger generation, adopted a wide variety of means to achieve personal autonomy and self-awareness. And, thanks in large measure to their parents' affluence, they enjoyed the luxury of experimenting with alternative lifestyles. For many of them, Oriental mysticism or charismatic Christianity provided invigorating alternatives to the status quo, as did a Dionysian combination of rock music, drugs, and sexual liberation. Collective urban living in hippie enclaves such as San Francisco's Haight Ashbury district, New York's East Village, or Atlanta's Fourteenth Street was the rage for a time, until conditions grew so crowded, violent, and depressing that residents migrated elsewhere. Rural living on communal or individual homesteads also attracted many of the bourgeois rebels. A member of one of the rural settlements explained why he discarded his car, stereo, toaster, and coffee maker in order to lead a simpler life: "This whole generation, all the people who are receiving these new energies and turning on, we don't want to be in the materialist bag anymore, and we don't want to get caught up in the nine-to-five career bag, the two-week vacation, barbecues-in-suburb bag."[16]

One indication of the revival of interest in homesteading simplicity was the paperback republication of Ralph Borsodi's *Flight from the City* and Scott and Helen Nearing's *Living the Good Life*. The latter had originally appeared in 1954 and had sold only a few hundred copies. Within a few years after its reprinting in 1970, however, a now eager public bought over 100,000 copies. Much like the Borsodis, the Nearings had left New York and taken up self-sufficient homesteading during the interwar years. But where Borsodi was a decentralist libertarian in his political outlook, Nearing (1883-1983) was a Tolstoyan socialist. As a young man he had found in Tolstoy his "counselor and guide." Thereafter, Nearing remembered, "I endeavored to simplify my life, and eventually become like him a vegetarian, a pacifist, and a socialist." The first step in such a personal program was to recognize that most of the trappings of life were merely status symbols devoid of intrinsic worth. "Since I did not intend to be and never was a status seeker, I must reduce wants and needs to a minimum." Soon after starting his career as an economics professor, however, Nearing discovered that his personal eccentricities and political sympathies irritated those around him. He was dismissed from two universities during World War I because of his radical pacifism and social activism. Cast out from the academic profession, Nearing joined the Communist Party in 1927, only to be defrocked three years later for espousing a theory of imperialism at variance with the Party line.[17]

Thus, in 1932, at age fifty, Nearing found himself blacklisted from teaching and unable to find publishers willing to print his writings. That the country was in the depths of the Great Depression further narrowed his options. Desperate for a livelihood, Nearing and Helen Knothe, a musician and vegetarian, decided that they must take control of their own fate, and they bought for $300 cash and an $800 mortgage a dilapidated sixty-five-acre farm in Vermont's Pikes Falls valley. Fifteen years later, with the death of Scott's estranged wife, the two homesteaders were married. The Nearings went to the country in order to create "a simple, satisfying life on the land, to be devoted to mutual aid and harmlessness, with an ample margin of leisure in which to do personally constructive and creative work." They were seeking "simplicity, freedom from anxiety or tension, [and] an opportunity to be useful and to live harmoniously."[18]

Anyone familiar with the Nearings' story thereafter knows how successful they were in cultivating such values and in living their version of the simple life. But it was not easy. Carving out a homestead in Vermont and then repeating the process twenty years later on the seashore at Harborside, Maine, were back-breaking endeavors, all the more so because they shunned the use of most labor-saving machines. "The machine has its function, especially on gigantic undertakings," Nearing explained. "Our project was not gigantic, but minute." Their one indispensable piece of machinery was a used pick-up truck. Otherwise they built their stone houses, cultivated their gardens, and cut their firewood all by hand. Machine tools, they believed with Ruskin, Morris, and the Arts and Crafts traditionalists, too often tended to displace "many of the most ancient, most fascinating, and most creative human skills." Their labor was therefore strenuous but also exhilarating, for they were for once their own bosses, and they knew that the work "was significant, self-directed, constructive and therefore interesting."[19]

Unlike so many other utopians, the Nearings thus successfully combined the visionary with the practical. The "value of doing something," they emphasized, "does not lie in its ease or difficulty, the probability or improbability of its achievements, but in the vision, the plan, the determination and the perseverance, the effort and the struggle which go into the project. Life is enriched by aspiration and effort, rather than by acquisition and accumulation." Gritty, determined, imaginative people, these puritan socialists planned carefully, kept systematic records, and adopted efficient productive methods. Yet they also scrupulously organized their days so as to alternate invigorating "bread labor" with leisure time for reading and writing, music, political activism, and fellowship with friends and their many visitors. Not content with commuter simplicity, they developed a self-sufficient family economy by practicing self-restraint, self-help, vegetarianism, and mutual aid. "We bought no candy, pastries, meats, soft drinks, alcohol, tea, coffee, or tobacco. We spent little on clothes and knickknacks. We lighted for fifteen years with kerosene and candles. We never had a telephone or radio. Most of our furniture was built in and handmade." Syrup from their own maple trees in Vermont and blueberry bushes in Maine provided the little cash income they needed for purchasing supplies and paying the mortgage. "We were not trying to make money," Scott recalled; "that is a game in which the sky is the limit. Instead, we ask ourselves: 'What is the least cash we can get by on during the next twelve months.'" The Nearings were so conscientiously indifferent to the lure of wealth that they sold their Vermont house for half its appraised value and deeded a forest tract to the town of Winhall for use as a community retreat.[20]

Scott Nearing, however, did not quite fit the saintly mold of a John Woolman or John Burroughs. His rugged simplicity was accompanied by an ideological dogmatism that led him to become an outspoken apologist for the totalitarian excesses of the socialist experiment in the Soviet Union. For a man so genuinely concerned with the betterment of humankind, he displayed some baffling moral blind spots. It is puzzling, for instance, that Nearing could admire Tolstoy and Stalin with almost equal fervor. Yet from the 1930s on, he doggedly defended almost every Russian foreign and domestic policy. Preoccupied with exposing the moral crimes of capitalism, he repeatedly ignored or minimized the crimes and moral bankruptcy of Stalinism. The "pacifist" Nearing, who once told his son that "he preferred not to be associated with the liquidation of any living thing," defended the Russian massacre of the Polish officer corps in the Katyn Forest as "a great social service," since it destroyed an aristocratic elite. Nearing also supported the Russian repression of the Hungarian revolt in 1956, claiming that the rebels were led by right-wing émigrés who had slipped back into the country from the West. As late as the 1970s, he continued to dismiss charges of Soviet persecution of Jews as "nonsense." How he could regard Russian actions with such complacency for so long remains a puzzle. Undoubtedly, the treatment he had received at the hands of university officials and government prosecutors during World War I served to sour his attitude toward the United States and incline him toward socialism. That is only understandable. But for him repeatedly to rationalize away the ruthless repression of civil liberties for the sake of the socialist experiment seems a baffling inconsistency.[21]

Yet Nearing the Soviet apologist was not the Nearing who inspired so many young middle-class seekers in the 1960s and 1970s. Most of those who visited the Maine homestead or who were transformed by reading *Living the Good Life* knew little or nothing of Nearing's ideological excesses. Nor did they seem to be aware of his old-fashioned personal morality. Nearing opposed the use of drugs as strenuously as he did the consumption of alcohol or tobacco. Hence, he must have been shocked to read a young communard's review of *Living the Good Life* in the *New Republic*, in which the book was praised along with "acid, [which] has given us the insight to look inward and not to be afraid of what we find." The Nearings, in fact, were quite taken aback at the jaded outlook of most of the disaffected bourgeois youth who flocked to see them. "Never before in our lives," they wrote, "have we met so many uncommitted, insecure, uncertain human beings." Their experiences with many such alienated rebels led them to conclude that self-sufficient homesteading was an alternative "confined rigidly to the few, rarely endowed and super-normally equipped men and women who are willing and able to live as altruists after being trained, conditioned and coerced by an acquisitive, competitive, ego-centric social system."[22]

Paul Goodman, the decentralist sociologist, novelist, and urban planner who developed an avid following among campus rebels in the 1950s and 1960s, was similarly concerned that the young dissenters were too often superficial and complacent in their vocational outlook. In writing prefaces for the new editions of both *Flight from the City* and *Living the Good Life*, he lectured his younger readers about the necessity of hard work and self-discipline. By reading how the Borsodis and Nearings went about establishing and maintaining their self-sufficient households during the 1920s and 1930s, he suggested, perhaps some of the hippies might learn the virtue of "puritan" discipline and thereby make their own alternative living experiments more than merely short-lived escapist indulgences.[23]

Too often, however, Goodman's warning went unheeded. Thousands of young and inexperienced romantics flocked to the countryside during the 1960s and early 1970s, eager to be liberated from parental and institutional restraints, to live in harmony with nature, and to coexist in an atmosphere of love and openness. "Out here," one of them sighed, "we've got the earth and ourselves and God above . . . we came for simplicity and to rediscover God." In the process many of them extended the spectrum of simple living to its practical limits—and beyond. All but a few of the utopian back-to-the-land experiments collapsed after a few months or a few years. The youthful populists were frequently the victims of their own liberationist philosophy and their bourgeois backgrounds. In their disgust for the modern work ethic, they tended to exchange the materialist hedonism of the consumer culture for the sexual and sensory hedonism of the counter culture. "The hippies will not change America," a journalist predicted, "because change means pain, and the hippie subculture is rooted in the pleasure principle."[24]

In fact, many of the intentional communities did produce more babies than bread. Pursuing an organic simplicity and allowing everyone to "do his thing" frequently meant that nothing got done. Impulse is a poor substitute for self-discipline when it comes to providing daily necessities. In a candid reflection, a young hippie confessed that "we are so stupid, so unable to cope with anything practical. Push forward, smoke dope. But maintain? Never. We don't know how." Initially intent upon detaching themselves from dependence on conventional society, many of the young rebels found themselves utterly dependent on it, and they were soon queued up at government offices, collecting welfare, unemployment compensation, and food stamps to help them survive the rigors of natural living. They had hoped to create a self-sustaining "lifestyle which unites a generation and love and laughter," but instead encountered increasing friction among themselves. Most of the communal settlements remind one of what Hawthorne said about Emersonian idealism—many bats and owls were attracted to its light. Drifters, runaways, addicts, and crazies soon crowded into the hippie settlements scattered across the country. A participant at Paper Farm, a commune in northern California that started in 1968 and failed by 1969, said of its residents: "They had no commitment to the land—a big problem. All would take food from the land, but few would tend it. . . . We were entirely open. We did not say no. We felt this would make for a more dynamic group. But we got a lot of sick people."[25]

The result of such openness and indolence was predictable. Just as had occurred at Fruitlands and other earlier collective utopias, many of the "New Age" communes suffered from a parasitic element intent on consuming but not contributing. A member of a mystical settlement in Oregon elaborated on the problem:

> You've eventually got to say: "Dig man! You want to eat, you got to work, like the rest of us, because that's what's happening here."
> And then they say, "That's just a copout man, we'll just lay around here and God will feed us."
> So I say, "O.K., you go find some other God, because this God ain't going to feed you unless you work."

Many of those who were willing to work and plan at communal living found themselves woefully unprepared for the demands of self-sufficient country existence. "We didn't know anything," a disillusioned communalist remembered. "We were déclassé hippies. We had no idea of history. We wanted to create a new economic order starting with us." But he and his friends had neither a program nor the practical knowledge sufficient for such a task. Most suffered from what youth psychologist Kenneth Keniston called the "fallacy of romantic regression" and were shocked at how demanding and uncertain life on the land could be. Ageless Mildred Loomis, who had joined Ralph Borsodi's homesteading movement during the 1930s, valiantly kept alive the School of Living idea at Heathcote, a homestead training center in Maryland. There she noticed that the most successful efforts at simple rural living were those attempted by couples or nuclear families. The young wayfarers who tried group living, she remarked, usually "discovered a fact rather surprising to them. That was their need for privacy. Almost all decided they wanted 'a place of their own,' and they moved on to find it."[26]

The superficiality and naïveté of many of the hippie communalists make them ready subjects for caricature. It is always easy to poke fun at utopians. But focusing only on the youthful follies of the hippies does not do justice to the complexity or the momentousness of the issues with which they were wrestling. Their quest for a more meaningful life that transcended materialism and embodied a personalist sense of community was indeed genuine, and in their effort to change things for the better, many communalists showed both courage and fortitude. Their search for the good life—though strewn with comic aspects—represented a profound stirring of youthful souls responding to intolerable social developments. And the refreshing zest for life that so many of them displayed redeemed much of their zaniness. As disturbers of the status quo, they provoked their elders and their peers to both outrage and reflection, and in the process helped change the cultural agenda. As Theodore Roszak recommended, "we must be willing, in a spirit of critical helpfulness, to sort out what seems valuable and promising in this dissenting culture, as indeed it mattered to us whether the alienated young succeeded in their project."[27]

In the midst of the incense and nonsense of the rural communes and ashrams, there were several success stories. The Vedanta monastic community in California, the Skinnerian Twin Oaks settlement in Virginia, and the many Bruderhof cells scattered across the country survived and flourished during the 1970s. Their common formula for success was a combination of intense commitment, structured labor organization, restrictive membership, and charismatic leadership. As Aldous Huxley pointed out a half-century before, "Don't imagine that a miscellaneous group can live together, in closest physical proximity, without rules, without shared beliefs, without private and public 'spiritual exercises,' and without a magnetic leader." These qualities were (and are) perhaps most clearly displayed in the largest and most publicized of the successful communes, The Farm, a thriving 1750-acre homestead in southwestern Tennessee.[28]

The Farm was the realized dream of Stephen Gaskin, a former Marine turned psychedelic professor of creative writing, who during the late 1960s began preaching in San Francisco a captivating blend of primitive Christian ethics and Zen philosophy. His spellbinding intensity quickly attracted a host of young followers who shared his vision of the good life. By 1970 Gaskin had grown convinced that it was necessary for him and his flock to leave the city and develop a more self-sustaining existence. So he led a caravan of thirty buses filled with some 250 men, women, and children out of the urban desert and into the promised land of rural Tennessee. There they set about organizing a commune. Their intention was to create a "spiritual community" in which each member lived simply and worked diligently for the benefit of all. "To develop an inexpensive and livable and graceful lifestyle," Gaskin emphasized, "is one of the most important things that we can pass on to humankind."[29]

No haven for the indolent, the libertine, or the indifferent, the Farm placed a high premium on work, marriage, and social service. Traditional family life was sanctified and personal morality regulated. No coffee, alcohol, or drugs (except marijuana) were allowed, and a vegetarian diet was required. And everyone must labor. "Don't ask for a mantra. Just hit the ball" was one of Gaskin's more memorable aphorisms. Reminiscent of the Puritans and Quakers, Gaskin preached the need to spiritualize labor, to "make *work* a meditation." In doing so he pinpointed the essential difference between the Farm and most other New Age communes. As a *New York Times* reporter recognized, Gaskin and the residents of the Farm "seem to have fulfilled their ideals of the '60s by turning dramatically away from the very freedoms that gave birth to those ideals. People who once promoted free love now ban adultery and insist upon marriage. Where they once lived off food stamps, they now work night and day."[30]

Gaskin quickly demonstrated a practical bent in establishing his agrarian utopia. In order to make the Farm as self-sufficient as possible, members were required to transfer their personal property to the collective and vow to lead a simple life. Hard work and careful planning enabled the settlers to raise most of their own food. The relatively small amount of cash needed to pay bills and buy necessities was raised by leasing acreage to local farmers and by members hiring themselves out as carpenters, painters, and handymen. Within a few years, the Farm also started a profitable publishing firm and several craft industries. Its own survival assured, the collective then turned to social service activities. "When we left San Francisco," Gaskin explained, "it wasn't to get a place to be, it wasn't to get a farm, it was to *make a difference*." To help make such a difference, the Farm established its own relief organization, PLENTY, which served as a mini-Peace Corps. It helped teach people in Guatemala and Africa how to grow soybeans and improve water management, and it established a free ambulance service in a Bronx ghetto. By 1980 the Farm had grown to include 1500 members, and a dozen or so satellite communities had been established across the country.[31]

The Farm's success, however, was more exceptional than representative. By the late 1960s it was apparent that the hippie phenomenon was beginning to lose its energy and its distinctive quality. The counter culture, like the earlier Arts and Crafts and back-to-nature movements, had developed both faddish and fashionable overtones, and much of the rebellion's original idealism was preempted by commercialization. Entrepreneurs were quick to see profits in protest. A clothing manufacturer used a picture of the Woodstock rock festival in an advertising layout. Underneath it read: "Granted, we're not hip to everything that's happening today, but what we are hip to, you might like." Another ad appealed to the youth movement's interest in nature and simplicity when it pictured a young man saying: "My world is evergreens and old blue jeans. Fresh, clean air. And *Dep* for my hair."

Retailers developed a banner business in faded blue jeans, surplus army jackets, beads, and sandals. Franchise health food stores and "head" shops appeared in shopping malls next to Nieman Marcus and Saks Fifth Avenue, and *Playboy* magazine featured a hippie playmate on its cover. Gyrating rock musicians made millions off their lyrical assaults on corporate capitalism. As one observer wrote, "the difference between a rock king and a robber baron was about six inches of hair." Many of the flower children themselves grew tired of their riches-to-rags existence and returned to school to become lawyers, doctors, politicians, and accountants. Such metronome behavior was most vividly displayed when a transformed Jerry Rubin, the Harpo Marx of the counter culture, became a Wall Street investment counselor.[32]

Superficially, at least, the tone of social aspiration in the United States changed markedly in the 1970s. Numerous commentators were struck by the sharp decline of social activism and a sharp rise in self-centeredness. Some called the period the "apathetic age." The "perfect symbol" of the post-Vietnam, post-Watergate years, said one critic, "was the Pet Rock, which just sat there doing nothing." Others detailed the aimless self-indulgence and social malaise that seemed to distinguish the seventies from the sixties. A 1969 *Time* cover story on California opened by declaring that "the good, godless, gregarious pursuit of pleasure is what California is all about." Journalist Tom Wolfe glibly labeled the 1970s the "me decade," and historian Christopher Lasch published a much-discussed, if little understood, study of the "culture of narcissism" in modern America. A compulsive egoism, an obsessive concern for physical and mental vitality, he argued, was eroding the bonds of mutuality necessary for maintaining a republican commonwealth. The status-achieving imperatives of corporate life and the consumer culture generated such a therapeutic mentality by displacing religion and tradition with a preoccupation with self-esteem and instant gratification. "To live for the moment is the prevailing passion—to live for yourself, not for your predecessors or posterity." As a result, the United States had become a "dying culture," held together only by a collective unhappiness and an individual pursuit of psychic survival. "After the political turmoil of the sixties," Lasch maintained, "Americans have returned to purely personal preoccupations." An anxious sense of inner emptiness led overwrought Americans to flock to psychiatrists, psychologists, and "human potential" counselors. Others found solace in fitness clubs or in self-help manuals such as *I'm OK, You're OK, Looking Out for Number One, The Joy of Pigging Out*, and *Winning through Intimidation*.[33]

In using such evidence to generalize about the spiritual deadness pervading American culture during the seventies, however, critics distorted as much as they illuminated the period's climate of opinion. There was far more continuity to American cultural behavior during the 1960s and 1970s than they implied. Co-existent with the public indifference and private narcissism was a continuing search on the part of a large segment of the public for a more personally meaningful *and* socially responsible existence than that offered by conventional affluent or corporate life.[34]

During the seventies, most of the young rebels and activists, now grown somewhat older, did abandon their more extreme eccentricities and re-enter the larger society. But as they did so, many of them retained a sceptical attitude toward the claims of the consumer culture and a mounting anxiety about the quality of the physical environment. A *New York Times* survey of college campuses late in 1969 revealed that many young people were transferring their attention from the antiwar movement to the environment. And in doing so they discovered that their ecological concerns were shared by an ever-widening segment of the population. In 1972 social analyst Daniel Yankelovitch described the "new naturalism" as comprising a vital new force animating the nation's youth: "Our children are urging us to stop our frantic rush to bend nature to the human will and to try instead to restore a vital—and more humble—balance with nature."[35]

This ecological conscience, for lack of a better term, blossomed during the 1970s into a major movement in the United States, a movement that served to sustain interest in the simple life as an alternative way of living. Theodore Roszak, for example, saw in the environmental movement the possibility of greatly enhancing the appeal of simple living beyond the alienated young. By providing "flesh-and-blood examples of low-consumption, high-quality alternatives to the mainstream pattern of life," serious enthusiasts could demonstrate to a sceptical nation that "ecologically sane, socially responsible living is *good* living; that simplicity, thrift and reciprocity make for an existence that is free and more self-respecting." He insisted that too many ecological zealots were foolishly wrapping simplicity in the "hair shirt of dismal privation, as if a healthy relationship with nature must mean grim, puritanical self-denial." As Roszak recognized, the ecological conscience was ideally animated not by a Franciscan absolutism but by the same idea of balance and proportion that had informed the simple life since ancient times. In this sense ecological simplicity shared many of the concerns about conscientious consumption that had motivated the turn-of-the-century nature movement. Enthusiasts in both eras were intent upon preserving the wilderness, conserving natural resources, and legislating responsible corporate behavior. Contact with nature was likewise deemed essential both for its therapeutic and transcendental effects. Thus microbiologist René Dubos called the ecological ethic a "religion based on harmony with nature as well as man."[36]

Yet the ecological simplicity of the 1970s differed in several important respects from its Progressive era counterpart. The turn-of-the-century movement was for the most part narrowly focused on the wasteful activities of the affluent. By the 1970s a far greater percentage of the population was sharing in the culture of abundance, and ecological activists directed much of their criticism at working class wastefulness and pollution. In addition, the phenomenon during the 1970s was also distinguished by a more global perspective and an almost apocalyptic immediacy. Typical of the alarmist tone that characterized much of the ecological debate was this prediction by Barry Commoner in his influential study, *The Closing Circle* (1971): "The present course of environmental degradation . . . is so serious that, if continued, it will destroy the capability of the environment to support a reasonably civilized society." Such dire warnings provoked many to question the growing social and personal costs of the Faustian drive toward unlimited economic expansion that had dominated Western culture since World War II. It was a shocking revelation to some that the United States, with only 6 percent of the world's population, was consuming a third of the world's natural resources.[37]

Such heedless consumption was increasingly portrayed as a mortal cultural threat. Many activists concerned with protecting the physical environment and promoting simpler and more restrained habits of living were powerfully stirred by the writings of Aldo Leopold, the saintly naturalist, biologist, forester, and conservationist, who had died in 1948. A year later, *Sand County Almanac*, a book of essays by Leopold, was published to an indifferent reception. When a paperback version was reprinted in 1973, however, over 270,000 copies were sold. The book included not only Leopold's detailed description of the changing of the seasons in the natural world but also his naturalist's plea for personal simplicity and social ecology. He complained that Westerners persisted in their "Abrahamic" attitude toward the natural world. "We abuse land because we regard it as a commodity belonging to us." Instead of such a myopic utilitarianism, he proposed a new, enlightened "land ethic" which would recognize "land as a community to which we belong" and therefore "use it with love and respect." The fundamental fact of both natural and human existence, Leopold stressed, was their necessary interdependence. Consequently, it was imperative that people quit viewing themselves as conquerors of nature deserving of all the spoils and recognize that such abuse of the land and its riches would ultimately lead to cultural suicide. "Nothing could be more salutary at this stage than a little healthy contempt for a plethora of material blessings." Future generations depended upon such a changed outlook toward the pursuit of happiness in the United States. The "problem we face," he maintained, "is the extension of the social conscience from people to the land." Such a "land ethic" entailed a human ethic. That is, the preservation of nature depended in large measure upon the way of life adopted by humans. As Leopold concluded, "we face the question whether a higher 'standard of living' is worth its cost in things natural, wild, and free."[38]

During the 1970s many others were asking the same question. Could the ecological web of life survive more decades of uncontrolled industrial growth and profligate consumerism? Even some economists began to say no. Kenneth Boulding stressed in an influential essay that the postwar "cowboy economy" of reckless expansion and exploitation would have to give way in the last quarter of the twentieth century to a new "spaceship economy" which recognized the fragile interconnectedness and finiteness of world resources. Another economist, Hazel Henderson, agreed that the conjunction between bigger and better could no longer be taken for granted. And she took some comfort in the fact that many Americans were beginning to adopt what she called "postindustrial values." Such values transcended "the goals of security and survival," Henderson told a 1972 White House conference. "They are, therefore, less materialistic, often untranslatable into economic terms, and, in turn, beyond the scope of the market economy. They constitute a new type of 'consumer demand,' not for products as much as for lifestyles." One proponent of such "postindustrial values" expressed the relationship between consumer behavior and environmental quality when he asserted that the "key ecological act that individuals can make is to reduce their income." Doing so would mean the first step toward a restoration of "Jeffersonian values: frugality, sharing, conservation, independence and simple living." The simple life was again rising from the catacombs of the consumer culture.[39]

The Arab oil embargo during 1973–74 and the ensuing price spiral gave added impetus to the resurrection. In the midst of the economic crisis, those promoting more measured patterns of living suddenly found their ideas being taken seriously by a capitalist society at the mercy of foreign manipulation. The energy crisis engendered a crisis of belief in the efficacy of the consumer culture, and self-restraint and self-reliance again became accepted societal virtues, as many of the same advertising agencies that earlier had promoted reckless consumer behavior were now hired by oil companies and public utilities to convince the public to buy less, heat less, and drive less. The Abundant Society was becoming the Modest Society.

Of course, earlier periods of war and depression had produced a similar response, but in those cases it had been commonly assumed that conservation was only a temporary necessity. A return to normality would also bring a return to high living. The energy crisis of the 1970s, however, brought with it the specter of permanent limits to American economic growth and standards of living. As England's Dr. Johnson once said, "When a man knows he is to be hanged in a fortnight, it concentrates his mind wonderfully."

The energy crisis certainly caught the attention of the American public. That the postwar era of cheap and abundant energy was over produced much wringing of hands and many omens of disaster, as experts catalogued the mounting "limits to growth." Affluence addicts went through withdrawal pangs, and the results were sometimes violent, as evidenced by the numerous clashes between frustrated drivers waiting in long lines for their gasoline ration. Public spokesmen worried that the gas shortage was a sign of permanent scarcities. Henry Ford II observed in the *New York Times* that the days of "high, wide and handsome" economic expansion were over. John Love, President Richard Nixon's energy chief, warned in 1973 that the embargo would force "a change of approach to our life-style and economy." Several years later, historian Ray Allen Billington was more conclusive in his assessment of the closing energy frontier: "We have reached the limits of the past type of life that we've been able to enjoy in this country." Future historians, he predicted, would see the 1970s as the turning point in American civilization. The increasing scarcity and expense of non-renewable resources would result in both a deep economic decline and a dangerous governmental expansion, as bureaucrats would be called upon to administer scarcity. "It may be a very long twilight, of course," Billington emphasized. "There's going to have to be a permanent adjustment in mentality, and I'm afraid it's going to take years or decades or even a century of agony before we adjust to it."[40]

Not all observers were so gloomy. As the English historian Arnold Toynbee reassured nervous Westerners in 1974, "A society that is declining materially may be ascending spiritually." Just as the Puritan divines had combined hope with dismay in their sermons, many commentators saw the possibility of a new social consciousness, a revolution of lowered expectations and enhanced virtue, emerging from the crisis. William Irwin Thompson, an innovative educator and prophetic historian, reflected this view. "As the Church lost the vision of its founder," he said, "so has the country lost the vision of its founding fathers, but now that industrial society is strangling in its own contradictions, we have our last chance to re-vision human society." Indeed, the surprising aspect of the energy crisis was the enthusiasm with which many observers welcomed it as a purgative and transforming event. "On the positive side," *Newsweek* asserted in March 1974, "the embargo and the action it prompted may well have brought about a permanent change in America's profligate life-style." James Reston of the *New York Times* agreed.

"The craziest notion that has hit this country in a long while," he observed, "is that shortages of gas, beef, and a lot of other things are bad for the American people."[41]

This hope that the energy and environmental crises would help promote a significant shift in American patterns of getting and consuming exhilarated those idealists already promoting simpler living. In a thoughtful analysis of the implications of an impending era of ecological scarcity, political theorist William Ophuls emphasized that the "earth is teaching us a moral lesson: the individual virtues that have always been necessary for ethical and spiritual reasons have now become imperative for practical ones." These virtues were the same as those cited earlier by Emerson and Thoreau, Muir and Burroughs: gentleness, frugality, humility, and simplicity. Ophuls suggested that such old values would become increasingly relevant as the environmental crisis worsened. The era of uncontrolled technological and industrial growth must necessarily give way to a "steady-state" society in which consumer demands and environmental resources would be balanced. This did not mean a static social condition. Instead, a "steady-state" society would be one governed by a dynamic equilibrium adjusting needs to resources. Growth would occur, but ideally only in those areas which posed no threat to the environment. Nor did the "steady-state" mean a forced return to primitive ways. As Ophuls argued, "A very good life—in fact, an affluent life by historical standards—can be lived without the profligate use of resources that characterizes our civilization." But this good life required that certain guidelines be followed, including "the preservation of a healthy biosphere, the careful husbanding of resources, self-imposed limitations on consumption, long-term goals to guide short-term choices, and a general attitude of trusteeship toward future generations."[42]

In this way, Ophuls, Herman Daly, and other advocates of the "steady-state" concept refurbished the Jeffersonian version of republican political economy and stressed its relevance to contemporary life. "Where this seems to lead," Ophuls concluded, "is toward a decentralized Jeffersonian polity of relatively small, intimate, locally autonomous, and self-governing communities rooted in the land (or other local ecological resources)." It was, as always, an arresting vision, and Jeffersonian simplicity witnessed a revival in the 1970s. Wendell Berry, the Kentucky poet, novelist, ecologist, and farmer, remarked that the old Jeffersonian "idea is full of promise. It is potent with healing and with health. . . . It proposes an economy of necessities rather than an economy based on anxiety, fantasy, luxury, and idle-wishing." Others agreed that old values were not necessarily decrepit values. Vincent Scully, a professor of architecture at Yale, explained:

I know it sounds corny, but I hope we'll return to the kind of environment envisaged by our forefathers for this continent—in tune with nature and the landscape. This idea requires that we get along with less, with a lot fewer material things. It leads to a sense of civilized, dignified self-sufficiency. . . . These are our virtues. They have been overlarded with the fat and hysteria of consumerism. But they could return.

Several observers pointed out that the oil embargo and its aftereffects were provoking forms of simpler living that promised to be more realistic and therefore more durable than those adopted by the youthful hippies during the 1960s. The new practitioners of enlightened self-restraint, according to one student of the subject, were not "extreme 'counterculture' youth who trek off into the hills or show a total commitment by joining an out-of-the-way live-in 'commune.' Rather, these are individuals who want to live in a sensible and responsible manner."[43]

It was such a "sensible and responsible" simplicity that Laurance Rockefeller promoted in the lead article in the February 1976 *Reader's Digest* entitled "The Case for the Simple Life-Style." This scion of great wealth turned businessman and environmentalist took great pleasure in noting the return of old-fashioned habits such as thrift and self-reliance in the face of the energy crisis and inflationary spiral. People were walking, car-pooling, or riding bicycles to work, conserving energy, installing woodstoves, recycling cans and bottles, reviving handicrafts, forming consumer cooperatives, planting vegetable gardens, and reassessing their priorities. "Americans in growing numbers," he reported, "are finding the satisfaction of material wants does not necessarily bring a sense of lasting well-being. Many long for something which will give a greater sense of purpose and meaning for their lives." But Rockefeller was quick to explain that the simple living he so admired was not that of the counter culture. He dismissed the hippies as "alienated pseudo practitioners" who chose to escape their responsibilities as citizens.[44]

What was needed, according to Rockefeller, was not such adolescent frivolity but a mature, deliberate attempt to engage in plainer living and higher thinking. This could be done by everyone, regardless of class, age, or circumstances. The simple life he proposed "involves reducing waste, and employing physical and spiritual capacities to the fullest. It does not necessarily involve radical change. For most, it does not mean renouncing modern conveniences or returning to nature. . . . It does mean reducing reliance on mechanical things and discovering the joy of self-reliance and the satisfaction of physical work." Thus Rockefeller saw great therapeutic value in simpler living within the mainstream of society, and in this sense he echoed many of the turn-of-the-century simplicity advocates. But he went beyond emphasizing the psychic benefits of such a life and revived the old argument of John Woolman and the Quakers which stressed that in a world of limits, more conscientious stewardship by the well-to-do would eventually benefit the less fortunate. "If advantaged Americans make fewer demands on limited resources," he declared, "there will, in the long run, be more for those who have access to very little, both in this country and throughout the world."[45]

Similarly, in addressing the frequent objection that any widespread revival of frugality would devastate the economy and increase unemployment, Rockefeller admitted that there would be sort-term dislocations. But in the long run, he predicted, the "return to less wasteful living is entirely consistent with economic growth." The market system would gradually adjust itself to changing consumer interests. New industries, such as solar heating, would create new investments and new jobs. Yet, Rockefeller emphasized in conclusion, the dilemma of modern man was not so much economic as it was spiritual and ethical. "We are faced with the moral challenge of simplifying our overly complicated, overly wasteful lives and forging a national commitment to an environmental ethic. . . . If we do it well, this personal and national commitment *can* enhance the spiritual life of every one of us."[46]

Rockefeller's contention that a mass movement toward simpler living was developing during the mid-1970s seemed to be borne out by a wide array of evidence. In 1977 a cultural historian wrote that the "idea of restraint, self-control, and revulsion against all sorts of excess is in ascendence everywhere." Students of public opinion and behavior were also struck by these trends toward simpler living. A Lou Harris poll concluded in 1977 that the "American people have begun to show a deep skepticism about the nation's capacity for unlimited economic growth, and they are wary of the benefits that growth is supposed to bring. Significant majorities place a higher priority on improving human and social relationships and the quality of American life than on simply raising the standard of living." Among the poll's particular findings was that most of the respondents were now more concerned with "learning to get our pleasure out of non-material experiences" than with "satisfying our needs for more goods and services." Harris summarized his evidence by suggesting that a "quiet revolution" was occurring in national values and personal aspirations.[47]

The Stanford Research Institute undertook a much more comprehensive study of changing American attitudes during the mid-1970s. It, too, noticed that "evidence is mounting that an increasing segment of the U.S. population is voluntarily taking up a simpler way of life." The report estimated that from four to five million adults were wholeheartedly committed to leading a simple life and that double that number "adhere to and act on some but not all" of its basic tenets. The core beliefs underlying the movement included spiritual commitment, civic involvement, human-scale technology and decision-making, ecological awareness, and conscientious consumption. Most of those "choosing to simplify their lives," the Stanford study indicated, "do not live in the backwoods or small rural towns; they live in the bigger cities and suburbs." They were white, well-educated, predominantly young (ages 18–39), middle- and upper-middle-class Americans seeking a way of life "outwardly simple but inwardly rich." Much of the ideological extremism that had colored the counter culture of the 1960s was now replaced by a deliberate search for practical expressions of simplicity. Far from being intent on destroying capitalism, these newly enlightened consumers were instead determined to improve the quality and humanness of the capitalist system. The "person living the simple life," the Stanford report noted, "tends to prefer products that are functional, healthy, nonpolluting, durable, repairable, recyclable or made from renewable raw materials, energy-cheap, authentic, aesthetically pleasing, and made through simple technology."[48]

Affluent Americans during the 1970s thus revived the ethic of conscientious consumption espoused earlier by the National Consumers League and other reformers during the Progressive era. "Voluntary simplicity is not poverty," one proponent explained to the Stanford researchers, "but it is searching for a new definition of quality—and buying only what is productively used." This emphasis on quality rather than quantity or showiness would supposedly benefit both the individual and larger society. As another respondent remarked, "I believe voluntary simplicity is more compassionate and conducive to personal and spiritual growth. I live this way because I am appalled that half the planet lives in dire poverty while we overconsume." The Stanford survey concluded that these changing attitudes toward the good life could prove to be the most significant social, economic, and political force during the next decade. It "could represent a major transformation of western values and signal shifts not only in values, but in consumption patterns, institutional operations, and national policies."[49]

Fueling the enthusiasm for various manifestations of simple living during the 1970s was a new genus of publications. Periodicals such as *Mother Earth News*, *The Whole Earth Catalog*, *Green Revolution*, *Rain*, and *Organic Gardening* detailed the methods of plainer, more self-reliant living to millions of subscribers. Books on the subject of simple living also abounded. Their titles revealed their message: *The Freedom of Simplicity*; *Enough Is Enough*; *Living Poor with Style*; *Beyond the Rat Race*; *Human Scale*; *Muddling Toward Frugality*; *No Bigger Than Necessary*; *A Guide for the Perplexed*; *99 Ways to a Simpler Lifestyle*.[50]

The most influential treatise on simple living was E. F. Schumacher's *Small Is Beautiful*, which enjoyed almost cult status. Schumacher, a German-born British economist, pointed out that modern economists and social scientists had established material growth (GNP) as the chief standard of societal progress. In the process, however, they tended to lose sight of humane values as well as the effects of such unrestrained expansion on the natural environment. Reflecting his attraction to the self-limiting aspects of Buddhist philosophy, he insisted that "since consumption is merely a means to human well being" rather than an end in itself, "the aim should be to obtain the maximum of well-being with the minimum of consumption." His thesis was engagingly simple. Modern man could better meet his spiritual needs by scaling down his material desires and his social structures. In Schumacher's ideal diminutive society, just as in Jefferson's or Mumford's, industries and communities would be planned according to "human scale," technologies would be made "more appropriate" to humane values, and thereby work and leisure would become more fulfilling. Small was therefore not only beautiful but healthier, cheaper, and ultimately more satisfying. That Schumacher failed to provide a convincing strategy for making small-ness the basis of social policy did not matter to the wildly enthusiastic audiences he addressed during an American speaking tour in 1977. His visionary program had struck a resonant note among many concerned idealists, and he was championed by a diverse array of prominent public figures, including Jerry Rubin, Elliot Richardson, Ralph Nader, Gary Hart, Jerry Brown, and Jimmy Carter.[51]

President Carter, in fact, invited Schumacher and his wife to the White House in 1977. The visit was more than ceremonial, for Carter had read *Small Is Beautiful*, as well as Amory Lovins's *Soft Energy Paths*, and had taken their common message to heart. The President decided that the energy and ecological crises required a sober reassessment of the American way of life. In his inaugural address he had told the nation, "We have learned that 'more' is not necessarily 'better,' that even our great nation has recognized limits." Shortly thereafter, he commented in an interview that the United States faced the prospect of being forced to change its basic patterns of work and consumption. The question was whether the public would make such adjustments "in a planned and rational way," or would have changes "forced on us with chaos and suffering by the inflexible laws of nature."[52]

This scenario became a recurring theme of the Carter presidency. To avoid the fate of President Ford's ill-fated appeal for public self-discipline in order to harness inflation—who could forget the Whip Inflation Now (WIN) buttons?—Carter sought to elevate the energy issue to the level of a do-or-die crisis. So he accepted Admiral Rickover's suggestion that he adopt William James's phrase the "moral equivalent of war" as the slogan for his energy program, hoping thereby to lead the country away from its wasteful habits and toward a more meaningful combination of material simplicity and felt spirituality.

But Carter was unable to translate his clarion call into effective public policies or to convince much of the public that such sacrifices were permanent necessities. His initial energy legislation was surprisingly anemic when com-pared with his apocalyptic rhetoric. One witty pundit charged that Carter's "moral equivalent of war" program should be abbreviated MEOW. Another characterized it as the "moral equivalent of Sominex." The clumsy political maneuvers and legislative inconsistency that plagued Carter's administration repeatedly frustrated his sincere desire to create a moral presidency. Like John Winthrop, William Penn, Thomas Jefferson, and Franklin Roosevelt, he found it far easier to preach simplicity than to establish it as a societal norm.

By July 1979 Carter had grown increasingly discouraged at his inability to forge a national consensus around the energy issue. Since 1977, his four televised speeches on the subject had drawn sharply diminishing audiences, and most of his legislative initiatives continued to flounder in Congress. It was in part this sense of growing impotence that led to Carter's abrupt cancellation of a scheduled televised speech on July 5 and his much publicized personal retreat to Camp David. There, after two weeks of reclusive meditation and discussion with invited representatives from all walks of life, Carter concluded that a "crisis of the American spirit" was enervating the national will.

Descending from the Catoctin mountains with this revelation in hand, the President addressed the nation on July 18 in an atmosphere of high drama. The citizenry and media had been kept waiting for almost two weeks while he had been in seclusion, and Carter's audience was large and expectant. He spoke less as a politician than as a lay preacher, determined to come to grips with the nation's paralyzing spiritual "malaise"—a term he took from his excited but superficial reading of Christopher Lasch's *Culture of Narcissism*. Whether he realized it or not, Carter drew upon the jeremiad tradition in presenting his sermon. "This is not a message of happiness or reassurance," he intoned, "but it is the truth and it is a warning." The nation had dangerously strayed from the ideal vision of the founding generation, he continued, and in order to survive it must again come to represent a cohesive spiritual commonwealth rather than a fragmented society of individuals and groups selfishly pursuing their own narrow interests. "All the legislation in the world can't fix what's wrong with America," Carter stressed. "It is a crisis of confidence. It is a crisis that strikes at the very heart, soul and spirit of our national will . . . [and] is threatening to destroy the social and political fabric of America."[53]

The heart of the problem, Carter had concluded, was that Americans had come to worship at the altar of Mammon. "In a nation that was proud of hard work, strong families, close-knit communities and our faith in God, too many of us now worship self-indulgence and consumption. Human identity is no longer defined by what one does but by what one owns." Yet, he contended, events of the decade had demonstrated that "owning things and consuming things does not satisfy our longing for meaning. We have learned that piling up material goods cannot fill the emptiness of lives which have no confidence or purpose." The nation was now at a crossroads, Carter maintained. Many still preferred "the path that leads to fragmentation and self-interest." But following that path would only result in continued conflict and stalemate. The other path, he claimed, would lead to a restoration of traditional American values·such as frugality, mutual aid, and spirituality. "We can take the first step down that path as we begin to solve our energy problem. Energy will be the immediate test of our ability to unite this nation."[54]

It was a unique message for a modern President to deliver. The tone seemed more appropriate to a John Winthrop or a Franklin Roosevelt. But

Carter obviously felt that such a dose of old-fashioned candor and morality was what the times demanded and the public expected. This is what he had been told by the national leaders he had invited to Camp David, and it was also the message he had received from his pollster-adviser, Patrick Caddell. In 1977 Caddell had claimed that the "idea that big is bad and that there is something good to smallness is something that the country has come to accept much more than it did ten years ago. This has been one of the biggest changes in America over the past decade."[55]

That may have been true, according to his surveys and those of the Stanford Research Institute and the Lou Harris organization. But was the change as widespread and as enduring as its advocates implied? Congress certainly did not see the energy crisis in the Jamesian terms Carter described, nor did much of the public. After Carter's dramatic speech, a Phoenix newspaper editorialized: "The nation did not tune in Carter to hear a sermon. It wanted answers. It did not get them." Indeed, Carter had implied that the national malaise was solely the result of individual selfishness and secularism. He totally ignored the fact that the country's dominant institutions—corporations, advertising, popular culture—were instrumental in promoting and sustaining the hedonistic ethic that he decried. The opposition to Carter's spiritual prescription was thus rooted both in the structure of the consumer culture and in the individuals immersed in it. So it should not have surprised the President and his advisers to learn that most Americans were not yet ready to see republican and Christian simplicity used as the basis of national social policy. Essentially, it seems, the much-ballyhooed "frugality phenomenon" of the 1970s was limited to middle- and upper-middle-class activists. Students, professors, environmentalists, consumer advocates, and idealists of various kinds were its most prominent and serious participants, and the predictions of a massive shift to simpler ways of living among the larger public were overstated. As the 1970s progressed, there were growing signs that the simplicity crusade was already beginning to wane. Citing a reviving interest in big cars among the consuming public, a University of Michigan economist concluded that the "American people obviously are not buying the argument that we have to turn into a nation of monks who live sparse and frugal lives." He failed to mention that marketing strategy might have had something to do with the public's rejection of frugality. In his view the consumer was a totally free agent in the marketplace, and "obviously," he concluded, "if the American people do not buy the austerity lifestyle argument, politicians in Washington had better reexamine their positions vis-à-vis expansion of energy supplies versus greater conservation."[56]

This lesson was not lost on Carter's political opponents. The results of the 1980 election demonstrated, in part, that the simple life had by no means driven the abundant life from the tangled field of American aspirations. Throughout the campaign, Ronald Reagan expressed only contempt for the claim made by Carter and John Anderson, the independent candidate, that the American energy and economic frontier was fast closing and that the public needed to adopt a permanent ethic of austerity. Reagan's outlook represented a classic illustration of the synthesis that had developed between the Protestant ethic and the spirit of capitalism since the seventeenth century. He combined an outspoken defense of conventional Christian morality with an equally enthusiastic endorsement of unfettered economic gain. In his speeches, Reagan frequently used Winthrop's metaphor of America as a "shining city on a hill" to characterize his own national vision. But his city was more gilded than that envisioned by the first Puritans. The emphasis of early Protestant moralists on the need for individuals to curb their quest for gain once a modest competency was attained seemed lost on him and his coterie of wealthy supporters.

Perhaps his own successful rise from humble beginnings to a position of wealth and power led Reagan to believe, with apparent candor, that anyone with enough pluck and energy would (and should) strike it rich. Those who failed to do so had only themselves to blame. Those who succeeded, he insisted, should be allowed to enjoy the fruits of their labors to the fullest. His political philosophy was thus grounded in the tradition of liberal individualism, a tradition that sought to maximize economic freedom and eliminate governmental restraints. Consequently, the idea that the consumer culture was out of control carried no weight with him. Reagan flatly rejected the conservationist argument that "we'll have to change our lifestyles, to start getting along with less, to accept a decline in our standard of living." Carter, he claimed, "mistook the malaise among his own advisers, and in the Washington liberal establishment in general, for a malady afflicting the nation as a whole." In his acceptance speech at the Republican convention, Reagan stressed that expansion, not retrenchment, would be the theme of his candidacy. "The Republican program for solving national economic problems," he concluded, "is based on growth and productivity." After promising to engineer a new era of prosperity, Reagan dramatically closed by asking the delegates to join him in a moment of silent prayer. It was a script Max Weber could have written.[57]

Reagan's steadfast refusal to believe that the United States had entered an age of limits, coupled with his disdain for the environmental movement, made him few friends among those professing the simple life. Yet Reagan was more complex in his political economy than most of his critics acknowledged. He frequently intertwined his adulation for liberal capitalism with an appeal to traditional republicanism. At times he could be strikingly Jeffersonian in his political stance. In a speech to Chicago business executives during the mid-1970s, for instance, he had called for "an end to giantism, for a return to the human scale—the scale that human beings can understand and cope with; the scale of the local fraternal lodge, the church congregation, the block club, the farm bureau." Such human scale activity would provide "a framework for the creation of abundance and liberty." Small thus seemed beautiful for Reagan, too. But it was a smallness limited primarily to social and governmental affairs rather than to business or consumer activity. If he was Jeffersonian in his sentimental political vision of a decentralized, self-governing republic, he was Hamiltonian in his refusal to emphasize any moral limits on the individual pursuit or consumption of wealth or on the size and influence of corporations.[58]

Just as so many proponents of the simple life had over the years been gripped by a nostalgic yearning for a golden age in the past, Reagan and many of his supporters looked wistfully back to the prosperous 1920s and 1950s as their ideal models for social and political renewal. Reagan once referred to the "golden years" of Eisenhower's administration and frequently cited Calvin Coolidge as his favorite president. By following Coolidge's example and reducing taxes and easing government regulation of business, he promised, the elixir of the market system would not only cure the energy problem but also bring about a new era of virtually cost-free material expansion that would spread its benefits to everyone. "Our aim is to increase national wealth so all will have more, not just redistribute what we have, which is just a sharing of scarcity."[59]

With their "more is more" philosophy to guide them, Reagan and his supporters quickly transformed the tenor of Washington public policy and social life. In his inaugural address the new President stressed his sharp philosophical difference with his predecessor. "If we look for the answer as to why for so many years we achieved so much, prospered as no other people on earth, it was because in this land we unleashed the energy and individual genius of men to a greater extent than had ever been done before." Individual freedom in the marketplace, not private restraint on behalf of the common-weal, was for Reagan the central political and social virtue. He thus bullishly reaffirmed the expansive ethic of liberal capitalism and set about reorganizing the government accordingly. Emphasis on conservation of natural resources and development of renewable energy sources was to be superseded by an aggressive policy of new oil exploration and exploitation. Reaganomics also promised new tax cuts for business and the affluent in the hope that the country would spend its way out of recession.[60]

At the same time, conspicuous consumption displaced conspicuous frugality in and around the White House. The chic simplicity of the Carterites—L. L. Bean boots, blue jeans, and plain cardigans—was out; the sumptuous chic of the Reaganites—Gucci bags, Galanos dresses, Dior gowns—was in. Nancy Reagan, who claimed in an interview to "tend toward simpler clothes," assembled a $25,000 inaugural wardrobe, including a $1,650-handbag. The rich and triumphant Republicans on parade at the numerous inaugural balls, dinners, and receptions reminded a reporter of the court at Versailles. Another characterized the inaugural atmosphere as a "bacchanalia of the haves." Even millionaire Republican party stalwart Barry Goldwater was dismayed at the "ostentatious" show. Other Republicans worried about the seeming contradiction between the Administration's stringent fiscal philosophy and its luxurious personal behavior. Maryon Allen, widow of Democratic Senator James Allen of Alabama and a *Washington Post* columnist, was more graphic—and partisan—in her disgust: "It made me sick—the racks of dresses and the fur coats they didn't even bother to pack, the lineup of private jets and the jeweled boots, the absolutely appalling overconsumerism, the insane jubilation."[61]

Yet many of the wealthy New Guard claimed that the public wanted such pomp and luster returned to the White House. Charles Wick, a millionaire and long-time Reagan associate who was appointed director of the International Communications Agency, argued that "economically pinched Americans of today enjoyed viewing the luxurious Washington way of life of the Reagan Administration members, much as Americans who suffered in the Depression enjoyed watching Hollywood stars in the movies." As Wick implied, for at least some well-to-do segments of the population, the revival of White House sanctioned high living was a godsend. One Washington socialite exulted: "Someone said when Reagan was elected you didn't have to be ashamed of what you have anymore. At the tea parties the children come in blue velvet and the ladies in three-hundred-dollar suits." The social reporter for the *Washington Post* likewise noted that since the "Republican aristocracy took over Washington," it was "safe again to put on diamonds, designer gowns and—speaking generally, the dog." Nor was the revival of opulence limited to the Washington social scene. A few months after the inauguration, *U.S. News and World Report* surveyed social life in a dozen major cities and announced that the "old less-is-more, down-with-materialism atmosphere that achieved a high-art patina during the Carter years has been brushed aside by the new ruling class. A flaunt-it-if-you-have-it style is rippling in concentric circles across the land." In an interview, a prominent sociologist emphasized that the stylish personal extravagance associated with the new administration had found a receptive audience across the country: "We're beginning to see a turn from deliberate simplicity to a more elaborate lifestyle."[62]

So the myth of ever-increasing material abundance and consumption continued to guide many Americans' aspirations. By 1983, economists caught up in the euphoric promises of Reaganomics and the first stirrings of recovery were resurrecting the predictive hubris of their predecessors in the 1920s and 1950s. The American standard of living, according to one forecaster, will "improve significantly this century and will continue to improve as far as the eye can see into the next century." Another bullish economist took considerable comfort in the historical propensity of Americans to define the good life in essentially material terms. "One thing about people in this country," he stressed in 1983, "they love to spend, and they're starting to do that now. This is not a flash in the pan. This might well hold true for many years to come." With F. Scott Fitzgerald's Jay Gatsby, such material optimists seemed eager to renew their belief in the "green light, the orgiastic future that year by year recedes before us. It eluded us then, but that's no matter—tomorrow we will run faster, stretch out our arms farther."[63]

By 1984 the economy had indeed grown dramatically and "big is better" bumper stickers began to displace those proclaiming "small is beautiful." But one should not exaggerate the resurgence of the corporate and consumer culture in the aftermath of the 1980 election. Many of the Reaganites did engage in vulgar displays of wealth and did proclaim a crassly materialist version of the good life. And, in so doing, they emboldened a prominent group of sympathizers to bring out their furs and diamonds. Yet the trend toward simpler and more ecologically sensitive ways of living begun in the 1960s did not die or even meekly fade away in the face of such conspicuous consumption. Rather, it continued to represent a significant alternative to the consumer culture and its pecuniary standards of value. To those who still dreamed of a republic of virtue and a moral economy, the attractions of simplicity remained compelling, well beyond the capacity of a single election or shift in public mood to dislodge.

Epilogue

The quick transition from Jimmy Carter's litany of limits to Ronald Reagan's promise of boundlessness provides a striking demonstration that Americans remain ambivalent about the meaning of the good life, as they have since the seventeenth century. From colonial days, the image of America as a spiritual commonwealth and a republic of virtue has survived alongside the more tantalizing vision of America as a cornucopia of economic opportunities and consumer delights. Yet the simple life as an enduring societal norm has never been realized. Espoused initially as a communal ethic, for all to embrace, it has in fact garnered only a relatively few serious adherents over the years. "Simplicity," observed the Quaker reformer Richard Gregg in 1936, "seems to be a foible of saints and occasional geniuses, but not something for the rest of us."[1]

Again and again, Americans have espoused the merits of simple living, only to become enmeshed in its opposite. People have found it devilishly hard to limit their desires to their needs so as to devote most of their attention to "higher" activities. This should not surprise us. Socrates pointed out centuries ago that "many people will not be satisfied with the simpler way of life. They will be for adding sofas, and tables, and other furniture; also dainties, and perfumes, and incense, and courtesans and cakes." He knew that all notions of moral excellence and spiritual commitment are by their very nature elitist, since few can live up to their dictates for long. Thoreau likewise noted that simplicity was for the few rather than for the many. He recognized at the beginning of *Walden* that the simple life he described would have little appeal to "those who find their encouragement and inspiration in precisely the present condition of things, and cherish it with the fondness and enthusiasm of lovers." Many Americans have not wanted to lead simple lives, and not wanting to is the best reason for not doing so.[2]

Though a failure as a societal ethic, simplicity has nevertheless exercised a powerful influence on the complex patterns of American culture. As a myth of national purpose and as a program for individual conduct, the simple life has been a perennial dream and a rhetorical challenge, displaying an indestructible vitality even in the face of repeated defeats. It has, in a sense, served as the nation's conscience, reminding Americans of what the founders had hoped they would be and thereby providing a vivifying counterpoint to the excesses of materialist individualism. During periods of martial, economic, or cultural crisis, it has been successfully invoked by statesmen, ministers, and reformers to help revitalize public virtue and stay the contagion of greed and indifference. The genuine sacrifices on the part of citizens during the two world wars and the oil embargo demonstrated the way in which simplicity has provided an emergency reservoir of moral purpose during times of crisis.

Likewise, the diverse exemplars of simple living—Woolman, Emerson, Thoreau, Burroughs, Muir, Bok, the Borsodis and the Nearings, as well as many others—proved that simplicity could be more than a hollow sentiment or a temporary expedient; it could be a living creed. Aspiring, despairing, yet persistently striving to elevate the nation's priorities, they dignified the ideal and invested it with relevance by practicing its tenets and by displaying an enlivening sense of wonder and an ennobling sense of purpose. As Emerson wrote in referring to the Transcendentalists, they served as "collectors of the heavenly spark, with power to convey the electricity to others." The historical prophets of simple living similarly provided through their lives and their dreams a wellspring of inspiration, a living legacy of an heroic conception of life that continues to move us. That they have represented a distinct minority does not detract from their significance. "It is not important," Thoreau recognized in *Civil Disobedience*, "that many be as good as you, as that there should be some absolute goodness somewhere."[3]

Today, thanks in large measure to models of simple goodness such as John Woolman and John Burroughs, most varieties of simple living persevere. The ideal may not move the millions, but it still seizes and nourishes ethically sensitive imaginations. Across the country, Amish, Mennonite, and Hutterite communities sustain a pietistic rural simplicity reminiscent of the early colonial settlements. Quakers and Christians of all denominations continue to bear witness to the power of Jesus's example by combining simplicity and service into a spiritual ethic of conscience. At the same time, thousands practice the homesteading ideal popularized by the Nearings, and poetic farmers such as Wendell Berry and Donald Hall revitalize the romantic naturalism and rural simplicity of Thoreau and Burroughs. At the other end of the spectrum, prominent conservative spokesman George Will professes an eighteenth-century philosophy of living based upon the patrician simplicity and civic humanism of a John Adams. And, in cities and suburbs, citizens of various political persuasions participate in cooperatives, encourage conscientious consumption, promote the conservation of natural resources, and seek greater self-reliance through mutual aid and home production. That the simple life has survived in such various forms testifies to the continuing attraction of its basic premise. It *can* be a good life. And it is this factor above all that explains its durability.

What does the future hold? As a rule historians should bypass the enticing briarpatch of cultural prophecy, but in this case, past experience does provide a reliable indicator of future behavior. Undoubtedly, the simple life will persist both as an enduring myth and as an actual way of living. There will always be Americans who prefer the pristine pursuit of goodness over the mere pursuit of goods. For simplicity to experience continued vitality, however, its advocates must learn from the ethic's historical strengths and weaknesses.

The weaknesses seem clear. Proponents of the simple life have frequently been overly nostalgic about the quality of life in olden times, narrowly anti-urban in outlook, and too disdainful of the benefits of prosperity and technology. "We have heard nothing but despair and seen nothing but progress," said the nineteenth-century English historian Thomas Macaulay, and his sentiment applies equally well to much of the cultural criticism in the United States. Because Americans have been so burdened by a peculiar sense of providentially assigned obligation, the despair felt by moralists in the face of the nation's material progress has been even more pronounced than that of their English and European counterparts. Perhaps it has been more warranted, as well, but too often the critics of American materialism have failed to give adequate recognition to the benefits of modern civilization and economic well-being.

After all, most of the "high thinking" of this century has been facilitated by prosperity. The expansion of universities, libraries, and research centers, the proliferation of learned publications, the democratization of the fine arts, and the ever-widening impact of philanthropic organizations—all of these developments have been supported by the rising pool of national wealth. This is no mean achievement. "A creative economy," Emerson once wrote, can be "the fuel of magnificence." The radical critics of capitalism and promoters of spartan rusticity among the advocates of the simple life would be well advised to acknowledge that material progress and urban life can frequently be compatible with spiritual, moral, or intellectual concerns. As Lewis Mumford, one of the sanest of all the simplifiers, stressed in *The Conduct of Life*: "It is not enough to say, as Rousseau once did, that one has only to reverse all the current practices to be right. . . . If our new philosophy is well-grounded we shall not merely react against the 'air-conditioned nightmare' of our present culture; we shall also carry into the future many elements of quality that this culture actually embraces."[4]

That the practices and prejudices of those advocating the simple life have occasionally been a sorry parody of their principles has also served to diminish the appeal of the simple life. Small can be both silly and bizarre. The lethal fanaticism of the Jonestown settlers and other apocalyptic survivalist groups that have fled the cities and taken up primitive communal living in the countryside reveals the way in which simplicity can be taken to destructive extremes. Moreover, too many advocates have pursued simplicity as a faddish impulse rather than as a sincere discipline. Stylish rusticity has always been quite fashionable among many affluent Americans, but only rarely has it been accompanied by a simplicity in the soul.

Cynics, however, are too often eager to dismiss the significance of simplicity because of the perversities and hypocrisies of some of its proponents. This is unfortunate, for in doing so they ignore the ethic's deep-seated spiritual appeal and the numerous examples of simple living constructively applied in the American experience. The simple life has shared the beauty of every other soaring ideal: the beauty of elevating human aspirations beyond the material and mundane and establishing a standard of conduct worthy of our effort. When the sceptics have had their say, the fact remains that there have been many who have demonstrated that enlightened self-restraint can provide a sensible approach to living that can be fruitfully applied in any era.

If this study has a moral, then, it is that the simple life, though destined to be a minority ethic, can nevertheless be more than an anachronism or an eccentricity. Although it has been most evident during times of national emergency, it requires neither an energy crisis nor a national calamity to make it appealing. What meaningful simple living does require is a person willing it for himself. Attempts to impose simple living have been notoriously ephemeral in their effects. For simplicity to be both fulfilling and sustaining, one must choose it, or, as the Puritans might have said, one must be chosen for it. "'Tis a gift to be simple," sang the Shakers, and the lyric still rings true.

If the decision to live a simple life is fundamentally a personal matter, then so, too, is the nature and degree of simplification. There is no cosmic guidebook to follow. Although some prominent enthusiasts have verged on asceticism or primitivism, they have been the exception rather than the rule. Simplicity in its essence demands neither a vow of poverty nor a life of rural homesteading. As an ethic of self-conscious material moderation, it can be practiced in cities and suburbs, townhouses and condominiums. It requires neither a log cabin nor a hairshirt but a deliberate ordering of priorities so as to distinguish between the necessary and superfluous, useful and wasteful, beautiful and vulgar.

Still, it is impossible to specify that this or that possession or activity is universally expendable. Simplicity is more aesthetic than ascetic in its approach to good living. Money or possessions or activities themselves do not corrupt simplicity, but the love of money, the craving for possessions, and the prison of activities do. Knowing the difference between personal trappings and personal traps, therefore, is the key to mastering the fine art of simple living. One of Gandhi's American friends once confessed to the Indian leader that it was easy and liberating for him to discard most of the superfluous clutter in his life and his household, but he could not part with his large collection of books. "Then don't give them up," Gandhi replied. "As long as you derive inner help and comfort from anything, you should keep it. If you were to give it up in a mood of self-sacrifice or out of a sense of duty, you would continue to want it back, and that unsatisfied want would make trouble for you." This means that simplicity is indeed more a state of mind than a particular standard of living. The good life, as Aldo Leopold pointed out, "boils down to a question of degree."[5]

Indeed it does. Determining and maintaining the correct degree of simplicity is not a simple endeavor. Human nature and the imperatives of the consumer culture constantly war against enlightened restraint. Nevertheless, simplicity remains an animating vision of vital moral purpose, for it is our dreams that energize us more than our abilities. In the quest for the good life the possible is as valid as the probable. And for those with the will to believe in the possibility of the simple life and act accordingly, the rewards can be great. Practitioners can gradually wrest control of their own lives from the manipulative demands of the marketplace and workplace. Then they can begin to cultivate a renewed sense of republican virtue, spiritual meaning, and social concern. Properly interpreted, such a modern simple life informed by its historical tradition can be both socially constructive and personally gratifying. This was the message that John Burroughs gave to the schoolchildren of New York City in 1911 when he wrote a letter at the request of the superintendent, explaining to the youngsters why he was so hale and happy at age seventy-four. "With me," he remarked, "the secret of my youth is the simple life—simple food, sound sleep, the open air, daily work, kind thoughts, love of nature, and joy and contentment in the world in which I live. . . . I have had a happy life. . . . May you all do the same." A sentimental creed, perhaps, but one that has repeatedly proven its worth to the moral health of the nation and the spiritual health of its practitioners.[6]

Notes

KEY TO ABBREVIATIONS

AA	Abigail Adams	JB	John Burroughs
AC	Andrew Carnegie	JCR	John Crowe Ransom
AJD	Andrew Jackson Downing	JD	John Dickinson
AL	Arthur Lee	JM	James Madison
AM	Arthur Morgan	JW	John Woolman
BR	Benjamin Rush	*LHJ*	*Ladies' Home Journal*
BSA	Boy Scouts of America	LM	Lewis Mumford
CEN	Charles Eliot Norton	RB	Ralph Borsodi
CM	Cotton Mather	RHL	Richard Henry Lee
EB	Edward Bok	RWE	Ralph Waldo Emerson
ELG	E. L. Godkin	SA	Samuel Adams
ETS	Ernest Thompson Seton	SJH	Sarah Josepha Hale
GS	Gustav Stickley	TJ	Thomas Jefferson
HDT	Henry David Thoreau	TR	Theodore Roosevelt
HM	Horace Mann	WJ	William James
JA	John Adams		

Chapter One: The Puritan Way

1. George Santayana, *Character and Opinion in the United States* (New York, 1920), 15; Edward Arber, ed., *Travels and Works of John Smith*, 2 vols. (New York, 1910), 1:212; "The Mayflower Compact," in Henry S. Commager, ed., *Living Ideas in America* (New York, 1964), 111. See also Louis B. Wright, *Religion and Empire:*

The Alliance Between Piety and Commerce in English Expansion, 1558–1625 (Chapel Hill, 1943); Michael Kammen, *People of Paradox: An Inquiry Concerning the Origins of American Civilization* (New York, 1973).

2. Thomas Aquinas, *Summa Theologica* (London, 1922), Book 2, Part 2, Question 61.

3. See R. H. Tawney, *Religion and the Rise of Capitalism* (New York, 1958), 20–32. On Calvin's social ethic see Georgia Harkness, *John Calvin: Man and His Ethics* (New York, 1931), 178–220; John T. McNeill, "Thirty Years of Calvin Study," *Church History* 17 (1948):232–35, and *The History and Character of Calvinism* (New York, 1954), 221–23.

4. John Calvin, *Institutes of the Christian Religion*, 2 vols. (Philadelphia, 1936), 1:791.

5. Max Weber, *The Protestant Ethic and the Spirit of Capitalism*, trans. Talcott Parsons (New York, 1958), 172, 163.

6. Huxley quoted in H. M. Robertson, *Aspects of the Rise of Economic Individualism: A Criticism of Max Weber and His School* (New York, 1959), 208. The literature on Weber's thesis is voluminous. I have found the following sources, in addition to Robertson and Tawney, most useful: Robert W. Green, ed., *Calvinism and Capitalism: The Weber Thesis and the Critics* (Boston, 1959); W. S. Hudson, "The Weber Thesis Re-examined," *Church History* 30 (1961):88–99; Gabriel Kolko, "Max Weber on America: Theory and Evidence," *History and Theory* 1 (1961): 243–60; Robert M. Mitchell, *Calvin's and the Puritans' View of the Protestant Ethic* (Washington, 1979); Kurt Samuelson, *Religion and Economic Action: The Protestant Ethic, the Rise of Capitalism, and the Abuses of Scholarship* (New York, 1961); Michael Walzer, "Puritanism as a Revolutionary Ideology," *History and Theory* 3 (1963):59–90.

7. Calvin, *Institutes*, 1:788, 785.

8. Ibid., 1:788–89.

9. The socializing process in Puritan New England has been richly treated in the following studies: James Axtell, *The School upon a Hill: Education and Society in Colonial New England* (New Haven, 1974); Bernard Bailyn, *Education in the Forming of American Society* (Chapel Hill, 1960); Timothy H. Breen, "Persistent Localism: English Social Change and the Shaping of New England Institutions," *William and Mary Quarterly* 3rd ser. 32 (1975):3–28; Arthur Calhoun, *A Social History of the American Family*, 3 vols. (New York, 1945), Vol. 1; Lawrence Cremin, *American Education: The Colonial Experience, 1607–1783* (New York, 1970); John Demos, *A Little Commonwealth: Family Life in Plymouth Colony* (New York, 1970); Sandford Fleming, *Children and Puritanism* (New Haven, 1933); Philip J. Greven, Jr., *Four Generations: Population, Land, and Family in Colonial Andover, Massachusetts* (Ithaca, N.Y., 1970); Kenneth Lockridge, *A New England Town: The First Hundred Years* (New York, 1970); Edmund S. Morgan, *The Puritan Family: Religion and Domestic Relations in Seventeenth-Century New England* (New York, 1966); Mary P. Ryan, *Womanhood in America* (New York, 1975), 21–135; Levin Shucking, *The Puritan Family: A Social Study from the Literary Sources* (London, 1969); Roger Thompson, *Women in Stuart England and America: A Comparative Study* (London, 1974); Michael Zuckerman, *Peaceable Kingdoms: New England Towns in the Eighteenth Century* (New York, 1970).

10. John Cotton, "A Christian Calling," in Perry Miller, ed., *The American Puritans* (Garden City, N.Y., 1956), 171. On the early Puritan social ethic in America, see Stephen Foster, *Their Solitary Way: The Puritan Social Ethic in the First Century of Settlement in New England* (New Haven, 1971); Philip J. Greven, Jr., *The Protestant Temperament: Patterns of Child-Rearing, Religious Experience, and the Self in Early America* (New York, 1977).

11. John Cotton, *A Practical Commentary, or An Exposition with Observations, Reasons, and Uses upon the First Epistle General of John*, 2nd ed. (London, 1658), 132; John Cotton, *The Pouring Out of Seven Vials*, 7 vols. (London, 1642), 6:39–40.

12. Edmund S. Morgan, *The Puritan Dilemma: The Story of John Winthrop* (Boston, 1958), 9.

13. Ibid., 10. I have taken the liberty of modernizing the spelling in this as well as later excerpts from colonial writings.

14. Massachusetts Historical Society, *The John Winthrop Papers*, 5 vols. (Boston, 1929–47), 1:193–94 (hereafter cited as *Winthrop Papers*); Morgan, *Puritan Dilemma*, 11; Ralph Barton Perry, *Puritanism and Democracy* (New York, 1944), 251. See also Greven, *Protestant Temperament*, 207.

15. *Winthrop Papers*, 2:14–17, 148; Richard Dunn, *Puritans and Yankees: The Winthrop Dynasty in New England* (New York, 1971), 4–5.

16. *Winthrop Papers*, 2:136.

17. Darrett Rutman, *Winthrop's Boston: Portrait of a Puritan Town, 1630–1649* (Chapel Hill, 1965), 245; James Hosmer, ed., *Winthrop's Journal: History of New England, 1630–1649*, 2 Vols. (New York, 1908), 1:134, 325 (hereafter cited as *Winthrop's Journal*).

18. Edgar A. J. Johnson, "Economic Ideas of John Winthrop," *New England Quarterly* 3 (1930):235–50; *Winthrop's Journal*, 1:144, 77.

19. Nathaniel B. Shurtleff, ed., *Records of the Governor and Company of the Massachusetts Bay in New England*, 5 vols. (Boston, 1853–54), 1:126 (hereafter cited as *Records*); Bernard Bailyn, *New England Merchants in the Seventeenth Century* (Cambridge, Mass., 1955), 39–44.

20. *Winthrop Papers*, 2:303.

21. Ibid., 3:216, 402–3. See also Rutman, *Winthrop's Boston*, 241–73.

22. *Records*, 3:243; 4:61–62; Gary North, "The Puritan Experiment with Sumptuary Laws," *Freeman* 24 (June 1974):341–55.

23. See J. R. T. Hughes, *Social Control in the Colonial Economy* (Charlottesville, 1976).

24. Shepard quoted in Larzer Ziff, *Puritanism in America* (New York, 1974), 144; Perry Miller, *Nature's Nation* (Cambridge, Mass., 1967), 27. On the transformation of the Puritan ethic during the seventeenth century, see Daniel W. Howe, "The Decline of Calvinism: An Approach to Its Study," *Comparative Studies in Society and History* 14 (1972):306–27; Robert S. Michaelson, "Change in the Puritan Concept of Calling or Vocation," *New England Quarterly* 26 (1953):315–36; Robert G. Pope, "New England Versus the New England Mind: The Myth of Declension," *Journal of Social History* 3 (1969):95–108; Darrett Rutman, "God's Bridge Falling Down: 'Another Approach' to New England Puritanism Assayed," *William and Mary Quarterly* 3rd ser. 19 (1962):408–21.

25. John Higginson, *The Cause of God and His People in New England* (Cam-

bridge, Mass., 1667), 11. See also Alan Heimert, *Religion and the American Mind* (Cambridge, Mass., 1966), 27, 423–26; Miller, *Nature's Nation*, 14–49.

26. Joseph B. Felt, *The Customs of New England* (Boston, 1853), 201–2; Rutman, "God's Bridge Falling Down," 412–16.

27. Carl Becker, *The Beginnings of the American People* (Boston, 1915), 120; Jack P. Greene, "Search for Identity: An Interpretation of the Meaning of Selected Patterns of Social Response in Eighteenth-Century America," *Journal of Social History* 3 (1970):189–220. Greene's interpretive synthesis provides an excellent overview of the turbulent changes affecting colonial thought and society during the eighteenth century.

28. James Russell Trumball, *History of Northampton*, 2 vols. (Northampton, Mass., 1898), 1:290–91; Richard L. Bushman, *From Puritan to Yankee: Character and the Social Order in Connecticut, 1690–1765* (New York, 1967), 189.

29. Eleazer Mather, *A Serious Exhortation* (Boston, 1671), 9, 17, 30; Peter Thacher, *The Fear of God Restraining Man from Unmercifulness and Inequity in Commerce* (Boston, 1719), 18.

30. Perry Miller was the first scholar to emphasize the jeremiad as a powerful mode of cultural expression. See his *New England Mind, The Seventeenth Century* (New York, 1939), *Errand into the Wilderness* (Cambridge, Mass., 1958), 8–9, 15, and *Nature's Nation*, 14–49. More recently, Sacvan Bercovitch has perceptively built upon and revised Miller's treatment, emphasizing the spirit of hope and affirmation that was coupled with the laments, as well as tracing the continuing prevalence of the jeremiad as a distinctive form of discourse in American culture. See *The American Jeremiad* (Madison, 1978). A fascinating, though needlessly obtuse, study of related themes is Martha Banta, *Failure and Success in America: A Literary Debate* (Princeton, 1978).

31. The debate over Puritan declension is thorny and tempestuous. As Robert Pope has shown, church membership figures for the second half of the seventeenth century seem to belie the ministerial claims of a decline in piety. But as contemporary experience reveals, church attendance is not necessarily a demonstration of inner piety. Nor does the fact that church membership increased during the last quarter of the seventeenth century invalidate the evidence that the Puritans (as well as the growing number of non-Puritans in New England) were indeed less inclined to follow the restraints inherent in the original *social* ethic. See Robert Pope, *The Half-Way Covenant: Church Membership in Puritan New England* (Princeton, 1969); Rutman, "God's Bridge Falling Down," 408–21.

32. Morgan, *Puritan Family*, 170.

33. Gary Nash, *The Urban Crucible: Social Change, Political Consciousness, and the Origins of the American Revolution* (Cambridge, Mass., 1979), 156. See also Lockridge, *New England Town*, and "Land, Population and the Evolution of New England Society, 1630–1730," *Past and Present* 39 (1968):62–80; Morgan, *Puritan Family*, 170; Conrad Arensberg, "American Communities," *American Anthropologist* 57 (1955):1150–51; Bushman, *From Puritan to Yankee*, 22–38, 135–43; Michaelson, "Change in the Puritan Concept of Calling," 315–36; Daniel Rodgers, *The Work Ethic in Industrial America, 1850–1920* (Chicago, 1974), 4–14.

34. On CM's social ethic see Virginia Bernhard, "Cotton Mather and the Doing of Good: A Puritan Gospel of Wealth," *New England Quarterly* 49 (1976):225–41; Richard F. Lovelace, *The American Pietism of Cotton Mather* (Washington, 1979),

146–97; Robert Middlekauff, *The Mathers: Three Generations of Puritan Intellectuals, 1596–1728* (New York, 1971), 191–99; Perry Miller, *The New England Mind, From Colony to Province* (Cambridge, Mass., 1953), 397–411.

35. CM, *A Christian at His Calling* (Boston, 1701), 42–43; CM, *The Good Old Way* (Boston, 1706), 8; CM, *Advice from Taberah* (Boston, 1711), 25.

36. CM, *Magnalia Christi Americana*, ed. Kenneth Murdock, 2 vols. (Cambridge, Mass., 1977), 1:14.

37. CM, *Bonifacius: An Essay upon the Good*, ed. David Levin (Cambridge, Mass., 1966), xiii, xxii; CM, *Good Old Way*, 28.

38. Kenneth Lockridge, *Settlement and Unsettlement in Early America* (Cambridge, Mass., 1981), 128.

39. CM, *Durable Riches*, 2 vols. (Boston, 1695), 2:2.

40. Worthington C. Ford, ed., *Diary of Cotton Mather*, 2 vols. (New York, 1957), 1:573.

41. Erik Erikson, "Identity and the Life Cycle," *Psychological Issues* 1 (1959): 28–29; Greene, "Search for Identity," 199; CM, *Some Account of the Earthquake That Shook New England* (Boston, 1727), 20–21, and *Good Impressions Produced by Earthquake* (Boston, 1727), 35–36; Thomas Prince, *Earthquakes, the Works of God and Tokens of His Just Displeasure* (Boston, 1727), 29.

42. John Webb, *The Duty of a Degenerate People To Pray for the Receiving of God's Works* (Boston, 1734), 124.

43. Bushman, *From Puritan to Yankee*, 185; Edwin Gaustad, *The Great Awakening in New England* (New York, 1957), 52.

44. Heimert, *Religion and the American Mind*, 56; Samuel Wigglesworth, *An Essay for Reviving Religion* (Boston, 1733), 25. See also Henry B. Parkes, "New England in the 1730s," *New England Quarterly* 3 (1930):397–419; Greene, "Search for Identity," 199–200.

45. Greven, *Protestant Temperament*, 70–71, 75–78. On Edwards see also Edward Davidson, *Jonathan Edwards: The Narrative of a Puritan Mind* (Boston, 1966); Perry Miller, *Jonathan Edwards* (New York, 1949); Paula Tracy, *Jonathan Edwards, Pastor: Religion and Society in Eighteenth-Century Northampton* (New York, 1979); Ola Winslow, *Jonathan Edwards, 1703–1758* (New York, 1940).

46. Arthur McGiffert, *Jonathan Edwards* (New York, 1932), 112–13. Interesting insights into Edwards's style of living are included in Leonard T. Grant, "A Preface to Jonathan Edwards' Financial Difficulties," *Journal of Presbyterian History* 45 (1967):27–32; Winslow, *Jonathan Edwards*, 115, 136, 216.

47. Winslow, *Jonathan Edwards*, 136; Whitefield quoted in Richard Bushman, ed., *The Great Awakening: Documents on the Revival of Religion, 1740–1745* (New York, 1970), 32; E. Williams and E. Parsons, eds., *The Works of President Edwards*, 8 vols. (London, 1817), 1:681; 2:164–65 (hereafter cited as Edwards, *Works*).

48. Blair and Whitaker quoted in Greene, "Search for Identity," 195; Heimert, *Religion and the American Mind*, 306, 31–34.

49. On the social effects of the Awakening, see Heimert, *Religion and the American Mind*, 45–53; Rhys Isaac, "Preachers and Patriots: Popular Culture and the Revolution in Virginia," in Alfred F. Young, ed., *The American Revolution: Explorations in the History of American Radicalism* (Dekalb, Ill., 1976), 125–58; Nash, *Urban Crucible*, 198–232; John W. Raimo, "Spiritual Harvest: The Anglo-American Revival in Boston, Massachusetts, and London, England," (Ph.D. diss., University

of Wisconsin, 1974), 64–76; Harry S. Stout, "Religion, Communications, and the Ideological Origins of the American Revolution," *William and Mary Quarterly* 3rd ser. 34 (1977):519–41.

50. Heimert, *Religion and the American Mind*, 12–14, 59–60, 306, 460–63; Gilbert Tennent, *A Solemn Warning to the Secure World from the God Of Terrible Majesty* (Boston, 1735), 102; Rhys Isaac, "Evangelical Revolt: The Nature of the Baptists' Challenge to the Traditional Order in Virginia, 1765 to 1775," *William and Mary Quarterly* 3rd ser. 31 (1974):353.

51. Nash, *Urban Crucible*, 208; Isaac, "Evangelical Revolt," 363; Charles Chauncey, *Enthusiasm Described and Cautioned Against* (Boston, 1742), 15.

52. Edwards, *Works*, 1:374, 387; Clarence E. Faust and Thomas H. Johnson, eds., *Jonathan Edwards: Representative Selections* (New York, 1962), 76, 77; Heimert, *Religion and the American Mind*, 57.

53. McGiffert, *Jonathan Edwards*, 113. See also Eugene F. White, "The Decline of the Great Awakening in New England: 1741-1746," *New England Quarterly* 24 (1951):35–52.

54. Bushman, *From Puritan to Yankee*, 189.

55. Anthony Trollope, *North America* (1862; rpt. New York, 1951), 235–36.

CHAPTER TWO: THE QUAKER ETHIC

1. Kai Erikson, *Wayward Puritans: A Study in the Sociology of Deviance* (New York, 1966), 107–36, 176–79. On early Quakerism see Hugh Barbour, *The Quakers in Puritan England* (New Haven, 1964); W. C. Braithwaite, *The Beginnings of Quakerism* (London, 1912); Howard Brinton, *Friends for 300 Years* (New York, 1952); E. Digby Baltzell, *Puritan Boston and Quaker Philadelphia: Two Protestant Ethics and the Spirit of Class Authority and Leadership* (New York, 1979).

2. Useful studies of Quaker social thought include Isabel Grubb, *Quakerism and Industry before 1800* (London, 1930); Rufus Jones, *Quakerism and the Simple Life* (London, n.d.).

3. L. V. Hopkin, comp., *A Day-Book of Counsel and Comfort, from the Epistles of George Fox* (London, 1937), 109, 90–91.

4. George Fox, *Gospel Truth Demonstrated* (London, 1706), 106.

5. Robert Barclay, *Apology for the True Christian Divinity* (London, 1678), proposition 15, pp. vii, 11.

6. Frederick B. Tolles, *Meeting House and Counting House: The Quaker Merchants of Colonial Philadelphia, 1682–1763* (New York, 1963), 38; Hopkin, comp., *A Day-Book*, 283.

7. Catherine Owens Peare, *William Penn* (Philadelphia, 1936), 43. On Penn see also Edward Beatty, *William Penn as Social Philosopher* (New York, 1939); Edwin Bronner, *William Penn's "Holy Experiment": The Founding of Pennsylvania, 1681–1701* (New York, 1962); Melvin B. Endy, Jr., *William Penn and Early Quakerism* (Princeton, 1973).

8. William Penn, "No Cross, No Crown," in Society of Friends, *Selected Works of William Penn*, 3 vols. (London, 1825), 1:333 (hereafter cited as Penn, *Works*).

9. Ibid., 370, 351–64.

10. Ibid., 341, 446, 480; William Penn to Wife and Children, 4 June 1682, ibid., 1:56.

11. Penn, "No Cross, No Crown," ibid., 1:495, 466. See also Joseph Dorfman, *The Economic Mind in American Civilization, 1606-1865* (New York, 1946), 78-92.

12. Penn, "Some Account of the Province of Pennsylvania," in Frederick Tolles, ed., *The Witness of William Penn* (New York, 1980), 116-17; Samuel Janney, *The Life of William Penn: With a Selection from His Correspondence* (Philadelphia, 1852), 255; Penn, "Some Fruits of Solitude," *Works*, 3:371.

13. Wesley F. Craven, *The Colonies in Transition, 1660-1713* (New York, 1968), 193; Claypoole quoted in Bronner, *"Holy Experiment,"* 82.

14. Beatty, *William Penn*, 284.

15. Minutes of Philadelphia Yearly Meeting, 1:54, 78, Department of Records, Philadelphia Yearly Meeting. See also Bronner, *"Holy Experiment,"* 50-69.

16. Gary B. Nash, *Quakers and Politics: Pennsylvania, 1681-1726* (Princeton, 1968), 91.

17. George Fox, *Epistles* (London, 1698), 503.

18. Penn quoted in Bronner, *"Holy Experiment,"* 206; R. W. Kelsey, "An Early Description of Pennsylvania: Letter of Christopher Sower," *Pennsylvania Magazine of History and Biography* 45 (1921):252-53.

19. Samuel Fothergill to James Wilson, 9 Nov. 1756, in George Crosfield, ed., *Memoirs of the Life and Gospel Labors of Samuel Fothergill* (Liverpool, 1843), 281-82; Carl Bridenbaugh, *Rebels and Gentlemen: Philadelphia in the Age of Franklin* (New York, 1965), 182.

20. See Tolles, *Meeting House and Counting House*, 109-43.

21. Penn to Wife and Children, 4 June 1682, *Works*, 1:57. On Penn's seeming double standard, see Beatty, *William Penn*, 167; Endy, *William Penn*, 358; Janney, *Life of William Penn*, 414-17.

22. Penn, "No Cross, No Crown," *Works*, 1:432.

23. Isaac Norris to Joseph Pike, 25 Feb. 1707, in Edward Armstrong, ed., "Correspondence between William Penn and James Logan," *Memoirs of the Historical Society of Pennsylvania* 10 (1872):259; Tolles, *Quakers and Atlantic Culture* (New York, 1960), 76-77, 79, 86-88. See also J. William Frost, *The Quaker Family in Colonial America: A Portrait of the Society of Friends* (New York, 1973), 187-211.

24. Tolles, *Meeting House and Counting House*, 230-43; Smith quoted in Amelia Gummere, ed., *The Journal and Essays of John Woolman* (New York, 1922), 267 (hereafter cited as *Journal and Essays*). On the decline of Quaker simplicity see, in addition to Tolles, Richard Bauman, *For the Reputation of Truth: Politics, Religion, and Conflict among the Pennsylvania Quakers, 1750-1800* (Baltimore, 1971), 19-34; Sydney James, *A People among Peoples: Quaker Benevolence in Eighteenth-Century America* (Cambridge, Mass., 1963).

25. On the Quaker revival see Tolles, *Meeting House and Counting House*, 234-43, and *Quakers and Atlantic Culture*, 89-113; Kenneth Carroll, "A Look at the Quaker Revival of 1756," *Quaker History* 65 (1976):63-80; Jack D. Marietta, "Wealth, War and Religion: The Perfecting of Quaker Asceticism, 1740-1783," *Church History* 43 (1974):230-41.

26. Churchman quoted in John Pemberton, *The Life and Travels of John Pemberton* (London, 1844), 28. Benezet quoted in Marietta, "Wealth, War and Religion," 236.

27. Phillips P. Moulton, ed., *The Journal and Major Essays of John Woolman* (New York, 1971), 49. This is the most authoritative edition of JW's famous *Journal* (hereafter cited as *JW Journal*).

28. Theodore Thayer, *Israel Pemberton: King of the Quakers* (Philadelphia, 1943), 126; George S. Brookes, *Friend Anthony Benezet* (Philadelphia, 1937), 223-24.

29. E. L. Griggs, ed., *Collected Letters of Samuel Coleridge*, 4 vols. (London, 1956), 1:302. On JW see also Edwin H. Cady, *John Woolman* (New York, 1965); Janet Whitney, *John Woolman, American Quaker* (Boston, 1942). Useful articles include William A. Christian, "Inwardness and Outward Concerns: A Study of John Woolman's Thought," *Quaker History* 67 (1978):88-104; Muriel Kent, "John Woolman: Mystic and Reformer," *Hibbert Journal* 26 (1928):302-13; Phillips P. Moulton, "The Influence of the Writings of John Woolman," *Quaker History* 60 (1971):3-13, and "John Woolman: Exemplar of Ethics," *Quaker History* 54 (1965):81-93.

30. *JW Journal*, 23-28.

31. Ibid., 29, 35.

32. See Rufus Jones, *The Quakers in the American Colonies* (New York, 1962), 397.

33. *JW Journal*, 38. On JW's opposition to slavery see Thomas E. Drake, *Quakers and Slavery* (New Haven, 1950), 54-60.

34. *JW Journal*, 96, 126; Janet Whitney, ed., *The Journal of John Woolman* (Chicago, 1950), 191.

35. *JW Journal*, 52-57.

36. Ibid., 53.

37. Ibid.; *Journal and Essays*, 118.

38. JW, "Serious Considerations on Trade," in *Journal and Essays*, 120; *JW Journal*, 54.

39. JW, "On Labour," in *Journal and Essays*, 388; JW, "On the Right Use of the Lord's Outward Gifts," ibid., 393.

40. JW, "A Plea for the Poor," in *JW Journal*, 240; JW, "Considerations on the True Harmony of Mankind," in *Journal and Essays*, 464.

41. JW, "Outward Gifts," in *Journal and Essays*, 394; *JW Journal*, 114-15; JW, "Considerations . . . ," in *Journal and Essays*, 443.

42. *JW Journal*, 112.

43. Ibid., 129, 127, 129.

44. Ibid., 129. See also Henry J. Cadbury, *John Woolman in England: A Documentary Supplement* (Philadelphia, 1971).

45. Ibid.

46. Ibid., 183.

47. Ibid., 185.

48. *Journal and Essays*, 320, 325, 323, 324.

49. WJ, *The Varieties of Religious Experience: A Study in Human Nature* (New York, 1902), 290.

50. *JW Journal*, 205.

51. Ibid., 60; Rufus Jones, *Quakers in the American Colonies*, 573, 574; Tolles, *Meeting House and Counting House*, 143.

52. Perry Miller, "The Shaping of American Character," *New England Quarterly* 28 (1955):445.

53. On Keayne see Bernard Bailyn, "The *Apologia* of Robert Keayne," *William and Mary Quarterly* 3rd ser. 7 (1950):569-87.

CHAPTER THREE: REPUBLICAN SIMPLICITY

1. Richard Hofstadter, *America at 1750: A Social Portrait* (New York, 1970), 162–64; Douglass Adair, "The Autobiography of Devereux Jarratt, 1732–63," *William and Mary Quarterly* 3rd ser. 9 (1952):360–63.

2. Eric Foner, *Thomas Paine and Revolutionary America* (New York, 1976), 20–25. On the changing social, economic, and demographic setting during the eighteenth century, see Joyce Appleby, "Liberalism and the American Revolution," *New England Quarterly* 49 (1976):3–26, and "The Social Origins of American Revolutionary Ideology," *Journal of American History* 64 (1977–78):935–58; J. E. Crowley, *This Sheba Self: The Conceptualization of Economic Life in Eighteenth-Century America* (Baltimore, 1974); Marc Egnal, "The Economic Development of the Thirteen Continental Colonies, 1720 to 1775," *William and Mary Quarterly* 3rd ser. 32 (1975):191–222; Charles Grant, "Land Speculation and the Settlement of Kent, 1738–1760," *New England Quarterly* 28 (1955):51–71; Jack P. Greene, "Search for Identity: An Interpretation of the Meaning of Selected Patterns of Social Response in Eighteenth-Century America," *Journal of Social History* 3 (1970):189–220; James Henretta, *The Evolution of American Society, 1700–1815* (Lexington, Mass., 1973); Alice Hanson Jones, *Wealth of a Nation To Be: The American Colonies on the Eve of the Revolution* (New York, 1980); Aubrey C. Land, "Economic Base and Social Structure: The Northern Chesapeake in the Eighteenth Century," *Journal of Economic History* 25 (1965):639–54; James T. Lemon and Gary B. Nash, "The Distribution of Wealth in Eighteenth-Century America: A Century of Change in Chester County, Pennsylvania, 1693–1802," *Journal of Social History* 2 (1968):1–24; Gary Nash, *The Urban Crucible: Social Change, Political Consciousness, and the Origins of the American Revolution* (Cambridge, Mass., 1979).

3. Douglass quoted in Greene, "Search for Identity," 202; Leonard Labaree, *Conservatism in Early American History* (New York, 1948), 52–53.

4. Jackson Turner Main, *The Social Structure of Revolutionary America* (Princeton, 1965), 209; Hunter D. Farish, ed., *Journal and Letters of Philip Vickers Fithian, 1773–1774* (Williamsburg, 1957), 27.

5. Carter and Nelson quoted in Robert Shalhope, *John Taylor of Caroline, Pastoral Republican* (Columbia, S.C., 1980), 37. See also John M. Hemphill, "John Wayles Rates His Neighbors," *Virginia Magazine of History and Biography* 66 (1958):305; Emory G. Evans, "Planter Indebtedness and the Coming of the Revolution in Virginia," *William and Mary Quarterly* 3rd ser. 19 (1962):519; Jan Lewis, *The Pursuit of Happiness: Family and Values in Jefferson's Virginia* (Cambridge, 1983).

6. On the relationship between Puritanism and republicanism, see "The Puritan Roots of American Whig Rhetoric," in Emory Elliott, ed., *Puritan Influences in American Literature* (Urbana, 1979), 107–27; Perry Miller, "From the Covenant to the Revival," in James Ward Smith, ed., *The Shaping of American Religion* (Princeton, 1961), 322–68; Edmund S. Morgan, "The Puritan Ethic and the American Revolution," *William and Mary Quarterly* 3rd ser. 24 (1967):3–42; Gordon S. Wood, "Rhetoric and Reality in the American Revolution," *William and Mary Quarterly* 3rd ser. 23 (1966):3–32.

The literature on republicanism and its social theory has grown dramatically in recent years. I have benefited most from the following studies: Bernard Bailyn, *The Ideological Origins of the American Revolution* (Cambridge, Mass., 1967); Cecilia Kenyon, "Republicanism and Radicalism in the American Revolution: An Old-

Fashioned Interpretation," *William and Mary Quarterly* 3rd ser. 29 (1962):153–82; Pauline Maier, *From Resistance to Revolution: Colonial Radicals and the Development of American Opposition to Britain, 1765–1776* (New York, 1972); Drew McCoy, *The Elusive Republic: Political Economy in Jeffersonian America* (Chapel Hill, 1980); J. G. A. Pocock, *The Machiavellian Moment: Florentine Political Thought and the Atlantic Republican Tradition* (Princeton, 1975); Robert Shalhope, "Toward a Republican Synthesis: The Emergence of an Understanding of Republicanism in American Historiography," *William and Mary Quarterly* 3rd ser. 29 (1972):49–80, and "Republicanism and Early American Historiography," *William and Mary Quarterly* 3rd ser. 39 (1982):334–56; Gordon S. Wood, *The Creation of the American Republic, 1776–1787* (Chapel Hill, 1969).

7. Morgan, "The Puritan Ethic," 7–8.

8. Wood, *Creation of the American Republic*, 47.

9. Gary B. Nash, "Social Change and the Growth of Revolutionary Urban Radicalism," in Alfred F. Young, ed., *The American Revolution: Explorations in the History of American Radicalism* (Dekalb, Ill., 1976), 30.

10. H. Trevor Colbourn, *The Lamp of Experience: Whig History and the Intellectual Origins of the American Revolution* (Chapel Hill, 1965), 22–23; Sallust, *The Conspiracy of Catiline*, trans. S. A. Handford (London, 1963), 182–83. See also Richard Gummere, *The American Colonial Mind and the Classical Tradition* (Cambridge, Mass., 1963); Charles F. Mullett, "Classical Influences on the American Revolution," *Classical Journal* 35 (1939):92–104.

11. Montesquieu, *The Spirit of Laws*, trans. Thomas Nugent (New York, 1900), book 5, sect. 1–5; book 7, sect. 1; Thomas Gordon, ed., *The Works of Sallust* (London, 1744), 87–116. On republicanism in English thought, see Colin Bonwick, *English Radicals and the American Revolution* (Chapel Hill, 1977); Z. S. Fink, *The Classical Republicans: An Essay in the Recovery of a Pattern of Thought in Seventeenth-Century England* (Chicago, 1962); Caroline Robbins, *The Eighteenth-Century Commonwealthmen: Studies in the Transmission, Development and Circumstance of English Liberal Thought from the Restoration of Charles II until the War for the Thirteen Colonies* (Cambridge, Mass., 1959).

12. Charles F. Adams, ed., *The Works of John Adams*, 10 vols. (Boston, 1850–56), 9:351 (hereafter cited as JA, *Works*); James Burgh, *Britain's Remembrancer* (Boston, 1759), 8–9, 14–15. On Burgh see Oscar and Mary Handlin, "James Burgh and American Revolutionary Theory," *Proceedings of the Massachusetts Historical Society* 73 (1961):38–57; Carla Hay, *James Burgh, Spokesman for Reform in Hanoverian England* (Washington, 1979); Robbins, *Eighteenth-Century Commonwealthmen*, 363–68.

13. Philip Hamer, ed., *The Papers of Henry Laurens*, 9 vols. (Columbia, S.C., 1968–), 7:226; AL to RHL, 4 Aug. 1769, in RHL, *Life of Arthur Lee*, 2 vols. (Boston, 1829), 1:205; AL to SA, 3 Dec. 1773, ibid., 1:261.

14. H. Trevor Colbourn, ed., "Pennsylvania Farmer at the Court of King George: John Dickinson's London Letters, 1754–56," *Pennsylvania Magazine of History and Biography* 86 (1962):255–59.

15. Wood, *Creation of the American Republic*, 110.

16. *Newport Mercury*, 7 Dec. 1767; "Atticus," *Maryland Gazette*, 4 May 1769; David Ramsay, *Fourth of July Oration* (1778), in H. Niles, ed., *Principles and Acts of the Revolution in America* (Baltimore, 1822), 64.

17. Morgan, "The Puritan Ethic," 8–18.

18. RHL to ?, 31 May 1764, in James C. Ballagh, ed., *The Letters of Richard Henry Lee*, 2 vols. (New York, 1911), 1:7 (hereafter cited as *Letters of RHL*); *Pennsylvania Gazette*, 17 May 1770.

19. *Boston Gazette*, 3 Oct. 1768; Stillman, *Artillery Sermon* (Boston, 1770), 25.

20. *Pennsylvania Journal*, 10 Dec. 1767, cited in Morgan, "The Puritan Ethic," 15; *New York Documentary History*, 4:344–45.

21. *Boston Gazette*, 2 Nov. 1767, 9 Dec. 1769; JD to AL, 31 March 1770, in RHL, *Life of Arthur Lee*, 2:300.

22. *South Carolina Gazette*, 1 June, 6 July, 21 Sept. 1769.

23. Paul Leicester Ford, ed., *The Life and Writings of John Dickinson*, 2 vols. (Philadelphia, 1895), 1:401; Gummere, *American Colonial Mind*, 108.

24. Marc Egnal and Joseph Ernst, "An Economic Interpretation of the American Revolution," *William and Mary Quarterly* 3rd ser. 29 (1972):23.

25. JA, *Works*, 2:265; AL to JD, 10 Jan. 1771, RHL, *Life of Arthur Lee*, 1:252.

26. Elizabeth Cometti, "Morals and the American Revolution," *South Atlantic Quarterly* 46 (1947):62–71; Maier, *From Resistance to Revolution*, 278–87.

27. Jacques Pierre Brissot de Warville, *New Travels in the United States of America*, 2nd ed. (London, 1797), 1:93; JA, *Works*, 1:673. For general background on SA, see Carl Becker, "Samuel Adams," *Dictionary of American Biography* (New York, 1928), 95–100; Pauline Maier, *The Old Revolutionaries: Political Lives in the Age of Samuel Adams* (New York, 1980), 3–50; John C. Miller, *Sam Adams: Pioneer in Propaganda* (Boston, 1936); William V. Wells, *The Life and Public Services of Samuel Adams*, 3 vols. (Boston, 1865); William A. Williams, *History as a Way of Learning* (New York, 1973), 303–21.

28. Becker, "Samuel Adams," 95.

29. Wells, *Samuel Adams*, 2:195.

30. Ibid.

31. *Independent Advertiser*, 5 Dec. 1748, 20 March 1749; Miller, *Sam Adams*, 18–20.

32. Lyman Butterfield, ed., *Diary and Autobiography of John Adams*, 2 vols. (Cambridge, Mass., 1961), 1:352 (hereafter cited as JA, *Diary and Autobiography*); JA, *Works*, 10:251, 308; 2:164, 308; "Philo Publicus," *Boston Gazette*, 1 Oct. 1764. See also Miller, *Sam Adams*, 59, 195.

33. *Boston Gazette*, 1 Oct. 1764, 8 Oct. 1764.

34. SA to Stephen Sayre, 16 Nov. 1770, SA to AL, 19 April 1771, in Harry A. Cushing, ed., *The Writings of Samuel Adams*, 4 vols. (New York, 1904), 2:58, 164 (hereafter cited as *Writings of SA*).

35. SA to AL, 9 April 1773, *Writings of SA*, 2:126; Wells, *Samuel Adams*, 2:194.

36. SA to William Checkley, 1 June 1774, SA to Thomas Young, 17 Oct. 1774, SA to Richard Randolph, 1 Feb. 1775, *Writings of SA*, 3:128, 154, 176.

37. JA, *Diary and Autobiography*, 3:262.

38. Ibid., 3:272; 1:72, 23.

39. On JA's "puritanism" see Philip J. Greven, Jr., *The Protestant Temperament: Patterns of Child-Rearing, Religious Experience, and the Self in Early America* (New York, 1977), 211, 214, 215, 223, 245, 252, 298, 304–5, 337, 346, 351, 359; McCoy, *Elusive Republic*, 70–72; Peter Shaw, *The Character of John Adams* (Chapel Hill, 1976), 33, 43, 55–57, 90, 101, 211–12.

40. JA, *Diary and Autobiography*, 1:41, 33, 45, 35.

41. Ibid., 1:25, 7–8; Shaw, *Character of John Adams*, 198.

42. JA, *Diary and Autobiography*, 1:181; Robert J. Taylor, ed., *The Papers of John Adams* (Cambridge, Mass., 1977), 106–7n; JA, *Diary and Autobiography*, 2:61–62.

43. Marx quoted in E. Digby Baltzell, *Puritan Boston and Quaker Philadelphia* (New York, 1979), 85; AA to JA, 13 April 1776, 16 Oct. 1764, in Lyman Butterfield, ed., *The Adams Family Correspondence*, 3 vols. (Cambridge, Mass., 1963), 1:377, 173 (hereafter cited as *Adams Family Correspondence*); Paul C. Nagel, *Descent from Glory: Four Generations of the Adams Family* (New York, 1983), 50. See also Edith B. Gelles, "Abigail Adams: Domesticity and the American Revolution" (Ph.D. diss., University of California, Irvine, 1978).

44. JA, *Diary and Autobiography*, 2:58; JA, *Works*, 4:116–17, 21, 37, 28, 54, 43.

45. JA to James Warren, 19 Oct. 1775, JA to Mercy Warren, 8 Jan. 1776, in Massachusetts Historical Society, *Warren-Adams Letters: Being Chiefly a Correspondence among John Adams, Samuel Adams, and James Warren*, 2 vols. (Boston, 1917–23), 1:146, 202 (hereafter cited as *Warren-Adams Letters*).

46. *Warren-Adams Letters*, 1:202; JA to AA, 3 July 1776, *Adams Family Correspondence*, 2:28. See also Shaw, *Character of John Adams*, 76–105.

47. George W. Corner, ed., *The Autobiography of Benjamin Rush* (Princeton, 1948), 83–84; BR, *An Oration* (Philadelphia, 1774), 102; David Hawke, *Benjamin Rush: Revolutionary Gadfly* (Indianapolis, 1971), 189, 203; Nathan Goodman, *Benjamin Rush: Physician and Citizen* (Philadelphia, 1934), 55.

48. Maier, *Old Revolutionaries*, 198; RHL to William Lee, 12 July 1772, RHL to JA, 8 Oct. 1779, *Letters of RHL*, 1:72; 2:155. For background on RHL I have relied primarily on Oliver Perry Chitwood, *Richard Henry Lee: Statesman of the Revolution* (Morganton, W.Va., 1967); Burton J. Hendrick, *The Lees of Virginia, Biography of a Family* (Boston, 1935); Maier, *Old Revolutionaries*, 164–200.

49. RHL to SA, Feb. 1776, *Letters of RHL*, 1:167–68; Greene, "Search for Identity," 218.

50. Otis quoted in Wood, *Creation of the American Republic*, 476, 416; Evarts Greene, *The Revolutionary Generation, 1763–1790* (New York, 1948), 270. See also McCoy, *Elusive Republic*, 76–104.

51. Henry Laurens to George Washington, 20 Nov. 1778, in Edward C. Burnett, ed., *Letters of Members of the Continental Congress*, 8 vols. (Washington, 1921–36), 3:500; John C. Fitzpatrick, ed., *The Writings of George Washington from the Original Sources*, 39 vols. (Washington, 1931–44), 13:335, 383, 467; 14:300; Octavius Pickering and C. W. Upham, *Life of Timothy Pickering*, 4 vols. (Boston, 1867–73), 1:376. See also Wood, *Creation of the American Republic*, 413–25.

52. SA to John Scollay, 20 March 1777, SA to Francis Lightfoot Lee, 1778, SA to Mrs. Adams, 28 Sept. 1778, in *Writings of SA*, 3:365; 4:19, 65.

53. SA to John Scollay, 30 Dec. 1780, SA to JA, 19 Dec. 1781, *Writings of SA*, 4:238, 270.

54. See Eric Foner, "Tom Paine's Republic: Radical Ideology and Social Change," in Young, *American Revolution*, 189–232; Nash, "Social Change," ibid., 3–36; Joseph Ernst, *Money and Politics in America, 1755–1775: A Study of the Currency Act of 1764 and the Political Economy of Revolution* (Chapel Hill, 1973).

55. E. P. Thompson, "The Moral Economy of the English Crowd in the Eighteenth Century," *Past and Present*, no. 50 (1971):76–136; Foner, *Thomas Paine*, 145–82.

56. Nash, *Urban Crucible*, 342–45; Foner, *Thomas Paine*, 36. See also McCoy, *Elusive Republic*, 90–104.

57. Foner, "Tom Paine's Republic," 203.

58. Foner, *Thomas Paine*, 62.

59. *Warren-Adams Letters*, 1:234; Foner, *Thomas Paine*, 136–37; Foner, "Tom Paine's Republic," 109.

CHAPTER FOUR: REPUBLICANISM TRANSFORMED

1. James Warren to JA, 27 Oct. 1783, Massachusetts Historical Society, *Warren-Adams Letters*, 2 vols. (Boston, 1917–23), 2:232; *Independent Chronicle*, 23 Nov. 1786; *Boston Gazette*, 24 Jan. 1785.

2. "Observer," *Massachusetts Centinel*, 15, 22 Jan. 1785. See also Gordon S. Wood, *The Creation of the American Republic, 1776–1787* (Chapel Hill, 1969), 421–25.

3. *Boston Gazette*, 30 Oct. 1780; SA to RHL, 3 Dec. 1787, in William V. Wells, *The Life and Public Services of Samuel Adams*, 3 vols. (Boston, 1865), 3:252–53.

4. Pauline Maier, *The Old Revolutionaries: Political Lives in the Age of Sam Adams* (New York, 1980), 48–49; James Warren to AL, 18 Dec. 1780, in RHL, *Life of Arthur Lee*, 2 vols. (Boston, 1829), 2:273.

5. BR to John Howard, 14 Oct. 1789, BR to Richard Price, 25 May 1786, in Lyman Butterfield, ed., *Letters of Benjamin Rush*, 2 vols. (Princeton, 1951), 1:528, 388.

6. BR, "Of the Mode of Education Proper in a Republic" (1798), in Dagobert D. Runes, ed., *The Selected Writings of Benjamin Rush* (New York, 1947), 90–91, 92. See also Hyman Kuritz, "Benjamin Rush: His Theory of Republican Education," *History of Education Quarterly* 7 (1967):432–51; David Tyack, "Forming the National Character," *Harvard Educational Review* 36 (1966):29–39.

7. TJ to BR, 21 April 1803, in Paul Leicester Ford, ed., *The Writings of Thomas Jefferson* (New York, 1897), 8:225–26 (hereafter cited as *Writings of TJ*).

8. TJ to William Short, 31 Oct. 1819, ibid., 10:143.

9. TJ to Henry Skipwith, 28 July 1787, in Julian Boyd, ed., *The Papers of Thomas Jefferson*, 19 vols. to date (Princeton, 1950–), 11:636; TJ to Dr. James Currie, 4 Aug. 1787, ibid., 11:682 (hereafter cited as *Jefferson Papers*).

10. TJ to Samuel Kercheval, 12 July 1816, *Writings of TJ*, 10:41.

11. TJ to John Rutledge, 6 Aug. 1787, *Jefferson Papers*, 11:701; TJ to Baron Geismar, 6 Sept. 1785, ibid., 8:499–500.

12. Karl Lehmann, *Thomas Jefferson, American Humanist* (New York, 1947), 208. See also Charles Flinn Arrowood, ed., *Thomas Jefferson and Education in a Republic* (New York, 1930).

13. Merle Curti, *The Social Ideas of American Educators* (New York, 1935), 36.

14. Charles F. Adams, Jr., ed., *The Works of John Adams*, 10 vols. (Boston, 1850–60), 5:432 (hereafter cited as JA, *Works*).

15. Ibid., 6:521, 274–75, 200; Philip J. Greven, Jr., *The Protestant Temperament: Patterns of Child-Rearing, Religious Experience, and the Self in Early America* (New York, 1977), 359.

16. Lyman Butterfield, ed., *Diary and Autobiography of John Adams*, 2 vols. (Cambridge, Mass., 1961), 4:123; Lyman Butterfield, ed., *Adams Family Correspondence*, 3 vols. (Cambridge, Mass., 1968), 1:114, 2:179; 3:311–12. See also Greven, *Protestant Temperament*, 176–77.

17. JA to James Warren, 4 July 1786, *Warren-Adams Letters*, 2:227.

18. JA, *Works*, 6:200.

19. JA, *Works*, 5:488; 6:95–97. See also Joyce Appleby, "The New Republican Synthesis and the Changing Political Ideas of John Adams," *American Quarterly* 25 (1973):578–95; John Howe, *The Changing Political Thought of John Adams* (Princeton, 1966), 102–32; Wood, *Creation of the American Republic*, 567–92.

20. JA, *Works*, 6:94, 97.

21. Ibid., 6:97, 104; Loren Baritz, *City on a Hill: A History of Ideas and Myths in America* (New York, 1964), 155.

22. Wood, *Creation of the American Republic*, 472, 475. On the changing attitudes toward republicanism in the aftermath of the Revolution, see John T. Agresto, "Liberty, Virtue, and Republicanism: 1776–1787," *Review of Politics* 39 (1977):473–504; Wood, *Creation of the American Republic*, 391–429, 469–564, 593–615.

23. JM to TJ, 19 March 1787, *Jefferson Papers*, 11:219; JM, "Federalist No. 10," in Jacob E. Cooke, ed., *The Federalist* (Middletown, Ct., 1961), 60 (all Federalist paper citations are from this edition); Greven, *Protestant Temperament*, 360.

24. Harold Syrett and Jacob Cooke, eds., *The Papers of Alexander Hamilton*, 27 vols. (New York, 1961–81), 10:80. The most penetrating treatment of Hamilton's economic and social outlook is Gerald Stourzh, *Alexander Hamilton and the Idea of Republican Government* (Stanford, 1970), especially chap. 3. See also Drew McCoy, *The Elusive Republic: Political Economy in Jeffersonian America* (Chapel Hill, 1980), 132–33, 146–52; John C. Miller, *Alexander Hamilton: Portrait in Paradox* (New York, 1959), 46–51; Lance Banning, *The Jeffersonian Persuasion: Evolution of a Party Ideology* (Ithaca, N.Y., 1978), 133–36.

25. On Hume's political and economic thought, see John B. Stewart, *The Moral and Political Philosophy of David Hume* (New York, 1963); Albert B. Glathe, *Hume's Theory of the Passions and Morals* (Berkeley, 1950); John Sekora, *Luxury: The Concept in Western Thought, Eden to Smollett* (Baltimore, 1977), 104–5, 110–11, 119–23.

26. Max Farrand, ed., *Records of the Constitutional Convention of 1787*, 4 vols. (New Haven, 1937), 1:376 (hereafter cited as *Records of the Constitutional Convention*); "Federalist No. 12," 73–74; "Federalist No. 6," 35.

27. William Vans Murray, "Virtue," *The American Museum and Repository*, 2nd ed. (Sept. 1787), 231; "Federalist No. 21," 134. On the "Court" party outlook in England, see Isaac Kramnick, *Bolingbroke and His Circle: The Politics of Nostalgia in the Age of Walpole* (Cambridge, Mass., 1968), 30–55, 127–37; J. G. A. Pocock, *The Machiavellian Moment: Florentine Political Thought and the Atlantic Republican Tradition* (Princeton, 1975), 462–505.

28. *Hamilton Papers*, 5:42; *Records of the Constitutional Convention*, 2:123.

29. RHL to Henry Laurens, 6 July 1779, *Letters of RHL*, 2:62–63.

30. JM to TJ, 18 June 1786, *Jefferson Papers*, 9:660; *Records of the Constitutional Convention*, 1:422–23; McCoy, *Elusive Republic*, 21–32. On JM, see also John T. Agresto, "A System without Precedent—James Madison and the Revolution in Republican Liberty," *South Atlantic Quarterly* 82 (1983):129–44.

31. *Records of the Constitutional Convention*, 1:392; McCoy, *Elusive Republic*, 237.

32. TJ, "Notes on the State of Virginia," in Merrill Peterson, ed., *The Portable Jefferson* (New York, 1975), 217. See also A. Whitney Griswold, "The Agrarian

Democracy of Thomas Jefferson," *American Political Science Review* 40 (1946):657–81.

33. TJ to Count Van Hogendorp, 13 Oct. 1785, *Jefferson Papers*, 8:633.

34. TJ to du Pont de Nemours, 18 Jan. 1802, in Dumas Malone, ed., *Correspondence between Thomas Jefferson and Pierre Samuel du Pont de Nemours, 1798–1817* (Boston, 1930), 40; TJ to George Washington, 15 March 1784, *Jefferson Papers*, 7:26.

35. *Hamilton Papers*, 10:80; Forrest McDonald, "How Conservatism Guided America's Founding," *imprimis* 12 (July 1983):6.

36. TJ to Tammany Society, 29 Feb. 1808, in Burton Spivak, *Jefferson's English Crisis: Commerce, Embargo, and the Republic* (Charlottesville, 1979), 204; TJ to Thomas Leiper, 21 Jan. 1809, *Writings of TJ*, 9:239. See also McCoy, *Elusive Republic*, 209–23.

37. Gallatin and Adams quoted in Spivak, *Jefferson's English Crisis*, 150–52.

38. Albert Gallatin to TJ, 28 May 1808, in Louis Sears, *Jefferson and the Embargo* (Durham, N.C., 1927), 91; Archibald Stuart to TJ, 28 Dec. 1808, in Spivak, *Jefferson's English Crisis*, 139.

39. Spivak, *Jefferson's English Crisis*, 159; TJ to Lafayette, 24 Feb. 1809, ibid., 137; TJ to James Jay, 7 April 1809, in Andrew Lipscomb, ed., *The Writings of Thomas Jefferson*, 20 vols. (Washington, 1903), 12:271.

40. TJ to JA, 28 Oct. 1813, in Lester Cappon, ed., *Adams-Jefferson Letters*, 2 vols. (Chapel Hill, 1959), 2:391. See also John Kasson, *Civilizing the Machine: Technology and Republican Values in America* (New York, 1976), 6–36; McCoy, *Elusive Republic*, 189–95, 253.

41. TJ to JA, 21 Jan. 1812, *Writings of TJ*, 9:333.

42. JA to TJ, 9 Oct. 1787, *Adams-Jefferson Letters*, 1:202–3.

43. JA to BR, 19 Sept. 1806, 18 April 1808, in John Schutz and Douglass Adair, eds., *The Spur of Fame: Dialogues of John Adams and Benjamin Rush, 1805–1813* (San Marino, Ca., 1980), 66, 108.

44. JA to TJ, 15 July 1813, 21 Dec. 1819, *Adams-Jefferson Letters*, 2:358, 551.

45. TJ to du Pont de Nemours, 31 Dec. 1815, 15 April 1811, *Jefferson-du Pont Correspondence*, 173, 132. See also McCoy, *Elusive Republic*, 204–8.

46. JA to TJ, 16 July 1814, *Adams-Jefferson Letters*, 2:436; JA, "Discourses on Davila," *Works*, 6:249–57; JA to John Taylor, ibid., 6:484, 517. In discussing Adams's and Jefferson's views of history, I have relied heavily on Stow Persons, "The Cyclical Theory of History in Eighteenth-Century America," *American Quarterly* 6 (1954):147–63.

47. TJ to JA, 1 Aug. 1816, JA, *Works*, 10:223; TJ to Peter Carr, 10 Aug. 1787, TJ to Joel Barlow, 24 Jan. 1810, Ford, *Works*, 4:428–29, 9:269.

48. Horace Bushnell, *A Discourse on the Tendencies of Human History* (New York, 1843), 29; Timothy Walker, "A Defence of Mechanical Philosophy," *North American Review 33* (1831):124. The best studies of the impact of technology upon nineteenth-century American thought are Kasson, *Civilizing the Machine*, and Leo Marx, *The Machine in the Garden: Technology and the Pastoral Ideal in America* (New York, 1964).

45. Clay quoted in Thomas Bender, *Toward an Urban Vision: Ideas and Institutions in Nineteenth Century America* (Baltimore, 1982), 41; Paul Goodman, "Ethics and Enterprise: The Values of a Boston Elite, 1800–1860," *American Quarterly* 18

(1966):437–51. See also Charles Sanford, "The Intellectual Origins and New-World-liness of American Industry," *Journal of Economic History* 18 (1958):1–16.

The literature on Lowell is extensive. I have benefited most from Thomas Dublin, *Women at Work: The Transformation of Work and Community in Lowell, Massachusetts, 1826–1860* (New York, 1979); Philip S. Foner, ed., *The Factory Girls* (Urbana, 1977); Hannah Josephson, *The Golden Threads: New England's Mill Girls and Magnates* (New York, 1945); Kasson, *Civilizing the Machine*, 53–106; Carl Siracusa, *A Mechanical People: Perceptions of the Industrial Order in Massachusetts, 1815–1880* (Middletown, Ct., 1979): Norman Ware, *The Industrial Worker, 1840–1860* (Chicago, 1964).

50. Bender, *Toward an Urban Vision*, 75; Donald Miller, *The Birth of Modern America, 1820–1850* (Indianapolis, 1970), 70.

51. "Girls at Waltham Factory," *American Traveler*, 8 Aug. 1821, p. 1; Siracusa, *A Mechanical People*, 98; Claudia Bushman, ed., *"A Good Poor Man's Wife": Being a Chronicle of Harriet Hanson Robinson and Her Family in Nineteenth-Century New England* (Hanover, N.H., 1981), 15.

52. Kasson, *Civilizing the Machine*, 77.

53. Siracusa, *Mechanical People*, 115; Foner, ed., *Factory Girls*, 81.

54. Miller, *Birth of Modern America*, 94; Catharine Beecher, *The Evils Suffered by American Women and American Children: The Causes and the Remedy* (New York, 1846), 5–12.

55. Ware, *Industrial Worker*, 41–42.

56. "Voice of Industry" (1847), in Foner, ed., *Factory Girls*, 89; Kasson, *Civilizing the Machine*, 99.

57. Alexis de Tocqueville, *Democracy in America*, ed. J. P. Mayer (Garden City, N.Y., 1969), 526–27. On Tocqueville and republicanism, see Ralph Lerner, "Commerce and Character: The Anglo-American as New-Model Man," *William and Mary Quarterly* 3rd ser. 36 (1979):3–26; Melvin Richter, "The Uses of Theory: Tocqueville's Adaptation to Montesquieu," in Richter, ed., *Essays in History and Theory: An Approach to the Social Sciences* (Cambridge, Mass., 1970), 90–101.

58. Ibid., 527, 540.

59. Ibid., 554.

60. Clarence H. Danhof, *Change in Agriculture: The Northern United States, 1820–1870* (Cambridge, Mass., 1969), 21–23.

61. William Gilmore Simms, *The Social Principle* (Tuscaloosa, Ala., 1843), 46; O. C. Gibbs, "Wealth the Stimulus to Labor," *Country Gentleman* 1 (14 April 1853):218–19. See also Arthur A. Ekirch, Jr., *The Idea of Progress in America, 1815–1860* (New York, 1944); Fred Somkin, *The Unquiet Eagle: Memory and Desire in the Idea of American Freedom, 1815–1860* (Ithaca, N.Y., 1967), 11–45.

62. Gallatin quoted in Henry Adams, *Life of Albert Gallatin* (Philadelphia, 1879), 653; *Washington Globe*, 29 April 1836.

63. Useful analyses of the transformation of republicanism during the nineteenth century include Rowland Berthoff, "Independence and Attachment, Virtue and Interest: From Republican Citizen to Free Enterpriser, 1787–1837," in Richard Bushman, ed., *Uprooted Americans: Essays to Honor Oscar Handlin* (Boston, 1979), 97–124, and "Peasants and Artisans, Puritans and Republicans: Personal Liberty and Communal Equality in American History," *Journal of American History* 69

(1982):579–98; Eric Foner, *Free Soil, Free Labor Free Men: The Ideology of the Republican Party before the Civil War* (New York, 1970).

64. TJ to Thomas Cooper, 9 Jan. 1816, Lipscomb, ed., *Writings*, 14:387.

CHAPTER FIVE: SIMPLICITY DOMESTICATED

1. Marvin Meyers, *The Jacksonian Persuasion* (Stanford, 1957), 16–32. See also John Ward, *Andrew Jackson: Symbol for an Age* (New York, 1955).

2. Bray Hammond, *Banks and Politics in America* (Princeton, 1957), 346; Meyers, *Jacksonian Persuasion*, 12. See also Hammond's two articles, "Banking in the Early West: Monopoly, Prohibition, and Laissez-faire," *Journal of Economic History* 8 (1948):1–25, and "Jackson, Biddle, and the Bank of the United States," *Journal of Economic History* 7 (1947):1–23.

3. Daniel Walker Howe, *The Political Culture of the American Whigs* (Chicago, 1979), 101–2; Orestes Brownson, *An Oration before the Democracy of Worcester, Delivered July 4, 1840* (Boston, 1840), 28.

4. Seward quoted in Rush Welter, *The Mind of America, 1820–1860* (New York, 1975), 278; *American Review* 1 (1845):95–98.

5. Rowland Berthoff, "Independence and Attachment, Virtue and Interest: From Republican Citizen to Free Enterpriser, 1787–1837," in Richard Bushman, ed., *Uprooted Americans: Essays to Honor Oscar Handlin* (Boston, 1979), 106. See also Berthoff, "Peasants and Artisans, Puritans and Republicans: Personal Liberty and Communal Equality in American History," *Journal of American History* 69 (1982): 579–98.

6. "On the Undue and Pernicious Influence of Wealth," *Southern Literary Messenger* 3 (1837):481.

7. "Simplicity," *Western Magazine and Review* 1 (July 1827):1; John Pierpont, *The National Reader* (Boston, 1827), 218.

8. Lyman Beecher, "The Gospel the Only Security of Eminent and Abiding Prosperity," *The American National Preacher* 3 (1829):147, 154.

9. Lyman Beecher, *Six Sermons on Intemperance* (Boston, 1829), 58; Barbara Cross, ed., *The Autobiography of Lyman Beecher*, 2 vols. (Cambridge, Mass., 1961), 1:253. On the evangelicals, see also Lois W. Banner, "Religious Benevolence as Social Control: A Critique of an Interpretation," *Journal of American History* 60 (1973): 23–41; Charles Cole, *The Social Ideas of the Northern Evangelists, 1826–1860* (New York, 1954); Clifford S. Griffin, *Their Brothers' Keepers: Moral Stewardship in the United States, 1800–1865* (New Brunswick, N.J., 1960).

10. Clifford S. Griffin, *The Ferment of Reform, 1830–1860* (New York, 1967), 3.

11. Bellows quoted in Roger B. Stein, *John Ruskin and Aesthetic Thought in America, 1840–1900* (Cambridge, Mass., 1967), 11; Neil Harris, *The Artist in American Society: The Formative Years, 1790–1860* (New York, 1966), 28–55.

12. John Ward, *Red, White and Blue: Men, Books, and Ideas in American Culture* (New York, 1969), 278; Harris, *Artist in American Society*, 167.

13. Harris, *Artist in American Society*, 209; Calvert Vaux, *Villas and Cottages* (New York, 1857), 26–27. A stimulating, innovative study of domestic architecture is

David Handlin, *The American Home: Architecture and Society, 1815–1915* (Boston, 1979).

14. Sedgwick quoted in Fredrika Bremer, *The Homes of the New World*, 2 vols. (New York, 1853), 1:46; James Fenimore Cooper, *The American Democrat* (New York, 1839), 144; AJD, "Influence of Horticulture," in AJD, *Rural Essays*, ed. George W. Curtis (New York, 1853), 15. A satisfactory biography of AJD remains to be published. Useful treatments of his ideas are in Edward Halsey Foster, *The Civilized Wilderness: Backgrounds to American Romantic Literature, 1817–1860* (New York, 1975), 62–66, 90–99; Harris, *Artist in American Society*, 208–16; Ward, *Red, White and Blue*, 170–81. The most extensive study is George B. Tatum, "Andrew Jackson Downing," (Ph.D. diss., University of Pennsylvania, 1950).

15. AJD, "On the Mistakes of Citizens in Country Life," *Rural Essays*, 123; "Moral Influences of Good Houses," ibid., 210.

16. Harris, *Artist in American Society*, 42–44. See also Eleanor Davidson Berman, *Thomas Jefferson among the Arts: An Essay in Early American Aesthetics* (New York, 1947).

17. AJD, "Moral Influences," 210; AJD, "Influence of Horticulture," 13–15; AJD, *The Architecture of Country Houses* (New York, 1850), v, 23.

18. John Maass, *The Victorian Home in America* (New York, 1972), 30; James Fenimore Cooper, *Home as Found* (New York, 1864), 132.

19. Ward, *Red, White and Blue*, 276; Maass, *The Victorian Home*, 30.

20. AJD, *Architecture of Country Houses*, 43, 138; AJD, "On Simple Rural Cottages," *Rural Essays*, 247.

21. AJD, *Architecture of Country Houses*, 258, 269, 37; AJD, "On the Mistakes of Citizens in Country Life," 126.

22. There is a rich literature on domesticity. See especially Ruth Bloch, "American Feminine Ideas in Transition," *Feminist Studies* 4 (1978):101–26; William Bridges, "Family Patterns and Social Values in America," *American Quarterly* 17 (1975):3–11; Nancy F. Cott, *The Bonds of Womanhood: "Woman's Sphere" in New England* (New Haven, 1977); Ann Douglas, *The Feminization of American Culture* (New York, 1977); Linda Kerber, *Women in the Republic: Intellect and Ideology in Revolutionary America* (Chapel Hill, 1980); Anne L. Kuhn, *The Mother's Role in Childhood Education: New England Concepts, 1830–1860* (New Haven, 1947); Glenda Riley, "The Subtle Subversion: Changes in the Traditionalist Image of Women," *Historian* 22 (1970):210–17; Mary P. Ryan, "American Society and the Cult of Domesticity, 1830–1860," (Ph.D. diss., University of California, Santa Barbara, 1971); Kathryn Kish Sklar, *Catharine Beecher* (New Haven, 1973); Barbara Welter, "The Cult of True Womanhood:1820–1860," *American Quarterly* 18 (1966): 157–74.

23. Charles Enfield, "Early Culture," *The Mother's Assistant* 14 (1849):31. See also Arthur Calhoun, *A Social History of the American Family*, 3 vols. (New York, 1945), vol. 2; Robert McGlone, "Suffer the Children: The Emergence of Middle-Class Family Life, 1820–1870," (Ph.D. diss., University of California, Los Angeles, 1971); Peter Slater, "Views of Children and Child-rearing during the Early National Period," (Ph.D. diss., University of California, Berkeley, 1970); Bernard Wishy, *The Child and the Republic: The Dawn of Modern American Child Nurture* (Philadelphia, 1968).

24. John S. C. Abbott, "The Father," *Parent's Magazine* 2 (1842):174. See also Kerber, *Women in the Republic*, 199–229.

25. Orin Howard, "The Mother, an Educator," *Mother's Assistant* 15 (1849):100.

26. Glenda Riley, "Origins of the Argument for Female Education," *History of Education Quarterly* 9 (1969):456; T. S. Arthur, *The Lady at Home: or, Leaves from the Every-Day Book of an American Woman* (Philadelphia, 1847), 177–78; Welter, "The Cult of True Womanhood," 157–63. See also Cott, *Bonds of Womanhood*, 85–89.

27. Catharine Beecher, *A Treatise on Domestic Economy* (Boston, 1841), 13; John S. C. Abbott, *The Mother at Home, or Principles of Maternal Duty* (Boston, 1835), 148.

28. Cott, *Bonds of Womanhood*, 47, 151.

29. Mrs. A. J. Graves, *Woman in America* (New York, 1855), 99; Harriet Beecher Stowe, *Uncle Tom's Cabin* (New York, 1852), 13–14.

30. Lydia Sigourney, *Letters to Mothers* (Hartford, 1838), 168. See also Robert Sunley, "Early Nineteenth-Century American Literature on Child Rearing," in Margaret Mead and Martha Wolfstein, eds., *Childhood and Contemporary Cultures* (Chicago, 1955), 150–67.

31. Lydia Maria Child, *The American Frugal Housewife* (Boston, 1836), 89.

32. SJH, *Northwood, A Tale of New England*, 2 vols. (Boston, 1827), 1:5; 2:146–47. Useful studies of SJH include Isabelle Webb Entrikin, *Sarah Josepha Hale and Godey's Lady's Book* (Philadelphia, 1946); Lawrence Martin, "The Genesis of Godey's Lady's Book," *New England Quarterly* 1 (1928):41–70; Riley, "The Gentle Subversion," 210–27; William R. Taylor, *Cavalier and Yankee: The Old South and American National Character* (New York, 1961), 96–99, 119.

33. SJH, *Northwood*, 1:167.

34. Ibid., 1:93; 2:7.

35. Ibid., 2:32, 152.

36. SJH, "Woman," *Ladies Magazine* 3 (1830):441, 42–43; 2 (1829):393–95.

37. Ibid., 4 (1831):67.

38. SJH, "The Conversazione," *Godey's Lady's Book* 14 (1837):1–5.

39. The two most comprehensive studies of Kirkland's life and writings are Langley Keyes, "Caroline Kirkland: A Pioneer in American Realism" (Ph.D. diss., Harvard University, 1935), and Daniel Riordan, "The Concept of Simplicity in the Works of Mrs. Caroline M. Kirkland," (Ph.D. diss., University of North Carolina, 1973).

40. Kirkland, "A Chapter on Hospitality," *Godey's Lady's Book* 32 (1846):224–25; "English and American Manners," *Sartain's Union Magazine* 4 (1849):404; Kirkland, "Chapter on Hospitality," 224–25.

41. Kirkland, *A New Home, Who'll Follow? Or, Glimpses of Western Life* (New York, 1839), 309; *Forest Life* (New York, 1842), 63; *A New Home*, 307; *Forest Life*, 59. See also John C. McCloskey, "Backcountry Folkways in Mrs. Kirkland's *A New Home*," *Michigan History* 40 (1956):297–308.

42. Child, *American Frugal Housewife*, 94; Calhoun, *A Social History*, 2:235–36.

43. Margaret Coxe, *Claims of the Country on American Females* (Columbus, Ohio, 1842), 26; "Success in Life," *Harper's New Monthly Magazine* 7 (1853):238; Adam G. Gurowski, *America and Europe* (New York, 1857), 382.

44. Graves, *Woman in America*, 162.

45. David J. Rothman, *The Discovery of the Asylum: Social Order and Disorder in the New Republic* (Boston, 1971).

46. Michael Katz, *The Irony of Early School Reform: Educational Innovation in Mid-Nineteenth Century Massachusetts* (Boston, 1968), 120.

47. HM quoted in Riley, "Origins of the Argument for Improved Female Education," 466; Joseph Kett, "Adolescence and Youth in Nineteenth-Century America," *Journal of Interdisciplinary History* 2 (1971):283–98.

48. Katz, *Irony of Early School Reform*, 213; Michael Katz, *Class, Bureaucracy and the Schools: The Illusion of Educational Change in America* (New York, 1971), 113. A good biography of Barnard is Vincent P. Lannie, *Henry Barnard: American Educator* (New York, 1974). The best general treatments of the early educational reformers are Merle Curti, *The Social Ideas of American Educators* (New York, 1935), and Clarence J. Karrier, *Man, Society, and Education: A History of American Educational Ideas* (Glenview, Ill., 1967).

49. Mary Mann, ed., *Life and Works of Horace Mann*, 5 vols. (Boston, 1867), 1:83 (hereafter cited as HM, *Works*). On HM see also Jonathan Messerli, *Horace Mann: A Biography* (New York, 1972).

50. HM, "The Necessity of Education in a Republican Government," *Works*, 2:187.

51. HM quoted in George E. Hardy, *Literature for Children* (New York, 1892), 5; Stanley K. Schultz, *The Culture Factory: Boston Public Schools, 1789–1860* (New York, 1973), 66.

52. HM, *Works*, 3:92; 1:151.

53. Ibid., 3:100; HM, *Lectures on Education* (Boston, 1845), 142–43; Kathleen Edgerton Kendall, "Education as 'The Balance Wheel of Social Machinery': Horace Mann's Arguments and Proofs," *Quarterly Journal of Speech* 54 (1968):15–16.

54. HM, *Works*, 3:92.

55. HM to Quincy quoted in Michael Fellman, *The Unbounded Frame: Freedom and Community in Nineteenth-Century American Utopianism* (Westport, Ct., 1973), 67.

56. Henry Tuckerman, "American Society," *North American Review* 81 (July 1855):30.

57. "Farming Life in New England," *Atlantic Monthly* 2 (1858):335–36; HM, *Works*, 4:271.

CHAPTER SIX: TRANSCENDENTAL SIMPLICITY

1. RWE, "New England Reformers," in Edward W. Emerson, ed., *The Complete Works of Ralph Waldo Emerson*, 12 vols. (Boston, 1903–4), 3:225 (hereafter cited as RWE, *Works*).

2. On Graham and other health reformers see Stephen Nissenbaum, *Sex, Diet & Debility in Jacksonian America: Sylvester Graham & Health Reform* (Westport, Ct., 1980); James C. Whorton, *Crusaders for Fitness: The History of American Health Reformers* (Princeton, 1982). The communitarian alternative is treated in Arthur Bestor, *Backwoods Utopias: The Sectarian and Owenite Phases of Communitarian Socialism in America, 1663–1829* (Philadelphia, 1950); Alice Felt Tyler, *Freedom's*

Ferment: Phases of American Social History from the Colonial Period to the Outbreak of the Civil War (New York, 1962).

3. William Ellery Channing, "The Present Age," in *The Works of William Ellery Channing*, 6 vols. (Boston, 1849), 6:171–72 (hereafter cited as Channing, *Works*).

4. RWE, "The Transcendentalist," *Works*, 1:335; Channing, "Self-Culture," *Works*, 2:372–75. The literature on Transcendentalism is extensive and uneven. The best recent treatments are Paul F. Boller, Jr., *American Transcendentalism, 1830–1860: An Intellectual Inquiry* (New York, 1974) and Anne Rose, *Transcendentalism as a Social Movement* (New Haven, 1981). Older, but still useful studies are Octavius B. Frothingham, *Transcendentalism in New England: A History* (New York, 1876), and Harold C. Goddard, *Studies in New England Transcendentalism* (New York, 1908).

5. See Arthur A. Ekirch, Jr., *Man and Nature in America* (Lincoln, Neb., 1973), 47–69.

6. RWE, "Nature," *Works*, 1:41–42; RWE, "Society and Solitude," ibid., 7:179.

7. William H. Gilman, et al., eds., *The Journals and Miscellaneous Notebooks of Ralph Waldo Emerson*, 16 vols. to date (Cambridge, Mass., 1960–), 8:108 (hereafter cited as RWE, *Journals*); RWE, "The Transcendentalist," *Works*, 1:340–41.

8. Octavius Brooks Frothingham, *Memoir of William Henry Channing* (Boston, 1886), 166; Henry W. Bellows, "The Influence of the Trading Spirit upon the Social and Moral Life of America," *The American Review* 1 (Jan. 1845):98.

9. RWE, *Journals*, 9:428; RWE, "Progress of Culture," *Works*, 8:229. On Emerson's debt to Puritanism, see Perry Miller, "From Edwards to Emerson," *New England Quarterly* 13 (1940):587–617; Wesley T. Mott, "Emerson and Thoreau as Heirs to the Tradition of New England Puritanism" (Ph.D. diss., Boston University, 1975).

10. RWE, "Domestic Life," *Works*, 7:121. For biographical information on RWE, I have relied primarily on Gay Wilson Allen, *Waldo Emerson: A Biography* (New York, 1981), and Ralph L. Rusk, *The Life of Ralph Waldo Emerson* (New York, 1949).

11. Rosalie Feltenstein, "Mary Moody Emerson: The Gadfly of Concord," *American Quarterly* 5 (1953):231–46.

12. RWE, "Mary Moody Emerson," *Works*, 10:399–433; Benjamin Emerson, *The Ipswich Emersons* (Boston, 1900), 78.

13. RWE, *Journals*, 7:444; RWE, "Boston," *Works*, 12:197, 210.

14. RWE, "Nature," *Works*, 1:9.

15. Ibid., 1:10.

16. RWE, *Journals*, 7:71, 404. RWE's ambivalence about his calling is perceptively discussed in Henry Nash Smith, "Emerson's Problem of Vocation," *New England Quarterly* 12 (1939):52–67.

17. Mott, "Emerson and Thoreau," 107; RWE, "Works and Days," *Works*, 7:158.

18. RWE, "The Young American," *Works*, 1:379; "Man the Reformer," ibid., 1:232; "The Conduct of Life," ibid., 6:126.

19. RWE, "Plato," *Works*, 4:53–58; "The Conduct of Life," ibid., 6:89, 134; "Society and Solitude," ibid., 7:116.

20. RWE, "Lecture on the Times," ibid., 1:227.

21. RWE, "Education," ibid., 10:133, 137; RWE, "Experience," ibid., 3:83.

22. RWE, "Self-Reliance," ibid., 2:50; RWE, "The Conduct of Life," ibid., 6:91.

23. RWE, "Man the Reformer," ibid., 1:245.

24. RWE, "Experience," ibid., 3:62; RWE, *Journals*, 13:38.

25. RWE, "Domestic Life," *Works*, 7:113; RWE, "Society and Solitude," ibid., 7:287; RWE, "Thoughts on Modern Literature," *The Dial* 1 (Oct. 1840):158.

26. RWE to Thomas Carlyle, 30 Oct. 1840, in Joseph Slater, ed., *The Correspondence of Emerson and Carlyle* (New York, 1964), 283–84; RWE, "Man the Reformer," *Works*, 1:247.

27. "Plan of the West Roxbury Community," *The Dial* 2 (Jan. 1842):364; Henry L. Golemba, *George Ripley* (Boston, 1977), 66; "Plan of the Roxbury Community," 364. On Brook Farm, see Georgiana Bruce Kirby, *Years of Experience, An Autobiographical Narrative* (Boston, 1887), 98–105; John Van Der Zee Sears, *My Friends at Brook Farm* (New York, 1912); Lindsay Swift, *Brook Farm* (New York, 1900); Zoltan Haraszti, *The Idyll of Brook Farm* (Boston, 1937).

28. RWE to George Ripley, 15 Dec. 1840, in Ralph L. Rusk, ed., *The Letters of Ralph Waldo Emerson*, 6 vols. (New York, 1939), 2:368–71 (hereafter cited as RWE, *Letters*); RWE, *Journals*, 7:408.

29. RWE, *Journals*, 3:319; 7:401; RWE, *Works*, 6:64.

30. Octavius Frothingham, *George Ripley* (Boston, 1883), 153; Sears, *My Friends*, 162. See also Caroline Dall, *Transcendentalism in New England* (Boston, 1897).

31. RWE to William Emerson, 21 Dec. 1840, 22 March 1841, *Letters*, 2:371, 387.

32. On Fruitlands see Louisa May Alcott, "Transcendental Wild Oats," *Independent* 25 (18 Dec. 1878):1569–71; Richard Francis, "Circumstances and Salvation: The Ideology of the Fruitlands Utopia," *American Quarterly* 25 (1973):202–34.

33. Rose, *Transcendentalism*, 118–19.

34. Paul Elmer More, *A New England Group and Others* (New York, 1921), 91–93.

35. Everett Webber, *Escape to Utopia: The Communal Movement in America* (New York, 1959).

36. Rose, *Transcendentalism*, 126.

37. RWE, *Journals*, 9:54, 8:311–12.

38. Ibid., 2:97, 6:451–52.

39. Ibid., 8:313; RWE, "Man the Reformer," *Works*, 1:252.

40. RWE, "Experience," *Works*, 3:64–66.

41. RWE, *Journals*, 9:69.

42. RWE, *Journals*, 5:453; 13:66.

43. The best survey of HDT's changing reputation is Wendell Glick, *The Recognition of Henry Thoreau* (Ann Arbor, 1969). See also Michael Meyer's excellent overview of twentieth-century attitudes toward HDT, *Several More Lives To Live: Thoreau's Political Reputation in America* (Westport, Ct., 1977). On HDT's concept of simple living see John C. Broderick, "Thoreau's Principle of Simplicity as Shown in His Attitudes Toward Cities, Government and Industrialism" (Ph.D. diss., University of North Carolina, 1953); Leo Stoller, "Thoreau's Doctrine of Simplicity," *New England Quarterly* 29 (1956):443–61.

44. Bradford Torrey, ed., *The Writings of Henry David Thoreau*, 20 vols. (Boston, 1906), 1:304–5 (hereafter cited as HDT, *Writings*); JB, "Henry D. Thoreau," *Century* (July 1882):375.

45. HDT, *Writings*, 15:155.

46. RWE, *Journals*, 7:498.

47. HDT, *Writings*, 2:16.

48. Mary Hosmer Brown, *Memories of Concord* (Boston, 1926), 101.

49. HDT, *Writings*, 8:319; 20:88.

50. For a provocative, if at times irritatingly speculative, analysis of HDT's childhood and adolescence, see Richard Lebeaux, *Young Man Thoreau* (Amherst, Mass., 1977).

51. HDT, *Writings*, 2:15; 12:426; 8:4; 2:241; 8:46. On HDT's Puritan strain, see Mott, "Emerson and Thoreau"; Egbert S. Oliver, "Thoreau and the Puritan Tradition," *ESQ* 44 (1966):79–86.

52. Edwin Moser, "Henry David Thoreau: The College Essays" (M.A. thesis, New York University, 1951), 183–85; HDT, *Reform Papers*, ed. Wendell Glick (Princeton, 1973), 156.

53. Franklin Sanborn, *The Life of Henry David Thoreau* (Boston, 1917), 288.

54. HDT, *Writings*, 8:164.

55. William Ellery Channing, *Thoreau the Poet-Naturalist* (New York, 1902), 18.

56. HDT, *Writings*, 2:76–77; 19:67–68; 8:193; 18:299.

57. RWE, *Journals*, 5:452.

58. Walter Harding and Carl Bode, eds., *The Correspondence of Henry David Thoreau* (New York, 1958), 53 (hereafter cited as HDT, *Correspondence*); Rose, *Transcendentalism*, 298.

59. Freneau, "The Pilgrim," in Philip M. Marsh, ed., *The Prose of Philip Freneau* (New Brunswick, N.J., 1955), 43.

60. HDT, *Writings*, 2:159, 185, 187.

61. Ibid., 21, 12, 44.

62. HDT, *Writings*, 7:253; 3:133, 9, 78. See also Philip Gura, "Thoreau's Maine Woods Indians: More Representative Men," *American Literature* 49 (1977):366–84; Albert Keiser, *The Indian in American Literature* (New York, 1933), 226; Roderick Nash, *Wilderness and the American Mind* (New Haven, 1967), 91–93; Robert Sayre, *Thoreau and the American Indians* (Princeton, 1977).

63. HDT, *Writings*, 2:226–31.

64. Ibid., 159–68.

65. Ibid., 166.

66. Ibid., 110–23.

67. HDT, *Writings*, 11:410–12.

68. Ibid., 9:296–97; 2:14. See also Nash, *Wilderness and the American Mind*, 92–95.

69. Ibid., 3:172; 18:334–35.

70. Ibid., 17:275; 2:34; HDT, *Correspondence*, 444.

71. HDT, *Writings*, 14:8; 4:229.

72. Ibid., 2:78–79; 6:260.

73. Ibid., 16:145; RWE, *Journals*, 12:241; HDT, *Writings*, 2:62.

74. William H. Channing, *The Civil War in America* (Liverpool, 1861), 90–91; Conway quoted in George M. Fredrickson, *The Inner Civil War: Northern Intellectuals and the Crisis of the Union* (New York, 1965), 73.

75. RWE, *Journals*, 8:398; Joel Porte, ed., *Emerson in His Journals* (Cambridge, Mass., 1982), 512; RWE, *Journals*, 15:351, 228–29.

76. CEN, "The Advantages of Defeat," *Atlantic Monthly* 8 (1861):361; "Editor's Table," *Harper's New Monthly Magazine* 24 (Dec. 1861):119.

77. J. M. Sherwood, "The Moral Causes of Our National Calamity," *National Preacher* 2 (1863):147; Henry Boardman, "Thanksgiving in War," quoted in James H.

Moorhead, *American Apocalypse: Yankee Protestants and the Civil War* (New Haven, 1978), 146.

78. George Fitzhugh, "Wealth and Poverty—Luxury and Economy," *DeBow's Review* 30 (1861):405; "Editor's Table," *Southern Literary Messenger* 32 (1861):402.

79. Mellon quoted in Harvey O'Connor, *Mellon's Millions* (New York, 1933), 23-24.

80. "The War and National Wealth," *Princeton Review* 36 (1864):458-59, 481.

81. Porte, ed., *Emerson in His Journals*, 530; RWE to Thomas Carlyle, 7 Jan. 1866, Slater, ed., *Correspondence of Emerson and Carlyle*, 548.

Chapter Seven: Patrician Simplicity—At Bay

1. Greeley quoted in John L. Thomas, *et al.*, *The Great Republic* (Boston, 1977), 831. On the process of modernization and its cultural effects, see Samuel P. Hays, *The Response to Industrialism, 1885-1914* (Chicago, 1957); T. Jackson Lears, *No Place of Grace: Antimodernism and the Transformation of American Culture, 1880-1920* (New York, 1981); Alan Trachtenberg, *The Incorporation of America: Culture and Society in the Gilded Age* (New York, 1982); Robert Wiebe, *The Search for Order, 1877-1920* (New York, 1967).

2. Rachel S. Thorndike, ed., *The Sherman Letters* (New York, 1894), 258; James quoted in John Ward, *Red, White and Blue: Men, Books, and Ideas in American Culture* (New York, 1969), 282.

3. Mark Twain, "The Revised Catechism," *New York Tribune*, 27 Sept. 1871; Rex Burns, *Success in America: The Yeoman Dream and the Industrial Revolution* (Amherst, Mass., 1976), 167. See also John Cawelti, *Apostles of the Self-Made Man: Changing Concepts of Success in America* (Chicago, 1955), 125-200; Irvin G. Wyllie, *The Self-Made Man in America: The Myth of Rags to Riches* (New York, 1954), 116-32.

4. William Dean Howells, "Certain Dangerous Tendencies in American Life," *Atlantic Monthly* 42 (1878):385, 387.

5. Octavius B. Frothingham, *Transcendentalism in New England: A History* (New York, 1876), xxviii; RWE, *Journals*, 14:258; Frothingham, *Transcendentalism in New England*, xv, xvii. For interesting discussions of the transformation of Transcendentalism after the Civil War, see George Fredrickson, *The Inner Civil War: Northern Intellectuals and the Crisis of the Union* (New York, 1965), 65-68, 98-112, and Anne Rose, *Transcendentalism as a Social Movement* (New Haven, 1981), 207-25.

6. Walt Whitman, *Democratic Vistas and Other Papers* (New York, 1888), 41-42, 80-81.

7. Gordon Milne, *George William Curtis and the Genteel Tradition* (Bloomington, Ind., 1956), 239; Henry Adams to Charles F. Adams, Jr., 21 Nov. 1862, in W. C. Ford, ed., *A Cycle of Adams Letters, 1861-1865* (Boston, 1920), 1:196. Useful general studies of the New England "Brahmins" include Geoffrey Blodgett, *The Gentle Reformers: Massachusetts Democrats in the Cleveland Era* (Cambridge, Mass., 1966); Van Wyck Brooks, *New England: Indian Summer, 1865-1915* (New York, 1940); Stow Persons, *The Decline of American Gentility* (New York, 1973); John G. Sproat, *"The Best Men": Liberal Reformers in the Gilded Age* (New York,

1968); John Tomisch, *A Genteel Endeavor: American Culture and Politics in the Gilded Age* (Stanford, 1971).

8. Henry Adams, *The Education of Henry Adams* (New York, 1931), 85; Charles F. Adams, Jr., *An Autobiography* (Boston, 1916), 15–16; WJ, "The Social Value of the College Bred," *McClure's* 30 (1908):420–21.

9. CEN, *Considerations on Some Recent Social Theories* (Boston, 1853), 19–20; Lowell to Edward Everett Hale, 11 Nov. 1890, in CEN, *The Letters of James Russell Lowell* (New York, 1894), 2:477 (hereafter cited as *JRL Letters*).

10. WJ to Mrs. Henry Whitman, 7 June 1899, in Henry James, Jr., ed., *The Letters of William James*, 2 vols. (Boston, 1920), 2:90 (hereafter cited as *James Letters*); CEN, "The Congress of Peace and the Liberty of Lausanne," *Nation*, 21 Oct. 1869, p. 336; ELG, *Nation*, 3 Oct. 1867, pp. 275–76; RWE, "The Progress of Culture," Edward W. Emerson, ed., *The Complete Works of Ralph Waldo Emerson*, 12 vols. (Boston, 1903–4), 8:218.

11. Rollo Ogden, ed., *The Life and Letters of Edwin Lawrence Godkin*, 2 vols. (New York, 1907), 1:11–12 (hereafter cited as *Life and Letters of ELG*); Curtis, "The Soldier's Monument," in CEN, ed., *Orations and Addresses of George William Curtis*, 3 vols. (New York, 1894), 3:53.

12. Hoar quoted in George Perry Morris, "Is American Character Declining?" *World's Work* 5 (1902):2778.

13. Holmes, *Autocrat of the Breakfast Table*, reprinted in David Levin and Theodore Gross, eds., *America in Literature*, 2 vols. (New York, 1978), 1:1487–88.

14. James Russell Lowell, "Sumptuary Laws," *North American Review* 103 (1866): 70; ELG, "Republican Simplicity," *Nation*, 4 March 1869, pp. 167–68; ELG, "The Economy and Simplicity of Our Forefathers," ibid., 16 March 1876, pp. 172–73; ELG, "The Vanity of Luxury," ibid., 2 May 1867, p. 347; ELG, "Our Love of Luxury," ibid., 18 April 1867, pp. 316–17. A good biography of ELG is William M. Armstrong, *E. L. Godkin: A Biography* (Albany, N.Y., 1978).

15. AC quoted in Robert Heilbroner, "Epitaph for the Steel Master," *American Heritage* 11 (Aug. 1960):4–5.

16. Ibid.

17. The best single source on AC is Joseph Wall's magisterial biography, *Andrew Carnegie* (New York, 1970).

18. AC, "Wealth," *North American Review* 148 (1889):653–64.

19. Ibid.

20. Ibid.

21. Ibid.; Wall, *Andrew Carnegie*, 812.

22. William Jewett Tucker, "The Gospel of Wealth," *Andover Review* 15 (1891): 645. See also Wall, *Andrew Carnegie*, 808–15.

23. "Mr. Carnegie at Skibo," *Independent* 56 (1904):1421–22.

24. AC, *Empire of Business* (New York, 1902), 136–40; "Two Rich Men," *Century* 26 (1883):308–9. See also Henry Potter, "The Gospel for Wealth," *North American Review* 152 (1881):513–22.

25. Matthew Josephson, *The Robber Barons* (New York, 1934), 339. See also Maury Klein and Harvey Kantor, *American Industrial Cities, 1850–1920* (New York, 1976), 204–42; Thorstein Veblen, *Theory of the Leisure Class* (New York, 1899).

26. The many reform movements of the Gilded Age are summarized in Paul Boller, Jr., *American Thought in Transition: The Impact of Evolutionary Naturalism, 1865–1900* (Chicago, 1969), 94–122.

308 NOTES

27. On Howells see Edwin Cady, *The Realist at War* (Syracuse, 1958); Clara Kirk and Rudolph Kirk, "Howells and the Church of the Carpenter," *New England Quarterly* 32 (1959):185–206; Kenneth Lynn, *William Dean Howells: An American Life* (New York, 1971); Kermit Vanderbilt, *The Achievement of William Dean Howells* (New York, 1968).

28. Howells, "Editor's Study," *Harper's New Monthly Magazine* 80 (1890):484; "The Editor's Easy Chair," *Harper's Monthly* 125 (1912):151; Howells to Edward Everett Hale, 28 Oct. 1888, in Mildred Howells, ed., *The Life in Letters of William Dean Howells*, 2 vols. (New York, 1928), 1:418.

29. Lowell to Thomas Hughes, 10 April 1890, *JRL Letters*, 2:447.

30. ELG to the *New York Daily News*, March 1869, in *Life and Letters of ELG*, 2:14–15.

31. ELG, "The Vanderbilt Memorial," *Nation*, 18 Nov. 1869, p. 432; ELG, "The Expenditure of Rich Men," *Scribner's* 20 (1896):495–501.

32. ELG, "Social Classes in the Republic," *Atlantic Monthly* 78 (1896):724; ELG, "Chromo-Civilization," *Nation*, 24 Sept. 1874, pp. 201–2.

33. ELG to Frederick L. Olmsted, 12 April 1865, 2 Aug. 1870, in William Armstrong, ed., *The Gilded Age Letters of E. L. Godkin* (Albany, N.Y., 1974), 26, 150; Armstrong, *E. L. Godkin*, 92.

34. Curtis, "The Centennial Celebration," in *Orations and Addresses of George William Curtis*, 3 vols. (New York, 1894), 3:128; ELG to CEN, 6 May 1871, in *Life and Letters of ELG*, 1:307; ELG to James Bryce, 17 Oct. 1887, Armstrong, ed., *Gilded Age Letters*, 359. See also Robert L. Beisner, "Gloom, Gloom, Gloom, and Scarce One Ray of Light: Ruminations of E. L. Godkin and Charles Eliot Norton," *American Heritage* 18 (Aug. 1967):67–71.

35. CEN, "America and England," *North American Review* 100 (1865):342–44; CEN to Chauncey Wright, 5 Dec. 1869, in Sara Norton and M. A. DeWolfe Howe, eds., *Letters of Charles Eliot Norton*, 2 vols. (Boston and New York, 1913), 1:371 (hereafter cited as *CEN Letters*).

36. CEN to ELG, 3 Nov. 1871, Charles Eliot Norton Papers, Harvard University; CEN, "The Intellectual Life of America," *New Princeton Review* 6 (1888):312–24. On Norton's relationship with English intellectuals, see John Henry Raleigh, *Matthew Arnold and American Culture* (Berkeley, 1961), and Roger B. Stein, *John Ruskin and Aesthetic Thought in America, 1840–1900* (Cambridge, Mass., 1967), 242–54.

37. WJ to Henry James, 11 April 1882, in *James Letters*, 1:318; WJ to H. G. Wells, 11 Sept. 1906, ibid., 2:260. For a more comprehensive treatment of WJ's promotion of the simple life, see William E. Leverette, Jr., "Simple Living and the Patrician Academic: The Case of William James," *Journal of American Culture* 6 (1984). The best general sources of information about WJ are Gay Wilson Allen, *William James* (New York, 1967); F. O. Matthiessen, *The James Family* (New York, 1948); Ralph Barton Perry, *The Thought and Character of William James*, 2 vols. (Boston, 1935).

38. WJ, *Varieties of Religious Experience* (New York, 1961), 254–55. See also, *James Letters*, 1:211, 2:193; WJ to ELG, 15 April 1889, WJ to Henry James, 9 May 1886, WJ to wife, 11 Nov. 1882, *James Letters*, 1:284, 252, 214.

39. WJ quoted in Robert Beisner, *Twelve Against Empire: The Anti-Imperialists, 1898–1900* (New York, 1968), 38.

40. Ibid.; WJ, *The Will To Believe* (New York, 1897), 187.

41. WJ, *Varieties*, 291–354; Beisner, *Twelve Against Empire*, 37.

42. CEN to ELG, 3 Nov. 1871, Norton Papers; "Harvard University in 1890," *Harper's New Monthly Magazine* 81 (1890):591; Vanderbilt, *Charles Eliot Norton*, 128, 129.

43. Vanderbilt, *Charles Eliot Norton*, 198, 199; CEN to John Ruskin, 17 July 1873, to G. W. Curtis, 14 July 1864, *CEN Letters*, 2:16, 1:273–74.

44. John Jay Chapman, *Memories and Milestones* (New York, 1915), 134–35; Arthur Sedgwick, "Words of a Contemporary," in *CEN Letters*, 2:444; CEN to Leslie Stephen, 13 Aug. 1895, ibid., 2:231–32.

45. Brooks, *Indian Summer*, 342.

46. WJ to John Jay Chapman, 18 May 1906, *James Letters*, 2:256; "On a Certain Blindness in Human Beings," in John McDermott, ed., *The Writings of William James* (New York, 1967), 642 (hereafter cited as *WJ Writings*); WJ to Alice James, 2 July 1887, WJ to Henry James, 12 April 1887, 6 June 1903, *James Letters*, 1:270, 267–68; 2:196.

47. WJ, "On a Certain Blindness in Human Beings," *WJ Writings*, 631.

48. WJ to Charles Renouvier, 5 Aug. 1883, to Mrs. Henry Whitman, 16 June 1895, *James Letters*, 1:229; 2:21.

49. CEN to Leslie Stephen, 3 June 1892, *CEN Letters*, 2:214; CEN, "The Intellectual Life of America," 312.

50. CEN to Leslie Stephen, 24 June 1898, *CEN Letters*, 2:270.

51. CEN to ELG, 17 Jan. 1900, Norton Papers; H. Adams, *The Education*, 313.

52. CEN to S. G. Ward, 13 March 1901, to Sir Mountstuart Grant-Duff, 19 April 1896, *CEN Letters*, 2:303, 242–43; CEN to J. B. Harrison, 17 May 1902, Norton Papers; ELG to CEN, 29 Nov. 1898, 12 Aug. 1900, Armstrong, *Gilded Age Letters*, 508, 539.

53. WJ, "Is Life Worth Living," in WJ, *The Will To Believe and Other Essays* (1897; rpt. Cambridge, Mass., 1979), 39–40; WJ, "The Moral Equivalent of War," *WJ Writings*, 667; WJ, *Varieties*, 285.

Chapter Eight: Progressive Simplicity

1. TR, *An Autobiography* (New York, 1913), 462–63. An excellent recent overview of the protean qualities of Progressivism is Daniel T. Rodgers, "In Search of Progressivism," in Stanley I. Kutler and Stanley N. Katz, eds., *The Promise of American History: Progress and Prospects* (Baltimore, 1983), 113–32. See also David Noble, *The Progressive Mind, 1890–1917* (Minneapolis, 1981).

2. Rho Fisk Zueblin, "Duties of the Consumer," *Craftsman* 7 (1904):95.

3. Macready Sykes, "Making a New American Boy through Woodcraft," *Everybody's Magazine* 23 (1910):473.

4. Cyrus Edson, "Nervous Exhaustion in Children," *Youth's Companion* 108 (1895):67. The growing prevalence of neurasthenia among the middle and upper classes was the subject of two prominent scientific studies. See George Beard, *American Nervousness* (New York, 1884), and S. Weir Mitchell, *Wear and Tear, or, Hints for the Overworked* (Philadelphia, 1871). The problem was a source of repeated discussion at the turn of the century. See "Editor's Study," *Harper's New Monthly Magazine* 89 (1894):799–801; Robert Grant, "The Art of Living," *Scribner's* 17

(1895):142–46; Edward Wakefield, "Nervousness: The National Disease of America," *McClure's* 2 (1894):305–7.

5. "Convalescence and the Strenuous Life," *Independent* 58 (1905):564–66; Gustave Michaud, "The Brain of the Nation," *Century* 49 (1904):46; "Making Life Worth Living," *Independent* 54 (1904):1044–45.

6. Henry D. Lloyd, *Wealth Against Commonwealth* (1894; rpt. New York, 1963), 171; Washington Gladden, *Working People and Their Employers* (New York, 1894), 68–69, 96; Washington Gladden, *The New Idolatry* (New York, 1905), 92.

7. Thorstein Veblen, *Theory of the Leisure Class* (1899; rpt. New York, 1954), 103, 200, 112.

8. Gilman quoted in Joseph Dorfman, *Thorstein Veblen and His America* (New York, 1934), 196.

9. Irene Sargent, "Private Simplicity as a Promoter of Public Art," *Craftsman* 2 (1902):210–11; John Spargo, "Edward Carpenter, the Philosopher," ibid., 11 (1906):55.

10. David Grayson (Ray S. Baker), *Adventures in Contentment* (New York, 1906), 111–12, 245–46. On Baker, see Robert C. Bannister, Jr., *Ray Stannard Baker, The Mind and Thought of a Progressive* (New Haven, 1966).

11. "What Salary Do You Need To Make You Happy?" *American Magazine* 84 (Oct. 1917):21.

12. Maud Nathan, *The Story of an Epoch-Making Movement* (Garden City, N.Y., 1926), xix; Zueblin, "Duties of the Consumer," 89.

13. John Farrell, *Beloved Lady: A History of Jane Addams' Ideas on Reform and Peace* (Baltimore, 1967), 57.

14. Jane Addams, *Twenty Years at Hull House* (New York, 1910), 73; Jane Addams, "Recent Immigration, a Field Neglected by the Scholar," *University Record* 9 (1905):280; Starr quoted in Jane Addams, *Democracy and Social Ethics*, ed. Anne Firor Scott (Cambridge, Mass., 1964), p. xxiii.

15. Addams, *Hull House*, 274–76; Aylmer Maude, "A Talk with Jane Addams and Tolstoy," *Humane Review* 3 (1902):216–17.

16. "Manners and Business," *Outlook* 79 (1905):166; "The True Prosperity," ibid., 76 (1904):636; Abram S. Isaacs, "Gentler Living," *North American Review* 192 (1910):101–6. Other examples include William F. Dix, "As a Man Prospers," *Independent* 72 (1912):362–63, and "Is the Cost of Living Really Increasing?" ibid., 73 (1912):1008; Alice Pearson, "Simplicity in Living," *LHJ* 25 (Dec. 1907):28; Maurice Francis Egan, "The Fine Art of Simple Living," *Century* 88 (1914):267–72; George P. Brett, "The Simple Life," *The World Today* 8 (1905):492–94; E. S. Martin, "Jostling the Simple Life," *Harper's Monthly* 114 (1906–7):950–53; Gwendolyn Talbot, "On Simplicity," *Living Age* 246 (1905):176.

17. EB, "How We Can Lead a Simple Life," *LHJ* 17 (Oct. 1900):18. The best study of EB is Salme H. Steinberg, *Reformer in the Marketplace: Edward Bok and the Ladies' Home Journal* (Baton Rouge, 1979). See also Frank L. Mott, *A History of American Magazines, 1885–1905* (Cambridge, Mass., 1957), 536–50, and James Playsted Wood, *Magazines in the United States* (New York, 1949), 105–17.

18. EB, *The Americanization of Edward Bok* (New York, 1921), 123–59.

19. Ibid., 374–75; Steinberg, *Reformer in the Marketplace*, 7.

20. Steinberg, *Reformer in the Marketplace*, 52.

21. Ibid., 67, 66.

22. "An Approaching Visit to America," *Independent* 54 (1904):543–44; *New York Times*, 11 Nov. 1904, 28 Sept. 1904.

23. EB, "The Voice of the World," *LHJ* 20 (Jan. 1903):16; EB, "The Simple Life Amid Plenty," ibid., 22 (Nov. 1905):18; EB, "The Value of Limitations," ibid., 22 (Dec. 1904):18.

24. EB, "What Is the Real Simple Life?" *LHJ* 28 (Sept. 1911):6; EB, "The Voice of the World," 16; EB, "The Simple Life Amid Plenty," 18.

25. Elting Morison, ed., *The Letters of Theodore Roosevelt*, 8 vols. (Cambridge, Mass., 1951–54), 3:486; 6:1003.

26. "The President's Rules for the Conduct of Life," *LHJ* 24 (Feb. 1907):21.

27. EB, "The Christmas That Remains," *LHJ* 18 (Dec. 1900):20.

28. EB, "A Simple Life Amid Plenty," 18.

29. EB, "In an Editorial Way," *LHJ* 24 (May 1907):6; EB, *Americanization*, 238, 243, 250; Ralph Adams Cram, "Country House of Moderate Cost," *LHJ* 18 (Jan. 1901):15. See also EB, "When We Build a Home," ibid., 22 (July 1905):16.

30. Frank Lloyd Wright, "In the Cause of Architecture," *The Architectural Record* 23 (March 1908):12, Wright, *The Autobiography of Frank Lloyd Wright* (New York, 1932), 163.

31. Louis Sullivan, "What Is Architecture?" *Craftsman* 10 (1906):143; Frank Lloyd Wright, "The Architect," *Brickbuilder* 9 (1900):126; F. L. Wright, "A Small House with 'Lots of Room in It,'" *LHJ* 18 (July 1901):15. See also Robert C. Twombly, *Frank Lloyd Wright: An Interpretive Biography* (New York, 1973), 48; Robert Crunden, *Ministers of Reform: The Progressives' Achievement in American Civilization, 1889–1920* (New York, 1982), 116–62.

32. EB, "Is It Worth While?" *LHJ* 17 (Nov. 1900):18; EB, In an Editorial Way," *LHJ* 24 (Feb. 1907):6; EB, "Is It Worth While?" 18. See also Max and Milly West, "How Shall We Furnish Our Houses," *LHJ* 24 (March 1907):13–14; EB, "Good Taste and Bad Taste in Tables," *LHJ* 23 (April 1906):37.

33. EB, "A Woman's Questions," *LHJ* 18 (April 1901):18.

34. Ibid.

35. Ruskin quoted in Mary Ann Smith, *Gustav Stickley: The Craftsman* (Syracuse, 1983), 11; John Ruskin, "A Joy Forever," in *The Works of John Ruskin*, 39 vols. (London, 1903–12), 16:134. The best general studies of the transatlantic Arts and Crafts movement are Isabelle Anscombe and Charlotte Gere, *Arts and Crafts in Britain and America* (New York, 1978); Robert Judson Clark, ed., *The Arts and Crafts in America, 1876–1916* (Princeton, 1972); Lionel Lambourne, *Utopian Craftsmen: The Arts and Crafts Movement from the Cotswolds to Chicago* (Salt Lake City, 1980).

36. Morris quoted in T. Jackson Lears, *No Place of Grace: Antimodernism and the Transformation of American Culture* (New York, 1981), 62; P. R. Thompson, *William Morris* (London, 1967), 254. See also Rho Fisk Zueblin, "A Visit to William Morris's Factory," *Outlook* 54 (1896):770–73.

37. EB, "Is It Worth While?" 18; EB, "The Voice of the World," 16.

38. For a comprehensive listing of the American Arts and Crafts organizations at the turn of the century, see Max West, "The Revival of Handicrafts in America," *U.S. Bureau of Labor Bulletin*, no. 55 (1904):1573–1622. See also Mabel Priestman, "History of the Arts and Crafts Movement in America," *The House Beautiful* 20 (Oct. 1906):15–16, ibid., (Nov. 1906):14–17; James Gilbert, *Work without Salvation:*

American Intellectuals and Industrial Alienation, 1880–1910 (Baltimore, 1977), 83–96; Lears, *No Place of Grace*, 59–96.

39. On GS, see John C. Freeman, *The Forgotten Rebel: Gustav Stickley and His Craftsman Mission Furniture* (Watkins Glen, N.Y., 1965); Smith, *Gustav Stickley*.

40. GS, "The Simplification of Life," in *Craftsman Homes* (New York, 1909), 1.

41. GS, "Home Training in Cabinet Work," *Craftsman* 8 (1905):86; Edward Pearson Pressey, *The Arts and Crafts and the Individual* (Montague, Mass., 1904), 11; Irene Sargent, "Private Simplicity as a Promoter of Public Art," *Craftsman* 2 (1902):210–11.

42. H. Langford Warren, "Our Work and Prospects," *Handicraft* 2 (1903):186. See also Daniel Rodgers, *The Work Ethic in Industrial America, 1850–1920* (Chicago, 1978), 76–82.

43. Rho Fisk Zueblin, "The Patronage of the Arts and Crafts," *Chautauquan* 37 (1903):268; Gwendolyn Wright, *Moralism and the Model Home: Domestic Architecture and Cultural Conflict in Chicago, 1873–1913* (Chicago, 1980), 129; Greene quoted in Anscombe and Gere, *Arts and Crafts*, 44. Lears accuses the Arts and Crafts movement of "accommodation" to mass-market commercialism and of giving only verbal allegiance to Morris's idealistic socialism. See *No Place of Grace*, 79–96.

44. Veblen, *Theory of the Leisure Class*, 162.

45. Alvan F. Sanborn, "The Scope and Drift of the American Arts and Crafts Movement," *Forum* 40 (1908):254–64; Lears, *No Place of Grace*, 86.

46. Irene Sargent, "In Praise of Country Life," *Craftsman* 3 (1903):265–74; Charles Richard Dodge, "Riches—and the Pursuit of Happiness," *Craftsman* 11 (1906): 232–37. See also Woods Hutchinson, "The Physical Basis of Brain Work," *North American Review* 146 (1888):522–31.

47. GS, "The Craftsman Idea," in *Craftsman Homes*, 194–205; Raymond Riordan, "A Visit to Craftsman Farms," *Craftsman* 23 (1912):155.

48. "In the Apple Orchard," *Independent* 55 (1903):2422. See also "Back to Nature," *Outlook* 74 (1903):305; Liberty Hyde Bailey, "What This Magazine Stands For," *Country Life in America* 1 (Nov. 1901):24; Louise Collier Willcox, "Outdoor Books," *North American Review* 183 (1906):116–24; Mabel Osgood Wright, "Life Outdoors and Its Effect upon Literature," *Critic* 42 (1903):308–11. The standard secondary treatments of the back-to-nature phenomenon at the turn of the century are William L. Bowers, *The Country Life Movement in America, 1900–1920* (Port Washington, N.Y., 1974); Roderick Nash, *Wilderness and the American Mind* (New Haven, 1973), 96–181; Peter Schmitt, *Back to Nature: The Arcadian Myth in Urban America* (New York, 1969).

49. "Suburbanism for the Professions," *Independent* 58 (1905):1317–19.

50. Background material on Muir's life can be found in William F. Badé, *The Life and Letters of John Muir*, 2 vols. (Boston, 1894); James M. Clarke, *The Life and Adventures of John Muir* (San Francisco, 1979); Stephen R. Fox, *John Muir and His Legacy: The American Conservation Movement* (Boston, 1981); John Muir, *The Story of My Boyhood and Youth* (New York, 1913); Nash, *Wilderness and the American Mind*, 122–40.

51. Badé, *Life and Letters*, 2:194; Edwin Way Teale, *The Wilderness World of John Muir* (Boston, 1954), xvi.

52. Nash, *Wilderness and the American Mind*, 124–25.

53. Jordan quoted in William F. Badé, "John Muir," in *Dictionary of American*

Biography (New York, 1948), 8:316; RWE quoted in Adeline Knapp, "Some Hermit Homes of California," *Overland* 35 (1900):3–6.

54. Muir, "The Wild Parks and Forest Reservations of the West," *Atlantic Monthly* 81 (1898):16; Nash, *Wilderness and the American Mind*, 128.

55. Fox, *John Muir*, 59; Teale, *Wilderness World*, 311; Nash, *Wilderness and the American Mind*, 129.

56. Fox, *John Muir*, 120.

57. Muir, "Wild Parks," 15–16.

58. "John Burroughs: Neighbor," *Outlook* 109 (1915):961; A. H. Pratt, "John Burroughs and His Friends," ibid., 109 (1915):225. On the many visitors to "Slabsides," see Clara Barrus, *Life and Letters of John Burroughs*, 2 vols. (Boston, 1925), 1:358–59, 365, 374, 2:7, 8, 19, 34, 76, 81–82, 95, 108, 142, 158 (hereafter cited as *JB Life and Letters*). Barrus was a physician who became JB's self-styled Boswell, editor, and companion in his last years. A comprehensive scholarly biography of JB remains to be written. For a sparkling brief portrait, see Paul Brooks, "The Two Johns— Burroughs and Muir," *Sierra* (Sept.-Oct. 1980):51–58. Also useful is Perry Westbrook, *John Burroughs* (New York, 1974).

59. Dallas Sharp, *The Seer of Slabsides* (Boston, 1921), 48, 50; Hamilton Mabie, "John Burroughs," *Century* 54 (Aug. 1897):563–65; *JB Life and Letters*, 2:147; JB, "Another Word on Thoreau," *The Writings of John Burroughs*, 23 vols. (New York, 1968), 23:106.

60. Clifton Johnson, "John Burroughs," *Outing* 37 (1901):593; JB, "The Gospel of Nature," *Century* 84 (1912):195–204; *JB Life and Letters*, 2:260.

61. *JB Life and Letters*, 2:134; Carpenter quoted in Gilbert Beith, ed., *Edward Carpenter: An Appreciation* (New York, 1973), 148–49.

62. JB, "What Life Means to Me," *Cosmopolitan* 40 (1905–6):654–58; *JB Life and Letters*, 1:360.

63. JB, "What Life Means to Me," 655–56; *JB Life and Letters*, 2:378.

64. JB, "What Life Means to Me," 658; "Worth-While People," *Cosmopolitan* 49 (1910):311.

65. Frederick Jackson Turner, *The Frontier in American History* (New York, 1920), 4.

66. TR, *The Strenuous Life: Essays and Addresses* (New York, 1905), 7–8, 18. See also George Fredrickson, *Inner Civil War: Northern Intellectuals and the Crisis of the Union* (New York, 1965), 229–38; Nash, *Wilderness and the American Mind*, 145–51.

67. Ralph Barton Perry, *Thought and Character of William James*, 2:312; WJ, "The Moral Equivalent of War," in John McDermott, ed., *The Writings of William James* (New York, 1967), 669.

68. Nash, *Wilderness and the American Mind*, 150–51.

69. The mixed motives behind the Country Life Movement are explored in Bowers, *Country Life Movement*, 30–44, and expressed in Liberty Hyde Bailey, "Some Aspects of the Country Life Movement," *North Carolina High School Bulletin* (1914):96–105; George W. Fiske, *The Challenge of the Country* (New York, 1913).

70. Bolton Hall, *Three Acres and Liberty* (New York, 1907), 19, 371–81; "Bolton Hall," *World To-Day* 17 (1909):685.

71. Hall, *Three Acres*, 374–75.

72. EB, "The American Man and the Country," *LHJ* 17 (July 1900):14; "The Tendency to Country Life," *LHJ* 16 (Dec. 1898):22.

73. EB, "Summers of Our Discontent," *LHJ* 18 (May 1901):16; "Prettiest Country Houses in America," *LHJ* 16 (Feb.-March 1899):10; Ashton Pentecost, "A $1500 Summer Cottage," *LHJ* 14 (Feb. 1897):19.

74. EB, "Summers of Our Discontent," 16.

75. "Camping in the Woodland," *New England Magazine* 18 (1898):737; Sigmund Spaeth, "Is the Boys' Camp Good for Boys?" *LHJ* 28 (June 1911):17, 62. See also Schmitt, *Back to Nature*, 96–114.

76. F. A. Crosby, "Boy Scouting—What It Really Is," *The World To-Day* 20 (1911):221; Edwin De Meritte, "The Vacation Camp for Boys," *Independent* 57 (1904):262–66; William C. Gray, *Musing by Camp-Fire and Wayside* (New York, 1902), 298, 299.

77. Ernest Ingersoll, "Practical Camping," *Outlook* 56 (1897):324.

78. ETS, *The Book of Woodcraft* (Garden City, N.Y., 1912), 3. On ETS, see Brian Morris, "Ernest Thompson Seton and the Origins of the Woodcraft Movement," *Journal of Contemporary History* 5 (1970):183–94; John H. Wadland, *Ernest Thompson Seton: Man in Nature and the Progressive Era, 1880–1915* (New York, 1978).

79. Ibid., v, 3, 5–7, 12, 18, 58, 572–75.

80. ETS, *Manual of the Woodcraft Indians* (Garden City, N.Y., 1915), 3; ETS quoted in Allan R. Whitmore, "Beard, Boys and Buckskins: Daniel Carter Beard and the Preservation of the American Pioneer Tradition," (Ph.D. diss., Northwestern University, 1970), 272–73; ETS, *The Birch Bark Roll of the Woodcraft Indians* (New York, 1906), 1–10. See also Schmitt, *Back to Nature*, 106–09; Wadland, *ETS*, 333–56.

81. *JB Life and Letters*, 2:97; Schmitt, *Back to Nature*, 106–14.

82. Walter Laqueur, *Young Germany: A History of the German Youth Movement* (New York, 1962), 6. See also Peter Stachura, *The German Youth Movement, 1900–1945* (New York, 1981).

83. Baden-Powell quoted in Schmitt, *Back to Nature*, 108. For an insightful comparison of the German and British youth movements, see John R. Gillis, "Conformity and Rebellion: Contrasting Styles of English and German Youth, 1900–1933." *History of Education Quarterly* 13 (1973):249–60. See also J. O. Springhall, "The Boy Scouts: Class and Militarism in Relation to British Youth Movements," *International Review of Social History* 16 (1971):125–58; Paul Wilkinson, "English Youth Movements, 1908–1930," *Journal of Contemporary History* 4 (1969):3–23.

84. The standard organizational history of the BSA is William D. Murray, *The History of the Boy Scouts of America* (New York, 1937). Two recent scholarly treatments are much more illuminating. See David Mcleod, "Good Boys Made Better: The Boy Scouts of America, Boys' Brigades and YMCA Boys' Work, 1880–1920," (Ph.D. diss., University of Wisconsin, 1973), and Carolyn Wagner, "The Boy Scouts of America: A Model and Mirror of American Society," (Ph.D. diss., Johns Hopkins University, 1979).

85. Beard quoted in BSA, *Scouting* (New York, 1914), 109; ETS, "The BSA," *Outlook* 95 (1906):630; *Boy Scouts of America: A Handbook* (New York, 1910), 1.

86. GS, "People Who Interest Us: Ernest Thompson Seton," *Craftsman* 19 (1910):67; "The Boy Scout Movement," *Chautauquan* 62 (1911):157; Norman Richardson and Ormand E. Loomis, *The Boy Scout Movement Applied by the Church* (New York, 1915), 73, 125.

87. *Letters of TR*, 7:229; Mcleod, "Good Boys Made Better," 26, 243–66. See also Harold P. Levy, *Building a Popular Movement: A Case Study of the Public Relations of the Boy Scouts* (New York, 1944); Schmitt, *Back to Nature*, 110–14; Wadland, *ETS*, 426–30.

88. Beard quoted in Schmitt, *Back to Nature*, 112; Wadland, *ETS*, 430; Wagner, "The BSA," 115.

89. Wadland, *ETS*, 431, 431–32.

90. Ibid., 442.

91. *Letters of TR*, 8:992–93.

92. TR, "A Message to All the Boys of America," *Boy Scout Yearbook* (1915), 47; "Seton Still Insists on Quitting Scouts," *New York Times*, 6 Dec. 1915.

93. ETS, "The Spirit of the Woods," *Century* 103 (1921):220.

94. "The Discrediting of Wealth," *Outlook* 84 (1906):108–9; "Successful Houses," *House Beautiful* 5 (1899):267; Eugene A. Clancey, "The Car and the Country Home," *Harper's Weekly*, 6 May 1911, p. 30. See also Schmitt, *Back to Nature*, 14–19.

95. Floyd Tillery, "Little Babbitts," *Forum* 84 (Dec. 1930):338–42; Horace C. Woodard, "Sneering at the Boy Scouts," ibid., 85 (Feb. 1931):xxii.

96. Henry S. Canby, "Back to Nature," *Yale Review* 6 (1917):755; EB, "Taking Short Views of Life," *LHJ* 25 (Sept. 1908):6.

Chapter Nine: Prosperity, Depression, and Simplicity

1. Wald quoted in Roland C. Marchand, *The American Peace Movement and Social Reform, 1898–1918* (Princeton, 1973), 223; Theodore H. Price, "The War-Induced Economy," *Outlook* 110 (1915):1003–4; David M. Kennedy, *Over Here: The First World War and American Society* (New York, 1980), 246. See also Allen F. Davis, "Welfare, Reform, and World War I," *American Quarterly* 19 (1967):516–33.

2. Ray S. Baker and William E. Dodd, eds., *War and Peace: Presidential Messages, Addresses and Public Papers*, 2 vols. (New York, 1927), 1:26; Hoover quoted in "Doing One's Bit by Economy," *World's Work* 34 (1917):130; Tom Schachtman, *Edith and Woodrow: A Presidential Romance* (New York, 1981), 151. See also Benedict Crowell, *How America Went to War* (New Haven, 1921).

3. "The Limits of Thrift," *New Republic*, 22 Dec. 1917, p. 198; "Thrift—Individual, Social, Governmental," *Outlook* 125 (1920):12.

4. Theodore H. Price, "Some Homely Economics," *Outlook* 122 (1919):399; Edwin Slosson, "Denim and Gingham," *Independent* 102 (1920):167.

5. "The Menace of Thrift," *Nation* 112 (1921):256; Clara Barrus, *Life and Letters of John Burroughs*, 2 vols. (Boston, 1925), 2:398; Kenneth S. Davis, *FDR: The Beckoning of Destiny: 1886–1928* (New York, 1971), 624.

6. Harding quoted in Charles R. Hearn, *The American Dream in the Great Depression* (Westport, Ct., 1977), 25.

7. Steffens quoted in William Leuchtenburg, *The Perils of Prosperity, 1914–1932* (Chicago, 1958), 202.

8. Ibid., 188; Charles Beard and Mary Beard, *The Rise of American Civilization*, 2 vols. (New York, 1927), 2:700.

9. EB, "When Money Is King and Business Our God," *World's Work* 48 (1924):479–82; EB, "The Greatest Word in the English Language," ibid., 49 (1924):60–62.

10. Glenn Frank, "Why Edward Bok Should Not Have Retired," *Century* 105 (1922):957–60; William Feather, "A Fourth of July Speech—New Style," *Nation's Business* 14 (July 1926):13–14. See also William Feather, "Why Boast of Not Making Money," *Nation's Business* 16 (November 1928):120.

11. James W. Prothro, *Dollar Decade: Business Ideas in the 1920s* (Baton Rouge, 1954), 61; Frankfurter quoted in William Harbaugh, "A Climate of Creativity," *New Republic*, 7 March 1983, p. 35.

12. Robert Lynd and Helen Lynd, *Middletown* (New York, 1929), 88.

13. Stuart Ewen, *Captains of Consciousness: Advertising and the Social Roots of American Culture* (New York, 1976), 57; R. Lynd and H. Lynd, *Middletown*, 82, 161. On advertising during the 1920s see also A. Michael McMahon, "An American Courtship: Psychologists and Advertising Theory in the Progressive Era," *American Studies* 13 (1972):9–18; David E. Shi, "Advertising and the Literary Imagination during the Jazz Age," *Journal of American Culture* 2 (1979):167–75.

14. Ewen, *Captains of Consciousness*, 86.

15. Sinclair Lewis, *Babbitt* (New York, 1922), 98, 222. See also Shi, "Advertising and the Literary Imagination," 169–70.

16. "Dare To Be a Babbitt," *Nation's Business* 13 (June 1925):40; *Nation's Business* 16 (Jan. 1928):29.

17. Donald R. McCoy, *Coming of Age: The United States during the 1920s and 1930s* (New York, 1973), 115, 116–30.

18. On the nostalgic appeal of rusticity and simplicity during the 1920s, see Roderick Nash, *The Nervous Generation: American Thought, 1917–1930* (Chicago, 1973), 77–90, 137–41.

19. Walter Lippmann, *A Preface to Morals* (New York, 1929), 153–55; Charles Stokes, "The Simple Life—And How!" *New Republic*, 10 July 1929, pp. 203–5.

20. Frederic Howe, *The Land and the Soldier* (New York, 1919), 6; Paul Conkin, *Tomorrow a New World: The New Deal Community Program* (Ithaca, N.Y., 1959), 51–52. On the soldier settlement plan, see also Bill G. Reid, "Proposals for Soldier Settlement during World War I," *Mid-America* 46 (1964):172–86, and "Franklin K. Lane's Idea for Veterans' Colonization, 1918–1921," *Pacific Historical Review* 33 (1964):447–61.

21. Dixon Wechter, *When Johnny Comes Marching Home* (Cambridge, Mass., 1944), 378; Bill G. Reid, "Agrarian Opposition to Franklin K. Lane's Proposal for Soldier Settlement, 1918–1921," *Agricultural History* 41 (1967):167–79.

22. The best background study of *I'll Take My Stand* remains Virginia Rock, "The Making and Meaning of *I'll Take My Stand*," (Ph.D. diss., University of Minnesota, 1961). See also Robert Crunden, ed., *The Superfluous Men: Conservative Critics of American Culture, 1900–1945* (Austin, 1977), and *From Self to Society, 1919–1941* (Englewood Cliffs, N.J., 1972); Alexander Karanikas, *Tillers of a Myth: Southern Agrarians as Social and Literary Critics* (Madison, 1969); Idus A. Newby, "The Southern Agrarians: A View after Thirty Years," *Agricultural History* 37 (1963):143–55; John L. Stewart, *The Burden of Time: The Fugitives and Agrarians* (Princeton, 1965), 91–171.

23. JCR, "Reconstructed but Unregenerate," in Henry N. Smith, intro., *I'll Take My Stand: The South and the Agrarian Tradition* (1930; rpt. Baton Rouge, 1977), 1; Warren quoted in Smith, intro., ibid., xxx.

24. JCR, "Reconstructed but Unregenerate," 12.

25. Forrest McDonald and Grady McWhinny, "The South from Self-Sufficiency to Peonage: An Interpretation," *American Historical Review* 85 (1980):1095–96.

26. William S. Knickerbocker, "Mr. Ransom and the Old South," *Sewanee Review* 39 (1931):228.

27. JCR, "Reconstructed but Unregenerate," 23.

28. Ibid., 5; "Introduction: A Statement of Principles," *I'll Take My Stand*, xlii; JCR, "Reconstructed but Unregenerate," 8.

29. Stark Young, "Not in Memoriam, but in Defense," *I'll Take My Stand*, 328.

30. "Introduction: A Statement of Principles," xlvi–vii.

31. Davidson discussed the relationship between the Borsodi homesteaders and the Nashville Agrarians in "Agrarianism for Commuters," *American Review* 1 (1933):238–42, and "'I'll Take My Stand': A History," ibid., 5 (1935):301–21; John Chamberlain, "Blueprints for a New Society," *New Republic*, 1 Jan. 1940, p. 14.

32. RB quoted in Mildred Loomis, "Ralph Borsodi: Reshaping Modern Culture," unpublished manuscript, 1978, pp. 48–50, School of Living, York, Pa. On RB's life and career, see also William E. Leverette, Jr. and David E. Shi, "Agrarianism for Commuters," *South Atlantic Quarterly* 79 (1980):204–18; William H. Issel, "Ralph Borsodi and the Agrarian Response to Urban America," *Agricultural History* 4 (1967):55–66; Richard P. Norris, "Back to the Land: The Post-Industrial Agrarianism of Ralph Borsodi and Austin Tappan Wright," (Ph.D. diss., University of Minnesota, 1976).

33. RB quoted in Mel Most, "The Rockland Homesteaders," *Bergen Sunday Record*, 24 June 1973.

34. RB, *This Ugly Civilization: A Study of the Quest for Comfort* (New York, 1929), 16, 17.

35. Ibid., 211, 246.

36. Ibid., 221, 257. Borsodi's elitism would lead him during the 1930s to suggest the benefits of engenics as a means of increasing the proportion of "quality-minded" citizens. Needless to say, this breeding program caused much discomfort for many of those who supported his decentralist philosophy, then and since.

37. Rexford Tugwell, review of *This Ugly Civilization*, in *Saturday Review*, 21 June 1930, p. 1143; RB, preface, in *Flight from the City*, 3rd ed. (New York, 1946), xv.

38. LM, *The Golden Day: A Study in American Experience and Culture* (New York, 1926), 282. Useful studies of LM include Van Wyck Brooks, "Lewis Mumford: American Prophet," *Harper's* 204 (June 1952):46–53; Charles I. Glicksberg, "Lewis Mumford and the Organic Synthesis," *Sewanee Review* 45 (1937):55–73; Park Dixon Goist, "Seeing Things Whole: A Consideration of Lewis Mumford," *Journal of the American Institute of Planners* 38 (1972):379–91.

39. Raymond Essen (LM), "Less Money and More Life," *Harpers's* 158 (January 1929):164; LM, *The Golden Day*, 279; LM, *Technics and Civilization* (New York, 1934), 319–20.

40. LM, "The Architecture of Escape," *New Republic*, 12 Aug. 1925, pp. 321–22.

41. On the "garden city" concept in Great Britain and the United States, see Patrick Geddes, *City Development: A Study of Parks, Gardens and Culture-Institutes* (Edinburgh, 1904), and *Cities in Evolution* (London, 1915); Ebenezer Howard, *Garden Cities of Tomorrow* (London, 1902); Roy Lubove, *Community Planning in the 1920s: The Contributions of the Regional Planning Association* (Pittsburgh, 1963).

42. LM, "The Theory and Practice of Regionalism," *Sociological Review* 20 (1928):137–39; LM, *The Culture of Cities* (New York, 1938), 492; LM, "Regions—To Live In," *Survey Graphic* 7 (1925):151–52.

43. On Radburn, see Lubove, *Community Planning in the 1920s*; Clarence Stein, *Toward New Towns for America* (New York, 1957).

44. B. D. Zevin, ed., *The Selected Addresses of Franklin Delano Roosevelt, 1932–1945* (Boston, 1946), 11–12 (hereafter cited as *Selected Addresses of FDR*); Samuel I. Rosenman, ed., *The Public Papers and Addresses of Franklin Delano Roosevelt*, 13 vols. (New York, 1941–45), 1:627, 632 (hereafter cited as *Public Papers of FDR*); Henry Wallace, *New Frontiers* (New York, 1934), 274.

45. *Selected Addresses of FDR*, 14; *Public Papers of FDR*, 10:151.

46. *Public Papers of FDR*, 5:438; Rexford Tugwell, *Political Science Quarterly* 75 (1960):261.

47. Frank Freidel, *Franklin D. Roosevelt: Launching the New Deal* (New York, 1973), 80, 81.

48. Frank E. Hill, *The School in the Camps: The Educational Program of the CCC* (New York, 1935), 8; Kenneth Holland and Frank E. Hill, *Youth in the CCC* (Washington, 1942), 89; Rexford Tugwell, *The Democratic Roosevelt* (New York, 1957), 331.

49. House Report 48, 73rd Congress, 1st sess., 10–11. On the TVA, see Charles Pritchett, *The Tennessee Valley Authority: A Study in Administration* (Chapel Hill, 1943).

50. North Callahan, *TVA: Bridge over Troubled Waters* (New York, 1980), 91, 57.

51. AM, *The Long Road* (Washington, 1936), 62–63. The best study of AM's moral outlook is Roy Talbert, Jr., "Arthur Morgan's Social Philosophy and the Tennessee Valley Authority," *East Tennessee Historical Society Publications* 41 (1969):86–99.

52. Callahan, *TVA*, 95; Talbert, "Morgan's Social Philosophy," 90.

53. AM, *Long Road*, xi.

54. Joseph G. Knapp, *The Advance of American Cooperative Enterprise: 1920–1945* (Danville, Ill., 1973), 326; Roy Talbert, Jr., "Arthur E. Morgan's Ethical Code for the Tennessee Valley Authority," *East Tennessee Historical Society Publications* 40 (1968):119–27.

55. Callahan, *TVA*, 35; Daniels quoted in Arthur Schlesinger, Jr., *The Coming of the New Deal* (Boston, 1959), 330.

56. AM, *The Making of the Tennessee Valley Authority* (Buffalo, N.Y., 1974), 156.

57. "Farms for Everybody," *New York World-Herald*, 1 Oct. 1933.

58. Conkin, *Tomorrow a New World*, 102–3.

59. M. L. Wilson, "The Subsistence Homestead Program," *Proceedings of the Institute of Public Affairs* 23 (1934):159; M. L. Wilson, "How New Deal Agencies Are Affecting Family Life," *Journal of Home Economics* 27 (1935):277. See also M. L. Wilson, "New Land-Use Program," *Journal of Land and Public Utility Economics* 10 (1934):3–12; Conkin, *Tomorrow a New World*, 73–130.

60. Knapp, *American Cooperative Enterprise*, 297.

61. Russell Lord and Paul Johnstone, eds., *A Place on Earth: A Critical Appraisal of Subsistence Homesteads* (Washington, 1942), 63–64, 183.

62. Conkin, *Tomorrow a New World*, 120–30.

63. See Edward S. Shapiro, "Decentralist Intellectuals and the New Deal," *Journal of American History* 58 (1972):938–57, and "American Conservative Intellectuals, the 1930s, and the Crisis of Ideology," *Modern Age* 23 (1979):370–80.

64. *New York Herald Tribune*, 24 Jan. 1938.

65. JCR, "Happy Farmers," *American Review* 1 (1933):526; Shapiro, "Decentralist Intellectuals," 946. See also Edward S. Shapiro, "The Southern Agrarians and the TVA," *American Quarterly* 22 (1970):791–806.

66. See RB, "Dayton, Ohio, Makes Social History," *Nation*, 19 April 1933, pp. 447–48, and "Subsistence Homesteads: President Roosevelt's New Land and Population Policy," *Survey Graphic* 23 (1934):11–14; "Homesteading Comes A-Cropper in Dayton," *Architectural Forum* 61 (1934):142–43; Oliver Baker, RB, and M. L. Wilson, *Agriculture in Modern Life* (New York, 1939), 269–83; Conkin, *Tomorrow a New World*, 107–8, 114, 121, 294, 333; Jacob H. Dorn, "Subsistence Homesteading in Dayton, Ohio," *Ohio History* (1969):75–93.

67. RB, "Land Tenure," *American Review* 7 (1936):556–63, and "Wanted: A School of Living," *Progressive Education* 12 (1935):20–23. RB's homestead communities received considerable attention. See George Weller, "Decentralized City Homesteads," *Commonweal*, 22 July 1938, pp. 341–44; "Design for Living," *Fortune* 18 (Oct. 1938):12, 18, 28; "Commuters Build a Model Colony," *New York Times*, 25 Oct. 1936.

68. Most, "Rockland Homesteaders," 7; RB, "Land Tenure," 556–63.

69. RB, *Flight from the City*, xiii.

70. See William E. Leverette, Jr. and David E. Shi, "Herbert Agar and *Free America*: A Jeffersonian Alternative to the New Deal," *Journal of American Studies* 16 (1982):189–206.

71. Bertram Fowler, *Consumer Cooperation in America: Democracy's Way Out* (New York, 1936), 293, 3.

72. See Edward S. Shapiro, "Catholic Agrarian Thought and the New Deal," *Catholic Historical Review* 65 (1969):583–99; Conkin, *Tomorrow a New Deal*, 294–303.

73. LM, Letter to editors, *Free America* 3 (Oct. 1939):16.

74. Ibid.; "Editorial Response," ibid., 17.

75. Conkin, *Tomorrow a New World*, 305–25.

76. Robert Bird, "Homestead Snarl; Homestead Trouble," *Commonweal* 32 (17 May 1940):70; Bob Gordon, "West Nyack Community Defies Time's Passage," *Sunday Journal News* (Rockland County, N.Y.), 4 Dec. 1977.

77. "Editorial," *Free America* 6 (May 1942):15; Dorothy Thompson, "The Volunteer Land Corps," ibid., 6 (June 1942):3–7; LM, "Decentralization: The Outlook for 1941," ibid., 5 (Jan. 1941):15.

78. Richard Lingeman, *Don't You Know There's a War On?* (New York, 1970), 247. See also John Morton Blum, *V Was for Victory* (New York, 1976).

79. "Editorial," *Free America* 9 (Winter 1945):2.

CHAPTER TEN: AFFLUENCE AND ANXIETY

1. Landon Jones, *Great Expectations: America and the Baby Boom Generation* (New York, 1980), 20; Eisenhower quoted in Henry Hazlitt, "Myth of Perpetual

Boom," *Newsweek*, 9 Nov. 1953, p. 77. See also David Potter, *People of Plenty* (Chicago, 1954).

2. "Is 'New Era' Really Here?" *U.S. News and World Report*, 20 May 1955, p. 21. William Leuchtenburg, *A Troubled Feast: American Society since 1945* (Boston, 1983), 138.

3. Meany quoted in Lawrence Wittner, *Cold War America: From Hiroshima to Watergate* (New York, 1978), 131; Leuchtenburg, *A Troubled Feast*, 55. See also Stephen Arnold and Denis Goulet, "The Abundant Society," In Ian Miles, ed., *The Poverty of Progress* (New York, 1982), 37–64.

4. Douglas T. Miller and Marion Nowak, *The Fifties: The Way We Really Were* (Garden City, N.Y., 1977), 117.

5. John A. Kouwenhoven, "Waste Not, Have Not," *Harper's* 218 (March 1959):72; Miller and Nowak, *The Fifties*, 117; Carey McWilliams, *The Education of Carey McWilliams* (New York, 1978), 199.

6. LM, *The Transformations of Man* (New York, 1956), 136, 149.

7. Henry Fairlie, "A Decade of Reaction," *New Republic*, 6 Jan. 1979, p. 16.

8. Leuchtenburg, *A Troubled Feast*, 182. See also Herbert Cross, "A Study of Values among Hippies," *Proceedings of the Annual Convention of the American Psychological Association* 5 (1970):449–50; John Howard, "The Flowering of the Hippies' Movement," *Annals of the American Academy of Political and Social Science* (1969):43–55.

9. Theodore Roszak, *The Making of a Counter Culture: Reflections on the Technocratic Society and Its Youthful Opposition* (Garden City, N.Y., 1969), 34; Charles Reich, *The Greening of America* (New York, 1970), 1–19.

10. Reich, *Greening of America*, 22, 92.

11. Roszak, *Counter Culture*, 208, 35, 47, 38.

12. Ibid., 50; Theodore Roszak, *Where the Wasteland Ends* (New York, 1972), xxxi; Roszak, *Counter Culture*, 82; Roszak, *Where the Wasteland Ends*, 427.

13. Reich, *Greening of America*, 242, 377, 248, 334.

14. Ibid., 276, 252–55.

15. Kennan quoted in Andrew Greeley, "The Redeeming of America According to Charles Reich," *America*, 9 Jan. 1971, p. 14; "Opinion," *Time*, 2 Nov. 1970, p. 13; Roszak, *Counter Culture*, 168, 159.

16. Keith Melville, *Communes in the Counter Culture* (New York, 1972), 11–12. On the communal movement see also Marguerite Bouvard, *The Intentional Community Movement: Building a New Moral World* (New York, 1975); Sara Davidson, "Open Land: Getting Back to the Communal Garden," *Harper's* 240 (June 1970):91–102; Hugh Gardner, *The Children of Prosperity: Thirteen Modern American Communes* (New York, 1978); Robert Houriet, *Getting Back Together* (New York, 1971); Rosabeth Moss Kanter, *Commitment and Community: Communes and Utopias in Sociological Perspective* (Cambridge, Mass., 1972); Sonya Rudikoff, "O Pioneers! Reflections on the Whole Earth People," *Commentary* 54 (July 1972):62–74; Lawrence Veysey, *The Communal Experience: Anarchist and Mystical Counter-Cultures in America* (New York, 1973); Benjamin Zablocki, *Alienation and Charisma: A Study of Contemporary American Communes* (New York, 1980).

17. Scott Nearing, *The Making of a Radical: A Political Autobiography* (New York, 1972), 29, 44.

18. Scott Nearing and Helen Nearing, *Living the Good Life: How To Live Sanely and Simply in a Troubled World* (New York, 1954), vii, 6.

19. Ibid., 39, 43.

20. Ibid., 197, 24–26; Nearing, *Making of a Radical*, 213; Helen Nearing, *The Good Life Album of Scott and Helen Nearing* (New York, 1974), 10; Nearing and Nearing, *Living the Good Life*, 185; H. Nearing, *Good Life Album*, 10–11.

21. Stephen Whitfield, *Scott Nearing: Apostle of American Radicalism* (New York, 1974), 191–92, 199, 211.

22. Scott Nearing and Helen Nearing, *Continuing the Good Life* (New York, 1979), 151.

23. Paul Goodman, preface, *Flight from the City*, by RB (New York, 1972), xi–xiv.

24. John C. Haughey, "The Commune—Child of the 1970s," *America*, 13 (March 1971):254; Jack Newfield, "One Cheer for the Hippies," *Nation*, 26 June 1967, p. 809.

25. Sandy Darlington, "Gimme Shelter," *Hard Times* 15 (Dec. 1969):3; Kanter, *Commitment and Community*, 180–81.

26. Richard Fairfield, *Communes, U.S.A.* (Baltimore, 1972), 107; "Ralph Borsodi Is Gone," *Mother Earth News* (Jan.-Feb. 1978):51; Mildred Loomis, "Ralph Borsodi: Reshaping Modern Culture," unpublished manuscript, 1978, School of Living, York, Pa., 378.

27. Roszak, *Counter Culture*, 39.

28. Huxley quoted in E. M. Halliday, "Our Forefathers in Hot Pursuit of the Good Life," *Horizon* 15 (Autumn 1973):115. On some of the successful communes, see Kathleen Kinkade, *A Walden Two Experiment: The First Five Years of Twin Oaks Community* (New York, 1973); Veysey, *The Communal Experience*, 207–78.

29. "A Good Look at the Farm," *Mother Earth News* (March-April 1980):140.

30. Ibid., 139; Kate Werner, "How They Keep Them Down on the Farm," *New York Times Magazine*, 8 May 1977, p. 74.

31. "A Good Look at the Farm," 141.

32. William L. O'Neill, *Coming Apart: An Informal History of America in the 1960s* (New York, 1972), 262. See "End of the Youth Revolt?" *U.S. News and World Report*, 9 Aug. 1971, p. 26; Peter Drucker, "The Surprising Seventies," *Harper's* 243 (July 1971):35–39.

33. Howard Junker, "Who Erased the Seventies?" *Esquire* 88 (Dec. 1977):152–55; *Time*, 7 Nov. 1969, p. 60; Tom Wolfe, "The 'Me' Decade and the Third Great Awakening," *New York*, 23 Aug. 1976, pp. 27–48; Christopher Lasch, *The Culture of Narcissism: American Life in an Age of Diminishing Expectations* (New York, 1978).

34. Peter Clecak, *America's Quest for the Ideal Self: Dissent and Fulfillment in the 60s and 70s* (New York, 1983). See also Peter N. Carroll, *It Seemed Like Nothing Happened: The Tragedy and Promise of America in the 1970s* (New York, 1982), 235–51; Daniel Yankelovitch, *New Rules: Searching for Self-Fulfillment in a World Turned Upside Down* (New York, 1981).

35. Gladwin Hill, "Environment May Eclipse Vietnam as College Issue," *New York Times*, 10 Nov. 1969; Daniel Yankelovitch, "The New Naturalism," *Saturday Review*, 1 April 1972, p. 32. For a comprehensive analysis of the origins of the environmental movement, see Donald Fleming, "Roots of the New Conservation Movement," *Perspectives in American History* 6 (1972):7–94. A convenient summary of the scholarly debate surrounding the environmental movement is David L. Sills, "The Environmental Movement and Its Critics," *Human Ecology* 3 (1975):1–41.

36. Roszak, *Where the Wasteland Ends*, 422; Dubos quoted in *Newsweek*, 26 Jan. 1970, p. 31.

37. Barry Commoner, *The Closing Circle* (New York, 1971), 217–18.

38. Aldo Leopold, *Sand County Almanac and Sketches Here and There* (New York, 1949), 203, ix.

39. Kenneth Boulding, "The Economics of the Coming Spaceship Earth," in Henry Jarrett, ed., *Environmental Quality in a Growing Economy* (Baltimore, 1966), 3–14; Hazel Henderson, "Redeploying Corporate Resources Toward New Priorities," in White House Conference on the Industrial World Ahead, *A Look at Business in 1990* (Washington, 1972), 23; Michael Phillips, "SRI Is Wrong about Voluntary Simplicity," *Co-Evolution Quarterly* (Summer 1972):32.

40. Ford quoted in Carter Henderson, "Living the Simple Life," *Human Resource Management* 16 (Fall 1977):23; Love quoted in "A Time of Learning to Live with Less," *Time*, 3 Dec. 1973, p. 29; Billington quoted in William K. Stevens, "Down-shifting America's Dream," *Charlotte Observer*, 8 July 1979.

41. Toynbee quoted in "How Will We React to an Age of Scarcity," *Conservation Foundation Newsletter* (Jan. 1975):8; William Irwin Thompson, *Evil and World Order* (New York, 1976), 13–14, and "Auguries of Planetization: Braving a New World," *Quest* (July-Aug. 1977):95; "The Embargo: Waiting for the End," *Newsweek*, 18 March 1974, p. 94; Reston quoted in John P. Sisk, "The Fear of Affluence," *Commentary* 57 (June 1974):61.

42. William Ophuls, *Ecology and the Politics of Scarcity: Prologue to a Political Theory of the Steady State* (San Francisco, 1977), 238; William Ophuls, "The Scarcity Society," *Harper's* 248 (April 1974):52; Ophuls, *Ecology and the Politics of Scarcity*, 13. On the "steady state" concept, see also Herman Daly, ed., *Economics, Ecology, Ethics: Essays Toward a Steady-State Economy* (San Francisco, 1973); Ezra J. Mishan, *The Cost of Economic Growth* (New York, 1967); "The No Growth Society," *Daedalus* 102 (Fall 1973).

43. Ophuls, *Ecology and the Politics of Scarcity*, 241; Wendell Berry, *The Unsettling of America: Culture and Agriculture* (New York, 1977), 14; Scully quoted in "Asking the Right Questions," *Newsweek*, 19 Nov. 1979, p. 142; George Marotta, "Voluntary Simplicity: A Style of Life Whose Time Has Come?" *Washington Post*, 23 Nov. 1980.

44. Laurance S. Rockefeller, "The Case for a Simpler Life-Style," *Reader's Digest* (Feb. 1976):61–65.

45. Ibid., 62, 63–64.

46. Ibid., 63, 65.

47. Louis Harris and Associates, *The Harris Survey*, 23 May 1977. On the growing popularity of simple living during the 1970s, see Duane Elgin, *Voluntary Simplicity: Toward a Way of Life That Is Outwardly Simple, Inwardly Rich* (New York, 1981); Carter Henderson, "The Frugality Phenomenon," *Bulletin of the Atomic Scientists* (34 (May 1978):24–27; Ronald Inglehart, *The Silent Revolution: Changing Values and Political Styles among Western Publics* (Princeton, 1977).

48. Duane Elgin and Arnold Mitchell, "Voluntary Simplicity: Life-Style of the Future," *Futurist* 11 (1977):200–209; Elgin, *Voluntary Simplicity*, 36–38.

49. Elgin, *Voluntary Simplicity*, 50; Elgin and Mitchell, "Voluntary Simplicity," 200.

50. Center for Science in the Public Interest, *99 Ways to a Simple Lifestyle* (Bloomington, Ind., 1977); John Cooper, *Finding a Simpler Life* (Philadelphia, 1974); Vernard Eller, *The Simple Life: The Christian Stance Toward Possessions* (Grand Rapids, Mich., 1973); Adam Finnerty, *No More Plastic Jesus: Global Justice and Christian Lifestyle* (Maryknoll, N.Y., 1977); Richard J. Foster, *Freedom of*

Simplicity (San Francisco, 1981); Arthur Gish, *Beyond the Rat Race* (Scottsdale, Pa., 1973); Andrew Greeley, *No Bigger than Necessary* (New York, 1977); Warren Johnson, *Muddling Toward Frugality* (San Francisco, 1978); Kirkpatrick Sale, *Human Scale* (New York, 1980); John Taylor, *Enough Is Enough: A Biblical Call for Moderation in a Consumer-Oriented Society* (Minneapolis, 1977).

51. E. F. Schumacher, *Small Is Beautiful: Economics As If People Mattered* (New York, 1973).

52. "Inaugural Address of President Carter," *Vital Speeches* 43 (1977):258–59; "Interview with the President Elect," *Professional Engineer Magazine* (Dec. 1976):9.

53. Jimmy Carter, "Energy Problems: The Erosion of Confidence," *Vital Speeches* 45 (1979):642–45.

54. Ibid.

55. Caddell quoted in Sale, *Human Scale*, 45.

56. "Nation's Newspaper Editorialists Split over Carter's Energy Talk," *New York Times*, 17 July 1979; "Riding Casually toward War," ibid.; "Consumer Resistance to Austere Lifestyle," *Intellect* (Nov. 1976):125.

57. Ronald Reagan, foreword, *The Conservative Decade: Emerging Leaders of the 1980s*, by James C. Roberts (Westport, Ct., 1980), vii; Reagan, "Acceptance Address," *Vital Speeches* 46 (1980):642.

58. Reagan quoted in Sale, *Human Scale*, 417.

59. Ronald Reagan, "The State of the Nation's Economy," *Vital Speeches* 47 (1981):292.

60. Ronald Reagan, "Inaugural Address," *Vital Speeches* 47 (1981):258–59.

61. "A First Lady of Priorities and Proprieties," *Time*, 5 Jan. 1981, p. 25; "The World of Nancy Reagan," *Newsweek*, 21 Dec. 1981, p. 22; Allen quoted in Ralph Nader, intro., *Reagan's Ruling Class*, ed. Ronald Brownstein and Nina Easton (New York, 1983), xv; Laurence Leamer, *Make Believe: The Story of Nancy and Ronald Reagan* (New York, 1983), 3.

62. Nader, *Reagan's Ruling Class*, xvi. Leamer, *Make Believe*, 290; "Flaunting Wealth—It's Back in Style," *U.S. News and World Report*, 21 Sept. 1981, pp. 61–62.

63. "A Saving Economy Will Produce a 'New Country,'" *U.S. News and World Report*, 9 May 1983, p. 23; "Interview with William Staton," *Business North Carolina* 3 (July 1983):44; F. Scott Fitzgerald, *The Great Gatsby* (New York, 1925), 218.

EPILOGUE

1. Richard B. Gregg, *The Value of Voluntary Simplicity* (Wallingford, Pa., 1936), 1.

2. *The Dialogues of Plato*, trans. B. Jowett, 2 vols. (New York, 1937), 1:636; Bradford Torrey, ed., *The Writings of Henry David Thoreau*, 20 vols. (Boston, 1906), 2:17.

3. Paul F. Boller, Jr., *American Transcendentalism, 1830–1860* (New York, 1974), 200; HDT, *Writings*, 4:362.

4. LM, *The Conduct of Life* (New York, 1951), 17–18.

5. Gregg, *Voluntary Simplicity*, 27; Aldo Leopold, *Sand County Almanac* (New York, 1949), vii.

6. Clara Barrus, *Life and Letters of John Burroughs*, 2 vols. (Boston, 1925), 2:156–57.

Index